"Responsibly covering an intricate and diverse theme like holiness throughout the Old Testament is a daunting task. One approach is for a mature scholar to synthesize a lifetime of discovery, another, to gather a community of scholars with expertise in various streams of Old Testament scholarship. This volume is able to do both, and the result is a volume that is sure to become foundational for future studies of this key theme in Old Testament theology. Be prepared for a canonical journey that will not only shape your theology but inspire you to holiness in your lives and communities."

—Mark J. Boda (PhD, Cambridge)
Professor of Old Testament
McMaster Divinity College

HOLINESS IN THE OLD TESTAMENT

A Textual and Thematic Analysis

MATT I. AYARS and
JOHN N. OSWALT
EDITORS

Holiness in the Old Testament: A Textual and Thematic Analysis

Published by Kregel Academic, an imprint of Kregel Publications, 2450 Oak Industrial Dr. NE, Grand Rapids, MI 49505-6020.

Cataloging-in-Publication Data is available from the Library of Congress.

ISBN 978-0-8254-4839-3

Printed in the United States of America

25 26 27 28 29 / 5 4 3 2 1

To Dr. Timothy Tennent,
in gratitude for his faithful service to the global church
and his tireless commitment to the message of holiness

CONTENTS

CONTRIBUTORS

Matt I. Ayars is the Lead Pastor of Wellspring Church and former President and Associate Professor of Old Testament at Wesley Biblical Seminary. He earned his PhD in OT from St. John's College of Nottingham and the University of Chester. Matt is the author and editor of several volumes, including *The Shape of Hebrew Poetry: Exploring the Discourse Function of Linguistic Parallelism in the Egyptian Hallel* (Brill, 2019) and *The Holy Spirit: An Introduction* (Seedbed, 2023). He is also a coauthor of *Holiness: A Biblical, Theological, and Historical Theology* (IVP Academic, 2023) and a coeditor of *Between the Psalms and the Twelve: Exploring the Nature and Shape of Composition* (Pickwick, 2025). An ordained elder in the Global Methodist Church, Matt's passion is for both ecclesial scholarship and the local church, especially the Methodist (Wesleyan-Arminian) tradition.

Craig G. Bartholomew is the Director of the Kirby Laing Centre for Public Theology in Cambridge. He is the editor and author of many books—most recently, *Listening to Scripture: An Introduction to Interpreting the Bible* (Baker Academic, 2023).

Daniel I. Block is Gunther H. Knoedler Professor Emeritus of Old Testament at Wheaton College. He earned a DPhil in Semitics (Classical Hebrew) from the University of Liverpool in 1982, under the tutorship of renowned Assyriologist Alan R. Millard. In addition to commentaries on Ezekiel (NICOT), Judges and Ruth (NAC), Deuteronomy (NIVAC), and Ruth (ZECOT), he has written three volumes of essays on Deuteronomy and two volumes on biblical theology: *For the Glory of God: Recovering a Biblical Theology of Worship* (Baker Academic, 2014), *Covenant: The Framework of God's Grand Plan of Redemption* (Baker Academic, 2021), and most recently a three-volume revised and expanded work, *Hearing the Gospel according to Moses: A Commentary on Deuteronomy* (Hong Kong: Inspirata, 2023–2024). Along with John Oswalt, he served as general reviewer for the New Living Translation of the Scriptures, with primary responsibility for the Pentateuch. His passion for Christ and his kingdom worldwide has been expressed through teaching and preaching on all continents—except Antarctica, which remains on his bucket list. His heaviest assignments have involved biblical education and pastoral training in Russia and China.

Scott A. Engebretson is an adjunct professor at Wesley Biblical Seminary and other institutions, teaching primarily in the areas of Old Testament and Biblical Theology. He has a PhD from Asbury Theological Seminary, a ThM from Princeton Theological Seminary, and an MDiv from Wesley Biblical Seminary. His undergraduate degree is a Bachelor of Urban Planning from the University of Cincinnati. His dissertation focused on the transition from the judges period to the monarchy, specifically analyzing urban planning design in ancient Israel and the surrounding region. Other research interests include the Israelite monarchy, archaeology, and biblical theology.

David G. Firth is a tutor in Old Testament and Academic Dean at Trinity College Bristol and a research associate of the University of the Free State. His doctoral research was on the Psalms at the University of Pretoria, which he completed while serving as a missionary in southern Africa. Along with his continued interest in the Psalms, he has researched and written on the OT's Historical Books, with a particular interest in their treatment of foreigners and the Spirit of God. He is also general editor of the Tyndale Old Testament Commentaries series and coeditor of the Baker Commentary on the Old Testament: Historical Books.

Victor P. Hamilton is Professor Emeritus of Old Testament studies at Asbury University in Wilmore, Kentucky. He taught there for thirty-six years, from 1971 to 2007. The university appointed him scholar-in-residence for the next five years, from 2007 to 2012. During those forty-one years, he was able to publish the following books: *Handbook on the Pentateuch*, 1st ed. (Baker Academic, 1982); *The Book of Genesis: Chapters 1–17* (Eerdmans, 1990); *The Book of Genesis: Chapters 18–50* (Eerdmans, 1995); *Handbook on the Historical Books* (Baker Academic, 2001); *Handbook on the Pentateuch*, 2nd ed. (Baker Academic, 2005); and *Exodus: An Exegetical Commentary* (Baker

Academic, 2011). All of the above books have been translated into at least one non-English language, and most have been reproduced in several languages. In addition to the above volumes, he has contributed to several one-volume study Bibles, Bible encyclopedias, and other reference tools for biblical studies. He was a member of the translation teams that produced the New King James Version (Thomas Nelson) and the New Living Translation (Tyndale). He is a graduate of Houghton College (BA), Asbury Theological Seminary (BD, ThM), and Brandeis University (MA, PhD). At Brandeis he was privileged to study under the late Semitist Cyrus H. Gordon. He is an ordained minister in the Wesleyan Church. He has been happily married to his wife, Shirley, since 1965. They have four adult children and thirteen grandchildren.

Peter C. W. Ho is Associate Professor of Old Testament and Academic Dean of the School of Theology, English at Singapore Bible College. His PhD is from the University of Gloucestershire, and his writings include *The Design of the Psalter: A Macrostructural Analysis* (Pickwick, 2019) and *Habakkuk and Zephaniah*, Asia Bible Commentary Series (Langham, 2024). He also coedited a volume, *Between the Psalms and the Twelve* (Pickwick, 2025), with Matt Ayars.

Jennifer M. Matheny is Associate Professor of Christian Scriptures at Baylor University's George W. Truett Theological Seminary. Jennifer earned her PhD from the University of Kent in Canterbury. She is author of *Judges 19–21 and Ruth: Canon as a Voice of Answerability* (Brill, 2022). Recent publications include "Tamar and Ruth: Dress as (Mis)communication and Inheritance Preservation," in *Dress and Clothing in the Hebrew Bible* (T&T Clark, 2022), and, coauthored with Amy Hale, "The Raging Prophet: Acceptance Commitment Therapy (ACT) as a Pathway Forward through Pain," in *When Psychology Meets the Bible* (Sheffield Phoenix, 2023).

John N. Oswalt is Faculty Emeritus of Old Testament studies at Wesley Biblical Seminary. He earned his PhD from Brandeis University. Dr. Oswalt returned to the Asbury Theological Seminary faculty in 2009 as visiting distinguished professor of Old Testament. This is his third term on Asbury Seminary's faculty, having first served from

1970 to 1982 as professor of Old Testament and Semitic languages and again from 1989 to 1999 as professor of Old Testament. He also served as president of Asbury College from 1983 to 1986, as a faculty member of Trinity Evangelical Divinity School from 1986 to 1989, and as a research professor of Old Testament at Wesley Biblical Seminary from 1999 to 2009. He is the author of eleven books, most notable of which is the two-volume commentary on the book of Isaiah in the NICOT (Eerdmans, 1986, 1998). His most recent book is *The Holy One of Israel: Studies in the Book of Isaiah* (Cascade Books, 2014). He has also written numerous articles that have appeared in Bible encyclopedias, scholarly journals, and popular religious periodicals. Dr. Oswalt is an ordained minister in the United Methodist Church, with membership in the Kentucky Annual Conference. He has served as a part-time pastor in congregations in New England and Kentucky and is a frequent speaker in conferences, camps, and local churches.

David B. Schreiner is Associate Professor of Old Testament and Inductive Biblical Studies at Asbury Theological Seminary. He earned his PhD in OT studies from Asbury Theological Seminary. He publishes and presents widely on issues of biblical interpretation, including those of history, culture, language, and the history of interpretation. He has published *1 and 2 Kings: A Commentary for Biblical Preaching and Teaching* (Kregel Ministry, 2022); *Ahab's House of Horrors: A Historiographic Study of the Military Campaigns of the House of Omri* (Lexham, 2023); and *Silhouettes of Scripture: Considering the Contextual Approach with Form Criticism* (Lexington Books, 2023). He has also recently published *Frigatebirds, Sea Lions, and Darwin: Musings on Evolution, Creation, and Ecology* (Wipf and Stock, 2025), as he continues to write *1 and 2 Kings* for The Bible in God's World series (Cascade Books, forthcoming).

Brian T. Shockey is Assistant Professor of Ministry and Director of the Accelerated Ministry Program at Palm Beach Atlantic University in West Palm Beach, Florida. Brian received his PhD in biblical studies (OT) from Asbury Theological Seminary. His research interests include the comparative method, implied ethics in biblical narrative, biblical law, discipleship, and pastoral ministry.

Terrance R. Wardlaw Jr. is a linguist and consultant. He and his wife, Sara, have five children and began serving overseas in 2001. Terry is interested in biblical languages, cognitive linguistics, discourse analysis, Relevance Theory, macroanalysis, exegetical method, translation theory, and the doctrine of Scripture. He has published three monographs related to the theme of creation within the Pentateuch and the Psalms: *Conceptualizing Words for "God" within the Pentateuch: A Cognitive-Semantic Investigation in Literary Context* (T&T Clark International, 2008); *Elohim within the Psalms: Petitioning the Creator to Order Chaos in Oral-Derived Literature* (Bloomsbury T&T Clark, 2015); and *Created Male and Female* (Wipf & Stock, 2020).

Paul D. Wegner is distinguished Professor of Old Testament at Gateway Seminary in Ontario, California, with a specialty in the book of Isaiah. He holds a PhD from Kings College, University of London, and his dissertation was titled "Messianic Expectation and Kingship in the Book of Isaiah 1–35." He was the PhD director at Gateway Seminary but has given that up to spend more time writing. He has two grown boys: the older one is a product chain manager for 3M, and the younger is doing a PhD at Princeton. He has two grandchildren, whom he thoroughly enjoys but who live too far away in Columbia, Missouri. Paul and his wife, Cathy, have been married for forty years and currently live in Highland, California. He enjoys fixing up his house, bike riding, and hiking in the hills around Highland. Previously, he taught at Phoenix Seminary and Moody Bible Institute. Some of his books include *The Journey from Texts to Translations: The Origin and Development of the Bible* (Baker, 1999); *A Student's Guide to Textual Criticism of the Bible: Its History, Methods and Results* (IVP Academic, 2006); *Wise Parenting: Guidelines from the Book of Proverbs* (Discovery House, 2009); and most recently *Isaiah* (IVP Academic, 2021).

INTRODUCTION

MATT I. AYARS AND JOHN N. OSWALT

The holiness of God and Israel's call to be holy are arguably at the theological center of the complex yet integrated and comprehensive theological vision of the OT. They are especially key themes in the Pentateuch, which has long been recognized as the theological foundation on which OT theology as a whole rests. Given this reality, the editors of this volume are aware of no single volume that offers a careful and thorough analysis and evaluation of the theme of holiness within the various corpora of the OT or as it relates to key theological themes and concepts spanning the OT. This volume aims at filling this gap; its vision is to clarify not only the notion of holiness, but also how it relates to the overall theological vision of the OT.

The volume comprises three parts: (1) introductory matter, (2) textual analyses, and (3) thematic analyses. The first section (introductory matter) establishes the meaning of the Hebrew term *qādôš* and frames the volume by highlighting its need and mapping its overall vision. The second section (textual analyses) explores the notion of holiness in the various parts of the OT (i.e., the Pentateuch, the Historical Books, the Wisdom Literature, and the Prophetic Books). Finally, the third section (thematic analyses) explores the notion of holiness as it relates to some of the major themes of OT theology (e.g., atonement, the Messiah, the Spirit of God, and election).

In the opening chapter, John Oswalt makes the case that the Hebrew root *qdš* signifies "qualitative otherness" in terms of both divine ontology as well as ethics. He argues that the common notion that *qdš* denotes something "set apart" cannot be demonstrated either from etymology or from usage. He further argues that Rudolf Otto's suggestion that "holy" in the OT means *mysterium tremendum* is fatally deficient, as it overlooks God's ethical purity as an essential part of the OT's conceptualization of God's holiness. In short, when the OT says that God is holy, it does not *merely* mean that he is "uncommon," in that he is uncreated or unlike other ANE "gods" (i.e., ontologically other). Rather, the OT reveals that at the heart of the holiness of God is the two-pronged notion of the eternality of God paired with his ethical purity. Because he is eternal and one, he is unchanging. His will is not mixed; therefore, neither is his ethical character. This definition of holiness, then, provides the explanatory power behind both the ceremonial and the ethical laws of Israel in the Pentateuch, as well as the Prophets' denouncing of empty ritual. Israel must bear God's likeness by being unmixed in its devotion to him, as expressed in both worship and everyday living. This moral perfection is only obtainable as the expressed outcome of a reconciled relationship with the one true God that yields a radical transformation of sinful humanity.

TEXTUAL ANALYSES

Holiness in the Pentateuch

Building on Oswalt's contribution, beginning with an exploration of the Sabbath, and moving through key stories in the Pentateuch, Matt Ayars explores how the Pentateuch conceptualizes the triconsonantal root *qdš*. Ayars posits that *qdš* not only captures the notion of transcendental monotheism but also its implications for ethics, human life, and the creation as a whole. Ayars reads key moments and notions in the Pentateuch (the Sabbath, God's personal name, the tabernacle, and atonement) as definitive polemic statements against Israel's ANE polytheistic milieu. Key for Ayars is human holiness not just as a response to God's holiness but as *the restoration of the image of God in humanity—a key notion for the fulfillment of God's plans and purposes for the creation as a whole*. God's intent was for creation to generate and sustain life, and the image of God in humanity was (and is) essential for that plan to be fulfilled. The covenant stipulations that contextualize many of the references to holiness in the Pentateuch are (1) the codification of the moral image of God, to be embodied by humanity, and (2) the mechanism through which sin is revealed.

Holiness in the Historical Books

Moving us into the Former Prophets, Brian T. Shockey explores the concept of holiness in the Historical Books by examining how God interacts with sinful humanity and demonstrates his love and mercy even toward those who fall short of his expectations. Shockey includes a survey of holiness language, an examination of key themes (as they relate both implicitly and explicitly to holiness), and an analysis of Samson and David as case studies for understanding holiness in the Historical Books.

Throughout the Historical Books, encounters between God and his servants highlight the importance of responding to God's holy presence with humility and deference. The text portrays God's holiness as the status quo and focuses on how it relates to ancient Israel's leaders and history. One early reference to holiness is found before the conquest of Jericho, where holiness language is used in connection with the location and spoils of war. Joshua plays a significant role in this narrative, demonstrating holiness in his leadership during this time.

Holiness in Ruth

Before moving past the Former Prophets, Jennifer Matheny explores how the notion of holiness is developed in the story of Ruth. The focus of the chapter is on holiness as embodied in acts of *ḥesed* (loving kindness)—for instance, Ruth's faithfulness to Naomi, Boaz's faithfulness to his kin via Ruth, and ultimately, YHWH's steadfast love to the rebel family and the foreigner. Yes, God is ontologically other as the uncreated Creator, but he is also other in that the quality of his moral character—which is best expressed in acts of *ḥesed*—is unlike human character, which waxes and wanes. His love is faithful and sure and directly related to his immutability and holiness.

Holiness in Ezra and Nehemiah

After investigating various issues related to the definition of holiness in the OT, David Schreiner explores the notion of foreignness and how it relates to holiness in Ezra and Nehemiah. He helpfully interprets the notion of otherness—defined within the framework of geoethnic politics and social relations during the postexilic period—in light of the policies of reform in postexilic Israel. Schreiner argues that the painful memory of exile inspired a renewed urgency for holiness, with the postexilic community fully committing itself to the teachings of Moses. Schreiner also argues that a comparison with the policy of *ḥērem*, which marked the conquest and colonization of Canaan, can bring these developments into sharper focus. Schreiner concludes that the unique economic, political, and social circumstances facing the postexilic community called for a remembering and reenvisioning of the reasons for and manners of holiness; God's covenant people faced new challenges as a rescued people living in an imperial context. He writes, "Standards were renewed and held with new rigor, and any hostility toward the community was to be met with intense opposition. Such a posture would have carved out a way forward for God's people, but the difficulty would be in whether it would accommodate YHWH's ambition to imprint his character on all people."

Holiness in the Wisdom Tradition

Craig Bartholomew explores the notion of holiness as it relates to the wisdom tradition. After establishing that wisdom is grounded in a theology of creation, Bartholomew develops the oneness, transcendence, and immanence of God as axes around which the very notion of living in harmony with the Creator revolves. He writes, "Wisdom is the discovery and following of God's ways in his world. God's transcendence or otherness and his immanence or availability for communion are central to the biblical notion of divine holiness. . . . Thus, far from being alien to wisdom, *God's holiness is the very thing that makes (human) wisdom possible*." He points out, then, that holiness, while a central focus in the Pentateuch, is inseparably connected to the overarching and integrated themes of the whole revelation of God in the OT, including the wisdom tradition (i.e., monotheism, transcendence, and immanence). Holiness, Bartholomew highlights, is not just about obedience to the 613 commands of the Torah; it is about being in fellowship with the Creator, who makes himself known for the sake of life-giving and life-sustaining community with his creation.

Holiness in the Psalms

Terrance Wardlaw first surveys the use of "holy" and related terms and their distribution in the Psalter. He notes that many occurrences are affiliated with the temple and the anticipation of the restoration of an ideal Zion. Departing from lexical considerations, he shifts to the theme of holiness as it unfolds across the Psalter as a collection. Wardlaw first considers Psalms 1 and 2 as the two-part introduction to the Psalter and its implications for holiness. He goes on to build the case that the Psalter anticipates an ideal David. He posits that "the prominence of David . . . and the law . . . in book 5 . . . suggests the restoration of holiness with covenant ethics through the messianic rule, the ascent of the elect to worship in holiness . . . , the willingness of a holy people to suffer for the Messiah . . . , and the eternal praise of the elect in holiness."

Holiness in the Prophets

Peter Ho discusses the theme of holiness in the Latter Prophets in view of Exodus 19:6. He traces terms related to holiness and the priesthood within "their larger structural-rhetorical contexts." While these texts often accentuate Israel's failure to keep holiness, they are always accompanied with a hopeful anticipation of redemption—a redemption accomplished by God alone, thereby fulfilling a final, true exodus experience. This exodus, however, is a deliverance from the power of sin. Ho also analyzes Isaiah as the prince of the Prophets, as far as holiness is concerned. In Isaiah it is the Holy One of Israel who will ultimately fulfill his redemptive purposes for Israel and the creation as a whole through his Servant. Ho also considers the vision of the final temple in Ezekiel and how the notion of holiness integrates with that vision. Ultimately, Ho says, it is through the work of the predicted and much-anticipated Messiah that God will fulfill his redemptive purposes and transform his people into a holy, royal priesthood.

THEMATIC ANALYSES

Holiness and Atonement

Victor Hamilton offers a detailed textual and linguistic analysis of the notion of atonement in the OT. Naturally, much of his essay focuses on the Pentateuch, the priesthood, and the temple. He analyzes various mechanisms for atonement for intentional and unintentional sin. Hamilton concludes with the following:

1. The commands from YHWH to his people via Moses to be holy are implicitly achievable.

    (1) Of all the divine attributes, the "only one for which he calls for emulation is holiness."

    (2) The holiness of God includes some of his incommunicable divine attributes (not just his ethical holiness, characterized

by *ḥesed*); not surprisingly, then, the demand for holiness among God's people does not include those incommunicable attributes (i.e., eternality, transcendence, and immutability in particular). That demand only relates to God's ethics.

(3) Leviticus and Deuteronomy use holiness language differently. In Leviticus, holiness is a call and future possibility, but in Deuteronomy, it is a present reality. This difference, notes Hamilton, is picked up in the NT, where imputed righteousness (i.e., justification in the Messiah) and imparted righteousness (i.e., the sanctifying work of the Holy Spirit) are distinguished.

(4) The holiness of God references not only his ontological otherness (as Otto has suggested), but also his ethical character (his *ḥesed*).

Finally, Hamilton suggests that atonement is the means through which a rebellious people return from captivity and are delivered from the power of sin—a feat only the Holy One of Israel is capable of.

Holiness and the Spirit of God

David Firth writes on the Spirit of God and holiness in the Samson story. One of the aims of his essay is to preserve a uniquely OT pneumatology. He writes, "Rather than reading back from the NT to the Old, we should read from the Old to the New and so understand why the language of holiness became so closely associated with the Spirit. This essay aims to lay some foundations for that." Through an analysis of the Samson story, Firth establishes that holiness can be associated with "patterns of disposition and behavior." The Samson story "points to YHWH's continued commitment to a people who continue to disappoint." Firth highlights the tension between Samson's birth narrative and Nazirite vow and his ritually unclean behavior. This is a man whom God chose to show favor, yet he never quite lives up to God's plans and expectations. Nonetheless, the Spirit of God comes upon him in unexpected moments—that is, while Samson is breaking his vows. Firth writes, "But if we are correct in seeing these [moments] as instances in which Samson acts without necessarily intending to breach his status, then we can understand the Spirit's work here as a gracious empowerment by YHWH, something that enables Samson to move toward Israel's deliverance." The point: the empowerment of God by means of the Holy Spirit is an act of grace. Implicit in that grace is a God whose love is steadfast. This is a God of holy love.

Holiness and the Messiah

Paul Wegner writes on holiness and the Messiah in the OT. By tracking the contexts from which messianic anticipation arises in the OT narrative, Wegner concludes that "God's unfolding plan for humankind's redemption was revealed over time: while the Messiah is never said to be holy, he is God's agent to sanctify or 'to make holy' fallen humankind." Wegner further explores the tension between the NT's vision of the Messiah—that is, as a high priest who reconciles humanity to a holy God—and the lack of language describing the Messiah as holy in the OT. The solution to that tension, Wegner posits, is the holy love of God.

Holiness and Salvation

Scott Engebretson demonstrates that at the heart of salvation, or "rescue" in the OT (as typified in the exodus event), is the restoration of God's presence with humanity. Through a careful evaluation of Genesis 1–11, Engebretson considers estrangement from God and the inbreaking of sin in creation as conditions needing redemption (i.e., needing to be "put right"). The putting right of creation requires reconciliation and unbroken fellowship with God. The mechanism for restoration and reconciliation is the covenant. Engebretson writes, "To summarize, the way of salvation requires divine patience in the face of sin (Noah), radical trust (Abraham), freedom from oppression and access to God's holy presence (Moses), and ultimately a sacrificial king who will make a way for people to truly experience God's presence and be transformed by his holiness (David)." To be "saved" in the OT, concludes Engebretson, is to be rescued from a state of sin and restored to the Edenic state of intimate fellowship with the God of holy love.

Holiness and Covenant

Dan Block explores the interrelatedness of holiness and covenant. After a helpful review of various terms pertaining to holiness, along with a probe into holiness as it relates to the call of Moses, Block concludes with the following: (1) Holiness, as understood in the context of covenants, is monergistic; that is, it is revealed and embodied only as a result of God's unconditional election of Abraham and his descendants. (2) Holiness is an imperative of the covenants and of the covenantal relationship between YHWH and his chosen people. And (3) "while the calls to covenant relationship and holiness are unconditional, both Israel's personal well-being and its fulfillment of the commission for which it had been ordained were contingent on the people demonstrating their holiness and righteousness within the covenant community and before a watching world."

Finally, the volume captures well the following:

1. The theology of the OT is remarkably integrated when analyzed with a focus on holiness.
2. Holiness in the OT is *qualitative otherness*.
3. The holiness of God is dynamic, referring to both incommunicable attributes (i.e., eternality, transcendence, and immutability) and communicable attributes (i.e., the steadfast love of God).
4. God commands his people to be holy (in reference to the communicable attributes), and that command is rooted in the human vocation to be divine image bearers.
5. The holy love of God is the basis on which he can be completely faithful to creation and to a covenanted yet rebellious people.
6. God's holy love is the basis of his covenants and of the transforming power of their reconciling purposes.
7. The Messiah is the agent through whom God's redemptive purposes for creation—namely, to restore it to its original ideal and to renew the image of God in humanity—are fulfilled.

PART 1

INTRODUCTORY MATTER

CHAPTER 1

"HOLINESS" (*QDŠ*) IN THE OLD TESTAMENT

JOHN N. OSWALT

Words (other than proper nouns) that utilize the root *qdš* occur in the OT some eight hundred times. The primary terms are the verb *qādaš* ("to be holy," which occurs most frequently in derived stem forms; 171 occurrences); the noun *qōdeš* ("holiness"; 470 occurrences); and the adjective *qādôš* ("holy"; 115 occurrences). The number of these occurrences is disproportionately higher than in any of the other known ancient Semitic languages.[1] The frequency of use suggests that the associated concept is of great importance in Hebrew thought.

THE MEANING OF THE WORD GROUP

In common parlance, the *qdš* word group is frequently said to refer to something "set apart." However, this meaning cannot be demonstrated from etymology or usage.[2] In Akkadian the corresponding adjective means "clean, pure, dedicated." In Ugaritic the comparable term is likewise used primarily in a cultic sense. In neither language are the terms widely used.[3] Kurt Goldammer offers a helpful definition: "The 'holy' is something [ontologically] different from [those using the term] and implies a *qualitative* distinction between the divine on the one hand and human beings and the world on the other."[4] Naudé says something similar when he points out the fundamental contrast between the holy and the common, the clean and the unclean, which is highlighted in Leviticus

1. See discussion in Naudé cited below.
2. See Jackie A. Naudé, "קדשׁ," *NIDOTTE* 3:885: "The theory that the original etymology was separation is now abandoned." See also W. Kornfeld, "קדשׁ [*qdš*]," *TDOT* 12:526.
3. This makes H. P. Müller's comments rather surprising—namely, that the description of a god as "holy" is particularly common in pre-Israelite Canaan (i.e., Ugarit) and that biblical hymns praising God's holiness betray a Canaanite influence ("קֹדֶשׁ *qdš* holy," *TLOT* 3:1110–11).
4. Kurt Goldammer, *Die Formenwelt des Religiösen: Grundriss der systematischen Religionswissenschaft* (Stuttgart: Alfred Kröner, 1960), 53; quoted in Kornfeld, "קדשׁ," 522, emphasis original.

10:10.[5] "Holy" does not so much connote "separate" as it does that which is qualitatively "other."

As Rudolf Otto has famously declared, to experience the holy is to experience awe, majesty, vitality, fascination, and even terror. Persons the world over recognize the existence of that which is beyond the normal realm of experience, and they often find these experiences accompanying an encounter with that "other."[6] The modern, secularized West has sought to reduce all experience to the common, but it has not succeeded. Rather, it has only replaced the holy with horror. The experiences that Otto associates with the holy, experiences we may argue are an essential part of human life, are now those that the reader or theatergoer experiences in reading a horror book or viewing a horror film. The "holy" has now been allied not with the clean but with the unclean, not with the life-affirming but with the life-destroying. This is the tragic result of the modern denial that any truly "other" can be found in life.

ANCIENT NEAR EASTERN CONCEPTS OF HOLINESS

In worldviews where the gods—though in some sense "other"—are still part of the natural order, rituals are effective only because of an assumed continuity between the human realm and the divine. Anything that can cause a breach between the two is labeled "unclean," and extensive rituals are prescribed to ensure that all unclean elements have been removed, both from the ritual utensils and from the ritual activities.[7] In this sense, uncleanness is an active reality that must be excluded from worship. It has no particular moral or ethical aspect, but it is simply that which makes rituals ineffective. This understanding of uncleanness is a result of the fundamentally dualistic understanding that tends to prevail in the world. We explain the vicissitudes of life by positing that reality has two poles: impersonal good (which is constructive) and impersonal evil (which is destructive). These two poles are in constant conflict. The gods themselves are caught up in this conflict, and they use magical powers on each other to try to appropriate one

5. Naudé, *NIDOTTE* 3:879.
6. Rudolf Otto, *The Idea of the Holy: An Inquiry into the Non-rational Factor in the Idea of the Divine and Its Relation to the Rational*, trans. John W. Harvey, 9th ed. (Oxford: Oxford University Press, 1928).
7. See, for instance, the "Ritual to Be Followed by the *Kalū*-Priest When Covering the Temple Kettle-Drum," *ANET* 334–38.

or the other of these forces. The unclean is the destructive force, and it must be excluded if the clean is to be effective. In this view, the unclean is not unholy, but simply represents the negative side of holiness. This view is captured well in what may be called Star Wars theology. "The Force" is the other—the holy. It is entirely impersonal and has light and dark sides. The challenge of life in the Star Wars world is to find out how to engage the light side and escape the dark side. Five thousand years ago, the Sumerians would have fully affirmed such a worldview and such a theology.

The absence of a moral and ethical component in the ANE conception of holiness is a necessary result of polytheism. All the gods, the good and the bad, are by definition "other"—holy. This fact excludes moral or ethical qualities from the concept of holiness. Mot, the Canaanite god of death and destruction, is just as holy as El, the beneficent progenitor of the gods. The perceptive reader will begin to recognize a disjunction here. Death is by definition unclean. So how can Mot be holy and unclean at the same time? The answer is contained in the dualistic worldview. If we still see a level of logical contradiction here, it is important to remember that in the so-called pagan theological system, logically contradictory concepts are quite permissible as long as they work to produce desired results.

So, for the Egyptian, the sun is a boat because, like a boat crossing the Nile, the sun crosses the sky. At the same time, the sun is a falcon because, like a falcon flying across the sky, the sun flies across the sky. The logical law of noncontradiction says that two things equal to a third thing must be equal to each other. So a boat is a falcon? Of course not. It is not a matter of logic, but a matter of what works. Thus, clean is holy, but so is unclean. While the holy is often the clean, this is not always the case in a dualistic understanding of reality.

THE BIBLICAL CONCEPT OF HOLINESS

General

At the outset, it must be observed that considerable similarity exists between biblical and nonbiblical understandings of holiness. In particular, many of the occurrences of the terms *qōdeš* and *qādôš* have to do with ritual purification. This is especially true in the books of Exodus and Leviticus. Persons and utensils engaged in the worship and service of YHWH must be dedicated (given over to his exclusive use) and purified, often with blood. The term "purified" (usually a translation of *ṭāhôr*) is important in this context. What does "unclean" mean in a setting where only one transcendent god is to be worshiped? First, the sacrificial system cannot be construed as a means of imitative magic, whereby the disposition of a god who is part of the cosmos is influenced in some way through the manipulation of material objects. The prophets railed against such a conception of sacrifice (e.g., Isa. 1:10–15; Jer. 7:21–23; Amos 5:21). Second, no force in the cosmos—or, more to the point, in YHWH—can effectively oppose YHWH's will.[8] So what does it mean to be unclean? What does it mean to be impure? Clearly, something unclean or impure does not correspond to the nature of YHWH. It is mixed, whereas he, both in his essence and in his character, is one. Thus, to make something clean or holy is to make it entirely one, with no mixture of anything that is inconsistent with the nature, purpose, and will of the Holy One.

In this regard, it is appropriate to say a word about the Hebrew concept of sin. In contrast to virtually all other ANE languages, which have relatively few (if any) words for sin, Hebrew has several such words. In ANE cultures, the primary offense against the gods was to infringe on their prerogatives. This infringement is expressed in Greek *hybris*, such as Icarus displayed when he sought to fly with the sun. By contrast, the Hebrew concept is much more nuanced, with more than half a dozen roots used to describe offenses against God and humans.[9] Here the offenses do not have so much to do with YHWH's prerogatives as with his will for human behavior, both toward him and toward other humans. Thus, the ultimate uncleanness, the ultimate unholiness, is the result of sin. This is seen clearly in Psalm 51, which is deeply concerned with uncleanness contracted as a result of sin. Here we see terminology similar to that found elsewhere in the ANE, though it is used in the service of a very different concept. Uncleanness is not some force contrary to the good life but rather a condition resulting from a failure to conform to God's will, whether intentional or unintentional. That failure—sin—will result

8. Amazingly, the one force that can oppose God's will is the human will. This reality is clear in Gen. 2, in YHWH's command to Adam concerning the tree, which suggests that Adam has the power to do what God does not want. Nothing else in the cosmos has such a capability.

9. These include *ḥṭ'*, *'wn, pš'*, *bgd*, *'wl, m'l, rmh*, and *šqr*, among others.

in death unless it is some way "covered" (*kāpar*) or "removed" (*sār*). A primary example is found in Isaiah 6. Isaiah's vision of the Holy God does not convict him of his finitude or his mortality but of the uncleanness of his lips. That is, his mouth has not been used in the service of God and his will. If it is to be so used, his sin will have to be covered and his iniquity will have to be taken away.[10]

Another example is found in Leviticus 10. In the previous ten chapters, YHWH spells out in detail how it is possible for his people, who have entered into covenant with him, to live in his presence and yet not be destroyed by his holiness. Aaron and his family have been designated as the mediators who would stand between YHWH and his people. In that regard, YHWH has made it clear that certain behaviors render a person clean in his presence and other behaviors render a person unclean—holy and unholy. All of this is directly connected with the divine will. Thus, there are holy and unholy oils, holy and unholy perfumes, holy and unholy fires. None of these items are holy in themselves; that is, they are not other in their essences. They are holy or unholy only if they conform to the will of the Holy One or not. But Aaron's sons do not make the connection between holiness and obedience. Thus, they prepare "strange" (*zārâ*, not of the household) fire and put it on the altar. It is fire "outside the family," fire that is not within the will of YHWH and, thus, unholy. YHWH's statement to Moses in the aftermath is significant: "By those who come near Me I must be regarded as holy" (Lev. 10:3 NKJV). To be a holy person is to be subject to the will of the Holy One.

All this is to say that although Israelite culture utilized some of the same terminology and practices that the neighboring cultures utilized, it did so in the service of a very different understanding of reality. As depicted in Israel's Scriptures, holiness is not merely ritual cleanness. Nor is ritual cleansing a way of neutralizing destructive cosmic forces. Rather, ritual cleansing is a way of both symbolizing and enforcing a profound truth about reality: *to defy YHWH's plan for creation is to render oneself*

10. The precise meaning of *ʿāwōn*, translated in the KJV with the now archaic word "iniquity," is difficult to ascertain. At one time, it was thought to have something to do with "twistedness," but more recently, it has been thought to connote the objective reality brought into existence by a sinful act; see *HALOT*, 2:800. Thus, it can be translated "guilt," but it is much more than merely guilt. It seems to express the cumulative effect of the sinful act; a reality now exists that must be counteracted in some way. Modern psychiatry may have succeeded in removing guilt from our collective psyche, but it has not removed *ʿāwōn*.

and everything one touches filthy, unable to exist in God's presence. So why sanctify the altar before its first use and annually thereafter? Doing so represents the truth that there is no cleanness except that to be found in obedience to the provision of the Holy God himself.

Only One Holy Being

These understandings all proceed from one earth-shaking revelation: YHWH is the only God (2 Sam. 7:22).[11] Hannah speaks the inescapable corollary of that truth: "There is no one holy like the LORD; there is no one besides you; there is no Rock like our God" (1 Sam. 2:2 NIV). What YHWH reveals to his people is that he is truly other. He is not merely a mysterious force within the cosmos. Rather, he is *completely other than the cosmos*. This truth is implicit in the second commandment. Why is making God in the shape of any created thing forbidden? Because he is other than all created things! Thus, as Hannah says, he alone is holy. Only one being transcends—is other than—every other being. All beings owe their existence to this being.

The recognition that YHWH is the only truly holy being in the universe may explain a remarkable feature of the book of Isaiah. The phrase "the Holy One of Israel" appears thirty-one times in the Bible, but twenty-five of those are found in Isaiah.[12] How are we to explain this phenomenon? It seems likely that it is the result of the overwhelming vision of YHWH recorded in Isaiah 6. There the prophet is forced to recognize the unique holiness of YHWH. That truth so impresses itself on him that it infuses his thinking from that point on. Why trust the nations when one can trust the Holy One? Why live in fear if one can have confidence in the Holy Being of the universe, the one who has singled Israel out among all the peoples of the world and voluntarily allied himself with her? Why believe that Babylon can hold his people captive when he has decreed otherwise? Why imagine that you can give light to the world unless your life is infused with the light of the Holy One?

11. See also Exod. 15:11 and Deut. 3:24, which pose rhetorical questions whose answers are clearly that no other gods exist. Deut. 4:35 says, "You were shown these things [the various experiences associated with Sinai] so that you might know that the LORD is God; besides him there is no other" (NIV).

12. The others are found in 2 Kings 19:22; Pss. 71:22; 78:41; 89:18; and Jer. 50:29; 51:5. Second Kings 19:22 is a duplicate of Isa. 37:23.

Holy Character

The ground-shaking truth that YHWH is the only truly holy being in the universe has some equally ground-shaking implications: it now becomes possible to define holy character, and such character is that of the Holy One. As mentioned above, it is impossible to define holy character in one way outside the Bible. Since all the gods, of whatever character, were considered holy, there could be no single holy character.[13] However, if only one holy being exists, it becomes possible to define holy character. It is the character of the Holy One. If YHWH's character were marked by brutality, cruelty, arbitrariness, or callousness, then holiness would include being brutal, cruel, arbitrary, or callous. But thankfully, YHWH's character is not marked by these things.

What is YHWH's character—his holy character? It is expressed in the concept of his holy name. The phrase "holy name" only occurs twenty-three times in the OT, but it provides the essential definition for the phrase "name of God," which appears much more frequently. The word "name" in the OT rarely refers only to a label, as it does normally in English. Rather, it refers to one's reputation, nature, and character, as in the English sentence "He has a good name in this community." "Holy name" occurs nine times in Ezekiel, seven times in the Psalms, three times in 1 Chronicles, three times in Leviticus, and once in Amos.[14] The occurrence in Psalm 103:1 is particularly instructive because the holy character mentioned there is clearly described in the following verses:

> Bless the Lord, O my soul,
>   and all that is within me,
>   bless his holy name.
> Bless the Lord, O my soul,
>   and do not forget all his benefits—
> who forgives all your iniquity,
>   who heals all your diseases,
> who redeems your life from the Pit,

13. This phenomenon is strikingly apparent in Otto's *The Idea of the Holy*. He brackets out any reference to moral excellence, saying that it is a derivative idea, not originally connoted by the term "holy." Thus, he feels it necessary to coin a replacement—namely, *numinous*, from the Latin *numen*; see pp. 6–8. But if one accepts the biblical view of reality, one cannot bracket out moral excellence. It is at the very heart of what holiness is.

14. Isa. 57:15 says, "whose name is holy" (NIV).

> who crowns you with steadfast love [*ḥesed*]
> and mercy [*raḥămîm*],
> who satisfies you with good as long as you live
> so that your youth is renewed like the eagle's.
> (Ps. 103:1–5 NRSV)

The Holy One is beneficial a source of flourishing; he is not a taker but a giver. He forgives, he heals, he redeems, he bestows undeserved love and compassion, he supplies all the good things one needs to live a fruitful and effective life. These realities define holy character. They embody his holy name.

In other instances, the holy name of God is displayed in the character of those who serve him. So it is the righteous, those who hate evil, who thank his holy name because he has given them light and joy (Ps. 97:10–12). It is those who remember, or abide by, YHWH's wondrous works and regulations (*mišpāṭîm*) who glory in his holy name (Ps. 105:3–5). In many ways, Psalm 145 is in its entirety a meditation on the holy character of YHWH. It begins with a statement of the psalmist's intention to bless the name of his God and King forever (v. 1), and it ends with the assertion that "all flesh will bless his holy name forever and ever" (v. 21 NRSV). Between these two verses are statements about YHWH's awesome power and majesty, *which are expressed in* his goodness and righteousness, his grace and compassion, his patience and his love, his goodness and trustworthiness, his providential care, and his attention to the cries of his people. What is holiness? Holiness is defined by these expressions. The holy character of YHWH can be summed up with six Hebrew terms, terms that are frequently associated with him and his behavior: *ṭôb*, *ʾĕmûnâ* or *ʾĕmet*, *ṣədāqâ*, *mišpāṭ*, *ṭāhôr*, and *ḥesed.*

Ṭôb, *"Goodness"*

First of all, YHWH is good. "O give thanks to the Lord, for he is good" (Ps. 107:1 NRSV). What does this verse mean? The term *good* in English has a very indefinite meaning, but in Hebrew, the sense is clear. "Good" is that which conforms to the constructive, beneficent purposes of the Creator. When God defines his creation as good in Genesis 1 (seven times, culminating in v. 31's "very good"), he means that the living, growing, productive universe is just as he has planned it. This is the significance of the knowledge of good and evil, bestowed by eating the fruit of the tree (2:17). It would involve the right to determine creation purposes for oneself and to shirk the transcendent Creator's definition of what is good.

So if "good" is that which conforms to creation purposes, how can the Creator himself be called good?[15] The answer to that question is that the statement is a testimony to the consistency of the Holy One's behavior. He only does that which keeps his own constructive creation purposes. But one might ask whether a great flood that wipes out every human being except one family is "good". When we compare the biblical account with what I take to be a corrupted Sumerian version of that account, we can see that, in fact, YHWH's action is good. According to the Sumerian tale, the gods intend to wipe out all humans because they are too noisy.[16] But one god has, we might say, a "fit of conscience" and alerts one human, who then manages to survive the flood. When the rest of the gods discover what has happened, they determine that the survivor who has become immortal by surviving will have to be isolated at the edge of the cosmos. Where the human race has come from is a question left unanswered and is a testimony to the fact that myths are not intended to be cognitive, but affective and effective. In contrast, the biblical narrative provides a coherent moral rationale for judgment and a clear redemptive purpose in preserving creation through Noah

In the biblical account, YHWH never intends to destroy humanity. Rather, by sending the flood, his intent is to demonstrate that if the corruption of humanity were ever addressed and creation restored to its original goodness, it would not be sufficient merely to destroy the human "bad actors." Thus, the intent of the flood is not to destroy, but to rule out one possible way to achieve a good humanity. In short, the Holy God can be trusted always to do that which is for the ultimate benefit of his creatures. He is good.

ʾĔmûnâ *or* ʾĔmet, *"Truth"*

A second feature of YHWH's holy character is "truth" (*ʾĕmûnâ* or *ʾĕmet*).[17] "The word of YHWH is right, and all his work is in truth"

15. See 1 Chron. 16:34; 2 Chron. 5:13; 7:3; 30:18; Ezra 3:11; Pss. 25:7, 8; 34:8; 86:5; 100:5; 106:1; 107:1; 118:1, 29; 135:3; 136:1; Jer. 33:11; Nah. 1:7. See also Gen. 50:20; Exod. 18:9; Pss. 73:1; 143:10.
16. See *ANET*, 104–6.
17. See Gen. 24:27; 32:10; Exod. 34:6; 2 Sam. 2:6; Pss. 30:9; 36:5; 40:10, 11; 57:3, 10; 61:7; 71:22; 86:11, 15; 88:11; 89:1, 2, 5, 8, 14, 33, 49; 91:4; 92:2; 96:13; 98:3; 100:5; 108:4; 115:1; 117:2; 119:75, 90; 138:2; 143:1; Prov. 16:6; Isa. 11:5; 25:1; 38:18, 19; Lam. 3:23; Hos. 2:20.

(Ps. 33:4 AT). *ʾĔmûnâ* and *ʾĕmet* are commonly translated "faithful" or "faithfulness" and frequently appear in parallelism with "steadfast love" (*ḥesed*, see below). They connote absolute, unfailing reliability. People displaying such character can be relied on in every situation. They will keep their word, no matter what; they can be depended on, even when keeping their word is not to their own benefit. YHWH's unqualified trustworthiness was astonishing to the Israelites. What god could ever be depended on? None. The gods were simply humans written large: better than humans in some regards, worse than humans in others. But the one thing the ancients knew is that they could not be trusted. On the contrary, YHWH could be trusted absolutely.

That being so, the Israelites could safely recline from their own management of their lives and "wait" for YHWH. This idea was not merely a matter of marking time, as it is in English. Rather, it was a confident expectation whereby one laid aside his or her own plans, resources, and understandings and looked forward to the unveiling of God's plans, resources, and surprising revelations. Such surrender was as difficult for ancient Hebrews as it is for those in the modern world. But those who will lay aside themselves and their own ways and look to God will discover that he is true, true to his word, and true to his people. He can be depended on.

Ṣədāqâ, *"Righteousness"*

A third aspect of YHWH's holy character is "righteousness" (*ṣədāqâ*).[18] That is, he can be trusted to do what is right in every circumstance. Although what is right might seem on the surface to be in conflict with what is good, further examination reveals that the two are harmonious. The Holy One sees beneath the surface and can be trusted to do what is in keeping with both his own integrity *and* the best ends of his creatures. Thus, it was right, after many years and many covenant breaches, to visit on the Israelites the accumulated results of their covenant breaking and exile them from their land. But would it be right for this God to abandon them and leave them there? Absolutely not. Why not? Because of his goodness. If he brings judgment, his ulti-

18. See Pss. 5:8; 7:17; 22:31; 31:1; 33:5; 35:24; 36:6; 50:6; 96:13; 97:6; 98:2, 9; 103:6, 17; 111:3; 143:1, 11; Isa. 9:7; 32:16; 33:5; 42:6, 21; 45:13; Jer. 9:24; Mic. 7:9.

mate purpose in that action is never destruction. His purpose is always refinement and redemption.

Thus, divine "righteousness" is often synonymous with "salvation."[19] See, for example, Isaiah 56:1: "Thus says the LORD: 'Keep justice, and do righteousness, for soon my salvation will come, and my righteousness be revealed'" (ESV). The treatment of the concept of righteousness has become confused as a result of Christian theology and its concept of imputed righteousness. We are justified before God and declared righteous because we confess our sins and accept that Jesus Christ died for us. We are not justified because of our right behavior. Thus far, we are in complete agreement. The problem arises when this concept is used to silence the OT's clear teaching that God enables his people to emulate him and to act righteously. YHWH demonstrates his holy character in both justification *and* sanctification. He expects that the world will see his righteousness—his right behavior—carried out in his people's lives (see Ezek. 36:23–27 and Isa. 56:1, the latter of which is quoted above). Because YHWH gives us his righteousness, we are expected to act in righteous ways. So Isaiah 61:11–62:2 (ESV) says:

> For as the earth brings forth its sprouts,
>   and as a garden causes what is sown in it to sprout up,
> so the Lord GOD will cause righteousness and praise
>   to sprout up before all the nations.
> For Zion's sake I will not keep silent,
>   and for Jerusalem's sake I will not be quiet,
> until her righteousness goes forth as brightness,
>   and her salvation as a burning torch.
> The nations shall see your righteousness,
>   and all the kings your glory,
> and you shall be called by a new name
>   that the mouth of the LORD will give.[20]

19. This raises an important interpretive issue. When Isaiah speaks of the "righteousness" of the redeemed exiles, the RSV and its derivatives will often translate the underlying term as "vindication" (e.g., Isa. 54:17; 62:1, 2). The idea is that YHWH has established that Israel is right before her former enemies. But more is possibly (probably?) involved than just judicial vindication; salvation will also issue in a new right character in God's people, one that will be displayed before the world (see Isa. 61:3, 10).

20. As noted above, the RSV tradition translates the second and third occurrences of *ṣədāqâ* in this passage as "vindication."

Mišpāṭ, *"Justice"*

A fourth characteristic of YHWH's "holy name" is *mišpāṭ*, conventionally translated as "justice" or "judgment."[21] As with so many Hebrew terms, this one has a large pool of potential meanings. It is based on the root *špṭ*. This root "signifies the action that restores *šālôm* to a community after it has been disturbed."[22] This understanding is, of course, quite different from the common idea that to do justice is to render a judicial decision. To be sure, to act in judgment is in part to restore *šālôm*. But giving judgment hardly exhausts what restoration involves. Every child who has wrestled with how Gideon is a "judge" (*šōpēṭ*) has dealt with that reality. In fact, that the Holy God is "just" is to say that God is passionately concerned about the well-being (*šālôm*) of his people. Such concern includes legal equity but extends far beyond that. *Mišpāṭ* is not so much about fairness, as we understand that concept today, as it is about the pattern of life that God has ordained for humans. Thus, his *mišpāṭîm* are not so much his "judgments" as they are his "regulations" (so the NLT). God can be trusted to work out his patterns of life, expressed in his regulations for life, for the good of his people. He is not arbitrary or callous; rather, he always works to mend the disturbed order, in which the powerful oppress the powerless, persons are treated as objects, and desire dissolves character.[23] Thus, to judge the nations with righteousness (Pss. 9:8; 96:13; 98:9) is to bring them into right order, to govern them in ways that accord with the nature of reality.[24] This understanding makes the statements in Isaiah that the Servant will bring justice (*mišpāṭ*) to the earth all the more startling (Isa. 42:1, 4). Who is this person who will do what only the Holy God can do?

---

21. Gen. 19:25; Deut. 16:20; 33:21; Pss. 9:7–8; 33:5; 37:28; 103:6; 119:149; 140:12; 146:7; Prov. 21:3; 29:26; Isa. 5:16; 30:18; 61:8; Jer. 5:4–5; 9:24; Mic. 3:8; Zeph. 3:5; Mal. 2:17.
22. *HALOT*, 4:1623.
23. Note the repeated statement that YHWH will judge the nations with righteousness. That is, YHWH will bring the nations into accord with his plan and do so in ways that are exactly right for everything and all concerned. For *mišpāṭ* as "plan," see Exod. 26:30, where Moses is instructed to build the tabernacle according to the *mišpāṭ* revealed to him on the mountain. See also 1 Kings 6:38 and Jer. 30:18. For *mišpāṭ* as "pattern of behavior," see 2 Kings 17:33–34, which speaks of the customs of the peoples who were transported into Samaria by the Assyrians.
24. The phrase "justice and righteousness" (*mišpāṭ ûṣədāqâ*) occurs in numerous OT passages. It is quite likely a device known as hendiadys, in which two items joined by a conjunction are intended to be taken as a single concept. Thus, the idea here may be "right order."

Ṭāhôr, *"Pure"*

The fifth term that describes the holy character of YHWH is *ṭāhôr*, "pure." While this term is rarely associated directly with God, it is *very* commonly related to items that are holy because of their association with him. The term is particularly related to holiness in six verses: Exodus 28:36, 30:35, 37:29, 39:30; 1 Kings 7:50; and 2 Chronicles 14:22. In each of these cases, an item must become pure to be associated with something holy (see also Lev. 24:4–6). Clearly, the idea is that the item in view must be all one thing and not mixed with something else in any way. The noun form is frequently used to convey this idea. When it is used in an ethical context, the idea of that which is unmixed seems to continue to be prominent. So David asks for a "pure heart" (Ps. 51:10 NIV), and Psalm 12:6 says that the words of YHWH are pure. A specific connection to YHWH is found in Habakkuk 1:13, where God's eyes are said to be too pure to look on evil. The point here is that to be holy is to be all one thing. It is not to be deceptive; it is not to speak out of both sides of the mouth. It is to be single minded, to have unmixed motives. Proverbs 30:12 speaks of those who are "pure in their own eyes but are not washed from their filth" (AT), whereas Psalm 24:3–4 says that the person who presumes to stand in the holy place must have clean hands and a pure heart, not having lifted his hands to a worthless idol or sworn deceitfully.[25]

Above we spoke of the distinctive ideas of the clean and the unclean in the OT. That which is associated with YHWH is clean, and that which is not associated with him is unclean. These concepts are expressed with *ṭāhôr* and its antonym *ṭāmēʾ*. Anything to be used in the service of YHWH must be clean. Anything that is unclean may not be so used. What is unclean? Something that is dirty; something that is in an unnatural state (e.g., shed blood); anything that is contrary to YHWH's *mišpāṭ*; anything that has not been atoned for with blood. When ethical behavior is involved, uncleanness particularly entails living in ways that are contrary to God's plan for life:[26] sexual activity outside the bonds of marriage (Gen. 34:5, 13, 27), worshiping other

25. Here "pure" translates the rare *bar*, which has the sense of "bright" or "transparent" and is thus synonymous with *ṭāhôr*.

26. Here the term "abomination" (*tôʿēbâ*) is significant. Whatever is contrary to *mišpāṭ* is abhorrent to God and is thus, by definition, unclean. See Mic. 3:9 for the conjunction of the two terms. See also Ezek. 43:8.

gods (Jer. 2:7–8), sacrificing children to them (Ezek. 23:37–38), and using things in ways clearly not intended by their nature (Lev. 11:44). In this regard, when Isaiah confesses that his lips are unclean, he seems to be saying that, unlike the lips of the seraphim, his lips have not always been used in the praise of God and are thus unholy.

Ḥesed, *"Unfailing Love"*

The final element that defines the holy character of YHWH in the OT is *ḥesed*. Here again we are confronted with a Hebrew term for which no single equivalent exists in the English language. It connotes a wide variety of behavior, ranging from kindness to self-denying love. The NIV uses no less than twenty-four different words or phrases to translate *ḥesed*. Of equal interest with the etymology is the lack of derivation.[27] To date, no cognate has been clearly identified in any other Semitic language. The term seems to be unique to the Hebrew Bible. Yet it occurs more than 250 times there. About three quarters of these occurrences relate to YHWH. It seems fair to say that the Hebrews discovered something in the character of God that was so unusual and remarkable that they needed to coin a new word to signify it.

Because *ḥesed* often occurs in covenantal contexts (e.g., David's treatment of Mephibosheth, reported in 2 Sam. 9), it has often been said that the term denotes "covenant love" and connotes the kind of mutual loyalty that a covenant enjoins on its participants. While that is certainly true as far as it goes, it by no means exhausts the meaning of the word. Upon further reflection, *ḥesed* is also that love that expresses itself in the determination of a superior to do good to an inferior, especially when the inferior does not deserve it. When the people of Israel considered the God who had laid hold of them and would not let them go, the God who is other than this world, they found that his *character* was as much other than human as his *essence* was other than the cosmos. Instead of a self-serving, grasping, and manipulative god, they found a God who cared more about his people than about himself; who delighted in giving them good things, which they did not deserve; who, far from manipulating them, delighted in empowering them instead. Here was one whose special favorites were the powerless in society:

27. John R. Kohlenberger III and James A. Swanson, *The Hebrew-English Concordance to the Old Testament* (Grand Rapids: Zondervan, 1998), 559.

the orphans, the widows, and the immigrants. After the Israelites had broken their covenant repeatedly for a thousand years and had finally reaped the results, they discovered that he still intended to preserve them and bless them. It is no wonder that the refrain of the returned exiles was "O give thanks to the LORD, for he is good, for his [*ḥesed*] endures forever" (Pss. 118:29; 136:1 NRSV; cf. 1 Chron. 16:34; Pss. 106:1; 107:1; 118:1; 136:2, 3, 26; Jer. 33:11; etc.).

It is suggestive that *ḥesed* first occurs in Genesis (19:19; 20:13; 24:1; etc.). Was it Abraham who coined the word, having discovered a self-denying love in the God who had called him from Haran and had cared for him in such remarkable ways? It would certainly be fitting if that were the case. The plea of Abraham's servant in 24:12 and similar passages—namely, that God would show him the same *ḥesed* that he has shown Abraham—suggests that Abraham and the servant had had some conversations about a God who was not out to get what he could from his human servants but was more interested in enhancing their lives. It is also interesting to imagine Naomi's conversations with Ruth and Orpah about the *ḥesed* of YHWH, which infuses the life of Ruth (Ruth 1:8; 3:10). The term is typically translated "kindness" in Ruth, and that is entirely appropriate, for what is kindness but undeserved favor shown to another?

HOLINESS AND MORAL EXCELLENCE

Rudolf Otto tells us that *The Idea of the Holy* was motivated by a concern over the bondage of orthodox Christianity to the rational.[28] Although he does not say it specifically, one suspects that that concern was linked with an apprehension about rationalistic biblical criticism and its effects on Christian faith. But in his concern to rediscover the nonrational aspects of vital religion, he disconnected the experience of the holy from ethical considerations. We may be grateful that he brought to light again the terror, the wonder, and the shock that a genuine encounter with the holy ought to have for us. The truth is that we humans have a terrible desire to domesticate God, to bring him down to our level, to make him useful. That was surely the sin of Nadab and Abihu. They did not realize that holiness is deadly to unprotected

28. Rudolph Otto, *The Idea of the Holy*, trans. J. W. Harvey (Oxford: Oxford University Press, 1925), 1–4.

humans. Their experience proved that we must never take the Holy One for granted.

That said, and indeed emphasized, Otto's attempt to abstract "holy" from ethical considerations was unfortunate. While the holy may be abstracted from the ethical in most religions of the world, it cannot be so abstracted in biblical religion. In fact, we will go so far as to say that in the only true expression of holiness, the biblical one, the holy and the ethical are indissoluble. The Holy One has made us with the purpose of sharing his holy character with us. How can we say such a thing, particularly when Otto has claimed that moral excellence is an unwarranted accretion to the actual meaning of holiness? We say it on the basis of the Scriptures. Let us retell the story that extends from Genesis through Leviticus.

Genesis tells us that YHWH created a people. He did so by demonstrating that if, in contrast to what took place in Eden, persons trust him, believe what he says, and do what he asks, they can experience divine blessing. But who is this YHWH who offers blessing? Is he another figure in the ANE pantheon? By no means! He is the only being who can truly be called God. But how can Abraham's offspring be brought to comprehend that amazing thought? It is especially problematic when we remember that, as Exodus tells us, these people were immersed in one of the region's most polytheistic cultures for several hundred years. The way YHWH revealed himself and the nature of reality to them was by means of a covenant. The covenant form that God used stipulated certain behaviors that a king required of his covenant partners. As the people, moved by their deliverance by YHWH from captivity, fulfilled these stipulations, they were learning who he was and what he was like. They were learning by doing. Here is one example: the first commandment requires that they honor no other god. No philosophical argument for monotheism is given here. Rather, a practical monotheism is encouraged, one that, if carried out at all faithfully, would lead almost inevitably to the conclusion that there are no other gods. So also, the second commandment teaches transcendence. Why can God not be captured in any form of this world? Because he is other than this world! It hardly needs to be said here that the only three monotheistic and iconoclastic religions in the world are dependent on the thirty-nine books that Christians call the OT.

But what is the purpose of this knowledge of God? Is YHWH simply desiring that people obey him? The answer to that question is to be found, in part, in the Bible's approach to sexuality. Sexual expression is carefully circumscribed in the Bible for two reasons. First, in the religion of all Israel's neighbors, sexual expression in one form or another was intimately tied to magical efforts to control fertility. Since YHWH, the only Holy One, transcends the cosmos, such efforts are not only misguided; they are wrong. Fertility is a gift, and it cannot be magically manipulated. Second, sexual expression is so carefully regulated (think of *mišpāṭ*) that it is intended to be an object lesson concerning the divine-human relationship. The sex act is often described as "knowing" one another, which is telling. Sexual activity among humans is always intended to express a God-ordained relationship. It is in an act of surrender and self-giving to one who is the same as us *yet different* that we truly find ourselves, and in the act of "knowing" that other, we become more truly ourselves. This is not an act whose terms we define for ourselves, nor is it an act in which we use our desires for our own purposes. But as we practice it within God's terms, it achieves the purposes for which God designed it. In the same way, God wants us to know him, *in order that* we may share his character.

So we find the statement that the people should make themselves holy and become holy people, because YHWH is holy (Lev. 11:44; 19:2).[29] Could this possibly mean that persons are expected to become transcendent in essence? The idea is ludicrous. But what then does it mean? Surely, it means that God expects his covenant partners not merely to fulfill covenant obligations but to share his holy character—that character that is as other than normal human character as divine essence is other than human essence. Is that possible in this life? The rest of the Bible, the Old and the New Testaments together, will address that question, but that such sharing is expected can hardly be doubted.[30] If there were any questions, they must certainly be laid to rest by Leviticus 19.

But before we turn to Leviticus 19, we must consider the context in which that chapter occurs—namely, chapters 18 and 20. These chapters,

29. Significantly, in neither of these references is the imperative used. The verbs are indicative. It is simply a matter of fact that the people will do what is necessary to make themselves holy.

30. See John N. Oswalt, *Called to Be Holy: A Biblical Perspective* (Grand Rapids: Zondervan, 1998).

with their sweeping prohibitions of any sexual activity outside heterosexual marriage, have grown increasingly controversial in our climate of sexual license. They are regularly dismissed as either the prudishness of rural people or the archaic requirements of a priest-ridden culture. In any case, we are told that they have no more relevance for modern Christians than do the restrictions of chapters 11–15. In fact, that is not the case. For one thing, the laws of chapters 11–15 are not enforced through the death penalty, whereas those in chapters 18 and 20 are. Clearly, the issues addressed in chapters 18 and 20 are not ceremonial, merely rendering one unclean. For another thing, chapters 11–15 are clearly intended, by their location, to be instructional in nature, coming as they do immediately after the deaths of Aaron's sons, Nadab and Abihu. Chapters 1–9 of Leviticus were designed to provide means whereby people could approach the Holy One and not be destroyed by his holiness. They should have taught that a hard and fast difference exists between the holy and the unholy. Clearly, Nadab and Abihu had not learned that lesson. If they had not, there was a very significant likelihood that the rest of the people had not either, thus the object of the lessons of chapters 11–15.

Some would say that since we certainly do not stone children for cursing their parents, the laws regulating sexual practices in Leviticus 18 and 20 are equally irrelevant. This is a rather striking category error. While the level of punishment associated with a prohibition says something about what God thinks of that prohibition's significance, it says nothing about the prohibition itself. Since we no longer stone children for cursing their parents, does that mean that children should be encouraged to curse their parents? Of course not. A family in which children dishonor their parents (whether the parents are worthy of honor or not) is a family that will not survive. That is as true today as it was in Moses's day.

What is communicated by encasing Leviticus 19 within statements about sexual ethics is that as a society's sexual ethics go, so go its ethics in general. That is, if illicit desire and its gratification are allowed to control a society, that society *cannot* mirror the holy character of God, who is self-giving, self-denying love. Chapter 19, beginning as it does with the statement that God's people are to be holy, proceeds to talk about the ethical expressions of holy character.[31] The expressions are

31. Mary Douglas, in her *Leviticus as Literature* (Oxford: Oxford University Press, 1999), argues that chapters 18 and 20 are intended to contrast with chapter 19, which she calls "the most important

delightfully mixed together, demonstrating that the compartmentalization of holy behavior is neither possible nor desirable.

Such behavior relates to the family (Lev. 19:3, 29), to religion (vv. 4–8, 12, 26, 30–31), to society (vv. 9–18, 20–22, 32–33), to the natural world (vv. 19, 23–28), and to business (vv. 35–36). To suggest, as Otto does, that holiness can be separated from ethics is to betray an unfortunate failure to consider the biblical text adequately. To be sure, it is equally wrong to suggest that holiness is only about ethics. It is not. Holiness is also about that which is radically, sometimes terrifyingly, other. But just as YHWH is radically other than the created cosmos, so is his character radically other than that which has come to characterize humanity. The wonder is that YHWH intends for his human creatures to be transformed into the likeness of that startlingly other character.

chapter in the book" (239). Chapter 19 displays "the pure and noble character of the Hebrew God," against the backdrop of "the libidinous customs of the very strange false gods" (238).

Part 2

TEXTUAL ANALYSES

Chapter 2

RESTORING PERFECTION: HOLINESS AND CREATION IN THE PENTATEUCH

MATT I. AYARS

INTRODUCTION: *'ĔLŌHÎM* IS ONE, TRANSCENDENT, SOVEREIGN, AND ETERNAL

The creation accounts found in Genesis 1–2 are distinct from its ANE counterparts. Deviating from the standard ancient Babylonian creation myths, Genesis 1–2 collectively reveals the following:

- God is not many but one.
- God is eternal.
- The creation is not eternal.
- The creation is not the result of warring deities, nor is it subject to fate and destiny.
- God created because it pleased him to do so.
- God is not dependent on the creation in any way.
- God did not create humans as servants or out of necessity.
- God created humanity simply because it pleased him to do so.

As a whole, then, what do the creation accounts of Genesis 1 and 2 affirm? They affirm that the one transcendent, sovereign, and eternal God created out of a desire to share life with his creatures. Genesis 1 and 2 not only contradict the claims of all other ANE creation myths; they are also pregnant with the key themes of the Pentateuch (as well as the remainder of the Scriptures). Beginning with an exploration of the Sabbath and moving through key stories in the Pentateuch, this chapter explores how the Pentateuch conceptualizes the triconsonantal root *qdš* as "qualitative otherness," which is inextricably linked to transcendental monotheism and its implications for ethics, human life, and the creation as a whole.

THE SABBATH IS HOLY

The first occurrence of *qdš* in the Bible is in Genesis 2:3, which says, "And God blessed the seventh day and sanctified [*wayəqaddēš*] it, for on it, he rested from all his work, which God created" (AT). Here God blesses and sanctifies the seventh day of creation, the Sabbath. The second half of the verse provides the rationale for God's blessing and sanctifying the Sabbath: "for on it, he rested from all his work, which [he] created." In other words, the seventh day is *distinct* (i.e., set apart) from the other days because God rested on it, whereas he actively created on the other days. A binarism is at work, distinguishing two types of days: (1) workdays and (2) rest days. The first six days comprise life-creating activity, yet the seventh day is one of rest from that activity.

While a qualitative difference exists between the six workdays and the Sabbath, these two categories of days share something in common: both support the generation and flourishing of life. The generation and flourishing of life are central themes of Genesis 1–2. In these two chapters, God creates life and systems that enable that life to flourish. In Genesis 1, God first creates habitations in which life can flourish (days 1–3), and then he fills those habitations with inhabitants (days 4–6). He then commands those inhabitants to propagate more life (vv. 22, 28). God's command to the first humans to cultivate and care for the creation is integral to the theme of the generation and flourishing of life. This theme also appears in Genesis 2, where God's creative activity climaxes with breathing the breath of life (*nišmat ḥayyîm*) into Adam (v. 7). The theme of life also resonates with the declaration that the tree of life (*ʿēṣ haḥayyîm*) is in the midst of the garden (v. 9) as well as in Eden's rivers, giving life to its surrounding lands (vv. 10–14). Altogether, God's good creation, as he intended it, is perfect and complete when teeming with self-propagating life.[1]

It is clear how six days of work generate life, but what about the day of rest? What do life and its flourishing have to do with the holiness of the Sabbath and, particularly, rest? The creation cycle is incomplete without rest because life cannot be properly sustained without balancing work with rest. The Sabbath protects life by guarding humanity against absorption in work. Blocher writes:

1. This notion is also emphasized in the fact that death is the consequence of violating God's rules (Gen. 2:17; 6:6–8, 13).

> Now what is the meaning of the Sabbath that was given to Israel? It relativizes the works of mankind, the contents of the six working days. It protects mankind from total absorption by the task of subduing the earth, it anticipates the distortion which makes work the sum and purpose of human life, and it informs mankind that he will not fulfill his humanity in his relation to the world which he is transforming but only when he raises his eyes above, in the blessed, holy hour of communion with the Creator. . . . The essence of mankind is not work![2]

In sum, rest is required for life to flourish, even when the cultivation of creation is the primary human vocation. Being absorbed in work ultimately hinders the flourishing of life.[3]

As noted above, this notion of rest being central in Genesis (and the rest of the OT) is unique from the extrabiblical ANE corpus. Many ANE myths reflect a worldview where the gods create humanity primarily to relieve themselves of the burdens of labor and to receive worship and service. Here are some notable examples:

1. Enuma Elish (Babylonian creation myth). In this myth, the gods create humans to perform labor so that the gods can rest. After the god Marduk defeats the chaos monster Tiamat and becomes the king of the gods, the other gods ask him to create humans to relieve them of their work. Humans are fashioned from the blood of the defeated god Kingu, and their purpose is to serve the gods by maintaining temples, offering sacrifices, and performing necessary work. It reads, "I will establish a savage, 'man' shall be his name. Verily, savage-man I will create. He shall be charged with the service of the gods that they might be at ease!"

2. Atra-Hasis (Akkadian/Babylonian flood and creation myth). In the Atra-Hasis myth, the gods originally toil to create canals and

2. Henri Blocher, *In the Beginning: The Opening Chapters of Genesis* (Downers Grove, IL: InterVarsity, 1984), 57.

3. Because creation is mutable (i.e., it has a beginning, is contingent, and subject to change), it is inherently finite and thus requires periodic renewal to sustain life. Rest—epitomized in the Sabbath—is the God-ordained rhythm that supports this need. It sustains the generative purpose of creation by making space for recovery, reflection, and relationship, all of which are essential in a creation that is not self-sustaining but directed toward flourishing in God.

perform other agricultural work, but they grow tired and rebel. To solve this problem, the god Enki (or Ea) proposes creating humans from clay and the blood of a slain god to take over these burdensome tasks. Humans are specifically created to work for the gods, providing food and offerings. It reads, "Belet-ili, the womb goddess, is present. Let the womb goddess create offspring, and let man bear the load of the gods!"

3. The Epic of Gilgamesh (Sumerian/Babylonian epic). While not primarily a creation myth, The Epic of Gilgamesh reflects a worldview in which humans serve the gods through labor and offering sacrifices. The gods take an active role in human affairs, and part of humanity's purpose is seen as appeasing the gods through worship and servitude.

4. Egyptian Creation Myths (Memphite theology). In some versions of Egyptian mythology, although humans are not explicitly created to be slaves, they are made to maintain the order of the cosmos (Ma'at) and serve the gods. The role of humanity is to perform rituals and provide offerings to sustain the gods' power and existence.

5. Eridu Genesis (Sumerian creation myth). Similar to the Atra-Hasis and Enuma Elish, in this Sumerian myth, humans are created to "carry the yoke" of labor for the gods, fulfilling a subservient role by providing for the needs of the divine.

In these myths, humanity's purpose is often utilitarian—humans exist to take on tasks the gods do not wish to do themselves, thus freeing the gods from the burden of labor and ensuring the continuous functioning of the cosmos and religious practices. These myths contrast with other creation narratives that ascribe a different purpose to human beings, such as the biblical account in Genesis, where humans are depicted as stewards of creation rather than slaves to the gods. In the biblical witness, the tyranny of work also distorts human meaning and humanity's vocation to be divine image bearers. The human vocation to cultivate and have dominion over the creation is one aspect of being created in the divine image. God's working six days a week and his resting on one are the model for human life. The Sabbath is a reminder that humanity's identity is not entirely wrapped up in work. Just as the Creator is more than the work he does, so is humanity. This day of rest, then, points to a reality about God and humanity. The consequence of divine image bearers failing to observe the Sabbath not only thwarts the sustaining of life; it also distorts the nature of the Creator.

The Sabbath and Human Rebellion

The risk of the tyranny of work exponentially increases with the consequences of sin in Genesis 3. As a result of Adam and Eve's disobedience, God pronounces a curse against them (vv. 16–19). Eve's consequence is that she will have pain in childbearing (v. 16). Adam's consequence is that he will have pain in cultivating the earth because the earth is now cursed (vv. 17–19). As Richter highlights, the curse of cultivation and childbearing is not as much physically burdensome, but emotionally and psychologically traumatic. Richter writes:

> This last bit of the curse is particularly poignant. Most read the phrase "by the sweat of your face" as having to do with difficult physical labor. But an article by Daniel Fleming of New York University has demonstrated that this phrase is actually an old ancient Near Eastern idiom having nothing to do with hard work. Rather, this idiom speaks of anxiety—perspiration-inducing *fear*. Where does anxiety fit into God's curse upon us? What we find in Genesis 3 is that because of the rebellion of the earth and the expulsion of Adam and Eve from God's presence, humanity will now live their lives in an adversarial world with a constant, gnawing undercurrent of dread that there will not be enough, that their labor will not meet the need.[4]

For both man and woman, bringing forth and sustaining life will be risky, onerous, burdensome, and painful due to their rebellion. Together as divine image bearers, their vocation of generating and sustaining life is one means by which they faithfully embody the likeness of God. By obeying the command to multiply and have dominion over

4. Sandra L. Richter, *The Epic of Eden: A Christian Entry into the Old Testament* (Downers Grove, IL: IVP Academic, 2008), 111.

creation, they participate in the life-generating and sustaining activity of the Creator. However, it is precisely in their faithful fulfillment of this vocation that they are cursed. The curse means that generating and sustaining life will be much more difficult and will demand much more effort. This demand heightens the risk of the tyranny of work.

Perhaps more importantly, the curse of Genesis 3 also thwarts humanity's witness to the nature of the Creator. In Genesis 1–2, God delights in his work, unlike the creating deities of the ANE and unlike humanity laboring under the burden of the curse. It is by strife, struggle, risk, betrayal, and pain that creation comes about in all other ANE creation myths (more below). In the Hebrew origin story, God is utterly unchallenged in his creative work. God's sovereignty shines through in the formulaic declaration "And God said, 'Let there be *x*,' and there was *x*. . . . And there was evening, and there was morning—the *n*th day." It is that simple. God wanted something to happen, so it did. Creation came about as a result of his unchallenged and perfect will, and he took delight in it. It was good. No other deity forced his hand. It was just as he intended, and life flourished. Ever since humans rebelled, however, they have looked more like the ANE gods, who were burdened by work and who struggled to keep death at bay. Humans were supposed to delight in their work and, in doing so, reflect the Creator's own delight in his work. Now it is not so. When they rest, however, they emulate the Creator, who also rested.

The life-preserving function of the Sabbath is heightened, then, when mapped onto the curse in Genesis 3. The Sabbath is the day on which the curse of toil is lifted. It is the day that brings relief from the curse. While the burden of strenuously fighting back death marks all the other days, the Sabbath is marked by life and peace. Moreover, when image bearers make the Sabbath holy by observing it, they continue to reflect the fact that they, like God, are more than the work they do.

As it is reflected in the OT, Egyptian slavery is the epitome of human life being absorbed in work and culminating in death, which is why, as we move forward in the story of the Pentateuch, the Sabbath is also mapped onto the Egyptian deliverance event.[5] Slavery in Egypt is a case study of what happens when the Creator's will is ignored. A

5. Interestingly, nearly half (47) of the OT occurrences of *šabbāt* (111) are in the Pentateuch. More than half of the Pentateuch occurrences are in Leviticus (25).

calendar with a day of rest at its center has special meaning for a nation delivered from generations of slave labor. Immediately following its deliverance from Egypt, God gives Israel an entirely new calendar that is centered not on work—but on rest. Redemption from a life of slavery means the reintegration of rest into the life of God's people and the flourishing of life as patterned after the Creator in Genesis 1. With the Sabbath in place, vocation returns to its proper place and meaning. Put another way, when Sabbath is in place, the vocational aspect of the image of God in humanity is redeemed and God's perfect creation is restored. With the image of God restored, so is humanity's effectiveness in fulfilling their vocation to be divine image bearers. This reality surrounding the sanctity of the Sabbath is a picture of what will come in the Sinai covenant.

The Holiness of the Sabbath and the Restoration of God's Purposes for Creation

Mapping the Sabbath onto the human vocation of Genesis 1–2, the curse of Genesis 3, and deliverance from Egyptian slavery suggests why the Sabbath plays a crucial role in the holiness manifesto[6] in Leviticus.[7] Leviticus 23:3 says, "Six days shall work be done, but on the seventh day is a Sabbath of solemn rest, a holy convocation. You shall do no work. It is a Sabbath to the Lord in all your dwelling places" (ESV). The Sabbath not only marks Israel as God's possession but also serves as a means of relief from the curse that is the tyranny of work, which culminates in death. God's holy people live according to the model of Eden, in which humans faithfully bear God's likeness, work is kept in its proper place, life flourishes, and God's will for the creation is fulfilled.

In sum, the Sabbath is not merely holy because it is a day of rest distinct from working days. The Sabbath is blessed and holy (i.e., qualitatively different) because it is a linchpin for fulfilling God's will for creation, specifically regarding the generation and flourishing of life. It

---

6. The "holiness manifesto" in Leviticus refers to the overarching theme and set of laws centered on holiness that shapes the theological and ethical framework of the book, particularly found in what is often called the "holiness code" (Lev. 17–26). The "manifesto" establishes a divine call for the Israelites to live in a way that reflects God's holiness, influencing every aspect of life—ritual, moral, and communal.
7. *Šabbāt* occurs thirteen times in Leviticus: 16:31; 23:3, 11, 15, 16, 32; 24:8; 25:2, 4, 6.

also enables humans to fulfill their vocation to bear the divine image. Absorption in work leads to death, the distortion of the image of God, and a fatal departure from God's will for his creation. Keeping work in its proper place and leaving room for rest, by contrast, lead to life. This Sabbath day, then, is qualitatively *different* from all other days. Beginning with the sanctification of the seventh day, we can safely say that holiness is *qualitative otherness*.

CLEAN DIRT

The noun *qōdeš* occurs in the Pentateuch for the first time in Exodus 3:5, which says, "Then [YHWH] said [to Moses], 'Do not come near; take your sandals off your feet, for the place on which you are standing is holy ground [*'admat-qōdeš*]'" (ESV). In the creation account, the root *qdš* applies to a day. Here it applies to dirt. The ground is cursed due to Adam's rebellion in Genesis 3, but here we find ground from which the curse has been lifted. Normally, ground is defiled by death, particularly desert ground, because the desert is the place where life cannot flourish. This ground, however, is clean; it is holy. The holy day and the holy ground together make up sacred time and space, both of which are key notions concerning YHWH worship at the tabernacle, which becomes the focus of the remainder of the Pentateuch. Accordingly, the burning bush and the holy ground around it prefigure the tabernacle later in Exodus. With the tabernacle in view, it is clear that God's presence in the bush renders the ground holy. There is nothing qualitatively different about this ground in and of itself. This ground is only made qualitatively different (i.e., sanctified) by the presence of the Holy One. This is evident in the symbol of fire, as Victor Hamilton points out: "Fire is a frequent medium by which God reveals himself. God's fire always does one of two things in Scripture. Either it destroys (think of Sodom and Gomorrah's fire), or it purifies (think of Isa. 6)."[8] Just as God's holy presence will later fill the tabernacle in the form of fire (Exod. 40:34–38), so his fiery, purifying presence fills the bush here. Likewise, as entering God's holy presence in the tabernacle requires special provision, Moses needs to remove his sandals to stand on holy ground.[9]

8. Victor P. Hamilton, *Exodus: An Exegetical Commentary* (Grand Rapids: Baker Academic, 2011), 46.
9. Many interpretations have been suggested regarding why Moses has to remove his sandals. My view is that Moses is required to remove his sandals because they are made from animal carcass, which we later learn is unclean. For an overview of the various explanations, see Hamilton, *Exodus*, 49.

Furthermore, it is worth noting that this holy ground is in the desert, which is the place where death reigns. We will see later how, on the Day of Atonement, the scapegoat takes the sin of the people out of the camp and into the wilderness because the wilderness is where sin belongs. The wilderness, which is also the desert, is the place where life cannot thrive. The desert is the place where the curse of human rebellion is most concentrated. Victor Hamilton sums the point up superbly:

> Normally, then, the wilderness is the antithesis of holiness. They go together like oil and water. The one thing that can transform common, unholy ground into extraordinary, holy ground is a theophany, a (spectacular) divine manifestation. And if God can transform unholy ground into holy ground by the glow of his presence, might he not also be able to transform an unholy life? What God can do with the ʾădāmâ, might he not also do with the ʾādām?[10]

The theophany of Exodus 3, which sanctifies the utmost of the unclean, provides hope that the curse can be lifted, a hope that extends to a people enslaved to death in Egypt. If the Holy One can reverse the curse of this unclean ground, then he can undoubtedly reverse the curse of the Israelites suffering under the tyrannical rule of Pharaoh. God creates life from nothing in Genesis 1–2. Can he also bring the dead to life?

"I AM": THE ETERNAL, TRANSCENDENT GOD

Meaningfully, God reveals his divine name to Moses in the immediate context of this theophany. Specifically, it suggests a correspondence between God's holiness and God's name. This correspondence is later made explicit in Deuteronomy's repeated declaration that the place of YHWH's name is the place of his presence and, therefore, the place of proper worship (Deut. 12:5, 11, 21; 14:23; 16:2, 6, 16; 26:2).[11] A first clear implication, then, is that the ground is holy because YHWH is holy. A second implication is that YHWH's name is vital in

10. Hamilton, *Exodus*, 49.
11. See Sandra L. Richter, *The Deuteronomistic History and the Name Theology*: *ləšakkēn šᵊmô šām in the Bible and the Ancient Near East*, BZAW 318 (New York: De Gruyter, 2002).

understanding what it means that YHWH is holy. If we are beginning to understand that holiness is qualitative otherness, then in what way is YHWH qualitatively other?

God tells Moses that he is I Am Who I Am (*ʾehyeh ăšer ʾehyeh*). While scholars have long debated the grammar and meaning of this name, a relatively high degree of consensus exists among both Jewish and Christian biblical scholars and theologians that the name—at least in part—refers to the *sovereignty*, *transcendence*, and *eternality* of God.[12] These aspects of the meaning of the name are wrapped up in the unbound essence of the grammar of the name. God, *unlike all created things*, is not limited by anything external to himself; nor is he bound by time or space or captured, contained, or equated with any created notion that a term could signify. He simply *is*. This aspect of God's being is profoundly *different* from the nature of creatures.

The name is not only grammatically unbound but also hinges on the operative "to be" verb, thereby indicating *life*. God *is*. He is the originator of life, and there has never been a time when he has not existed. He is life from eternity to eternity. He is pure life, with no admixture of finitude and certainly not death. It is precisely these qualities that make God qualitatively different from anything or anyone created.

There are, then, two ontological categories: (1) the uncreated and (2) the created. The created is finite, bound by time and space, entirely dependent on the creation for survival (e.g., food, oxygen), mutable, and therefore transformable toward the good and the bad (i.e., corruptible). The uncreated is qualitatively different in that he is infinite, unrestricted by time and space, immutable, and therefore eternally one. In sum, the unbound name of God attests to his eternality and therefore his qualitative differences from all things created.

THE COVENANT AND THE FIRST COMMANDMENT: EXCLUSIVE MONOTHEISM AND HOLINESS

Of all the ways the one true God could have delivered his chosen people from the tyrannical grip of Pharaoh, why plagues? If God could harden Pharaoh's heart (Exod. 4:21; 7:3; 14:4, 17), he certainly could have softened his heart as well. Why, then, the burden of the ten plagues? The answer is simple: the ten plagues reveal that YHWH is

12. b. B. Bat. 73a; b. Ber. 9b; ʾAbot R. Nat. A 34.2; Sep. Torah 4.1; Exod. Rab. 3.6.

superior to the Egyptian pantheon (and certainly superior to Pharaoh). Many other sources have offered a robust exposition of how the ten plagues demonstrate the fact that YHWH, the God of the Hebrews, is superior to the false gods of the Egyptian pantheon.[13] A rehearsal of those details is beyond the scope of this chapter. Here I wish to state that, on the one hand, the plagues serve to loosen Pharaoh's grip on God's people; on the other hand, they make a mockery of imposter deities associated with various aspects of nature (the sun, the Nile, bulls, etc.). Moses summarizes the point in his declaration "Who is like you, O Lord, among the gods? Who is like you, majestic in holiness, awesome in glorious deeds, doing wonders?" (Exod. 15:11 ESV). Numbers 33:3–4 likewise says, "On the day after the Passover, the people of Israel went out triumphantly in the sight of all the Egyptians, while the Egyptians were burying all their firstborn, whom the Lord had struck down among them. *On their gods also the Lord executed judgments*" (ESV, emphasis added). Ultimately, as the plagues come to a climax with the killing of the firstborn and the crossing of the Red Sea, it becomes clear that YHWH is sovereign over death.[14] Morales helpfully writes:

> the signs and wonders worked in Egypt are to be understood within a *theology of creation*, revealing YHWH as Creator. Egypt is steadily de-created until Pharaoh's hosts are submerged in the waters of chaos, whereas Israel emerges from those waters re-created.[15]

As Israel moves out of the Red Sea into freedom, God makes a covenant (*bərît*) with the nation for the sake of restored fellowship. "Cutting" (*kārat*) a covenant means making a blood oath. The sacrificial ritual of the covenant demonstrates that death is the consequence of breaking the covenant, thereby underlining the exclusive nature of the relationship. The covenant becomes a means by which YHWH teaches

13. For a very interesting and helpful take on this topic, see Ziony Zevit, "Three Ways to Look at the Ten Plagues," *Bible Review* 6 (1990): 16–23, 42.
14. As a body of water, the Red Sea symbolizes chaos and death in the ANE. For God to exercise complete control over the Red Sea is to demonstrate that he is superior to death.
15. L. Michael Morales, *Who Shall Ascend the Mountain of the Lord? A Biblical Theology of the Book of Leviticus*, NSBT 37 (Downers Grove, IL: IVP Academic, 2015), 78.

Israel about his qualitative otherness and its implications for humans in general and the nation in particular. More specifically, as summarized in the Decalogue and the Shema, the covenant stipulations communicate to Israel the same principles revealed in Genesis 1 and 2 and in the divine name: YHWH is the one transcendent, sovereign, and eternal God. The basis for Israel's restored relationship with YHWH is therefore its *exclusive recognition of YHWH as the one true God.* So the theology of Genesis 1 and 2, along with the ten plagues, informs the opening of the Decalogue:

> I am the Lord your God, who brought you out of the land of Egypt, out of the house of slavery. You shall have no other gods before me. You shall not make for yourself a carved image, or any likeness of anything that is in heaven above, or that is in the earth beneath, or that is in the water under the earth. You shall not bow down to them or serve them, for I the Lord your God am a jealous God, visiting the iniquity of the fathers on the children to the third and the fourth generation of those who hate me, but showing steadfast love to thousands of those who love me and keep my commandments. (Exod. 20:2–6 ESV)

YHWH demands exclusive worship, which he merits because he has demonstrated his superiority and sovereignty over all the so-called gods through the plagues. The violation of this covenant stipulation results in death precisely because rebellion against the one who is pure life—and likewise the life giver—naturally results in the breaking of fellowship with the source of life (more below in the section on atonement). Furthermore, YHWH prohibits making carved images. Later in the Pentateuch, we see that in the holy of holies is not a carved image but a box—a mercy seat (*kappōret*)—associated with the invisible presence of God with his people. The qualitative otherness of God appears in both the demand for exclusive worship and the prohibition against carved images. Carved images represent the deity. Since YHWH is utterly different from the creation in his very ontology (being uncreated)—and since he is not continuous with the creation in any way—no created object can come close to representing him accurately. Making a carved image representing YHWH is prohibited and diametrically opposed to who he is. He is *not* synonymous or continuous with creation, nor can he be contained by it. He is eternal, which means he is infinitely more than all created things. Not only this, but when taken in tandem with monotheism, he is the *only being* in this ontological category.

The Shema, then, becomes Israel's definitive declaration concerning the oneness of God. Deuteronomy 6:4–5 says, "Hear, O Israel, YHWH our God, YHWH is *one*. You are to love YHWH your God with *all* your heart, and with *all* your soul, and with *all* your strength" (AT, emphasis added). This declaration, which one could strongly argue is at the center of the Pentateuch's theology, teaches that God is qualitatively other in that he is one and that he has called Israel to live in a way that corresponds to his oneness through its undivided, unmixed devotion to him. His utmost superiority, sovereignty, and oneness absolutely prohibit the nation's affection from being divided between him and false gods. To worship YHWH alongside other "deities" is to deny his very divinity. These notions are further teased out in the building of the tabernacle, the ceremonial laws of Leviticus, and the notion of atonement.

THE TABERNACLE, CEREMONIAL LAWS, ATONEMENT, AND HOLINESS

As the exodus story progresses, it becomes apparent that the aim of Israel's deliverance from Egyptian slavery is not merely freedom from external oppression. The goal of the exodus is the redemption and the restoration of what has been lost in Eden: fellowship with God, the divine-image-bearing vocation of humanity (by extension), and ultimately *life*. In other words, the exodus aims to restore the perfection of God's creation. The frequency and location of the occurrence of the root *qdš* in the Pentateuch are telling. The statistics are as follows:

Book	Number of Occurrences	Percent of Total
Genesis	5[16]	2%
Exodus	57	28%
Leviticus	92	46%
Numbers	36	18%
Deuteronomy	12	6%

16. Four of the five occurrences in Genesis are *qədēšâ*, meaning "cult prostitute."

Seventy-five percent (149) of the total occurrences of *qdš* in the Pentateuch are in Exodus and Leviticus. Furthermore, 86 percent of the occurrences of *qdš* in Exodus are in chapters 26–40, which, in large part, detail the instructions for building the tabernacle. *Qdš* in Leviticus occurs ninety-two times in connection with instructions to the priests and worshipers in and around the temple.

These statistics reveal that holiness in the Pentateuch is most closely associated with *God's presence in the tabernacle*. In short, God delivers the Israelites to make his dwelling place among them (Exod. 25:8; 29:45–46; Lev. 26:11), which is why the story's focus shifts from getting Israel out of Egypt to the construction of the tabernacle. Most of the occurrences of *qdš* in the Pentateuch can be found in and around the instructions for building the tabernacle and the ceremonial laws regulating access to YHWH's holy presence.

The Tabernacle

A few observations can be made regarding the relationship between the tabernacle and holiness. First, that so much of the exodus story is spent on detailed instructions for building the tabernacle emphasizes the notion that the final aim of the exodus event is not the event itself, but rather the restoration of God's presence among his people (Exod. 29:45). The whole purpose of deliverance is restoring the divine-human relationship that was lost in Eden. Relating to holiness, the restoration of the divine presence is prefigured in the burning bush episode in Exodus 3. Just as the divine presence there sanctifies the ground around the bush (and presumably the bush itself), so the divine presence in the tabernacle means sanctified space. God's unmixed nature necessitates a pure and holy place for his dwelling and, by extension, a holy people.

Related to this, the construction of the tabernacle also parallels the creation account in Genesis 1–2. The creating activity of the Spirit in Genesis 1–2 is remembered through the Holy Spirit's inspiration of Bezalel (Gen. 1:2; Exod. 31:1–6; 35:31), who is empowered to be the chief artisan-builder of the tabernacle. Victor Hamilton observes, "It should not escape us that the first individual filled with God's Spirit was not a patriarch, a lawgiver, a prophet, or a judge, but an artisan, Bezalel, supervisor of the tabernacle project."[17]

---

17. Victor P. Hamilton, *Handbook on the Pentateuch*, 2nd ed. (Grand Rapids: Baker Academic, 2005), 220.

The parallel between Genesis 1–2 and the construction of the tabernacle is the result of the tabernacle being presented within the broader narrative as the new creation. The tabernacle is the place where the curse of Genesis 3 is lifted and God's perfect, life-sustaining creation is restored. Ultimately, the reality of the tabernacle means sharing in the life-giving divine presence that was lost in Genesis 3. The covenant community is the representative head of the new creation and therefore the restoration of the exclusive worship of YHWH as the one true God—a summation of holiness restored to the divine image bearers. In sum, it is the sanctification of both people and space.[18]

The moral profile of YHWH being built into the covenant stipulations illustrates that the restoration of Eden is the whole goal of the covenant. To remain God's people, Israel must align itself with the ethical purity of YHWH as detailed in the covenant stipulations. At the heart of the covenant stipulations is the faithfulness of YHWH, a key character trait that must be embodied in his people as his witness to the world. Certainly related to faithfulness is YHWH's goodness and righteousness. Together, these characteristics support the generation and the sustaining of life as God has intended it within his creation. Plainly put, as the representative head of the new creation, God's people bear the moral image of the giver of life. Where the curse of sin lies, there the corruption of life and ultimately death lie as well. Those who are reconciled to the giver of life and live according to his commands live where the curse is lifted, and life can be properly generated and sustained as God originally intended for his image bearers and the creation as a whole. This is the notion at the heart of Leviticus 11:45: "For I am the Lord who brought you up out of the land of Egypt to be your God. You shall therefore be holy, for I am holy" (ESV).

Also worth noting is that the designs for the tabernacle are entirely God's. No human architect is involved in the design of the place of God's presence. This results in the repetition of the phrase "and

18. A few scholars have defended the view that the tabernacle is intended to be a microcosm of the new creation (esp. see G. K. Beale, *The Temple and the Church's Mission: A Biblical Theology of the Dwelling Place of God*, NSBT 17 [Downers Grove, IL: IVP Academic, 2004]). Such approaches draw on interpretations from Josephus and Philo to posit that the tripartite structure of the tabernacle is intended to symbolize the visible creation (the outer court), the heavenlies (the inner court), and the invisible dimension where God's presence resides (the holy of holies). These observations are indeed compelling; however, no clear support in the immediate context of the Scriptures themselves can be found for these interpretations.

they did," interlaced throughout the tabernacle building narrative. The implication here is that this sanctified-space-and-people project requires complete (unmixed) human obedience. This is in contrast to the rebellion in Genesis 3. If the tabernacle is a new Eden, then Israel, as the representative head of the new creation, is entirely obedient in carrying out the instructions of God in the place of the new creation. Where Adam failed, Israel succeeds.

Finally, Israel's journey out of Egypt begins and ends with building projects. As slaves in Egypt, Israel built edifices at the command of the tyrannical Pharaoh, who—like those in Genesis 11—sought to make a name for himself. Egypt was the place of the curse, the place where death reigned supreme, human labor was not balanced with Sabbath rest, and life was unsustainable. Egypt was the place where the sum of Israel's existence was work and the image of God was distorted.

In typical OT fashion, the reality of Egyptian slavery parallels the building of the tabernacle in the wilderness, but with essential differences. The key difference is that the tabernacle project, while located in the desert (the place of the curse), is a new creation where the life-giving presence of the Holy Creator is restored and the curse of death lifted. Quite ironically, death reigns in Egypt, a country overflowing with natural resources and security; all the while, it is in the desert—a place devoid of natural, life-sustaining resources—that Israel encounters the Holy Creator of life, who is pure life and in whom no corruption, decay, or death exists. The garden of true life is in the desert, and the place of curse and death is in the garden that is Egypt. The point of this contrast is that life comes from a living relationship with YHWH and nothing else. Life, or human purpose and meaning, is not the product of an impersonal, mechanical system. Rather, life as God intends is rooted in an intimate relationship with him. The outcome of that life is the fulfillment of the true human vocation of bearing God's image.

Ceremonial Laws

Ceremonial laws are those that directly relate to the Pentateuch's prescribed form of worship. This form of worship includes ritual and ceremonial practice, the religious calendar, and the structure of the priesthood. These laws function as a detailed and powerful object lesson with one central teaching point that can be summarized in the repeated refrain of Leviticus: "Be holy because I, the Lord your God, am holy."[19]

The fundamental view behind the ceremonial laws of Israel and the notion of holiness therein are definitively distinct from their ANE counterparts. As is noted in the opening chapter of this volume, impurity (i.e., the profane) in the ANE is "simply that which makes rituals ineffective." The standard ANE view is that the universe works *mechanically*, not *personally*. Holiness in ceremony and ritual has everything to do with achieving desired results through the manipulation of the universe and nothing to do with one's personal relationship with the gods. An assumed continuity exists between the material and the immaterial, which one can manipulate. However, what God reveals to Israel is diametrically opposed to this view. Holiness in the ceremonial life of Israel is deeply personal and wrapped up in the moral and ethical qualities of YHWH. Moreover, as we saw above, God is qualitatively different in that he is *one*.

But how do the ceremonial laws of Israel communicate the oneness of God to Israel? Every person, object, utensil, and vessel used in worship has to correspond to the nature of YHWH. Impure people and vessels must be purified (*ṭāhôr*) or dedicated *entirely* (without mixing). Pollution must be completely absent. Corresponding to the moral and ethical qualities of YHWH, *there must be perfect oneness* because God is perfectly one and his will is perfectly one. Once again, this object lesson reinforces that morality is *not* plural, a notion completely foreign to ancient Israel's neighbors.

The ceremonial laws repeatedly suggest that no part of life is untouched by the notion of purity or oneness. From the highly sacramental to the mundane spheres of life, everything is framed by the question "Clean or unclean?"[20] The ceremonial laws bring home the message that God is different in that he is one in his ethics; he is morally consistent in his will, his purposes, his nature, and his desire for life and its flourishing. The natural outcome of such a reality is that to be his people, his holy habitation, Israel must be holy, as he is holy.

19. Lev. 11:44, 45; 19:2; 20:7, 26; 21:6, 8.

20. As scholars have thoroughly documented elsewhere, the three main categories regarding Israel's ceremonial life are *holy*, *clean*, and *unclean*. The scope of this essay is not to rehearse the technicalities of these categories but to explore the broader theological notions informing the reality of categories of cleanness.

The nation is to share in his likeness, to live a life of full devotion to God, with undivided hearts (Deut. 6:4–5).

What makes people and instruments unclean is the mixture of death with life. Humans lose their eligibility for sharing in the life of God in Genesis 3. God instructs Adam and Eve to eat any vegetation in the garden except that from the tree of the knowledge of good and evil. He explains that on the day they eat of it, they will surely die (*môt tāmût*; Gen. 2:15–17). Deceived by the serpent, they eat of the tree and are subsequently cast out of the garden (i.e., God's presence). But what happens in this story that makes them ineligible to continue in God's presence? Is it their act of disobedience? Is it the nature of the tree itself and what it symbolizes (i.e., the knowledge of good and evil)? Is it their loss of innocence (evident in the shame of their nakedness)?

While the text does not answer this question explicitly, the implicit answer is *death*. God warns Adam and Eve that on the day they eat of the forbidden tree, they will *die* (Gen. 2:17).[21] Furthermore, the serpent challenges this very declaration. He sows deceit at the heart of the matter. He tells the first humans that they will *not* die if they eat from the tree. Further still, upon casting Adam and Eve out of the garden, God places a barrier between them and the tree of life. While other elements are certainly present (e.g., the loss of obedience, shame, rebellion, the knowledge of good and evil), death and life pervade the story. One can conclude that Adam and Eve are no longer eligible to live in God's presence because he is pure life and in him there is no death; by contrast, death is now a part of their existence. They are a mixture of death and life, whereas God is entirely life. God is *one* in that he is pure life. There is no admixture of death with God like there is with Israel and the created order. This view is strongly affirmed through the themes of the creation story mentioned above—namely, life and the flourishing of life. The entire creation account is geared to demonstrate that God's desire for creation is life and its flourishing. This means that death is the antithesis of God's purpose for his perfect creation. Death is the contaminator.

Repeatedly in the ceremonial laws, death defiles. For example:

21. That the infinitive absolute phrase *môt tāmût* here is emphatic further supports this view.

> "These are unclean for you among all the swarming creatures. Whoever touches them when they are dead will be unclean until evening" (Lev. 11:31 CSB).
>
> "Every person, whether the native or the resident alien, who eats an animal that died a natural death or was mauled by wild beasts is to wash his clothes and bathe with water, and he will remain unclean until evening; then he will be clean" (Lev. 17:15 CSB).
>
> "He must not go near any dead person or make himself unclean even for his father or mother" (Lev. 21:11 CSB).
>
> "Whoever touches anything made unclean by a dead person . . . will remain unclean until evening and is not to eat from the holy offerings unless he has bathed his body with water" (Lev. 22:4, 6 CSB).

These verses not only demonstrate that ceremonial laws communicate the qualitative otherness of God in his oneness; they also demonstrate, more specifically, that there is absolutely no death in him. God is pure life with no admixture of death or decay, which is why all things and people related to the temple and service in the temple must be pure (i.e., without mixing). Yes, God is one in the sense that there are no other uncreated beings, but he is also one in that he is entirely and purely life.

Cleansing by Blood: Atonement[22]

The looming question, then, is: How can that which is "mixed" (i.e., unclean or impure) enter the presence of YHWH, who is pure life? The Pentateuch answers that question with the notion of atonement. Atonement (*kippur*) is the provision made for the impure to share life with the pure by way of "covering over," "removing," or "blotting out" (*māḥâ*) the contaminant. Blood sacrifice is required for entry into

22. A much more robust exploration of atonement and how it relates to holiness is explored in another chapter in this volume. As a result, the scope of the investigation here is limited to atonement as it relates specifically to the concepts that we have explored thus far.

God's presence throughout the covenant stipulations. The shedding of blood is what purifies the contaminant of death. But why blood? Why can water not purify? The answers to these questions have everything to do with sin. Informed by Genesis 3, sin can be generally defined as the refusal to live according to God's plans and purposes. Rebellion against God means breaking fellowship with him and, therefore, separation from him who gives life and is life itself. Death is the natural result of being separated from God as the giver of life. *Atonement is the reversal of this consequence.* Blood sacrifice is required to restore fellowship with God. Similar to the message inherent in "cutting a covenant," we learn from the covenant stipulations regarding blood sacrifices that blood is the "life" of the sacrifice (Gen. 9:4; Lev. 17:11, 14; Deut. 12:23). Only life—symbolized in blood—can blot out death.

The notion of atonement is best illustrated in the ritual practice and observance of the Day of Atonement (Lev. 16). James Mays helpfully describes the Day of Atonement as "the climax and crown of Israel's theology of sanctification."[23] The Day of Atonement was the mechanism through which God offered to cleanse Israel from all its sin and defilements. Allen Ross writes, "The revelation of the removal of sin and defilement is also clearly presented here in the scapegoat. All the sins of the people were confessed and transferred to the victim, which was then led outside the camp. All sin was removed by this substitute."[24] The scapegoat carrying the people's sin to the wilderness is symbolic of sin being sent to the place of the curse, the place of death.

The blood of the sacrifice sprinkled on the ark of the covenant is also significant. Inside the ark are the Ten Commandments, which summarize the covenant stipulations. The meaning of blood sprinkled on the ark of the covenant has two prongs. On the first prong, worshipers acknowledge that they have violated the covenant and that the consequence for covenant violation is death. On the second prong, the blood sacrifice satisfies the requirement of death due to their rebellion against God. As the ark symbolizes God's presence with his people, this ritual demonstrates that this restored fellowship is only possible with the blotting out of sin-guilt from God's people (i.e., expiation)

23. James L. Mays, *The Book of Leviticus, the Book of Numbers*, Layman's Bible Commentary 4 (Atlanta: John Knox, 1977), 52.
24. Allen P. Ross, *Holiness to the Lord: A Guide to the Exposition of the Book of Leviticus* (Grand Rapids: Baker Academic, 2002), 314.

and the satisfaction of the covenantal stipulations and the wrath of God (i.e., propitiation). The animal sacrifice is a substitute for God's people, satisfying the consequence of rebellion against God, which is death.

With atonement, then, *life blots out death*. Symbolized in blood, life accounts for death by covering it and making it possible to restore fellowship with God. Furthermore, the ultimate outcome of restored fellowship between God and his image bearers is that God's plans and purposes for creation are restored.

Nevertheless, where does the oneness (i.e., unmixed) nature of God come into play in the broader scheme of atonement? As mentioned above, God is pure life and there is no death in him. Should death come into his presence, it is consumed because life "purges" death. A worshiper who is a mixture of death and life and who enters God's pure-life presence will be consumed. Death, however, is purged from a worshiper whose sin has been covered with life blood. The covering of sin-guilt with blood, then, restores God's purposes for namely life and the flourishing of life through the eradication of the contamination that is death.

CONCLUSION: HOLINESS AS QUALITATIVE OTHERNESS

This chapter's exploration of holiness in the Pentateuch affirms Oswalt's thesis, developed in the opening chapter of this volume, that qualitative otherness is at the heart of the root *qdš*. The OT's—and especially the Pentateuch's—claim that God is one is a polemic declaration in its ANE context. The OT distinctly declares that YHWH is superior to all other "gods" (Exod. 18:11; Deut. 4:28; 6:4; 10:17; 32:17). Furthermore, YHWH is the God who transcends the creation, and it is because he is the one true God that his character—which is repeatedly revealed in the OT as "good" (*ṭôb*),[25] "true" (*ʾĕmûnâ* or *ʾĕmet*),[26] "right" (*ṣədāqâ*),[27] "just" (*mišpāṭ*),[28] "faithful" (*ḥesed*),[29] and

25. Gen. 50:20; Pss. 25:8–9; 31:19; 34:8; 107:1.

26. Pss. 33:4; 100:5; 135:3; Jer. 33:11.

27. Pss. 5:8; 7:17; 22:31; 31:1; 33:5; 35:24; 36:6; 50:6; 96:13; 97:6; 98:2, 9; 103:6, 17; 111:3; 143:1, 11; Isa. 9:7; 32:16; 33:5; 42:6, 21; 45:13; Jer. 9:24; Mic. 7:9.

28. Gen. 19:25; Deut. 16:20; 33:21; Pss. 9:7–8; 33:5; 37:28; 103:6; 119:149; 140:12; 146:7; Prov. 21:3; 29:26; Isa. 5:16; 30:18; 61:8; Jer. 5:4–5; 9:24; Mic. 3:8; Zeph. 3:5; Mal. 2:17.

29. Gen. 24:27; 39:21; Exod. 15:13; 20:6; 34:6–7; Num. 14:18–19; Deut. 5:10; 7:9, 12; 1 Sam. 20:14–15; 2 Sam. 2:6; 7:15.

"pure" (*ṭāhôr*)[30]—determines the moral code for the created order. Morally speaking, then, creation is not a pluralistic order. *One* moral standard is defined by the one transcendent God.

Furthermore, God's will is naturally and inextricably linked to his moral character. His character is one; therefore, his will is one. It is precisely because of his character that his will for creation (and particularly his image bearers) is to embody and reflect his moral attributes (i.e., goodness, faithfulness, etc.). Driving his will for creation is the overall purpose of flourishing life, which directly corresponds with his holiness. Anything that deviates from his will is a detriment to the flourishing of life and is therefore prohibited, unholy, impure, or unclean.

In the introduction to his translation and commentary on the Babylonian Talmud, Jacob Neusner claims that the Torah is ultimately instruction on restoring the perfection of the world.[31] Neusner is spot-on. Creation was originally perfect because the Creator was perfect. It was whole, complete, lacking nothing, and completely free from faults, defects, and contamination because *he* was whole, complete, lacking nothing, and completely free from faults, defects, and contamination. It was teeming with life because the Creator was life. Considering humanity's rebellion against the Creator, the Torah is instruction on restoring to a state of perfection the world contaminated by human sin and rebellion. Put another way, the Pentateuch is instruction on *holiness*. It teaches the way to align with the Holy One and his purposes.

Understood this way, holiness in the Pentateuch is not merely one of many theological motifs working together in a broad, complex mosaic that creates a comprehensive and coherent theological system. Holiness, instead, is at the heart of the Pentateuch. Holiness as the restoration of creation's perfection—especially the restoration of the perfection of God's image bearers and his fellowship with them—is the controlling theological motif and the ultimate aim of the instruction (*tôrâ*) that is the Pentateuch.

30. Exod. 28:36; 30:35; 37:29; 39:30; 1 Kings 7:50; 2 Chron. 14:22.

31. Jacob Neusner, *The Babylonian Talmud: A Translation and Commentary* (Peabody, MA: Hendrickson, 2011), xxiv.

CHAPTER 3

THE CURIOUS CASE OF HOLINESS IN THE HISTORICAL BOOKS

BRIAN T. SHOCKEY

The concept of holiness is of central importance to the OT, both with respect to the revealed character of God and the prescribed lifestyle for the Israelites. Within the Historical Books, holiness language occurs in a variety of places, including references to God, his temple, and its furnishings. Perhaps more notable is the absence of holiness language in connection with the people of God—people called in the Pentateuch to exemplify the holiness of their God. If Israel truly was called to be holy as God was holy (Lev. 19:1), why are the narratives filled with flawed characters who fail to live up to their God's standards?

While it is possible that this absence of "holy character" results from a disinterested narrator, it is also possible, perhaps even likely, that these portrayals are intentional. If so, one might argue that the narrator invites the audience to consider what may be learned from the interactions of a holy God with sinful humanity—how God calls and embraces not only those who live as he intends, but also those who strive for holiness and fall short. Viewed in this way, portions of the Historical Books use holiness to both demonstrate the surpassing moral and ethical character of God and to reveal his steadfast love and mercy for those he sets apart to serve and to lead his people.

This chapter will explore the concept of holiness in the Historical Books through a survey of holiness language, a brief examination of key themes, and an investigation of two representative characters who demonstrate the narrative technique suggested above.

PRELIMINARY MATTERS

Before exploring the concept of holiness in the Historical Books, some attention must be given to the boundaries of the corpus and the terminology used. As will be shown below, the use of holiness language varies throughout the texts included in the Christian canon, which is largely based on the LXX. The categorization of a text as part of the Historical Books is descriptive rather than prescriptive, which frees the reader from the need to seek a universal or unifying theme within the group as a whole. Therefore, it is not problematic to find variant uses of holiness terminology within different subsections of the group. Rather than seeking a singular witness within the Historical Books, alignment should instead be expected between members of the Historical Books that have demonstrable compositional, contextual, or historical connections. That said, this study will eschew discussions of compositional history, save for general comments where necessary, in favor of a more synchronic, canonical approach to the text.[1]

Some discussion of the term "holiness" is also warranted, as it has at times carried different connotations in scholarly research.[2] This study envisions a concept of holiness that is at the same time descriptive of a divine "otherness," cultically relevant, and ethically prescriptive. Put another way, holiness in ancient Israel was not only important for the needs of the religious system, but also descriptive of a certain moral purity—distinct from surrounding cultures—which was itself predicated on the discrete moral character of the Lord: his holiness. While not every reference to holiness should be seen as explicitly addressing all three of these aspects, their interdependence suggests that they should be held together. For example,

1. Awareness of portions of the Levitical material during the compositional process of the Historical Books is accepted as a presupposition to the arguments herein. Scholarly opinions on the development of the biblical material—matters of date, authorship, oral tradition, and scribal practice—vary in the field. The arguments presented here do not require a particular ordering of the Pentateuchal material, nor do they require the canonical form of the material to be fully realized prior to the composition of the Historical Books. They simply require an understanding of ancient Israel that includes holiness as a core cultural value. A full exploration of compositional and cultural concerns and their bearing on the plausibility of this assumption, however, is outside the scope of this essay. At *minimum* it seems the concept of holiness was not unknown to the audience of the Historical Books, nor was it deemed completely irrelevant, regardless of how one construes the compositional timeline. For discussions of the Pentateuch's composition, see B. T. Arnold, "Pentateuchal Criticism, History Of," *DOTP* 622–31; Jan C. Gertz et al., eds., *The Formation of the Pentateuch*, FAT 111 (Tübingen: Mohr Siebeck, 2016); and Sara J. Milstein, *Tracking the Master Scribe: Revision through Introduction in Biblical and Mesopotamian Literature* (New York: Oxford University Press, 2016).

2. For a survey of holiness in the OT and representative views, see M. C. Lyons, "Holiness," *LBD*; David P. Wright, "Holiness: Old Testament," *ABD* 3:237–49; John Goldingay, *Israel's Life*, vol. 3 of *Old Testament Theology* (Downers Grove, IL: IVP Academic, 2009), 607–22; and John Oswalt, *Called to Be Holy: A Biblical Perspective* (Nappanee, IN: Evangel, 1999), 9–38.

one cannot consider the otherness of God apart from his character. Neither can one consider the specialized purpose of certain items or people without a concern for the God for whom they have been set apart. Holiness language referring to people or things is exclusively reserved for a connection with God. Nothing in Israel is holy apart from the Lord.

DISTRIBUTION OF HOLINESS LANGUAGE IN THE HISTORICAL BOOKS

Explicit references to holiness in the Historical Books derive from the Hebrew root *qdš*. The text primarily uses the nominal form, *qōdeš*, and the verbal form, *qādaš*, to refer to holiness.[3] The adjectival form, *qādôš*; the related terms *miqdāš* ("sanctuary") and *qādēš* ("shrine attendant" or "prostitute"); and the locations *qādēš*, *qādēš barnēʿa*, and *qedeš* ("Kadesh," "Kadesh Barnea," and "Kedesh") are also present, albeit at a much lower frequency.

These latter terms are less relevant to the current study because they lack a specific connection to the concept of holiness in Israel. The references to *qədēšîm* in the Historical Books are viewed negatively by the narrator and would not be considered holy because of their association with another religious system.[4] The locational terms are also of limited value, as the naming of these locations, regardless of their narrative significance, occurs outside the story.[5] These terms will therefore be excluded from the following discussion.

3. For an overview of the term *qdš* and its use in the OT, see Oswalt's essay in Chapter 1 of this volume.
4. The etymology of the word *qədēšîm*, however, serves as a helpful reminder that the concept of holiness was not unique to ancient Israel. Other religious systems also considered certain things and roles as "holy" because of their connection to their deity. This supports the idea that holiness is properly understood as a culturally bound concept, which in Israel requires an association with YHWH. Further, recent research has suggested that the association of *qədēšîm*, as well as the related *qədēšâ*, with temple prostitution should be discarded in favor of a broader understanding of these terms as representative of men and women consecrated for religious service. This interpretation suggests that the *qədēšîm* may indeed be considered within Israel's religious framework. For an exhaustive study of the relevant comparative data, see Phyllis A. Bird, *Harlot or Holy Woman? A Study of Hebrew Qedešah* (University Park, PA: Eisenbrauns, 2019).
5. Kadesh and the city of Kadesh Barnea were likely viewed as holy at the time they were named—perhaps due to a specific encounter with the Lord or a specific religious purpose. Kedesh initially appears to be of more value since it is identified as a refuge city in Josh. 20:7. The text, however, does not indicate that the city was named when it was set apart for this purpose. Further, several other cities lacking *qdš* in their name were also set apart as refuge cities at the same time, which argues against this suggestion.

Considering the distribution of the remaining terms across the Historical Books yields interesting results (see fig. 3.1). Chronicles accounts for more than half of the overall references to holiness in the corpus, while Ezra, Nehemiah, and Kings together account for more than a quarter of the total. Neither Ruth nor Esther gives explicit reference to holiness. Dividing the same material in accordance with the Jewish canon, the books identified as the Former Prophets (Joshua, Judges, Samuel, and Kings) account for 29 percent of the occurrences, whereas the books included in the Writings (Ruth, Esther, Chronicles, Ezra, and Nehemiah) host 71 percent of the references. The Former Prophets are demonstrably less interested in holiness, which raises questions about the importance and the understanding of the concept in these texts. Chronicles, Ezra, and Nehemiah, by contrast, exhibit a much greater attentiveness to the topic—particularly its relevance for Israel's religious system.[6]

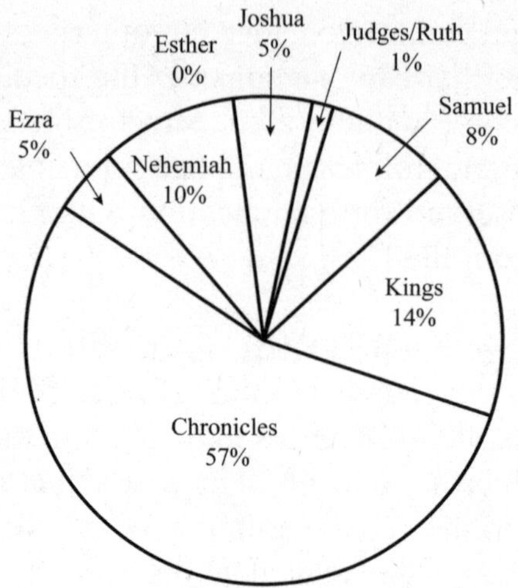

Figure 3.1 References to Holiness in the Historical Books

Shifting the focus to the narrative context of the terms reveals that the majority (70 percent) are used in connection with Israel's temple. This includes references to the temple itself, furnishings for the temple, and donations specifically given for the temple. The remaining 30 percent may be subdivided into five domains: holy things, holy times, holy places (other than the temple), holy people, and the holy nature

6. While efforts to prove shared authorship between Chronicles, Ezra, and Nehemiah have fallen short, similarities in the proposed cultural context for the final form of these books at least provide a starting point from which to evaluate the importance of holiness for these texts in contrast to those of the Former Prophets. For a brief summary of arguments pertaining to the compositional relationship of these books, see Lisbeth S. Fried, "Textual History of Ezra-Nehemiah," in *Writings*, vol. 1C of *Textual History of the Bible: The Hebrew Bible*, ed. Armin Lange and Emmanuel Tov (Leiden: Brill, 2016), 603–4. See also Israel P. Loken, "The Relationship between Chronicles, Ezra, and Nehemiah," in *Ezra and Nehemiah*, EEC (Bellingham, WA: Lexham, 2011).

of God. References to holy people are, as one might expect, largely linked to the priesthood rather than nonpriestly characters.[7]

Returning to the distribution of these terms with the added element of context clarifies the broader divisions noted earlier. References associated with the temple occur with greater frequency in the Writings than they do in the Former Prophets (cf. eighty-six occurrences with twenty-four occurrences, respectively), whereas the other references are more balanced between the two groups (cf. twenty-four occurrences with twenty occurrences). This usage suggests a more central role for the holiness of the temple and the religious system in the Writings than in the Former Prophets.

Explicit references to holiness aside, one must also consider whether the audience might associate other terminology with holiness.[8] At least two general categories of terms warrant comment. The first category includes terms associated with divine choice. Throughout the Historical Books, individuals are selected or set apart for specific leadership roles and responsibilities. This selection is at times implied by the narrative and at other times indicated via a proclamation from God or a formal anointing by a priest. Regardless of how the choice is indicated, these scenes are relevant for a discussion of holiness in the corpus because they portray individuals who are set apart from the general population and associated with God for a specific, holy purpose.

The second category of terms is more problematic. If, as assumed above, holiness contains a moral or ethical dimension, it stands to reason that any language associated with righteous behavior would also need to be considered. Holiness has often been equated with righteousness by biblical interpreters. John Wesley, for example, writes,

7. References to holiness in people other than the priests and Levites include the consecration of the Israelites prior to crossing the Jordan (Josh. 3:5), the consecration of the Israelites prior to Achan's judgment (Josh. 7:13), the consecration of Jesse's sons (1 Sam. 16:5), and the Shunammite woman's reference to Elisha (2 Kings 4:9).

8. During the formation of the biblical text, the creators of the text would have been aware of the intertextual network of information available to their audience. They were thus able to utilize this information—the audience's general knowledge of culture, theology, oral tradition, and literature—strategically as they communicated with their audience. Modern interpreters are likely only aware of a fraction of the cultural backdrop of the text and are left at a disadvantage. For discussion of intertextual networks and biblical interpretation, see David M. Carr, "The Many Uses of Intertextuality in Biblical Studies: Actual and Potential," in *Congress Volume Helsinki 2010*, ed. Martti Nissinen, VTSup 148 (Leiden: Brill, 2012), 505–35. See also the discussion of intertextuality in comparative studies in Brian T. Shockey, "Beyond Comparison: A Process for Comparing Israelite and Ancient Near Eastern Literature" (PhD diss., Asbury Theological Seminary, 2021), 132–37.

"'The upright man,' throughout the Scripture, is a truly good man; a man of integrity, a holy person."[9] One can certainly quibble over the subtle distinctions between these terms, but here they are (perhaps rightly) flattened together. After all, is it possible to imagine an individual, in any given cultural context, who is considered holy but not upright? Can a person be holy and yet be without integrity? Surely, the concept of holiness as defined above requires some association of the upright individual with God, but that association need not use explicit holiness language to indicate behavior consistent with a holy lifestyle. The opposite is also true; characters demonstrating behavior inconsistent with holiness need not be explicitly identified as "unholy" for the audience to perceive them as such. Herein lies part of the genius of the biblical narrative. The audience is invited—I daresay expected—to interpret the actions of the narratives' characters in light of the biblical portrayal of their holy God and his instructions.[10]

A full exploration of holiness in the Historical Books, then, would need to consider not only language related to righteousness but also the ethical behavior of the characters in the narrative. This daunting task would, unfortunately, likely dilute and diminish the significance of the holiness terminology surveyed above. The present study will, therefore, attempt to balance the explicit references to holiness with these implicit references via representative case studies, selected from characters who are clearly set apart by the Lord.

Reviewing the distribution data, then, yields several helpful observations for understanding the concept of holiness in the Historical Books. First, Chronicles, Ezra, and Nehemiah seem to use explicit holiness language to focus on holiness in connection with the temple. Second, explicit references to holiness outside the temple context are infrequent in these books and, as such, may provide useful information regarding the audience's contextual understanding of holiness. Third, the Former Prophets generally avoid explicit references to holiness and instead

9. John Wesley, *The Works of John Wesley*, 3rd ed. (London: Wesleyan Methodist Book Room, 1872), 9:399.

10. For an introduction to the literary analysis of characters, see Robert Alter, *The Art of Biblical Narrative*, rev. ed. (New York: Basic Books, 2011), 114–30; Meir Sternberg, *The Poetics of Biblical Narrative: Ideological Literature and the Drama of Reading* (Bloomington: Indiana University Press, 1985), 321–41; Adele Berlin, *Poetics and Interpretation of Biblical Narrative* (Sheffield: Almond, 1983), 23–42; and Shimon Bar-Efrat, *Narrative Art in the Bible* (Sheffield: Sheffield Academic, 1997), 47–92.

invite the audience to explore the presence or absence of the concept through the portrayal of key characters in the narratives themselves. Examinations of these key characters benefit from a summary knowledge of the explicit references to holiness in the text. Themes found in passages containing explicit references will be explored first, followed by an analysis of the representative characters of Samson and David.

HOLINESS THEMES (EXPLICIT) IN THE HISTORICAL BOOKS

The Historical Books maintain the portrayal of God as holy, as defined in the Pentateuch. This portrayal is conveyed through a handful of explicit references to his holiness and the holiness of his name, as seen in Joshua 24:19, 1 Samuel 2:2, 1 Chronicles 16:10, and 29:16. The text gives little explanation for God's holiness; the audience is expected to be aware of God's holy nature and what it entails from the Pentateuch. God's character is also consistent with that revealed in the Pentateuch—he is morally upright, faithful, and pure throughout the text.[11] Encounters between God and his servants reflect this reality, as people respond to God's holy presence with appropriate humility and deference.[12] The Historical Books accept God's holiness as the status quo, and they display interest in how his holiness relates to ancient Israel's leaders and history.

One of the earliest references to holiness in the Historical Books is found shortly before the conquest of Jericho. Here holiness language is explicitly employed in connection with location and the spoils of war. At some point after the observance of Passover, Joshua encounters an angel near Jericho, who identifies himself as the captain of the Lord's army. The angel instructs Joshua, "Remove your sandals from your feet, for the place where you are standing is holy" (Josh. 5:15 NASB1995). Once Joshua assumes the proper posture, instructions are

11. Cf. Matt Ayars, Christopher T. Bounds, and Caleb T. Friedeman, *Holiness: A Biblical, Historical, and Systematic Theology* (Downers Grove, IL: IVP Academic, 2023), 40–51. Ayars, Bounds, and Friedeman use different terminology to describe their theological understanding of holiness in the Pentateuch, but they nonetheless advance a similar argument—namely, that the Historical Books continue to portray Israel's God within the framework previously established.

12. Gideon bows down upon hearing the interpretation of God's promise from a dream (Judg. 7:15); Saul bows down before Samuel's spirit (1 Sam. 28:14); the captain of the guard bows down before Elijah (2 Kings 1:13); etc. Note also the comment of the narrator in 2 Kings 17:32, who reminds listeners of their responsibility to bow down in worship to the God who brought them out of Egypt.

given from the Lord himself in Joshua 6:1–5. Presumably, the presence of the Lord (or his representative) alters the status of this location, which would not have otherwise been considered holy.[13] Once it is associated with God, his holiness elevates the status of the space—it is holy because *he* is holy and present at that time and location. Joshua, now aware of this holy status, behaves in a manner consistent with the sacred space by removing his sandals.[14]

A second reference to holiness occurs when Joshua instructs the Israelites regarding the spoils of the conquered city.

> The city shall be under the ban, it and all that is in it belongs to the Lord. . . . But as for you, only keep yourselves from the things under the ban, so that you do not covet them and take some of the things under the ban, and make the camp of Israel accursed and bring trouble on it. But all the silver and gold and articles of bronze and iron are holy to the Lord; they shall go into the treasury of the Lord. (Josh. 6:17–19 NASB1995)

A distinction is made here between items that are *ḥērem*, under the ban, and items that are *qōdeš*, holy. Both are set apart but in very different ways.[15] Items that are *ḥērem* are marked for destruction, and they serve no further purpose for the people of God on earth. Items that are holy are given an elevated status and presumably a new purpose in connection with God's people. The identification of these items with the Lord is what renders them holy, not the items themselves.

Taken together, the references to holiness in Joshua 5 and 6 reinforce an understanding of holiness that is intimately connected with Israel's God. *God's presence and purposes elevate the status of ordi-*

---

13. Scholars have offered a range of interpretations for the specific referent of Josh. 5's "holy ground." Some opt for a more localized interpretation of the site of the encounter, others for the city of Jericho itself, and still others for the entire promised land. For a summary of the arguments, see Thomas B. Dozeman, *Joshua 1–12: A New Translation with Introduction and Commentary*, AYB 6B (New Haven, CT: Yale University Press, 2015), 329–30.
14. This narrative evokes Moses's encounter with God at the burning bush (Exod. 3:5), where Moses likewise arrives at a space made holy because of its association with the presence of the divine.
15. Dozeman (*Joshua 1–12*, 377) follows the helpful argument of Robert L. Hubbard Jr., who notes that "as God's exclusive property, *ḥerem* enjoys the highest degree of holiness" (*Joshua*, NIVAC [Grand Rapids: Zondervan Academic, 2009], 198). While it may seem unusual to understand items that are *ḥērem* as holy, their association with God places them in this category, although functional differences remain regarding how this holiness is understood.

nary things to the realm of the holy, even if they are not used in an explicitly religious context. Once something has received an elevated status, a new set of rules applies. Just as Joshua is required to remove his shoes on holy ground, a holy status bestowed on other things also requires special behavior.

An example of this phenomenon is found in the curious incident in 2 Chronicles 8:11, which involves Pharaoh's daughter and the ark of the covenant. According to the text, Solomon does not want his Egyptian wife to dwell in the palace of his father, David, because the ark has entered the building and made it holy. While the ark is only explicitly identified as holy in 2 Chronicles 35:3, it has clearly been associated with God's presence since its construction.[16] It is described as the place where God pledges to meet with Moses (Exod. 25:22), appearing in a cloud above the mercy seat (Lev. 16:2). Thus, the entry of the ark into David's palace would symbolize the entry of God himself, and it is therefore not surprising that Solomon would categorize the location as holy.

Pharaoh's daughter, for her part, first appears in 1 Kings 3:1, where she marries Solomon in connection with an alliance between Israel and Egypt. Given that Solomon's wives later lead him into idolatry, it seems plausible that Pharaoh's daughter retained her Egyptian faith, which would have limited her ability to enter places regarded as holy in Israel.[17] This creates a housing problem, as Solomon's marriage to the Egyptian princess occurs prior to the construction of the temple, the city wall, and his palace.[18] As the text reports, she is brought to Jerusalem to live while the building projects are completed, but a specific location for her home is not provided. Likely, the ark of the covenant was still in David's palace at the time of Solomon's marriage, elevating its status and preventing it from being used as a home for his non-Israelite wife.

---

16. See, for example, the associations of the ark with God in 1 Sam. 5–6.
17. Cf. Andrew E. Hill, *1 and* 2 *Chronicles*, NIVAC (Grand Rapids: Zondervan Academic, 2003), 404; contra Raymond B. Dillard, who argues that Pharaoh's daughter is prohibited from the presence of the ark because she is a woman (*2 Chronicles*, WBC 15 [Dallas: Word, 1987], 65). If Dillard's argument is right, it modifies the specific reason for Solomon's prohibition but does not change his concern for the violation of holy space.
18. According to 1 Kings 7:1, Solomon's palace took thirteen years to complete. Undoubtedly, certain sections of the palace complex, perhaps including a home for Pharaoh's daughter, were completed and occupied while the project was ongoing. That said, housing for Pharaoh's daughter was still likely a problem for many years.

While the precise location of the ark prior to its deposit in the temple cannot be determined for the entire period of Solomon's marriage, it seems less likely that the palace would be reckoned as categorically holy if the ark had been moved to a new location. Support for this claim can be found by examining the experience of the Philistines when they temporarily steal the ark from Israel. While the ark of the covenant resides in their pagan temple, the statue of Dagon falls down before it, and sickness afflicts the people (1 Sam. 5). Once the ark is returned and a guilt offering made, the symptoms leave the people (1 Sam. 6).[19] The effects do not linger, except in the minds of the people who now recognize the power and supremacy of Israel's God. A similar change of status may have occurred with David's palace, which would have returned to its "non-holy" status once the ark of the covenant had departed. Either way, the incident involving a home for Pharaoh's daughter confirms the witness of the Historical Books regarding God's presence. Things become holy when they are in or associated with that presence.

The temple itself is the ultimate illustration of this concept.[20] As the singular resting place for God's holy presence, the temple provides a central hub for religious activity and worship. When God's presence fills the temple, God himself declares, "I have chosen and consecrated this house that My name may be there forever, and My eyes and My heart will be there perpetually" (2 Chron. 7:16 NASB1995). The temple exemplifies holiness not only because of its association with God's presence and blessing but also because of its specific cultic function. It is regularly referenced as holy in the text, with particular attention given to the most holy place, where the ark of the covenant is kept.[21] This designation is not surprising given the importance of holiness in the religious system as recorded in Levitical law. Holiness

19. Interestingly, the ark is returned to Israel on a *new* cart, which is pulled by two *newly* yoked cows. Newness language here is consistent with a sense of purity and is associated with holy items used in connection with God for a special purpose.

20. For a general overview of the temple, see Carol Meyers, "Temple, Jerusalem," *ABD* 6:350–69; J. Monson, "Solomon's Temple," *DOTHB* 929–35.

21. Because the innermost part of the temple is literally named the "holy of holies," the identification of holiness language here is perhaps misleading. The location itself, as the functional resting place of God's presence, would have been afforded holy status automatically, even had it not been named as such. It seems likely that the use of holiness language here is therefore more pragmatic than an attempt by the narrator to assign an elevated status to the space. Despite this, the decision to name this location as the holy of holies is intentional, and thus the presence of holiness language must be acknowledged, albeit with appropriate nuance.

language referencing the temple furnishings and utensils, the Lord's treasury, and the priesthood would also be expected here due to their elevated status in association with the temple, just as they had received elevated status in connection to the tabernacle.

The establishment of Jerusalem as the site for the permanent temple necessitates a change in the responsibilities of the Levites, who are no longer required to move the tabernacle from place to place. Revised instructions are given by David, who reaffirms the role of the Levites in the religious system and their permission to handle holy things:

> For their office is to assist the sons of Aaron with the service of the house of the Lord, in the courts and in the chambers and in the purifying of all holy things, even the work of the service of the house of God, and with the showbread, and the fine flour for a grain offering. . . . They are to stand every morning to thank and to praise the Lord, and likewise at evening, and to offer all burnt offerings to the Lord. . . . Thus they are to keep charge of the tent of meeting, and charge of the holy place, and charge of the sons of Aaron their relatives, for the service of the house of the Lord. (1 Chron. 23:28–32 NASB1995)

The holiness of the Levitical priests is evidenced in their ability to serve in close proximity to the presence of God and their special responsibilities for holy items in the religious system. Explicit references to the holiness of the priesthood are less common in the Historical Books, usually occurring in connection with worship or religious renewal. This phenomenon may be observed when the priest Jehoiada places Joash on the throne in the aftermath of the wicked reign of Ahaziah and his mother, Athaliah. Here the priests and Levites are described as the only ones allowed to enter the house of the Lord because they are holy (2 Chron. 23:6). A similar circumstance occurs during the reign of Hezekiah, who returns Judah to the Lord following the idolatry of his father, Ahaz. Hezekiah commands the priests to consecrate themselves—to make themselves holy—as they purify the temple and restore proper worship in Israel (2 Chron. 29:5). A third example is found when Ezra leads a group of Israelites back to Jerusalem following the exile. Ezra sets apart twelve priests and gives them charge of the utensils and offerings for the restoration of the temple, reminding them that they (and their utensils) are holy to the Lord (Ezra 8:28). In each of these cases, the shift toward religious renewal is what reminds people of the elevated status of the priests and their special function in the religious system.

Holiness language used for specific utensils or offerings also occurs in connection with religious reforms or restoration, where it appears necessary to instruct the people regarding what is set apart. This language can be found in the transition from the tabernacle to the temple, when the holy utensils are moved from one location to the other (2 Chron. 5:5), when the Israelites return the holy utensils from exile (Ezra 8:28), and when they reestablish their covenant with God in Jerusalem (Neh. 10:33). Utensils and offerings are also identified as holy when the status of the items plays a role in the plot of the narrative. In one instance, the holiness of the temple utensils is noted to make clear the seriousness of Athaliah's sin when she uses the utensils in the worship of Baal (2 Chron. 24:7). In another example, the holiness of the showbread given to David and his men is highlighted, perhaps to illustrate their purity as they flee from Saul (1 Sam. 21:4–6). Even through the audience might already assume the utensils and showbread are "holy" by association, their prominence in the narrative warrants the use of more intentional language to reinforce the point of the story.

HOLINESS THEMES (IMPLICIT) IN THE HISTORICAL BOOKS

The narratives in the Historical Books are framed around the basic theological reality of God's holiness and the implication that God's presence and purpose can categorically elevate and make holy something secular. The passages examined above demonstrate this principle with respect to locations, things, and the Levitical priests. A tension arises when the principle is applied to God's people, who are clearly associated with God and should be afforded a holy status but exhibit lifestyle characteristics inconsistent with the standards of holiness previously revealed in the Pentateuch. What is one to make of this dissonance? Is it possible that the importance of holiness for God's people has been overstated or misunderstood? Is holiness perhaps only of significance for certain segments of the population (such as the priesthood noted above) or certain seasons of the nation's development?

It seems more likely that the narratives use the apparent absence of holiness among God's people as a strategy to engage the audience in reflection (or conversation) concerning the concept in Israel's history—to judge for themselves the correlation between God's intent and the reality of the human experience. Meir Sternberg highlights the importance of these types of gaps in narratives, noting that

> a literary work consists of bits and fragments to be linked and pieced together in the process of reading: it establishes a system of gaps that must be filled in. This gap-filling ranges from simple linkages of elements, which the reader performs automatically, to intricate networks that are figured out consciously, laboriously, hesitantly, and with constant modifications in light of additional information disclosed in later stages of the reading.[22]

In the Historical Books, the audience discovers that the gap between God's holy ideal and the flawed leaders of the narrative allows other aspects of God's character—namely, his grace and mercy—to come into focus. Holiness is not absent from the text but is instead a contextual concept that the audience may use to evaluate characters' actions.

This concept is reinforced in Joshua 24, where God is first explicitly referenced as holy in the Historical Books. When Joshua renews the covenant between God and his people, he reminds them of the gap between their behavior and the holy character of God. He warns,

> "You will not be able to serve the Lord, for He is a holy God. He is a jealous God; He will not forgive your transgression or your sins. If you forsake the Lord and serve foreign gods, then He will turn and do you harm and consume you after he has done good to you." The people said to Joshua, "No, but we will serve the Lord." Joshua said to the people, "You are witnesses against yourselves that you have chosen for yourselves the Lord, to serve Him." And they said, "We are witnesses." (Josh. 24:19–22 NASB1995)

22. Sternberg, *Poetics of Biblical Narrative*, 186.

As the Historical Books bear witness, the Israelites are not able to faithfully serve God nor live in accordance with his standards of holiness. Despite their choice to serve the Lord, each subsequent generation (with a few exceptions) moves further away from the ethical and moral standards of God's design. Yet the people remain "a holy people to the LORD. . . . His own possession out of all the peoples who are on the face of the earth" (Deut. 7:6 NASB1995). This reality creates an inconsistency in the categorization of the Israelites. On one hand, they are categorically holy, set apart for and associated with the Lord. But on the other hand, they are categorically *not* holy, pursuing a lifestyle unreflective of the Lord's character. The back and forth movement between these two categories occupies a place of prominence in the telling of Israel's history. God's people repeatedly turn away from a holy lifestyle, in contrast to the unchanging holiness and promises of God. This tension can be seen in both the nation of Israel as a whole and many of those specifically called to lead it. Samson and David function as representative samples from this group, as they display clear evidence of being set apart and, at the same time, exhibit behavior inconsistent with God's holy standards.

CASE STUDY #1: SAMSON

Samson's birth occurs during the period of the judges, after forty years of Israel's punishment at the hands of the Philistines for its unfaithfulness. Following the pattern of previous judges, the audience expects Samson to deliver the Israelites from their oppression. Samson is born to a barren mother, who is instructed to raise him as a Nazirite, specifically set apart for the Lord (Judg. 13:5). The story implies that details of the Nazirite vow are no longer known, as Samson's father petitions the angel to provide instructions for how Samson is to live. According to Numbers 6, the Nazirite lifestyle is a life of holy dedication to the Lord.[23] Voluntary restrictions regarding diet and the cutting of hair mark this lifestyle, along with a special attentiveness to ritual cleanliness. For the term of the vow, the person is considered as consecrated to the Lord—as holy—by the community.[24]

23. For an overview of the Nazirite vow, see Baruch A. Levine, *Numbers 1–20: A New Translation with Introduction and Commentary*, AB 4 (New Haven, CT: Yale University Press, 2008), 229–35.

24. This association may find further support in the use of "holy one" to refer to Samson in LXX Vaticanus. See Stuart D. Chepey, "Samson the 'Holy One': A Suggestion Regarding the Reviser's Use of ἅγιος in Judg 13,7; 16,17 LXX Vaticanus," *Biblica* 83 (2002): 97–99.

Samson's lack of participation in the vow raises questions about any assumed correlation between his holy status and the condition of his heart. As an adult, Samson's desire to marry a Philistine, which would have been categorically prohibited by his vow, only serves to heighten the tension between his behavior and his status as a Nazirite. His parents recognize the problem and advise him to take a wife from his own people, but he is not deterred (Judg. 13:3). Instead, on the way to meet his prospective Philistine wife, he again exhibits behavior inconsistent with his status as a Nazirite by touching and eating honey from the carcass of an animal (14:8–9). While this act, and the riddle devised from it, ultimately become the basis for a conflict with the Philistines, little in Samson's behavior appears "holy." His subsequent attack on the Philistines at Ashlekon is motivated by anger, not a calling to deliver God's people. Samson himself suggests that this violence is unjustified when he comments that he will be blameless in his *next* attack against the Philistines, because they have given his wife to another man (15:3). In the next instance, however, Samson again fights to avenge, not to deliver God's people. He slaughters his enemies without considering the broader consequences of his actions. When he is called to account by the men of Judah and handed over to the Philistines, God empowers him, and he kills a thousand men with the jawbone of a donkey. Only at this point, exhausted from battle, does Samson indicate a snarky awareness of God's deliverance. Samson is, in short, an overconfident, self-serving brute—the opposite of a holy, God-serving Nazirite.[25]

Despite this characterization, the end of the story clarifies that throughout Samson's life he has been aware that he was dedicated to the Lord and has, at minimum, honored the instruction to refrain from cutting his hair. His hair, an external marker of his dedication to the Lord, carried with it a blessing and an empowerment. When he is tricked into revealing this fact and his hair is cut, the power and blessing of God are temporarily removed.[26] Interestingly, Numbers 6

25. Cf. the similar assessments of Trent C. Butler, *Judges*, WBC 8 (Nashville: Thomas Nelson, 2009), 356–60; Daniel I. Block, *Judges, Ruth*, NAC 6 (Nashville: Broadman & Holman, 1999), 470–71; and K. Lawson Younger Jr., *Judges and Ruth*, NIVAC (Grand Rapids: Zondervan Academic, 2002), 309–10.

26. Cf. Butler, *Judges*, 350; Block, *Judges, Ruth*, 461–62. See also Jeremy Schipper's argument that Samson knowingly allows his hair to be cut because he mistakenly thinks he can get along without the strength God has given him ("What Was Samson Thinking in Judges 16:17 and 16:20?," *Biblica* 92 [2011]: 60–69).

specifies that when Nazirites' hair, which "symbolizes their dedication" (v. 9 NIV), is defiled, those affected are to shave their head and make atonement to the Lord. After this, the period of dedication must be restarted, but there appear to be no additional negative consequences. As with other sins, forgiveness and mercy are offered. So it seems with Samson that once his head is shaved, his period of dedication begins anew, and after praying to the Lord (albeit for revenge), his strength returns.[27]

The dissonance in Samson's story raises questions about the relationship between categorical holiness and upright behavior. While the narrator does not appear to approve of Samson's behavior, the latter's lack of holiness does not disqualify him from accomplishing God's special purpose of judgment against the Philistines, nor does it prevent his inclusion among the examples of faith highlighted in the New Testament by the writer of Hebrews (Heb. 11:32). Instead, God works through Samson's imperfections to accomplish his purposes and deliver his people. In addition, the difference between Samson's behavior and status reveals how far removed the Israelites' religious awareness is from their covenantal consciousness generations earlier (recall Josh. 24). Given the lack of knowledge of the Nazirite vows by Samson's parents, it is not surprising that Samson's life fails to reflect the dedication that might formerly have been expected of a Nazirite. As noted above, Samson is aware of his dedication to the Lord and, in his own way, has tried to honor that dedication with the growth of his hair.[28] Perhaps God is simply willing to receive the dedication that Samson is able to offer, given the context in which he finds himself. This would suggest that holy behavior, rather than being a standard against which God's leaders are judged, is a contextual concept that reveals their shortcomings and creates space where God may graciously choose to intervene.

---

27. Following James L. Crenshaw (*Samson: A Secret Betrayed, a Vow Ignored* [Atlanta: John Knox, 1978], 501), Block notably sees the return of Samson's hair as evidence of hope in the narrative (*Judges, Ruth*, 463).
28. Younger (*Judges and Ruth*, 320) suggests that Samson's awareness of his Nazirite vow in Judg. 16:17 implies he has knowingly violated the other requirements of his vow with his prior behavior. While this is possible, Samson's awareness of one aspect of the vow does not necessarily require an awareness of the entirety of its stipulations.

CASE STUDY #2: DAVID[29]

David is presented in the biblical narrative as a character in tension—both a man who sought to honor and obey God and an imperfect leader who was guilty of sin. Like Samson, his behavior at times seems inconsistent with the role for which God has set him apart. The narrator's choice to portray David as a foil to Saul fosters an expectation among the audience that highlights this inconsistency. Saul is cast off because he rejects the word of God (1 Sam. 15:23), but David is chosen because God has evaluated and (presumably) approved of his inner character, his heart (1 Sam. 16:7). When Samuel anoints David, setting him apart and divinely authorizing him to serve as king, the audience expects that his character will reflect the character of God—that unlike Saul, he will live a holy life. Instead, David is full of contradictions; he is a king known as much for his hymns of praise as for his cries of confession, as much for his deeds of deliverance as for murder and sexual sin. Three familiar episodes from David's life offer a helpful perspective on this nuanced portrayal.

The first episode, mentioned earlier, narrates the consumption of the consecrated bread by David and his companions while fleeing from Saul. By this point in David's life, he has largely displayed exemplary character, particularly in his efforts to respect the current anointed king of Israel. Upon his arrival at Nob, David asks the priest, Ahimelech, for food to sustain his men:

> The priest answered David and said, "There is no ordinary bread on hand, but there is consecrated bread; if only the young men have kept themselves from women." David answered the priest and said to him, "Surely women have been kept from us as previously when I set out and the vessels of the young men were holy, though it was an ordinary journey; how much more then today will their vessels be holy?" So the priest gave him consecrated bread. (1 Sam. 21:4–6 NASB1995)

29. The following case study examines a composite picture of David culled from material found throughout the Historical Books. There are, of course, variations between the portrayal of David found in 1–2 Sam. and that of 1–2 Chron., but both present David, to a certain degree, as a flawed character. The differences between these two sources will be briefly discussed at the conclusion of the present section. See also P. E. Satterthwaite, "David," *DOTHB* 198–202; and David M. Howard Jr., "David (Person)," *ABD* 2:46–47.

This bread would normally be reserved solely for members of the priesthood (Exod. 29:32–34; Lev. 24:9). Ahimelech, however, bends the rules and treats David and his men as having the same elevated, holy status as the priests. Surprisingly, he seems singularly interested in one aspect of their behavior, sexual abstinence, and no other dimensions of ethical conduct are considered.[30] David is quick to answer and proclaim his men as holy, although his response could simply be motivated by a desire to acquire food. Either way, here holiness is afforded to David and his men based on a single quality (sexual abstinence) in connection with David's explanation that he and his men are on an official task from the king.

This task itself is also problematic in the immediate context, as no such task is given to David in the preceding chapter. To gain access to and consume the holy bread, David lies to the priest. This lie, rather than David's consumption of the showbread, is what ultimately leads to the death of Ahimelech and his family (1 Sam. 22:6–23).[31] A lack of consequence to David and his men for eating the showbread perhaps indicates that their needs in the moment have outweighed the command to keep the showbread solely for the priesthood.[32] Despite the lies, death, and cultic violation, God mercifully does not reject David as his choice for the next king of Israel. Kyle McCarter argues that the overall narrative sequence (including the death of the priests and citizens of Nob) actually presents David in a positive light as the preserver of the priesthood through his protection of Abiathar.[33]

---

30. Most commentators assume this singular focus relates to fitness for holy war in connection with the so-called special assignment from the king concocted by David. See, for example, David Toshio Tsumura, *The First Book of Samuel*, NICOT (Grand Rapids: Eerdmans, 2007), 530–31; Harry A. Hoffner Jr., *1 and 2 Samuel*, EEC (Bellingham, WA: Lexham, 2015), on 1 Sam. 21:5–7.

31. Cf. P. Kyle McCarter Jr., *I Samuel: A New Translation with Introduction and Commentary*, AB 8 (Garden City, NY: Doubleday, 1980), 365–67.

32. McCarter points to the NT interpretation of this event "as an instance of an excusable violation of cultic regulation (cf. Matt. 12:3–4; Mark 2:25–26; Luke 6:3–4)" (*I Samuel*, 349). In the three Gospel accounts where this story is raised, Jesus uses it to engage the Pharisees in discussion around the appropriate application of biblical law. Jesus acknowledges that a law has been violated but suggests this violation was appropriate given the circumstances. Reasons justifying Ahimelech's decision to give the showbread to David and his companions are not given, but Jesus's appeal to the incident suggests that neither he nor the Pharisees would criticize Ahimelech's behavior. This allows Jesus to use Ahimelech's approach to the situation as an example of compassion, mercy, and grace which Pharisees should emulate when faced with similar legal questions. For discussion see Darrell L. Bock, *Luke 1:1-9:50*, BECNT (Grand Rapids: Baker Academic, 1994), 523–25; W. D. Davies and Dale C. Allison, *A Critical and Exegetical Commentary on the Gospel according to Saint Matthew*, ICC, 2 vols. (London: T & T Clark, 2004), 2:310–11.

33. McCarter, *I Samuel*, 367.

A second interesting episode is found when David is prohibited from building the temple. Desiring to erect a permanent house for the ark of the covenant (2 Sam. 7), David is interrupted by the Lord, who indicates that he has not asked David to undertake the project and that he is not able to complete it. While holiness is not explicitly mentioned, the implication remains that something is categorically wrong with David that prevents him from participating in the construction of the temple. As we see later, David does make extensive preparations for the building of the temple, but the task cannot begin until his reign ends. The text offers two reasons for this reality. Kings suggests that David is unable to complete the building project because he is actively engaged in warfare during his reign (1 Kings 5:3). It is not logistically possible for David to complete a major building project while he establishes and secures the boundaries of the nation itself—a task that takes the duration of his life. Chronicles offers a similar reason but emphasizes the character of the man. David is a man of war who has "shed so much blood on the earth" before God, whereas Solomon would be a man of peace (1 Chron. 22:8–9 NASB1995).

David's association with war, then, appears to have both practically and categorically prevented him from building the temple. This situation, however, is not presented solely as a negative evaluation of David's character but also as a reflection of God's distinct purpose for David. After gently rebuking him for overstepping his boundaries, God uses this opportunity to remind David of his faithfulness and to form a new covenant with him. David's lack of categorical holiness becomes an opportunity for God to reveal his promise to David's family—specifically, that despite their sins in the future, God's love will never depart from David's family and David's kingdom will endure (2 Sam. 7:15–16).

A third episode illustrating David's inconsistent character is found in the story of David and Bathsheba (2 Sam. 11–12).[34] Here David abuses his kingly power to sleep with the wife of Uriah the Hittite. From the outset it is important to note that the focus in the narrative,

34. The narrative of David and Bathsheba has been the frequent subject of study and at times presented as an exemplar for narrative criticism. For a brief overview of the passage, see David Toshio Tsumura, *The Second Book of Samuel*, NICOT (Grand Rapids: Eerdmans, 2019), 172–99; P. Kyle McCarter Jr., *II Samuel: A New Translation with Introduction and Commentary*, AB 9 (Garden City, NY: Doubleday, 1984), 277–309; or Baruch Halpern, *David's Secret Demons: Messiah, Murderer, Traitor, King* (Grand Rapids: Eerdmans, 2001), 34–38.

both in the account of the incident and in the subsequent prophetic rebuke, is wholly on the sin of David. Bathsheba is not presented as complicit in the sin, nor is she punished for her actions as would be expected if she was a willing participant.[35] David is the guilty party—a king who uses his power to take what he wants, flagrantly disregarding the commands of God and the rights of those around him. David's actions here might be better described as rape than adultery.[36] In either case, the narrative presents David's sin as abhorrent to God. He has coveted another man's wife, taken her, slept with her, lied about it, and then had a man killed to cover it up.

David's actions in the narrative are presented in stark contrast to the behavior of Bathsheba and Uriah.[37] The audience meets Bathsheba in the context of her purification in accordance with Levitical law.[38]

35. Deuteronomy 22:22–27 indicates that both the man and the woman caught in adultery are to be put to death for their sin. The equal punishment seen here is consistent with the way the act of adultery is handled in other ancient civilizations. Mercy, when requested by the adulterous woman's husband, must also be equally applied (see Samuel Greengus, *Laws in the Bible and in Early Rabbinic Collections: The Legal Legacy of the Ancient Near East* [Eugene, OR: Cascade, 2011], 48–59, for a survey of the relevant extant data). The law in Deuteronomy assumes that any sexual activity taking place within the city (presumably within earshot of others) is consensual unless the woman has cried for help. Concessions are made for accusations of rape that take place outside of the city. In these instances, only the man receives the death penalty while the woman is given the benefit of the doubt because there is no one around to hear her cry for help. Second Samuel 11, however, despite being set in the city, does not contain any record of Bathsheba's cries for help. Why then, does the punishment focus only on David? Alexander I. Basili has argued that Bathsheba does in fact receive punishment via the death of her son ("Was It Rape? The David and Bathsheba Pericope Re-examined," *VT* 61 [2011]: 1–15.). However, she is not included in the prophetic rebuke, implying that she should be seen more as a victim than an accomplice.

36. Determination of the specific nature of David's sin in this instance is complicated by its proximity to Amnon's rape of Tamar in 2 Sam. 13:11–17. Tamar clearly protests Amnon's actions, which the text describes as oppressive and violent. Basili rightly observes that this language is consistent with other biblical depictions of rape that also include language indicating force or violence ("Was It Rape?" 3–6). The description of David's sin against Bathsheba, however, does not include this type of language, which perhaps explains why many interpreters inquire about Bathsheba's role in the incident and refer to the act as adultery. Evidence in the text can be construed to make the case for rape or adultery but is insufficient to completely eliminate the possibility of either. Moreover, as Bill Arnold recognizes, the episode is "an intensely *literary* presentation, in which the blame is carefully and deliberately placed only on David. The narrator is uninterested in the possibility [of Bathsheba's guilt] and simply defers the question, making it impossible for us to speculate about her motives" (*1 & 2 Samuel*, NIVAC [Grand Rapids: Zondervan, 2003], 526 n.33).

37. David P. Wright, "David Autem Remansit in Hierusalem: Felix Coniunctio!," in *Pomegranates and Golden Bells: Studies in Biblical, Jewish, and Near Eastern Ritual, Law, and Literature in Honor of Jacob Milgrom,* ed. David P. Wright, David Noel Freedman, and Avi Hurvitz (Winona Lake, IN: Eisenbrauns, 1995), 217–24.

38. Bathsheba's purification is attributed here to the seven-day period of ritual cleansing prescribed for women following menstruation, as in Lev. 15:19, rather than purification from a discharge resulting

The language of purification here draws the audience's attention to the concept of holiness and heightens their awareness to the sinful nature of David's actions. The earlier emphasis on sexual purity in relation to the showbread is also instructive here. Unlike the earlier episode, where David and his men abstain from sexual activity and are deemed holy by the priest, here it is Uriah who is presented as a man who is "clean," having abstained from sexual relations with his wife during the military campaign. David's actions here are anything but holy. Not only does he remain home from war and engage in sexual activity—he does so with another man's wife!

The visit of Nathan the prophet to convict David of his sin draws further attention to the dissonance in David's behavior. In brief, the king is presented as so unaware of his sin that he zealously condemns the character in Nathan's parable without realizing that he himself is the subject of the story. To his credit, when confronted directly with his sin and his punishment, he does repent and seek the Lord. Although David is punished for his actions, God forgives him of his sin and remains faithful to the promises he had made to him in the past. Once again, God's grace and mercy shine brightly against David's failure to live a morally and ethically holy life. David's actions have consequences, but God's promises and presence in his life remain.

Before proceeding, it is important to note a crucial difference in how the books of Samuel and Chronicles present David's sin against Bathsheba. While the event and its consequences are covered in great detail in 2 Samuel, Chronicles completely omits them. This difference has led to the common idea that Chronicles portrays David as a holy, perfect king, in contrast to Samuel's portrait of him as a flawed leader. Support for this view is found in the arguably more sanitized depiction of the end of his reign (1 Chron. 28–29). Here he is presented as a strong leader who prepares the kingdom for his son, contributes to the preparations for the construction of the temple, and leaves a legacy of wealth and honor. Indeed, the portrayal of David in Chronicles is more positive, but to describe him as a perfectly holy king seems to overstate

from intercourse, as in Lev. 15:18. This detail is included as an aside to indicate that the pregnancy must be the result of David's sexual sin rather than any prior encounter with Bathsheba's husband. For further discussion, see Tsumura, *The Second Book of Samuel,* 177–78; Wright, "David Autem Remansit," 218-19; Basili, "Was It Rape?," 13; and McCarter, *II Samuel*, 286.

the case.[39] The Chronicler does not shy away from mentioning David's warfare or his problematic census, suggesting the portrayals in each book reflect a difference of degree and focus rather than an alternate version of the king.[40]

This variance likely stems from the different social context and theological emphasis of the Chronicler. If Chronicles presents the history of Israel (and portions of its religious system) to an audience attempting to make sense of its past in light of its return from exile, it seems more appropriate to highlight positive traits that its leaders should aspire to rather than rehash the negative traits that led to the exile itself. In addition, as noted above, the Chronicler displays a heightened interest in the construction of the temple as well as the holiness of the structure and the items associated with it. The two kings associated with the building of the temple, David and Solomon, are presented in a noticeably positive light by the Chronicler, perhaps in keeping with the holiness theme. This positive portrayal further serves to legitimize the Davidic monarchy for a new age.[41] That said, the fact that David retains some of his imperfections in this context reinforces the idea that even God's anointed leaders need his grace and forgiveness.[42] "Perfect" leaders are not those completely without sin, but those who repent of their sin and are reminded of the gracious and compassionate character of their God.

CONCLUSION

The Historical Books engage the concept of holiness via both explicit terminology and the implications of narrative storytelling. First, the historical narratives generally maintain the importance of holiness

39. See, for example, the arguments made by Sara Japhet (*I and II Chronicles: A Commentary*, OTL [Louisville: Westminster John Knox, 1993], 48) or Ralph W. Klein (1 Chron*icles: A Commentary*, Hermeneia [Minneapolis: Fortress, 2006], 44).

40. This argument assumes a certain unity to the final form of Chronicles, suggesting that intentionality lies behind the portrayal of David, regardless of the compositional process. For a short summary of possible explanations for the inclusion of these negative elements, see Gary N. Knoppers, "Images of David in Early Judaism: David as Repentant Sinner in Chronicles," *Biblica* 76 (1995): 450–53.

41. See, for example, David Noel Freedman, "The Chronicler's Purpose," *CBQ* 22 (1961): 436–42. Freedman notes, "The city of Jerusalem, the temple, the priesthood, and the ordinances for worship in song and sacrifice, all . . . center in the person of David, and his descendants" (437). See also Yossi Leshem, "'And David Was Sitting in Jerusalem': The Accounts in Samuel and Chronicles," *HUCA* 87 (2016): 49–60, which argues that messianic expectations also contribute to this depiction.

42. Cf. Knoppers, "Images of David," 454.

for the Israelite religious system in the Pentateuch. Where questions might be raised regarding proper practice due to a change of circumstance, explicit terminology is employed to ensure that the standards of holiness are maintained, particularly with respect to the temple and its associated utensils and offerings. Rather than repeating the Pentateuchal material, the Historical Books rely on the presence of this information in the cultural memory of the audience. The absence of the material in the text may actually signal that it was more important for the community, not less.

Second, holiness is intentionally linked with the presence and purposes of God. A connection with God elevates people and things to categorical holiness. God sets things (and people) apart, and things are set apart for God. In both cases, the association with God is what is significant, not the tasks, objects, or persons themselves.

Finally, the presentation of imperfect leaders in the narratives creates a tension that is subsequently resolved by the mercy and grace of God. As Joshua accurately predicts, Israel and her leaders cannot uphold the standards of a holy God. Although their decisions and actions have consequences, the expectation of holiness allows God to intervene and show his faithfulness to them. By inviting the audience to consider God's mercy and grace in connection with his holiness, the Historical Books remind their readers that their own failure to fully embody holy character does not disqualify them from God's promise and love.

Chapter 4
HOLINESS IN RUTH
JENNIFER M. MATHENY

The book of Ruth appears as a simple rural story with a warm readerly welcome after the violent final chapters of Judges. This scroll experienced early acceptance in the Christian and Jewish tradition.[1] As an embraced text, it is important to note that Ruth is not revered as a traditional holiness text. However, upon closer inspection, its story reveals nuanced and complex characteristics, displaying a social holiness lived and observed by its characters within their unique chronotope (i.e., their unique time-space). Ruth offers a powerful voice in the canon of Scripture, one in which the term "holiness" may be absent, yet one that nevertheless illustrates holiness *embodied* and *performed* by unexpected people on the margins of society. Unfortunately, Ruth has been marginal in major volumes of OT theology, often forgotten and sometimes even absent in their indexes.[2] Might this marginalized story reveal something about social holiness through an unexpected agent?

If holiness is expressed by loving God and neighbor, as many have suggested,[3] Ruth's extraordinary acts of *ḥesed* ("loving kindness")

1. For a fuller discussion, see Jennifer M. Matheny, "Ruth's Chronotope in the Canon," in *Judges 19–21 and Ruth: Canon as a Voice of Answerability*, BibInt 200 (Leiden: Brill, 2022), 128–49.
2. Amy Erickson and Andrew R. Davis note that "in the following works, Ruth does not appear at all in the index of citations: Brevard Childs, *Biblical Theology of the Old and New Testaments* (1993); James Barr, *The Concept of Biblical Theology* (1999); Walter Brueggemann, *Theology of the Old Testament* (1997); Reinhard Feldmeier and Hermann Spieckermann, *God of the Living* (2011)" ("Recent Research on the Megilloth (Song of Songs, Ruth, Lamentations, Ecclesiastes, Esther)," *CurBR* 14 [2016]: 308). Thankfully, the trend has been shifting. "Volumes with a significant use of Ruth include the following: Paul R. House's *Old Testament Theology* (1998) lists 13 references to Ruth. John Goldingay's three-volume *Old Testament Theology* (2009) lists a total of 65 references to Ruth. Bruce K. Waltke's *An Old Testament Theology: An Exegetical, Canonical, and Thematic Approach* (2007) contains 139 citations of Ruth. An interest in Ruth's particular contributions to Old Testament theology has advanced and may possibly increase, as illustrated with the above treatments in House, Goldingay, and Waltke. Lau and Goswell have dedicated an entire monograph to the theology of Ruth, focusing on major themes such as 'famine', 'land', 'redemption', 'covenant', 'kingship' (2016: 3)" (Jennifer M. Matheny, "Ruth in Recent Research," *CurBR* 19 [2020]: 14–15).
3. Jason Vickers writes, "Indeed, Wesley repeatedly said that what really mattered in religion was love for God and love for neighbor. Moreover . . . he was convinced that obedience followed a change of heart. It was the consequence of a right ordering of one's affections. Yet there is a real sense in which

toward Naomi, her mother-in-law, are exemplars of holiness. The entire community witnesses these acts of *ḥesed* (Ruth 2:11–12; 4:14–15). Although they may appear insignificant on a surface level, Ruth's actions alter Israel's political and theological trajectories. No wonder this gem of a story has sparked much scholarly discussion regarding its genre.[4] Perhaps the ambiguity on this matter is one of the book's strengths. It is a story of holiness lived and expressed in actions of *ḥesed* amid surprising conversations, commitments, and encounters (Gen 39:21; 32:10; Josh. 2:12–14; Ruth 2:8–9).

"Holiness" (Heb. *qdš*), as defined in the opening chapter of this volume, is "qualitative otherness."[5] Accordingly, holiness is profoundly relational, concerning humanity's relationship with God (Exod. 19:10–11; Lev. 11:44–45), one another (Lev. 19–20), and the rest of creation (Gen. 1:26; 2:3, 15; Num. 33:33; Ps. 24:1). In Exodus, God reveals plans for a tabernacle so that he can dwell with humanity, an Edenic representation of cosmic realities.[6] Within this structure is the holy of holies, the inner sanctum of the most sacred of spaces. Leviticus reveals that this program of holiness is attentive to relationships, a reality communicated by the recurring refrain "Be holy, because I am holy" (Lev. 11:44–45; 19:2; 20:7 NASB). Within ancient pastoral and religious contexts, key signs, symbols, and rituals were "key to the pursuit of holiness," and they are still key to that pursuit "because [they remind] us that we are physical creatures who learn through embodied acts of worship."[7] Though the rituals through response in Leviticus

obedience and love are in a dialectical relationship in Wesley's theology" (*Wesley: A Guide for the Perplexed*, Guides for the Perplexed [London: T&T Clark, 2009], 101).

4. "The genre (type of literature) of Ruth has been a vital part of the discussion of Ruth's purpose and function in the Old Testament. Proposals have identified the book of Ruth as similar to everything from a charming and idyllic story or a nursery tale to a historical narrative. But the genre of a text also encompasses its shared social location, intended function, and rhetorical aim. Ruth ends with a genealogy that bridges into the future Israelite monarchy by giving the lineage of King David" (Jennifer M. Matheny, "The Faithful Love of God," in *Encountering the God of Love: Portraits from the Old Testament*, ed. Brad E. Kelle and Stephanie Smith Matthews [Kansas City, MO: Foundry, 2021], 82–83). I argue for the possibility of Ruth as a *māšāl* ("proverb"). See Matheny, *Judges 19–21 and Ruth*, 143.

5. For a detailed discussion, see John Oswalt's essay in this volume.

6. See Sandra L. Richter, *The Epic of Eden: A Christian Entry into the Old Testament* (Downers Grove, IL: IVP Academic, 2008).

7. Mark W. Scarlata, *A Journey through the World of Leviticus: Holiness, Sacrifice, and the Rock Badger* (Eugene, OR: Cascade, 2021), 20. Purity laws are regulations for individuals and the community, but importantly, impurity is not equated with moral failure.

pertain to Israel in their ancient context, Terence Fretheim notes that they are also "*cosmic* in scope."[8] Purity regulations are part of Israel's life and worship, but holiness involves a call for ethical living that embodies life-giving, dynamic avenues of blessing and wholeness for all of creation.

What does holiness look like when it extends from the appointed priests to the entire nation? The prophets call Israel back to the very core of what it means to live a holy life. God as holy is wholly other, yet Israel is called to be holy. Brad Kelle writes, "Israel must practice purity and justice."[9] Francis Landy describes the mystery of difference and presence by appealing to Hosea 11:9: "God's difference from humanity ('For I am God and not human') is manifested by his presence in humanity ('in your midst holy')."[10] How is this holiness worked out within relationships? The prophets' admonitions revolve around caring for others well through the sharing of resources and the establishment of justice. Jeremiah reveals that "faithfulness to God and Torah is bound to caring for the oppressed, the orphan, the widow and the marginalized. When so much is physically lost (temple, land), a שׁוב ('return') to relationships may seem impossible, yet later in the text, hope is offered through language of healing, exodus imagery, new covenant, and a Davidic king (Jer. 31–33)."[11]

Can a story have anything to do with holiness if it lacks explicit words for holiness? Though the story of Ruth contains zero occurrences of the root *qdš*, it does reveal actions of *ḥesed*. The highest quality of God's holy character is *ḥesed*.[12] Even in exile, after the loss of key markers of identity (i.e., the temple and the land), it is through liturgy and the call to love God and neighbor that relational holiness remains an identifier of a true Israelite. Loving God and neighbor is at the theological heart of the OT (Deut. 6:4–5; Matt. 22:37–40).

8. Terence E. Fretheim, *God and World in the Old Testament: A Relational Theology of Creation* (Nashville: Abingdon, 2005), 129, emphasis original.

9. Brad E. Kelle, *Telling the Old Testament Story: God's Mission and God's People* (Nashville: Abingdon, 2017), 101.

10. Francis Landy, *Hosea*, RNBC (Sheffield: Sheffield Academic, 1995), 18.

11. Jennifer M. Matheny and Amy E. Hale, "The Raging Prophet: Acceptance Commitment Therapy (ACT) as a Pathway Forward through Pain," in *When Psychology Meets the Bible*, ed. Heather A. McKay and Pieter van der Zwan, Bible in the Modern World 83 (Sheffield: Sheffield Phoenix, 2023), 243–44.

12. Rabbi Simlai writes that the Torah begins with *ḥesed* and ends with *ḥesed*, from God clothing Adam and Eve to Moses's burial (b. Soṭah 14a, 6).

Essentially, holiness is relational. Wesley writes, "Disperse abroad, give to the poor: deal your bread to the hungry. Cover the naked with a garment, entertain the stranger, carry or send relief to them that are in prison. Heal the sick; not by miracle, but through the blessing of God upon your seasonable support. . . . Defend the oppressed, plead the cause of the fatherless, and make the widow's heart sing for joy."[13]

The story of Ruth reveals what it means to live out holiness before God and within community. Scarlata writes that "holiness is a *communal* endeavor."[14] Through risk, hospitality, and generosity, Ruth reveals a powerful and intimate story of imaginative possibilities. Wesley captures the interplay of love and holiness as he asks, "What is holiness? Is it not, essentially, love? The love of God and of all humankind? . . . Love is holiness wherever it exists."[15]

ḤESED

One of the defining characteristics of YHWH is *ḥesed*.[16] The Hebrew term is difficult to define. In our English translations, it has been translated as "love" (NIV, ESV, NLT, MSG), "loving kindness" (KJV) "loyalty" (NIV, ESV, NLT), "steadfast love" (ESV, NRSVUE), and "unfailing love" (NIV, NLT). It occurs more than 250 times in the OT and is found in every major section: Law, Prophets, and Writings. Many scholars note that *ḥesed* is one of most important theological terms in the OT.[17] Studies of *ḥesed* grapple with questions of origin and agency (human and divine), and the answers are inconclusive.[18] Brian Britt suggests that *ḥesed* "is a fundamentally ambiguous term . . . and that biblical authors used [its ambiguity] to express the

13. John Wesley, "Upon Our Lord's Sermon on the Mount, Discourse VIII," in *John Wesley's Sermons: An Anthology*, ed. Albert C. Outler and Richard P. Heitzenrater (Nashville: Abingdon, 1991), 252.
14. Scarlata, *Journey through the World*, 16, emphasis added.
15. Wesley, "Upon Our Lord's Sermon on the Mount," 252.
16. See the section on *ḥesed* in Oswalt's chapter in this volume.
17. See Robin Routledge, "*Hesed* as Obligation: A Re-Examination" *Tyndale Bulletin* 46 (1995): 179–96; John H. Hayes, "Covenant and Hesed," in *Interpreting Ancient Israelite History, Prophecy, and Law*, ed. Brad E. Kelle (Eugene, OR: Cascade), 282–91; Michael Card, *Inexpressible: Hesed and the Mystery of God's Lovingkindness* (Downers Grove, IL: IVP Books, 2018); Nelson Glueck, *Hesed in the Bible*, trans. Alfred Gottschalk (Cincinnati: Hebrew Union College Press, 1967); Katherine Dobb Sakenfeld, *The Meaning of Hesed in the Hebrew Bible: A New Inquiry*, HSM 17 (Missoula, MT: Scholars Press, 1978).
18. See Gordon R. Clark, *The Word "Hesed" in the Hebrew Bible*, LHBOTS 154 (London: Bloomsbury Academic, 2015); idem, "Hesed—A Study of a Lexical Field," *ANES* 30 (1992): 34–54.

complexities of the divine-human relationship."[19] The ambiguity of this term is one of its strengths.

From early studies, which view *ḥesed* as an obligatory activity, to more recent ones, which see it as a relational activity that can exceed obligation, the term has received much scholarly attention.[20] A brief survey of its use demonstrates that it encompasses many of the other terms often associated with it: "truth," "mercy," "compassion," "justice," "covenant," and "holiness." The psalmist trusts in God's *ḥesed* (Ps. 13:5), and in Lamentations 3, the poetry shifts as a brief respite in suffering liturgy (v. 22). Because of it, God is unlike other gods (2 Chron. 6:14) and is proclaimed as the source of commitment, everlasting covenant, and faithfulness (Isa. 55:3). The book of Hosea calls for *ḥesed* because when it is lacking, injustice exists (4:1). In 1 Samuel 15, *ḥesed* describes the reason why hands of vengeance and violence are restrained (v. 6). In the Psalms, God's *ḥesed* is something longed for (109:21; 117:2; 147:11), asked for, and praised (100:5); it protects, supports, and comforts (119:41, 76, 159).

Ḥesed captures the greatest sense of God's loving nature, as witnessed often in stories. It is particularly embodied in the story of Ruth. For Mildred Bangs Wynkoop, holiness is a dynamic process. Wynkoop writes, "The human element in the Bible to which the divine speaks is the common life blood that keeps the divine meaningful to all who partake of life. The story is the flesh around the idea. It preserves the idea from becoming so detached and irrelevant and intellectualized that it loses all contact with reality."[21]

Wynkoop notes that this phenomenon "saves justification and sanctification from abstraction."[22] This rings true for the theological idea of

19. Brian Britt, "Unexpected Attachments: A Literary Approach to the Term חסד in the Hebrew Bible," *JSOT* 27 (2003): 293.

20. Some of the key early studies include Nelson Glueck, *Das Wort Hesed im alttestamentlichen Sprachgebrauche als menschliche und göttliche Gemeinschaftgemasse* (Giessen: Alfred Töpelmann, 1927); Boone M. Bowen, "A Study of Chesed" (PhD diss., Yale University, 1938); and Katharine Doob Sakenfeld, *The Meaning of Hesed in the Hebrew Bible: A New Inquiry* (Leiden: Brill, 1978). More recently, see Gordon R. Clark, *The Word "Hesed" in the Hebrew Bible*, BAC (New York: Bloomsbury Academic, 2015).

21. Mildred Bangs Wynkoop, *An Existential Interpretation of the Doctrine of Holiness* (Portland, OR: Western Evangelical Seminary, 1958), 40, https://digitalcommons.georgefox.edu/cgi/viewcontent.cgi?article=1032&context=gfes.

22. Wynkoop, *Existential Interpretation*, 40. I am thankful for first hearing this quote from a paper delivered by Rev. Dr. Johan Tredoux in celebration of the fiftieth anniversary of Wynkoop's *A Theology of Love: The Dynamic of Wesleyanism* (Kansas City, MO: Beacon Hill, 1972) at the

holiness as well. Holiness is exemplified by acts of *ḥesed* in the story of Ruth. Although terms for holiness do not occur in this narrative, the ideal is lived out in extraordinary acts of *ḥesed*, accounting for its ethical nature and revealing the possibilities of extravagant love within community. Ruth's story reveals that daily moments, which may initially appear insignificant and small like yeast, are really what contribute to a notable story. One of the chief ways God's people exemplify holiness is by representing him in their everyday interactions. The Holiness Code (Lev. 17–26) admonishes Israel to be holy, as YHWH is holy. The prophet Jeremiah proclaims, with intense emotion, how Israel has broken the covenant and so failed in this endeavor. In key texts that mention Jeremiah's or the Lord's anger (i.e., Jer. 4:4; 6:11; 7:20; 10:25; 18:20; 21:5; 21:12; 25:15; 30:23; 32:31; and 32:37), all refer to Israel breaking the covenant and perverting justice, especially against the marginalized and the oppressed. These are acts that violate God's desire for Israel's conduct, which includes caring for the immigrant, the widow, and the oppressed (Deut. 27:15–25). In Jeremiah's famous temple sermon (found in Jer. 7), Judah is given a detailed list of how it should amend its ways (vv. 5–7). For instance, it is not to oppress the refugee, the orphan, or the widow. It is to refrain from shedding innocent blood and chasing after other gods. God's *ḥesed* is revealed in Jeremiah, even after all that the people have done in breaking the covenant (33:11). God describes God's self as, "I am *ḥāsîd*" (3:12)[23] and twice describes God's self as *ḥesed* in the poetic passage that is referred to as the grace formula (*Gnadenformel*) in Exodus 34:5–6. In Ruth what is profound is that God's *ḥesed* is revealed through a Moabite widow to an Israelite widow and their deceased. Her acts of *ḥesed* embody the Bible's holiness ethic. How does one *perform* holiness? By acts of *ḥesed*.

The book of Ruth explicitly uses the term *ḥesed* three times (Ruth 1:8; 2:20; 3:10). It also gives an example of the interplay between divine activity and human activity. Schipper notes that 2:20 "explicitly associates YHWH with *ḥesed*."[24] Yet upon closer inspection, the verse

conference "A Theology of Love, Celebrating the 50th Anniversary of Mildred Bangs Wynkoop's *A Theology of Love*," November 12, 2022.

23. This adjectival form of *ḥesed* is worth noting as it is from the root *ḥesed* and is a related adjective. See also Karen Nelson, *Hesed and the New Testament* (University Park, PA: Eisenbrauns, 2023), 1–6.

24. Jeremy Schipper, *Ruth: A New Translation with Introduction and Commentary*, AYB 7 (New Haven, CT: Yale University Press, 2016), 31.

reveals some intentional ambiguity. That is, the act of *ḥesed* in view may also be attributed to Boaz. Perhaps it is both God and Boaz, and this ambiguity highlights the social holiness, a working of God's activity through human agents, in which *ḥesed* and holiness are a tangible expression through community participants.

YHWH'S *ḤESED* REVEALED THROUGH ORPAH AND RUTH

Violence hums in the backdrop of Ruth 1:1, which situates the storyline within the time of Judges: "in the days the judges were judging" (AT). Within this era of darkness comes an intimate story of a family in need. Death and despair hang in the balance in the opening scenes. Judges ends with the death of multitudes amid a civil war, and Ruth opens with the death of all its male characters. It is within this harsh context that holiness blossoms through acts of courage and generosity (i.e., *ḥesed*) by unlikely women, including Moabite widows. To demonstrate the extraordinary significance of these displays of *ḥesed*, it will help to highlight key literary features of Ruth (e.g., intentional ambiguity and female agency), together with the book's intentional setting within the period of the judges.

Ruth and Orpah appear to be unusual agents of *ḥesed*, especially when the story is placed in canonical dialogue with Judges 19–21. Anyone foreign or deemed other is oppressed in the final chapters of Judges. Women are nameless and voiceless and experience a frightening amount of gendered violence. The violence against women and foreigners juxtaposes with Orpah and Ruth's alternative vision of remarkable generosity. One example of the negative attitude toward foreigners in Judges is the Levite's refusal to lodge in Jebus precisely because it is a city of *foreigners* (19:12). This heightens the irony when the town of Benjamin, a familial place where the Levite decides to lodge, turns out to be a city of violence. Violence is witnessed in the dismemberment of the Levite's *pîlegeš* ("concubine" or "secondary wife"), who remains nameless throughout the story. After a civil war against the tribe of Benjamin, women are kidnapped to repopulate the tribe. Both the violence to women and the attitude toward the foreigner are excessive and heighten in irony as Judges comes to an end.

Through a canonical and intertextual lens and in contrast to the actions of Judges 19–21, Orpah's and Ruth's actions of *ḥesed* are quite extraordinary. This interpretive key allows readers to witness social holiness during a dark season and through an unexpected people.

Naomi commands Ruth and Orpah to return to Moab, their ancestral home: "Then Naomi said to two of her daughters-in-law, 'Go and return, each of you, to the house of her mother. May YHWH treat *ḥesed* with you, just as you have done with the dead and with me. May YHWH give to you that you may find rest, each of you in the house of your husband.' Then she kissed them, and they lifted their voice and wept" (Ruth 1:8–9 AT). Naomi has nothing to offer her daughters but this beautiful prayer. She invokes the covenant name of Israel's God to act out of *ḥesed* for them, just as they have acted out of *ḥesed* for her and for those who have died. Even though the story does not list what these acts of *ḥesed* include, a close reading will unpack some of the ways these acts are demonstrated and witnessed by the community in Bethlehem. Wynkoop rightly asserts that getting into the flesh of the story helps the reader to avoid theological abstraction.[25] In Ruth holiness is displayed through self-sacrificing acts of *ḥesed.*

One of the most powerful and well-known scenes in the book of Ruth is when Ruth pledges herself through an oath commitment to Naomi:

> "Do not plead with me to leave you and return after you. For wherever you go, I will go; wherever you live, I will live; your people will be my people, and your God my God. Wherever you die, I will die, and there I will be buried. May the YHWH do [this] to me, and more also, if even death will divide us." But when she saw that she was determined to go with her, she ceased speaking to her. (Ruth 1:16–18 AT)

Such covenantal language expresses Ruth's unwavering desire and reveals her *ḥesed* for Naomi, which she and Orpah previously demonstrated (Ruth 1:8–9). Ruth's continued demonstration of *ḥesed* will be revealed through sacrificial actions that go beyond the call of duty. Her oath will be followed by a journey alongside Naomi, during her season of grief, loneliness, and need.

25. Wynkoop, *A Theology of Love*, 150–59.

Ruth's oath is unique in the OT. It is the only oath of significance spoken by a woman. Jonathan speaks a similar oath to David in 1 Samuel 20:13, likewise invoking the Lord's covenant name, and "given the situation, both parties [undermine] themselves to enact the oath. For Jonathan and David, Jonathan is forfeiting his role and succession as king, giving allegiance to David. For Ruth, she is risking a future with her people to return to a foreign land where she has pledged to be with Naomi in a covenant similar to a marriage contract."[26] What is interesting in Jonathan's oath to David is that Jonathan requests that *ḥesed* be demonstrated to him and his family. *Ḥesed* is expressed through a covenant oath. David will go on to fulfill this promise after Jonathan is deceased (2 Sam. 9). These types of oaths are found only on the lips of male leaders in the OT, with only one exception: Ruth.

Although the word *ḥesed* does not occur in Ruth's oath to Naomi (as it does in 2 Sam. 9), Ruth performs acts of *ḥesed* both beforehand and afterward (Ruth 1:8; 3:10). Ruth is committed to Naomi and Naomi's God, YHWH. Against the backdrop of Judges 19–21, Ruth's oath is unexpected. Whereas every woman is nameless and silent in Judges 19–21, Ruth speaks boldly. The oath mentioned in Judges 21:5 results in *ḥērem* being executed on Jabesh-Gilead. Here an oath spoken by a woman *to* a woman will lead to new life. David fulfills his oath to Jonathan. Ruth desires to fulfill her commitment by journeying with Naomi to Bethlehem.

Lest the incredible movement of Ruth to Bethlehem be overlooked, we would do well to remember that ancient households were communal and kinship oriented. The text does not discuss Ruth's tribal affiliations in Moab, but she indeed could have been leaving a very large, supportive household. To pledge herself to Naomi without the possibility of an immediate heir is provocative. Her yes to "return"[27] with Naomi to Bethlehem places her in a vulnerable and risky situation, exemplified by the threat of violence in the fields in Ruth 2. Ruth's display of *ḥesed* is one of risk, loyalty, and determination.[28]

---

26. Matheny, *Judges 19–21 and Ruth*, 163; cf. Judy Fentress-Williams, *Ruth*, AOTC (Nashville: Abingdon, 2012), 52.
27. For Naomi, this is a return to her homeland, but for Ruth, the Moabite, this is foreign soil.
28. Ruth "clings" (*dbq*) to Naomi (Ruth 2:8, 21, 23). This is the same verb used in Genesis to imply marriage (2:24).

God's people demonstrate holiness by loving God and neighbor and taking care of the foreigner, the orphan, and the widow (Deut. 6:4–5; 10:18). The use of both oath language and *ḥesed* reveals a social holiness embodied by Orpah and Ruth. Even though Orpah returns to Moab, the initial actions of *ḥesed* performed by both Orpah and Ruth will continue throughout the story. (The message of caring for the widow appears in the NT as well, as we see in James 1:27.) In this moving scene at the end of Ruth 1, roles are reversed when a Moabite widow cares for an Israelite widow.

ḤESED EXPRESSED THROUGH HUMAN AND DIVINE ACTS OF GENEROSITY

Ruth continues to demonstrate *ḥesed* to Naomi as the two begin a new life together in Bethlehem, Naomi's hometown. Naomi is well known, a fact demonstrated at the end of Ruth 1 as she enters town. The women of Bethlehem exclaim, "Is this Naomi?" (v. 19 AT). Naomi's downcast state is also revealed in this scene: "Then she said to them, 'Do not call me Naomi; call me Mara. For the Almighty has greatly embittered me. I walked away full, but YHWH has caused me to return empty. Why do you call me Naomi? YHWH has answered against me; the Almighty has answered me and brought this brokenness upon me'" (vv. 20–21 AT).

Demonstrating love for a neighbor in a difficult situation is not easy, especially when he or she is grieving or depressed. Doing so is one of the world's greatest acts of sacrifice. But Ruth is also in a season of grief. The emotional energy needed to honor her oath must have been exceedingly great for Ruth. One can easily envision Ruth waking up each day to endure curt remarks, rants of despair, and perhaps even heavy silence from a bitter and grieving Naomi. Grief is messy. Yet in this context, the reader is reminded that Ruth loves Naomi. In fact, Naomi is the only person Ruth is explicitly said to love in the story: "Then the women said to Naomi, 'Blessed is YHWH, who did not remove from you a redeeming one this day, and may his name be famous in Israel! May he be to you a restorer of life and a support for you in old age because your daughter-in-law, who loves you, she has given birth to him'" (Ruth 4:14–15 AT). I envision Ruth keeping her oath and expressing holiness through love hour by hour and minute by minute.

The economic challenges facing widows in the ancient world should not be minimized. One way forward for widows was for a kinsman-redeemer (*gō'ēl*) to offer resources. Without children, an inheritance was impossible. In the biblical story, inheritance is connected to land and memory. If a widow died without children, the memory of her family would be lost. A redeemer, then, could restore by redeeming persons or property. Some examples include purchasing back family land that has been lost through indebtedness (Lev. 25:25–28), avenging the blood of one murdered (Deut. 19:6, 12),[29] and freeing someone from servitude (Lev. 25:47–55). A redeemer, according to levirate customs (Gen. 38:11; Deut. 25:5–7), can be a family member who procreates with the widow for the deceased brother and, thus, continues the family line. Inheritance rights are not assumed in these legal texts.[30] Ruth 2:1 alerts the reader that Boaz is a kinsman, a relative of Naomi. Although he is not her nearest kinsman, he is one possible redeemer.

Ruth places herself in vulnerable positions to glean in the nearby fields, providing sustenance for her and Naomi. Gleaning is mandated by Israelite law, yet Ruth is aware that it still depends on the favor of others. In Ruth 2:20, she states to Naomi that she will glean in a field where she "finds favor" in the eyes of the owner. This text reminds the reader of Ruth's vulnerability as a foreign, widowed woman. In a previous conversation with his foreman, Boaz instructs him to keep her safe and to tell the other men to refrain from touching her. While Ruth gleans, Boaz notices her. He approaches her and invites her to glean safely in his fields. Ruth is grateful, and she identifies herself as a foreigner and speaks in deference to Boaz: "How have I found favor in your eyes, that you take notice of me, a foreigner?" (Ruth 2:10 AT).[31] Schipper offers insight into this scene:

> According to her statement, Ruth assumes that her successful gleaning depends on the favor of others rather than on the

29. Although ancient laws allowed for acts of vengeance, it is important to note that the first murder in the Bible reveals YHWH's compassion and relationship with creation and humanity in important ways. Though YHWH exiles Cain after Abel's murder (rather than killing him), he provides a mark of protection for him (Gen. 4). For a helpful treatment of this topic, see Matthew R. Schlimm, *From Fratricide to Forgiveness: The Language and Ethics of Anger in Genesis*, Siphrut 7 (Winona Lake, IN: Eisenbrauns, 2011), 135–43.

30. Pentateuchal law ultimately reminds Israel that all creation belongs to YHWH, the true Redeemer. This is evidenced in the laws and liturgical practices related to the Sabbath and the Jubilee year. See Jacob Milgrom, "Jubilee: The Priestly Response to Economic Justice," in *Leviticus: A Book of Ritual and Ethics*, CC (Minneapolis: Fortress, 2004), 298–316.

31. Ruth's use of "take notice" (*nākar*) and "foreigner" (*nokrî*) here represents a play on words.

> faithful application of legally mandated provisions for aliens. Even if Ruth is aware of the Pentateuchal gleaning laws, and that is not certain, there is no reason to assume that she would have faith that the residents of Bethlehem would follow these laws in a fair or just manner, especially considering that a kindred redeemer has yet to step forward in accordance with Pentateuchal law. Whether in ancient Israel or the contemporary United States, it is often only the socially privileged who assume that the law will protect them. As the story continues, Ruth may have to resort to other methods for support.[32]

Ruth returns home after her day of gleaning with an abundance of all she has gathered.[33] As already discussed in this essay, Naomi's response reveals an intentional ambiguity regarding the word *ḥesed*: "'The Lord bless him!' Naomi said to her daughter-in-law. 'He has not stopped showing his kindness [*ḥesed*] to the living and the dead'" (Ruth 2:20 NIV). Considering the backdrop of violence in this scene and in Judges, human choice and agency becomes even starker. In Judges the refrain "they did what was right in their own eyes" signals violence and evil (Judg. 21:25 AT). In Ruth 2, Boaz's favor results in provision and sustenance for these two widows.

Life as a widow in the ancient world was difficult. Women did not have equal rights, as they do in many parts of the world today. The fact that various types of widows existed in the ANE gives insight into Ruth and Naomi's situation and their search for a redeemer (*gōʾēl*). The plight of two widowed women involves the realities of seeking daily provisions. Previously, scholars identified three different types of widows in the ancient setting. As I have written elsewhere, the work of Steinberg and EunHee Kang illuminate the realities:

> [Naomi] Steinberg shows the challenging economic realities and identifies three markers for the widow (אלמנה; אשה אלמנה; אשה המת),

32. Schipper, *Ruth*, 115.

33. Newly picked or gleaned grains could not be consumed without a lengthy process of preparation. Carol L. Meyers writes, "Producing flour was a laborious task in the days before the invention of milling. Using stone grinding tools, which are ubiquitous in the excavation of Israelite dwellings, it would take a person at least two to three hours every day to feed a family of six" ("The Importance of Bread," in *The Biblical World of Gender: The Daily Lives of Ancient Women and Men*, ed. Celina Durgin and Dru Johnson [Eugene, OR: Cascade Books, 2022], 6).

demonstrating how each identifier connects to a unique hardship. The necessity to provide financial care for widows in ancient Israel as an ethical and community obligation is minimal and found only in Deuteronomy (14:29; 24:17, 19, 20–21; and 26:12–13). Steinberg searches for important variances with each term in order to grasp the particular economic disadvantage or advantage associated with them in the biblical text. Steinberg summarizes her findings in the following ways:

> *ʾalmānâ*—a widow with limited economic support,
>
> *ʾiššâ-ʾalmānâ*—an inherited widow with sons,
>
> *ʾēšet-hammēt*—an inherited widow without sons.[34]

Focusing on Ruth, EunHee Kang explores the question, concluding that Ruth is one of two possibilities: (1) a widow (*ʾalmānâ*)—a widow with limited economic support—or (2) a wife of the dead (*ʾēšet-hammēt*)—an inherited widow without sons.[35] The phrase "the wife of the dead" is employed in Ruth 4 and could indicate, according to Kang, a unique situation that is in suspension and can be altered if a levirate marriage comes about. The scene at the city gate highlights the phrase, as Boaz warns the unnamed redeemer of the financial cost of accepting the levirate role: "Then Boaz said, 'On the day you buy the field from the hand of Naomi, with it you must buy Ruth the Moabitess, the wife of the dead, to raise the name of the dead upon his inheritance'" (v. 5 AT).

As the scene plays out, the unnamed redeemer admits that the role is too costly; accordingly, he refuses to redeem the family. The phrase "the wife of the dead" is intentionally ambiguous, as it could refer to Ruth or Naomi.[36] Kang's research reveals that the status of a widow, as the wife of the dead, can be altered once a levirate

---

34. Matheny, *Judges 19–21 and Ruth*, 202. See Naomi Steinberg, "Romancing the Widow: The Economic Distinctions between the *ʾalmānâ*, the *ʾiššâ-ʾalmānâ*, and the *ʾēšet-hammēt*," in *God's Word for Our World: Biblical Studies in Honor of Simon John De Vries*, ed. J. Harold Ellens et al., 2 vols. (New York: T&T Clark International, 2004), 1:327–46.
35. Matheny, *Judges 19–21 and Ruth*, 195–220 and EunHee Kang, "The Dialogic Significance of the Sojourner, the Fatherless, and the Widow in Deuteronomy through an Analysis of Chronotope Using Bakhtin's Reading Strategy" (PhD diss., Graduate Theological Union, 2009), 85.
36. Intentional ambiguity, by the way, is a key literary feature throughout Ruth.

marriage is consummated. Either way, it also reveals that this phrase most likely refers to Ruth.

ḤESED REVEALED THROUGH RISK AND IMAGINATION

One of the most interesting and evocative scenes in the story is the episode of Ruth and Boaz on the threshing floor (Ruth 3:7–13). As a widow or, more specifically, a "wife of the dead," Ruth seeks a change in status by making a request of the unsuspecting Boaz. The approach at midnight (v. 8) reveals that Naomi and Ruth wish the request to be private. Legal requests are given before the elders and witnesses in the light of day. This reality suggests that Ruth's request is unusual and that it comes about as a result of the widows' initiative. Moreover, midnight represents moments of reckoning and major trajectory shifts in the OT. For example, midnight is when Israel is released from bondage and the firstborn is struck down (Exod. 11:4; 12:29), when Samson's power is displayed (Judg. 16:3), and when Job is judged (Job 34:20).[37] In brief, the timing of Ruth's request suggests that something significant is taking place. This is a key scene that will alter the future of these widows and, eventually, the future of Israel and the world, leading to the lineage of Jesus.[38]

Ruth's request extends beyond Naomi's initial instructions to ask for redemption, as she also asks for marriage. This additional request reveals a creative agency and boldness on Ruth's part. If Boaz accepts, a future inheritance of land and name will continue for Naomi's family.[39] Boaz is not a brother but a relative, so he is not duty bound within the legalities of the levirate marriage (Deut. 25:5–10). Sarah Derck writes, "Simply put, no one was required to preserve Elimelek's line."[40] Although Ruth's request is under the cover of darkness, indi-

37. Cf. 1 Kings 3:20. See also Jack M. Sasson, *Ruth: A New Translation with a Philological Commentary and a Formalist-Folklorist Interpretation*, 2nd ed., BibSem 10 (Sheffield: Sheffield Academic, 1995), 74.

38. The "midnight motif" can also be found in Judg. 16:3; 1 Kings 3:20; and Job 34:20. See Matheny, *Judges 19–21 and Ruth*, 186–87.

39. Kirsten Nielsen (*Ruth*, OTL [Louisville: Westminster John Knox, 1997], 75) notes that the redeemer role focuses on property rights and is "not duty bound" to include marriage (Lev. 25:24–34, 47–55; Jer. 32:7–12; 1 Kings 21:3; Deut. 19:6, 12).

40. Sarah B. C. Derck, Joseph Coleson, and Elaine Bernius, *Ruth, Song of Songs, Esther: A Commentary in the Wesleyan Tradition*, NBBC (Kansas City, MO: Beacon Hill, 2020), 41.

cating that she does not want to be seen, it is still a risk, since threshing floors are not private spaces. Boaz's response reveals that Ruth's double request needs to be kept secret until he makes a public request at the city gate. He notes that there is a closer redeemer whose right precedes his own, but he expresses that he is willing to redeem the widows if the closer kinsman refuses (Ruth 3:13). Boaz proclaims that Ruth's *ḥesed* is even greater than before! She imagines a new way forward through her twofold request, one that extends beyond legal duty and can only be answered by one with *ḥesed* in return. Similar to God's generosity with Israel, Boaz will graciously fulfill all that Ruth requests. In our modern contexts, it can be difficult to imagine the risk and creativity that Ruth exhibits in departing from Naomi's instructions and making such a bold request. But Boaz notices this reality and deems it a response marked by *ḥesed.*

CONCLUSION

Nina Henrichs-Tarasenkova remarks on Wesley's attention to the story of Ruth:

> Wesley rarely spoke of the importance of Ruth in his writings, but when he did, his focus was on Ruth's words of commitment (1:16–17). Thus, Ruth's words might be echoed in hymns 17 and 221 found in "A Collection of Hymns for the Use of the People Called Methodists" (WJW 7:102, 359), which aims to "reinforce what was the professed aim of the four volumes of *Sermons*" (WJW 7:55). Furthermore, one of Wesley's journal entries might indicate Ruth's importance for Wesley when he recorded after he had preached a sermon on "those words of Ruth" at Darlaston, "The flame of love seemed to melt many hearts. What has God done for Darlaston! How are the last become first!" (WJW 24:12). It is primarily in his *Notes on the Book of Ruth* that one finds what Wesley thought of the book. In the introduction he recorded that Ruth was designed "to lead us to Providence, acknowledging God in all our ways; To lead to Christ, who descended from Ruth."[41]

41. Nina Henrichs-Tarasenkova, "Ruth," in *Wesley One Volume Commentary*, ed. Kenneth J. Collins and Robert W. Wall (Nashville: Abingdon, 2020), 183.

In the end, the woman Ruth is given the highest praise, as one worth more than seven sons and comparable to the matriarchs (i.e., Leah, Rachel, and Tamar). Naomi, in Ruth 1, does not realize that the *ḥesed* she receives from Orpah and Ruth will continue in acts of *ḥesed* by Ruth, YHWH, and Boaz. The emptiness Naomi proclaims to the women of Bethlehem in chapter 1 is answered by canticles of praise for Ruth in chapter 4: "Then the women said to Naomi, 'Blessed is YHWH, who did not remove from you a redeeming one this day, and may his name be famous in Israel! May he be to you a restorer of life and a support for you in old age because your daughter-in-law, who loves you, she has given birth to him. She is better for you than seven sons'" (vv. 14–15 AT). Ruth ends with a birth story that responds to the ending of Judges. Judges ends with a refrain: "There was no king in Israel; everyone did as they saw fit" (Judg. 21:25 AT). The genealogy at the end of Ruth points to King David and even to Jesus (see Matt. 1:1–17). The story of Ruth displays social holiness, embodied and performed through courageous acts of *ḥesed*. On a larger theological-political horizon, this steadfast, faithful love of God embodied by Ruth gives hope to a nation in exile. Through a poor, marginalized Moabite widow, God's redeeming and restorative love is witnessed and given voice. YHWH's defining characteristic of holiness is bound up with his *ḥesed* (Exod. 34:6–7; Jer. 3:12)—the theological heart and hope of the OT (Ruth 2:20; Ps. 136; Lam. 3:22).

Chapter 5

OBEDIENCE AND SEPARATION AS HOLINESS INITIATIVES

IN EZRA, NEHEMIAH, AND THE SECOND TEMPLE PERIOD

DAVID B. SCHREINER

A certain level of irony surrounds the concept of holiness in the Bible. For a concept so ubiquitous across the canon, the semantics of the concept remain rather elusive. Simply put, "holiness is never defined in Scripture."[1] In one respect, this phenomenon can be explained by the following proposition: since this concept was so ingrained in the ANE worldview, the biblical writers likely assumed a certain level of familiarity on their readers' part.[2] While somewhat helpful, this explanation does not ameliorate the difficulties for contemporary readers. Nevertheless, one can still sketch a preliminary framework of the concept and how it operates by means of the biblical and extrabiblical data.[3] First, holiness is associated with a variety of things, including divine beings, humans, objects, places, times, and more. Second, holiness is closely linked with certain biblical Hebrew lexemes and concepts, such as *qdš*, *bdl*, *tnk*, *ḥrm*, *nzr*, and *ʿbr*, as well as cleanliness, purity, and their opposites. Third, the OT, particularly in texts historically associated with priestly traditions, attests to a complex system of rituals and actions that affect holiness. Fourth, attempted definitions of holiness are diverse, though this is to be expected as the methodologies employed to understand the concept have proven remarkably varied.

Linguistically, interpreters often single out *qdš* to explain holiness, suggesting that the root signifies something "separated" from the common for a specific purpose, while being put in some proximity to the divine (i.e., dedication to the divine). However, some voices, including

1. Kent Brower, "Holiness (*qdš*, *hagios*)," in *Global Wesleyan Encyclopedia of Biblical Theology*, ed. Robert D. Branson (Kansas City, MO: Foundry, 2020), 171.
2. For useful summaries, see M. C. Lyons, "Holiness," *LBD*; Jackie A. Naudé, "קדשׁ," *NIDOTTE* 3:877–78; and David Wright, "Holiness (Old Testament)," *ABD* 3:237.
3. Wright, "Holiness (Old Testament)," still functions as a worthy starting point.

one in this volume, have highlighted the fallaciousness of such an angle of investigation.[4] Beyond question, however, monolithic approaches will continue to struggle to clarify the complexities associated with the concept. Recent research into holiness has solidified the reality that it is one of the most sophisticated concepts in the Bible.

This essay engages this complex conversation by focusing on a particular aspect of holiness that is especially characteristic of the Old Testament books set in the Second Temple period (the period between the construction of the temple after the exile in 516 BC and its destruction in 70 AD)—namely, the notion of separation as a major "denotation of holiness."[5] In Ezra and Nehemiah, *exclusivity* defines much of the community's boundaries, a reality most clearly shown in Ezra's marriage requirements and in particular aspects of Nehemiah's reforms.[6] Yet the impetus for such exclusive reforms have been explained in various ways. On the one hand, Lisbeth Fried exemplifies the socioeconomic and political line of argumentation when she contends that the intermarriage ban seeks to control economic resources flowing through the temple.[7] On the other hand, A. Philip Brown privileges the biblical text and, thus, the theological explanation when he links the rationale to idolatry, the abandonment of the covenantal ideal, and the realization that the community is on the verge of revisiting the exile.[8] However, both camps of research have benefits. Because the reforms of Ezra and Nehemiah have theological and nontheological stimuli behind them, how the two interact merits exploration and analysis.

Nevertheless, this investigation was initially inspired by those who emphasize the theological explanations for the reforms of Ezra and Nehemiah. In my estimation, the association between foreignness and the community's propensity to put itself at risk by covenantal infidelity,

---

4. See John Oswalt's essay in this volume, "'Holiness' (*qdš*) in the Old Testament," which references Naudé.
5. Brower, "Holiness," 173.
6. Matthew Thiessen describes Ezra 9–10, alongside Neh. 13:23–30, as one of the "central texts" for Ezra's and Nehemiah's exclusionary reforms ("The Function of a Conjunction: Inclusivist or Exclusivist Strategies in Ezra 6.19–21 and Nehemiah 10.29–30?," *JSOT* 34 [2009]: 66).
7. Lisbeth S. Fried, "No King in Judah? Mass Divorce in Judah and in Athens," in *Political Memory in and after the Persian Empire*, ed. Jason M. Silverman and Caroline Waerzeggers, ANEM 13 (Atlanta: SBL, 2015), 381–402.
8. A. Philip Brown, "The Problem of Mixed Marriages in Ezra 9–10," *BSac* 162 (2005): 437–58.

emphasized in both Ezra and Nehemiah, inversely echoes elements of the *ḥērem* initiative of the settlement period, that is, the period where Israel settles in the promised land (ca. 1200 BC). Consequently, it is possible to consider the dynamics of holiness inherent in Ezra and Nehemiah's reforms by using the *ḥērem* initiative in Joshua as a foil.[9] This essay, therefore, will juxtapose perceptions of foreignness in Joshua, Ezra, and Nehemiah with perceived threats to the community's covenantal compliance. This juxtaposition will be accomplished by examining the *ḥērem* concept in Joshua after discussing the reform programs of Ezra and Nehemiah. From there, the essay will ponder how separation came to define the community's pursuit of holiness. This essay will suggest that the significance of separation as a criterion of holiness in Ezra's and Nehemiah's reforms may be clarified by Joshua's discussion of the *ḥērem* initiative. The rationale for such a development is undoubtedly linked to the Babylonian exile, but it may also be linked to a dynamic process of identity formation in an increasingly complicated imperial context. All of this implies that the implementation of holiness—not to be confused with the standard of holiness—is a contextualized phenomenon.

DEFINING HOLINESS

Before this essay can proceed, it is prudent to articulate a working definition of holiness. However, as mentioned above, this is a difficult task, and the difficulty is comparative at its core. In short, the broad attestation of the root *qdš* across the ANE has encouraged many to define the biblical concept predominantly in light of the larger ANE thought world. Without a doubt, this initial inclination is laudable. As comparativists have long advocated, concepts should be considered with a sensitivity to what binds them to their larger cultural milieu. However, it is also important to explore how concepts differ within each particular culture. In the case of holiness, the broad attestation of this concept often results in a definition that essentially communicates "being set apart."[10] In other cases, holiness is defined by the closely associated concepts of cleanliness and

9. Consequently, this essay accepts the well-known, close association between holiness and *ḥērem*; as the essay will discuss, obedience to divine initiatives represents the heart of holiness.

10. For example, "The Old Testament word *holiness* essentially conveys the notion of 'separation' from the mundane for service and/or worship to YHWH, who himself is wholly separate from his creation." Andrew E. Hill and John H. Walton, *A Survey of the Old Testament*, 3rd ed. (Grand Rapids: Zondervan Academic, 2009), 132.

uncleanliness or purity and impurity.[11] In a few cases, holiness even becomes synonymous with the results of ritualistic actions.[12] All of these definitions reflect a commitment to understanding the biblical concept within the context of the ANE.

However, at what point do the biblical dynamics push readers to consider a radical departure from the prevailing worldview? John Oswalt, in his contribution to this project, suggests such a scenario when he emphasizes the distinctiveness of holiness in the OT. If polytheistic assumptions fundamentally affect ideas of holiness in other cultures, then a monotheistic worldview—with its radical break from polytheism—certainly influences the biblical understanding of holiness. By implication, this reality suggests that conversations about the biblical concept must tilt the balance in favor of the differences—albeit in a responsible way. Put differently, the OT's monotheistic context implies that we should prioritize the biblical data while remaining aware of the Bible's (and Israel's) larger cultural context.

For Oswalt, holiness is fundamentally a qualitative statement.[13] Holiness has everything to do with someone's or something's association with the divine "other." Thus, if things or people are in alignment with the divine—however defined—they are holy. Conversely, if they are not in alignment, they are unholy. And if the biblical witness presents YHWH monotheistically, then holiness becomes synonymous with the character of YHWH. In other words, holiness in the Bible is a statement applied to people or things that are in alignment with the character and will of YHWH, the Holy One of Israel. Extrapolating from this, obedience to the will of YHWH goes a long way in establishing and explaining holiness. As Oswalt says, "To be a holy person is to be subject to the will of the Holy One."[14] Consequently, conversations about holiness in the Second Temple literature should address more than temple instruments set aside for particular purposes, architecture that represents spiritual realities, or rituals that connect the participant to the divine. Holiness conversations should also address actions and policies, whether

11. Lyons, "Holiness."

12. Lyons, "Holiness."

13. Oswalt, "Holiness," quotes Goldammer: "The 'holy' is something totally different from [those invoking the concept] and implies a *qualitative* distinction between the divine on the one hand and human beings and the world on the other"

14. Oswalt, "Holiness."

on a personal, local, or national level. Simply put, if actions or policies conform to the will or revelatory teachings of YHWH, then they are holy. If they do not, then they are unholy. With this point established, it becomes clear how the reforms of Ezra and Nehemiah are critical in understanding holiness in the Second Temple period.

THE REFORMS OF EZRA AND NEHEMIAH

Ezra does not appear in the book of Ezra until chapter 7. However, the narrative moves quickly upon his appearance, beginning with a short genealogy and briefly describing his character and context of ministry (7:1–10). The text traces Ezra's lineage through Phineas and eventually to Aaron (vv. 1–5), and it describes him as *sōp̄ēr māhîr bətôrat mōšeh* ("a scribe skilled in the teaching of Moses," v. 6 AT), determined to study and implement the community's ethos (v. 10). Yet he does not travel to Yehud alone, nor does he come without imperial sanction (vv. 6–9). It is with Ezra's imperial authorization that his reforms gain more of their effectiveness.

Ezra 7:11–26 recounts the official correspondence (*paršegen hanništəwān*) sent from King Artaxerxes, and it is in this passage that Ezra's administrative authority to facilitate all necessary reforms is articulated. This correspondence appears in two distinct sections, the first of which (vv. 13–20) articulates the purposes of Ezra's journey with two infinitives construct (*ləbaqqārāʾ*, *ləhêbālâ*) alongside a passive participle (*šəlîaḥ*). The group of returnees, led by Ezra, is to inquire about Judah and Jerusalem and to infuse the temple apparatus with the necessary financial stimulus. Yet the key criterion for Ezra's social inquiry is the phrase *bədāt ʾĕlāhāk* ("according to the law of your God," v. 14 AT).[15] With this, Ezra's reforms fuse divine and earthly agents and social, economic, and theological concerns (vv. 14–15).

Ezra 7:16–20 goes into detail regarding the economic component of the reforms. In short, Ezra is to have access to whatever financial resources he desires, so long as they bolster the temple establishment. This agenda is critical because the Persian imperial structure would have required a functioning temple.[16] Nevertheless, the tone of the letter

15. The prefixed *bə* on the construct chain should be understood as an instrumental use. *HALOT*, 2:1830.

16. Within historical context, the temple was an integral component of a larger program to restore productivity for the sake of the empire. The temple would not only reinforce local identity and practical loyalty; it would also facilitate the movement of the required tribute. For a useful summary

shifts in verses 21–26. There the decree specifically addresses the treasurers (*ḡizzabərayyāʾ*, v. 21) and Ezra (*ʾant ʿezrāʾ*, v. 25), linking direct exhortation with explicit recipients. This not only intensifies the imperial decrees but also puts the scope and authority of Ezra's reforms beyond question. Most importantly, the imperial correspondence establishes an intricate connection between the spiritual, social, and economic facets of the reform. They are all inextricably linked. By implication, holiness—understood as conforming to the will of YHWH—appears to be affected by the imperial system governing God's people.

Ezra 8 recounts Ezra's departure for, approach to, and arrival at Jerusalem. In chapter 9, the issue of reform comes back into focus. On the one hand, *ûkkallôt ʾēlleh* in verse 1 communicates that this chapter's events occur sometime after Ezra's arrival, initial ceremonies, and preliminary dissemination of imperial information (8:31–36), although internal referencing suggests a time of approximately four months between Ezra's arrival and the start of his famous reforms (cf. 7:9; 10:9). Nevertheless, the details of verses 1 and 2 suggest that the local officials (*haśśārîm*) come to Ezra out of a concern for the erosion of the community's identity by means of marriage practices:

> After completing these things, the officials approached me, saying, "The people of Israel, the priests, and the Levites have not been separated[17] from the people of the lands, conforming[18] to their abominations—belonging to the Canaanites, the Hittites, the Perizzites, the Jebusites, the Ammonites, the Moabites, the Egyptians, and the Amorites. Because they took some of their daughters for themselves and for their sons, they have mixed up the holy seed with the people of the lands, and

of Persian imperial policy and its impact on the cult in Jerusalem and other local traditions, see Rainer Albertz, *Israel in Exile: The History and Literature of the Sixth Century* B.C.E., trans. David Green, SBLStBl 3 (Atlanta: Society of Biblical Literature, 2003), 113–32.

17. The form *nibdəlû* is a *niphal* perfect third common plural of *bdl*. A reflexive reading is also possible, which would render the clause "The people of Israel, the priests, and the Levites have not separated themselves from the people of the lands."

18. The prefixed *kə* fundamentally communicates agreement or comparison. In this instance, the agreement exists in Israel's conformity to the abominable practices of its neighbors. The translation here deviates from the tradition of translating this prefix as "like" or "as" to accommodate this nuance. Franz Rosenthal, *A Grammar of Biblical Aramaic*, 6th ed., PLO 5 (Wiesbaden, Germany: Harrassowitz, 1995), 37–38.

> the action of the officials and elders has been first in this disloyalty." (Ezra 9:1–2 AT)

Much has been said about the marital dynamics of Ezra's reforms. After being stupefied by the state of affairs (Ezra 9:3–4), Ezra prays and admits the danger of the situation. According to his prayer (vv. 5–15), he understands intermarriage as not only gross disobedience but also a revisitation of the same practices that secured the exile in the first place. And while Ezra prays, "confessing, weeping, and falling in front of the house of God," a crowd gathers around him as a sign of solidarity (10:1 AT).[19] Among the crowd, Shecaniah eventually speaks up and suggests that the community "cut a covenant" (*nikrāt-bərît*) with the expressed purpose of excommunicating (*ləhôṣîʾ*) women and children in accordance with Torah (v. 3). Such a plan resonates positively with Ezra and the community at large, for upon Ezra's official exhortation (vv. 10–11), the people oblige to enter into this agreement. Then, by the first day of the first month, after three months of deliberation (vv. 16–17), all the questionable marriages are terminated.

This essay is not the place to offer a thorough examination of the theological, cultural, and social dynamics (or even the legitimacy) of Ezra's program of marital termination. Instead, the following elements are emphasized. First, the text explains the rationale for the program of marital termination theologically. The threat of revisiting the tragedy of the exile is so great that Ezra accepts Shecaniah's proposal and facilitates what can only be described as a drastic program of divorce. The text emphasizes that the actions are to be done according to the Torah (*kattôrâ yēʿāśeh*, Ezra 10:3). By implication, second, holiness and separation are inextricably linked. On this point, the text is clear. The community is at risk because of its failure to keep outside influences from eroding its holiness.[20] Therefore, failing in this program of separation would not only be generally disobedient; it would also demonstrate a commitment to undermining holiness and a return to the perpetual defiance of the preexilic period. Third, the fusion of imperial authorization with the desires of YHWH—the fact that YHWH

19. The text states that they too wept intensely (*kî-bākû hāʿām harbēh-bekeh*).

20. This association is explicitly clarified in Ezra 9:2, where the clause *wəhitʿārbû zeraʿ haqqōdeš bəʿammê hāʾărāṣôt* articulates the result of the marital decisions.

works through the Persian imperial system—suggests that standards of holiness can be occasioned through diverse mechanisms, perhaps even secular mechanisms. Here the imperial infrastructure influences the procurement of holiness. Fourth, ethnicity, insofar as it reinforces unholy practices, is understood to be an existential threat to the community's holiness.

Like Ezra's reforms, Nehemiah's reforms enjoy imperial sanction. While the book of Nehemiah lacks the copies of official decrees that the book of Ezra displays, King Artaxerxes is nevertheless said to bolster Nehemiah's efforts. According to Nehemiah 1:6 and 1:8, the king is pleased to send Nehemiah to Jerusalem and grant him the necessary documentation to verify imperial support. In fact, verse 9 divulges how Nehemiah's support is further bolstered by a military contingent, a reality that proves critical when Nehemiah faces intense opposition.

However, Nehemiah's reforms are ostensibly more extensive than Ezra's. Whereas the book of Ezra largely emphasizes Ezra's marriage reforms, Nehemiah's reforms are theological, physical, and economic. In the case of the physical reforms, Jerusalem's walls are the focus. After three days of being in Jerusalem, Nehemiah secretly inspects the wall under the cover of darkness (Neh. 1:11–16). This reconnaissance, in turn, inspires him to defy all outside antagonism (vv. 19–20; 4:1–23) and systematically rebuild the city walls (3:1–32). In the end, after fifty-two days of continuous and contentious work, the wall is repaired (6:15). Yet Nehemiah's reforms are also economic. On the one hand, the economic situation is dire. According to chapter 5, much of the population has incurred crippling debt. The problem, however, is internal; that is, members of the community have been exploiting other members of the community. In response, Nehemiah strategically uses his position as governor to encourage them to forgo interest payments and restore the resources that have been sold to stave off the looming economic crisis. Nehemiah also shares his rightful provisions with others as an act of solidarity. Finally, Nehemiah encourages the leadership to give capital to the treasuries (7:70–73[69–72]). Nevertheless, the most comprehensive element of Nehemiah's reforms is the theological component.

According to Nehemiah 7:73[72]–8:1, the theological reforms begin with the public teaching of Ezra at the Water Gate in the seventh month.

Encouraged by the people "to bring out the book of Moses's teaching" (*ləhābîʾ ʾet-sēper tôrat mōšeh*, 8:1 AT), Ezra explains the Scripture—using a group of assistants (v. 7)—throughout much of the day, as the people listen attentively (v. 3). Eventually, the people feel compelled to praise and worship, and it is when they feel that way that the day is recognized as holy. "Today is holy to YHWH your God" (*hayyôm qādōš-hûʾ layhwh ʾĕlōhêkem*, v. 9 AT) is the declaration. This realization then spurs the community to recommit itself to remembering the Lord's salvation through national assemblies. However, the impact of this moment is most clearly seen in the written document drafted to register the community's "agreement" to embark on a new way of life (9:38[10:1]).[21]

The Hebrew phrase in Nehemiah 9:38[10:1] is *ûbəkol-zōʾt ʾănaḥnû kōrtîm ʾămānâ*, and particular attention must be given to the object *ʾămānâ*, an alternative way to denote a covenant.[22] This agreement results in a separation from the peoples of the lands, but specific application is made to marriage as well (10:28[29]). Thus, under the penalty of a curse, the community vows not to give its daughters to the peoples of the lands, nor to take their daughters for its sons (v. 30[31]). All of this is to align with the Torah and, more explicitly, "to carefully do all the commands of YHWH our Lord, with his ordinances and statutes" (*lišmôr wəlaʿăśôt ʾet-kol-miṣôt yhwh ʾădōnênû ûmišpāṭāyw wəḥuqqāyw*, v. 29[30] AT).

So separation, as dictated by the Lord's authoritative teaching, is also a fundamental concern for Nehemiah's reforms. But does it have the same link to apostasy as it does in Ezra's reforms? Here Nehemiah 9:38[10:1] is critical. The phrase *ûbəkol-zōʾt* can be translated as "Now because of all of this," where the demonstrative pronoun refers back to the "great distress" (*ṣārâ gədôlâ*) in the previous verse. That distress is the current imperial context in which God's people find themselves. This situation, as recounted in the prayer and confession of chapter 9, is the result of the exile and the history of perpetual disobedience to

21. So H. G. M. Williamson, who notes that writing is a guarantee of authenticity and preservation against later alteration (*Ezra, Nehemiah*, WBC 16 [Dallas: Word, 1985], 332).

22. The object *ʾămānâ* occurs only two times in the OT (Neh. 10:1; 11:23). However, many commentators agree that its corresponding verb, *krt*, establishes it as an alternative way to speak of a covenant. See, for example, Israel Loken, *Ezra and Nehemiah*, EEC (Bellingham, WA: Lexham, 2011). However, others argue that *ʾămānâ* (rather than the customary *bərît*) exhibits a particular nuance. For example, Williamson (*Ezra, Nehemiah*, 332) points to a "voluntary . . . and unilaterally binding promise or agreement."

the Lord's desired way of life. Consequently, the logic of Nehemiah is similar to that of Ezra; the current situation is ultimately the result of gross and perpetual disobedience at all levels of society. Thus, obedience to the Lord's authoritative teaching will not only demonstrate lessons learned but also hopefully invert the current imperial context. Applied to holiness, the reforms are again similar. Holiness hinges on obedience, and it will remain if the community obeys the authoritative teaching that was originally facilitated through Moses and that imprints God's holy character on his people.

In summary, holiness in Ezra and Nehemiah is fundamentally concerned not only with obedience to YHWH's authoritative teaching but also separation from hostile, foreign influences. Moreover, both books closely associate Persian governance and the reforms that would ultimately facilitate a particular level of holiness.[23]

THE CONCEPT OF *ḤRM* IN JOSHUA

Seventy-eight salient instances of the root *ḥrm* occur in the OT, and twenty-seven of those appear in the book of Joshua.[24] It has cognate attestation across the ANE,[25] but its appearance in the Mesha Inscription has been championed as a particularly important occurrence due to its similarities with the biblical examples.[26] In addition, Lauren Monroe has argued that an Arabic occurrence should be read in a manner similar to the Moabite occurrence.[27] Regardless, the biblical data remains the prime context for understanding the semantics of this concept.

Of the seventy-eight instances of the root, fifty occur as a verb and twenty-eight as a nominal form. All the verbal occurrences are

23. For a concise summary describing the reforms of Ezra and Nehemiah in terms of Persian interests, see Pierre Briant, *From Cyrus to Alexander: A History of the Persian Empire*, trans. Peter T. Daniels (Winona Lake, IN: Eisenbrauns, 2002), 583–84.

24. Search data here was compiled through the Bible Word Study function of Logos 9. According to Logos, the root occurs a total of 114 times, but 36 occurrences are associated with the geographic notations Hermon, Harim, Hormah, and Baal-Hermon. Thus, they have been excluded from this discussion.

25. *HALOT*, 1:353–54.

26. In particular, see Philip D. Stern, "The Implications of the Mesha Inscription," in *The Biblical Ḥerem: A Window on Israel's Religious Experience*, BJS 211 (Atlanta: Scholars, 2020), 19–56; Arie Versluis, "Devotion and/or Destruction? The Meaning and Function of חרם in the Old Testament," *ZAW* 128, (2016): 233–46.

27. Lauren A. S. Monroe, "Israelite, Moabite and Sabaean War-*ḥērem* Traditions and the Forging of National Identity: Reconsidering the Sabaean Text RES 3945 in Light of Biblical and Moabite Evidence," *VT* 57 (2007): 318–41.

causative. Forty-seven appear in the *hiphil* stem, with only three in the *hophal*. Versluis has argued that among the verbal occurrences, the sense "almost always belongs to the semantic domain of destruction and devastation."[28] Moreover, the object "mainly concerns human beings," and "the extent of the destruction differs," although it is often "total."[29] Regarding the nominal forms, Versluis is correct to note a greater difficulty in categorization. For example, while the nominal forms of the root semantically overlap with words for holiness and purity, they certainly do not always denote corollary concepts.[30] Eventually, Versluis suggests that the "idea of separation," fundamentally describing the nominal forms, "may be useful."[31] While such a suggestion is on target, it does appear too simplistic. In short, one must consider matters of genre when describing the *ḥērem* concept, particularly with respect to Joshua's employment of the term.[32] Therefore, it is preferrable in this context to leave the Hebrew word untranslated,[33] acknowledging that it refers to a cultic sphere and a militaristic sphere of application. The former reference denotes something identified for a particular cultic purpose, and the latter signifies something targeted for destruction for a variety of reasons.

Within Joshua, fourteen verbal and thirteen nominal instances of the root occur.[34] The verbal occurrences are all *hiphil* verbs that point to a militaristic application. Therefore, Joshua 8:26 recounts how Ai and all its inhabitants are to be subjected to *ḥērem*. Similarly, there are statements about Jericho (6:18), Hazor (11:11–12), and several cities

28. Versluis, "Devotion and/or Destruction?," 236.

29. Versluis, "Devotion and/or Destruction?," 235.

30. Versluis, "Devotion and/or Destruction?," 235–36. For example, Versluis ponders whether *ḥrm* is the opposite of holy or pure, ultimately suggesting that while some examples appear to convey such a relationship, inconsistency prevents any well-founded conclusion.

31. Versluis, "Devotion and/or Destruction?," 236.

32. In short, Joshua is an example of conquest literature (cf. K. Lawson Younger Jr., *Ancient Conquest Accounts: A Study in Ancient Near Eastern and Biblical History Writing*, JSOTSup 98 (Sheffield: Sheffield Academic, 1990). Therefore, statements of absolute destruction or devastation—irrespective of the object—must be understood as having a particular rhetorical function. This realization effectively complicates any simplistic categorization, and it appears to be a consideration that Versluis ignores. Categories based on application may be a preferrable way of organizing this complex concept.

33. The cultural, historical, and linguistic variables inherent to the term are both well-known and complicated. This is not the place to attempt a novel explanation, other than to say that Versluis's work clearly lays out the difficulties.

34. Verbal occurrences: Josh. 2:10; 6:18, 21; 8:26; 10:1, 28, 35, 37, 39, 40; 11:11, 12, 20, 21. Nominal occurrences: Josh. 6:17, 18 (3x); 7:1 (2x), 11, 12 (2x), 13 (2x), 15; 22:20.

throughout the northern and southern theaters of conflict (10:28–40; 11:20–21). In two instances, Rahab and Adoni-Zedek recount the Israelite *ḥērem* leveled against polities in the Transjordan (2:10; 10:1).

Joshua 6–7 is critical for understanding the *ḥērem* concept in the book. Specifically, 6:17–18 states: "And the city shall be *ḥērem* to the LORD, it and everything that is in it. Only Rahab, the prostitute, will live, she and everyone who is with her in the house, because she hid the spies whom we sent. Only keep from the *ḥērem*, lest you be *ḥēremed* when you take from the *ḥērem* and make the army of Israel as *ḥērem* and throw it into ruin" (AT). According to these verses, the city and everything in it—save Rahab and everyone in her house—has been categorized as "*ḥērem* to the LORD." Thus, it is all off-limits. However, the exhortations of verse 18 demonstrate that the classification of *ḥērem* may be transferred to the one who violates the stipulations of the *ḥērem* ("lest you be *ḥēremed*"). With the onset of chapter 7, the text will proceed to document how Achan's conscious looting of the plunder brings this scenario to life. Achan's willful violation of the *ḥērem* (in taking an article of clothing) is shown to have deadly consequences, not only for him but also for his family and the people at large.[35] Thus, Achan becomes a paradigm of disobedience, referred to on occasion to underscore the importance of obedience to YHWH's specific directives (e.g., Josh. 22:20).

However, Achan is poetically connected with Rahab in the book of Joshua. Just as Achan becomes a paradigm of conscious disobedience and abandonment of the community's ethical standards, Rahab, the Canaanite *zônâ* ("prostitute"), who is subjected to the *ḥērem*, becomes a paradigm of obedience. As Frank Anthony Spina demonstrates, the narrative of Joshua 1–12 intricately intertwines the fates of these two characters,[36] and at the heart of this sequence is the siege of Jericho and its aftermath. Jericho is where these two characters' futures and relationships are determined, and the entire literary unit is fused together with recurrences of *ḥērem*.

35. In a sense, one can understand Achan's experience as the historical corollary to certain Deuteronomic texts (Deut. 7:2, 26; 13:17).

36. Frank Anthony Spina, "Reversal of Fortune: Rahab the Israelite and Achan the Canaanite," *BRev* 17 (2001): 24–30, 53–54.

Joshua 1–12									
Conquest (1:1–12:24)									
Preparation 1:1–5:12			Jericho and Ai 5:13–8:35			Conquest Expanded 9:1–11:23			List of Kings 12:1–24
Encouragement (1:1–18)	Spies (2:1–24)	Crossing into the Promised Land (3:1–5:12)	Jericho (5:13–6:27)	Ai (7:1–8:29)	Ebal (8:30–35)	Gibeon and Israel (9:1–27)	Southern Campaign (10:1–43)	Hazor (11:1–23)	
	X		XXX XXX	XX XX XXX XXX			XXX XXX	XX XX	
Each "X" represents an occurrence of the nominal and verbal forms of the root *ḥrm*.									

The *ḥērem* concept assimilates with the concept of holiness, but not because of any inherent connection to an idea of "separation" or "being set a part." Rather, the *ḥērem* concept in Joshua is a holiness concept because it exhibits a foundational connection with Yahwistic directives. In other words, obedience to *ḥērem* is tantamount to being holy because the call to honor the *ḥērem* stipulations comes directly from YHWH and is foundational to Israel's settlement in the promised land. Simply put, honoring the *ḥērem* initiative would enable the perpetual establishment of YHWH's people in the promised land,[37] the place where they would channel his character to the world (Gen. 12:1–9).[38]

---

37. One must consider the testimony of Deuteronomy on this topic. According to several passages (7:2, 26; 13:16, 18; 20:17), *ḥērem* is applied to particular polities because of the syncretistic temptations they represent. The application of *ḥērem* is explicitly linked to the abominable practices (*tô'ēbâ*) that these peoples may teach Israel (20:17) or to the religious syncretism facilitated by intermarriage (7:2). In these cases, a policy of zero tolerance must be adopted, as violation of the *ḥērem* will result in the judgment of the violator and the community (7:26; 13:16–18). In other words, Deuteronomy presents the violation of any *ḥērem* as a scenario that may put the nation at risk.
38. Also see David B. Schreiner, "Reading Joshua 2–7, 2 Kings 5, and Acts 5:1–11 Comparatively," *WTJ* 58.1 (2023): 105–20.

CORRELATING EZRA, NEHEMIAH, AND JOSHUA

If holiness is linked to the subjugation of one's will to the Holy One, per Oswalt, then in Ezra, Nehemiah, and Joshua, holiness hinges on an ability to honor specific Yahwistic directives. In the case of Ezra and Nehemiah, holiness is contingent on being in alignment with a series of theological, physical, economic, and social reforms. Such reforms are designed to reinforce the community's foundation and its ability to progress YHWH's agenda in an increasingly complex imperial context. In the case of Joshua, holiness is linked to honoring the *ḥērem* initiative that is a critical component to Israel's settlement activity. Adherence to the program ensures the eradication of hostile spiritual influences, signifies acceptance of YHWH's ownership of the nation and land, and establishes the boundaries of the community. In each case, what is right and what is wrong, what aligns with YHWH's will and what does not, are clearly delineated. In short, the paths of holiness and unholiness are clear.

Nevertheless, these two contexts are starkly distinguished. In Ezra and Nehemiah, foreignness appears inherently hostile. In a sense, therefore, foreign influences are basically equal to unholiness. Moreover, intermarriages with their foreign influences appear to be the quintessential examples of unholy action. Thus, separation from outside influences becomes optimal for the community. What is more, only one direction of movement exists; hostile, foreign influences are purged from the community, with no reentry. These realities are different from what is seen in Joshua. There foreignness should not be understood as inherently bad. Rahab's salvation and eventual inclusion in the community puts the point beyond question. What matters above all for the book of Joshua is obedience, which is crystallized most pointedly in loyalty to the *ḥērem* initiative. Joshua teaches that honoring the *ḥērem* stipulations protects the community and ensures that its vitality in the promised land translates into fulfilling the mission of God—that is, being a blessing to the world, a precious possession, a kingdom of priests, and a holy nation. Yet Joshua also teaches that the stipulations of *ḥērem* are not absolute; they may be lifted with confession and a commitment to live by God's authoritative teaching, as in the case of Rahab. Yet Achan's story shows that *ḥērem* may also be imposed in light of gross disobedience and a rejection of YHWH's desires. Again, obedience is the premium quality.

In terms of holiness, therefore, both consistency and inconsistency exist across these three books. Holiness is intimately connected with obedience to YHWH's directives, regardless of one's sociohistorical context, as their implementation will channel the character of the Holy One of Israel. However, in the Second Temple books, holiness tellingly embraces a commitment of separation. In the Second Temple period, separation was largely dictated by considerations of ethnicity. This reality raises the question of why. Why has ethnic separation risen to a criterion on par with obedience in defining so much of what holiness is?

ON THE RISING IMPORTANCE OF SEPARATION

On the one hand, the implications of the Babylonian exile were certainly part of the equation. As this essay has suggested, the apostasy and syncretism that secured the exile were fostered to a great degree by intermarriage with local Canaanite populations. Therefore, intermarriages in the Second Temple period threatened to thrust the community down a familiar, tragic path. In other words, a strict program of separation, particularly via endogamy (marrying within a certain community), was thought to help ensure that the spiritual integrity of the community would not be compromised. On the other hand, the fact that Ezra and Nehemiah were underwritten with imperial support created something of a paradox. Imperial sanction increased the odds that the community's identity was eventually overwhelmed by Persian concerns. Therefore, the community had to strike a balance between accepting imperial support (due to its lack of political status and resources) and remembering the traditions that anchored them to the preexilic period. A policy of separation from the "other," particularly in the context of marriage (but certainly not restricted to it), allowed God's people to forge an identity that would be distinguishable within an imperial context without being antagonistic toward it. The settlement period not only lacked the imperial variable; it also presented opportunities for God's people to assert their sociopolitical influence throughout the promised land, particularly in wake of the Late Bronze Age collapse. Thus, the book of Joshua remembers a time when the community dictated more in the sociopolitical sphere and when the other did not present an existential threat.[39]

39. For up-to-date treatments of the Late Bronze Age Collapse and the subsequent era that allowed the polities of Canaan, Mesopotamia, and the Mediterranean basin, which included Israel, to endure, see Eric Cline, *1177 B.C.: The Year Civilization Collapsed*, rev. ed. (Princeton, NJ: Princeton University Press, 2021); idem, *After 1177 B.C.: The Survival of Civilizations* (Princeton, NJ: Princeton University Press, 2024).

Another way to explain the rise of separation is to discuss sites of memory and periodization.[40] A *site of memory* refers to something—whether a place, a thing, a concept, or even a person—that is remembered for its symbolic value in relation to a community's identity. Consequently, the Israelite individuals Joshua, Ezra, and Nehemiah can be understood as "sites" of memory, as leaders who, through their programs of strict obedience to divine directives, became symbols of holiness and the community's identity. *Periodization*, by contrast, contextualizes a site of memory at the onset of a new era. Applied to these three leaders, periodization explains how they each ministered during critical eras in Israel's history. More specifically, Joshua led God's people through the initial phases of the settlement period, whereas Ezra and Nehemiah led the community during the turbulent fifth century BCE, a period that functioned as something of a watershed moment in Persian history.[41] And it is precisely that turbulent context that may clarify Ezra's and Nehemiah's preference for separation. Because their reforms construed the Persian king as a "high-value outsider,"[42] separation, particularly endogamy, could not only have prevented imperial concerns from consuming Yehudan identity; it could also have functioned as a clarifying agent within a dynamic cultural response that pitted God's people against their connection to the imperial system.[43]

---

40. Ehud Ben Zvi has recently applied these concepts to Alexander the Great, while also pointing to an application with Cyrus. Ehud Ben Zvi, "Alexander the Great as Site Memory in Hellenistic Judah in the Context of Mnemonic Appropriations of 'High Value' Outsiders," in *The Hunt for Ancient Israel: Essays in Honour of Diana V. Edelman*, ed. Cynthia Shafer-Elliot et al. (Bristol, CT: Equinox, 2022), 476–95.

41. The turmoil of the fifth century altered imperial policy. See Briant, *From Cyrus to Alexander*, 515–692.

42. A "high-value outsider" offers "cultural capital . . . to enhance the cultural capital of the local group" (Ben Zvi, "Alexander the Great," 485).

43. The Batavians may offer an informative parallel here. With the sanction of the Roman Empire, an immigrant group merged with indigenous populations in the frontier region of the Rhine delta, in Gaul's northern periphery. This polity became known as the Batavians, and at the heart of their political structure was the *stirps regia*, a dynastic family descended from Julius Civilis and supported by the imperial apparatus. Their sense of identity was forged through a dynamic process that considered Batavian relationships with the other (i.e., Rome) and traditional ideologies. Nico Roymans (*Ethnic Identity and Imperial Power: The Batavians in the Early Roman Empire*, AAS 10 [Amsterdam: Amsterdam University Press, 2004]) describes a process of Roman stereotyping that would engender a Batavian response. Particularly appealing for understanding Persian-period Israel are the issue of imperial sanction (i.e., a high-value outsider), the use of dynastic families to support local and imperial concerns, and self-awareness as a result of responding to outside perceptions. It is possible to view holiness concepts alongside other traditions to clarify Israel's identity in this dynamic process. More research is in order.

Most importantly, what is observed here becomes a framework for much of the postexilic period moving forward. In so many ways, the Second Temple period marked a struggle to maintain an enduring sense of identity in a sequence of imperial contexts that became increasingly difficult to navigate. These contexts would simultaneously offer opportunity and hostility, while also requiring a certain degree of participation. Thus, it should not be surprising to see that the Second Temple period became a period of increasing diversity with respect to the identity of God's people. For example, Jozef Tiño has shown how early Jewish texts from different eras, yet written within the same social institution, discuss particular issues with divergent convictions.[44] Perhaps this is crystalized by the observed aversion among scholars of early Judaism to speak about "normative Judaism."[45] Nevertheless, N. T. Wright and Michael Bird are correct to argue that despite a diversity of expression across early Judaism, broad agreement remained on critical issues.[46]

---

44. Jozef Tiño, "An Elaboration of Some Theological Issues of Second Temple Judaism in Chronicles and Jubilees," *Communio Viatorum* 59 (2017): 25–47. According to Tiño, the shift from the Persian to the Hellenistic imperial systems was the catalyst for the observed divergent convictions within the same institution.

45. John Collins, "A Contested Field: Half a Century of Study of Second Temple Judaism," *JSJ* 50 (2019): 437–59.

46. N. T. Wright and Michael F. Bird, *The New Testament in Its World: An Introduction to the History, Literature, and Theology of the First Christians* (Grand Rapids: Zondervan Academic, 2019), 137–38. James C. VanderKam ("Judaism in the Land of Israel," in *Early Judaism: A Comprehensive Overview*, ed. John J. Collins and Daniel C. Harlow [Grand Rapids: Eerdmans, 2012], 70–94) also espouses continuity among diversity. First, widespread agreement existed that the Torah imparted on early Jews a narrative that anchored their heritage in real space and time, although disagreements centered on how Jews were to translate those realities into practical action. Second, all Jews agreed that one's cultic expressions were to be organized by honoring an intricately crafted system that featured public proclamations as well as personal piety. In fact, such convictions appear to have led to the elevated concern for cleanliness and ritual purity observable in the Second Temple period, a concern that may have risen to a level of obsession. See Gary M. Burge and Gene L. Green, *The New Testament in Antiquity: A Survey of the New Testament within Its Cultural Contexts*, 2nd ed. (Grand Rapids: Zondervan Academic, 2020), 81. With respect to the temple and the promised land, the third issue—namely, the shadow of the Diaspora—complicates perceptions. On the one hand, a widespread longing existed among Jews to return to the promised land. Thus, Isaiah could long for the gathering of redeemed Israel (43:5) as it looked upon Zion in its approach (60:4). And such a turn of events would lead to an age of peace, abundance, and dominance (Zech. 8:9–13). Later, 2 Maccabees (1:27–29), Tobit (14:5–7), and Baruch (5:5) anxiously await the return of all Israel to the promised land. On the other hand, a primary concern for those in the Diaspora was how to remain a faithful Jew in a foreign context, a question that bred its own diverse repertoire of answers (Wright and Bird, *New Testament in Its World*, 167). Consequently, it seems that Erich S. Gruen is on target when he suggests that a "Jerusalem or not" posture misses the mark: "Jerusalem as a concept and reality remained a powerful emblem of Jewish identity—not supplanted by the Book or disavowed by those who dwelled afar. It appears again and again in the text of the Second Temple authors as a symbol of highest appeal. Yet this

It seems, therefore, that the Second Temple period produced a dialectic between ideological unity and diversity when it came to expressions of Judaism. Diverse expressions and convictions existed in relation to other common expressions and convictions. Holiness was also expressed in this context—and with a similar dynamic. On the one hand, certain categories of actions became clear, immediate, and broadly attested expressions of a commitment to channeling the holy character of YHWH. For example, one's tithing, even from distant reaches of the Diaspora,[47] showed a commitment to facilitating the agenda of the Holy One through economic expression and the allocation of resources. Pilgrimages to major festivals, even across long distances, became expressions not only of one's perceptions of sacred space but also of one's desire to experience YHWH's holy presence. And the abject rejection of paganism became perhaps the clearest expression of one's acceptance of monotheistic ideas. On the other hand, expressions of holiness were not uniform. For example, the endogamy advocated in the reforms of Ezra and Nehemiah was not shared across early Judaism. Tobit appears to advocate endogamy, akin to Ezra and Nehemiah (Tob. 4:12–13), but Gruen has wondered if this expression is something of a parody, particularly since Tobit's final testament envisions the conversion of the Gentiles (Tob. 14:3–11).[48] Less controversial, Joseph and Aseneth offer a creative commentary, at least in part, on the parameters for what constitutes an acceptable marriage to a Gentile.[49] Thus, Daniel Gurtner is on target when he says,

> So while many things can be indicated about readership from this—the elevation of gentile converts in Jewish communities, the problem of Jewish identity in a gentile context, the presentation of Aseneth as an ideal proselyte, and so on—the thrust seems to be that it is permissible for diaspora (Egyptian) Jews to pray for the conversion of non-Jews and to marry converted gentiles.[50]

---

tenacious devotion did not entail a widespread desire to pull up stakes and return to their fatherland" ("Judaism in the Diaspora," in Collins and Harlow, *Early Judaism*, 113–14).

47. See Gruen's discussion, which references a documented tendency among Jews to provide funding to the Jerusalem temple from all parts of the ancient world (Gruen, "Judaism in the Diaspora," 114–15).
48. Gruen, "Judaism in the Diaspora," 107.
49. *OTP*, 2:177–247.
50. Daniel M. Gurtner, *Introducing the Pseudepigrapha of Second Temple Judaism* (Grand Rapids: Baker Academic, 2020), 317. Obviously, the key factor in Joseph and Aseneth is conversion. The

So ultimately, holiness in the Second Temple period could be understood as a microcosm of early Judaism. Just as various expressions within Judaism shared a common essence, so various expressions of holiness arose from a common commitment to embody the character of YHWH in thought, word, and deed. Yet this discussion does not suggest that standards of holiness change based on the dynamics of one's context. To the contrary, holiness is absolute because it stems from YHWH's character. Different sociohistorical contexts cannot change that. Rather, the implementation and expression of holiness can change. The Second Temple period, because of its unique issues, encouraged the community to emphasize aspects of holiness that had always been present but that had become more critical for the longevity of God's people. At the heart of this reality was a looming uncertainty, even skepticism, about the place of God's people in the world. In the settlement period, Israel's future was bright, and opportunities to influence its neighbors could have seemed endless. In the Second Temple period, particularly during the fifth century when Greece and Egypt were becoming increasingly problematic for Persia, uncertainty about the viability of God's people in an imperial context was increasing. Therefore, holiness must have taken on a new sense of urgency. Standards were renewed and held with new rigor, and any hostility toward the community was to be met with intense opposition. Such a posture would have carved out a way forward for God's people, but the difficulty would be in whether it would accommodate YHWH's ambition to imprint his character on all people.

Egyptian princess's conversion *permits* Joseph's marriage. Therefore, Barclay is correct to note the qualification inherent in this vision. See John M. G. Barclay, *Jews in the Mediterranean Diaspora: From Alexander to Trajan (323 BCE–117 BCE)* (Berkeley: University of California Press, 1999). And in this sense, Joseph and Aseneth embodies the spirit of Joshua's use of the *ḥērem* directive. Nevertheless, the book is distinctly more lenient than the rigidly endogamous visions of Ezra and Nehemiah, which produces the inevitable question of why things changed.

Chapter 6

HOLINESS AND THE WISDOM TRADITION

CRAIG G. BARTHOLOMEW

INTRODUCTION

We read the Bible through lenses provided by the guild of OT studies to a greater extent than we realize. A legacy of historical criticism is to envision law, prophecy, cultus (holiness), and wisdom as independent streams within OT Israel and thus within the OT itself. This, I think, is one major reason why it struck me as unusual—albeit intriguing!—when I was asked to write this chapter. Holiness tends to be associated with the so-called Holiness Code (Lev. 17–26) and the cultus, having little to do with wisdom. The different strands of the OT certainly are different, but once we step back and think about how culture works, it makes little sense to think of them as operating independently. Like humans, culture pushes toward unity, and it is hard, for example, to imagine Israelites being instructed in Torah by a priest in the temple (see Eccl. 5:1–7 [4:17–5:5]) without them realizing that such instruction makes them wiser. Indeed, from Deuteronomy's perspective (see Deut. 4:6), it is precisely the manifestation of the *Holy* God amid his people at Sinai (Exod. 19:1–Num. 10:10) that results in Israel's wisdom and understanding among the nations.

This chapter uses this insight to revisit the major OT Wisdom Books (Proverbs, Job, and Ecclesiastes) to see if, in fact, holiness is far more present in OT wisdom than often realized. Similar to the way metaphors work, bringing together holiness and wisdom has the potential to spark fresh insights into both. To begin with, we need a sense of what we mean by *holiness* and what we mean by *wisdom*.

HOLINESS

The word "holy" occurs 614 times in the ESV, 431 of which are in the OT.[1] "Holiness," by contrast, occurs 34 times, and 22 of those are in the OT. Holiness is both an attribute of God and a (potential) characteristic of things within the creation. In Genesis 2:3, for example, the seventh day is made holy (*qādaš*), in the sense of setting it apart from the other days because God rests on this day, and his people are to do the same. In Exodus 3:5, the ground on which Moses stands is said to be holy; in Exodus 12, Israel is instructed to keep a holy assembly. At Sinai, God says to the Israelites through Moses that they will be a "holy nation" (*gôy qādôš*, Exod. 19:6).

The language of holiness is by no means restricted to Israel but is widely attested in the ANE. Theodore Lewis, for example, asserts that "the widespread concept of holiness (*qdš*) in multiple Northwest Semitic cultures from the Late Bronze Age forward demands a closer look by historians of Israelite religion, and not just those interested in priestly understandings of ritual and cultic holiness."[2] Mark Smith similarly notes the widespread use of holiness in the ANE, underscores just how fundamental it is to the idea of deity, and says of shrine objects and processes in West Semitic texts, "They are marked and demarcated for holiness, and divinity is perceived to partake fully of holiness. In turn, the presence of divinity imparts holiness to those places."[3]

Smith notes that Rudolf Otto's concept of the *mysterium* captures only one side of the ANE experience of holiness. He quotes van der Toorn in this respect: "Occasional doubts could not rob them [i.e., ANE citizens] of the conviction that the gods dwelled in the same universe as they did and were to a large extent subject to the same forces and moved by the same reasonings."[4] This qualification is important because it alerts us to the fact that while the OT unsurprisingly adopted

---

1. The ESV translation is used throughout this essay.
2. Theodore J. Lewis, *The Origin and Character of God: Ancient Israelite Religion through the Lens of Divinity* (Oxford: Oxford University Press, 2020), 575. See also his references to additional sources in n. 2 on page 575; F. van Kappen and K. van der Toorn, "Holy One," *DDD* 415–18; and Mark S. Smith, *The Origins of Biblical Monotheism: Israel's Polytheistic Background and the Ugaritic Texts* (Oxford: Oxford University Press, 2001), 93–97. Smith sees apartness as something new that Israel introduced to the concept of holiness (*Origins of Biblical Monotheism*, 86).
3. Smith, *Origins of Biblical Monotheism*, 93.
4. Karel van der Toorn, *Sin and Sanction in Israel and Mesopotamia: A Comparative Study*, SSN 22 (Assen, Netherlands: Van Gorcum, 1985), 23, quoted in Smith, *Origins of Biblical Monotheism*, 95.

the vocabulary of holiness—Israel was a latecomer in the ANE—we should not assume that such an adoption went unchanged. The criteria of both similarity *and* dissimilarity need to be invoked. It is true that in the ANE the gods were immanent in the sense that they were part of "the creation." This description, however, was (and is) not the case with YHWH. Exodus 15:11 poses the question "Who is like you, O Lord, among the gods?" and throughout Exodus, we have YHWH acting powerfully and sovereignly in and outside of Egypt, contexts brimming with thousands of different gods.

As is often noted, the holiness of God is a relational concept:[5] things become holy in relation to God. Fundamentally, God *himself* is regularly described as holy. In the Song of Moses, for example, following the exodus, God is described as "majestic in holiness" (*neʾdār baqqōdeš*, Exod. 15:11). This phrase is found only here in the OT. "Majestic" is a *niphal* participial form of *ʾādar*, with the meaning of "majestic" or "glorious," a kind of superlative of "holy" (*qādôš*).[6] Clearly, in Exodus 15, YHWH's holiness is related to or has become evident in his acts of defeating Pharaoh and of liberating his people from Egypt; indeed, in verse 6, his right hand is described using the word translated as "majestic" in verse 15—namely, *ʾādar*. "Right hand" is anthropomorphic language that evokes the reality of God acting in his world on Israel's behalf. Related to God's holiness is his character as the living God who acts within the world.[7] Certainly, his power is in view, as is his superiority to all other gods, but so too is his character in hearing the cry of the oppressed and in acting on their behalf.

Of course, the holiness and sovereignty of God relates to the question of the origins of monotheism in Israel. Lewis says, for example, that "the worshipers in Exodus 15, Psalm 68, Psalm 89, and 1 Samuel 2 . . . acknowledge YHWH's awesome power (with

5. Herman Bavinck, *Reformed Dogmatics*, vol. 2, *God and Creation*, ed. John Bolt, trans. John Vriend (Grand Rapids: Baker Academic, 2004), 216, observes that "at present everyone acknowledges that the concept of holiness in the Old and the New Testament expresses a relation of God to the world."

6. *ʾĀdar* is also used of YHWH's right hand in Exod. 15:6. William H. C. Propp, *Exodus 1–18: A New Translation with Introduction and Commentary*, AB 2 (New York: Doubleday, 1999), 527, says that the phrase "in holiness" is "is quintessentially polyvalent." He asserts that "we are invited to equate holy temple, holy mountain, holy heaven, the gods and the abstract concept of holiness" (*Exodus 1–18*, 528). Lewis, *Origin and Character of God*, 615, translates the phrase as "feared in holiness."

7. See Craig G. Bartholomew, *The Old Testament and God*, OTOQG 1 (Grand Rapids: Baker Academic, 2022), 397–409.

the fear of lethal holiness in Exod. 15 and Ps. 89), yet they do not then proceed to engage in a series of ritual precautions in order to approach the Unapproachable."[8] However, Exodus 15 leads on to the Sinai event, Psalm 68:24–27 speaks of the procession into the temple, and Psalm 89:15 refers to an engagement in festivities. The argument from silence is a weak one and depends to a large extent on the failure to affirm the Sinai event as historical. Once we read Exodus as a whole and take Sinai as historical,[9] many of these false dichotomies disappear. Furthermore, even if theoretical monotheism has not appeared, monotheism is present in principle. As YHWH says in Exodus 19:5, "All the earth is mine." Yehezkel Kaufmann asserts that "the revelation of the name YHWH at the bush opens the battle with paganism and establishes the contrast between Israel and Egypt. It is the beginning of the monotheistic revolution in Israel."[10]

The word "holy" only occurs once in Exodus 19–24—namely, in 19:6: "holy nation." However, the absence of the vocabulary does not for a moment mean that the reality is lacking.[11] The Sinai event is drenched in the holiness of God and articulates a rudimentary gradation of cultic holiness, a gradation that is fleshed out in detail once the tabernacle is built and the priesthood established.

Scholars reach for different passages in the OT to articulate the holiness of God, such as Isaiah 6:1–7. All of these are valuable, but in the OT, all paths lead to and from Sinai, and the Sinai event enables us to identify the key aspects of God's holiness:

- At Sinai divine holiness is an attribute of the living God, who is alive, other, powerful, and yet deeply personal; who graciously reveals himself to the Israelites and speaks to them and particularly to Moses.
- God's holiness is also awesome and scary. God's sensory revelation in smoke, fire, and the trembling of the mountain evoke

8. Lewis, *Origin and Character of God*, 603.
9. See Craig G. Bartholomew, *The God Who Acts in History: The Significance of Sinai* (Grand Rapids: Eerdmans, 2020), and Bartholomew, *Old Testament and God*, 438–43.
10. Yehezkel Kaufmann, *The Religion of Israel: From Its Beginnings to the Babylonian Exile*, trans. Moshe Greenberg (Chicago: University of Chicago Press, 1960), 225.
11. The Sinai narrative concludes in Num. 9:14, and "holy" occurs often in Exod. 25–Num. 9.

his transcendence and otherness, understandably evoking fear among the people (Exod. 19:16).[12]

- Holiness relates to God as *Deus revelatus* and *Deus absconditus*. He descends on the mountain but is hidden in thick cloud, thereby both revealing and hiding himself. Barth asserts that "in revealing himself, God reveals himself as the hidden God, but the hidden God reveals himself. And just because he is gracious God shows his Holiness, and as the Holy God he manifests his grace."[13]
- The holiness of God is what necessitates the establishment of boundaries around the mountain (Exod. 19:12) and the need for the Israelites to purify themselves (vv. 10–11).
- YHWH's holiness is the reason for Sinai being both fearful and invitatory.[14] In Exodus 19:17, Moses brings the people to meet God (cf. v. 4). The Israelites are invited to become God's people through a covenant that yields communion with him (ch. 24).
- Finally, God's holiness is full of ethical significance. The Decalogue is at the heart of Sinai and sets forth the ethos of the good neighborhood,[15] whereby the Israelites will become like God.[16]

Not surprisingly, therefore, Theodorus Vriezen asserts that "holiness is the quality most typical of the belief in God in the Old Testament." He goes on to say that "the holiness of God is not only the central idea of the Old Testament faith in God, but also the continuous background to the message of love in the New Testament. In this respect the two are in complete agreement, and here the Christian faith is based on the revelation of God in the Old Testament."[17]

When it comes to parts of the creation being holy, it is important to note, as several scholars have pointed out, that the opposite of "holy" is not "profane" (common) but rather "unclean."[18] Alan

---

12. On transcendence and holiness, see Karl Barth, *The Doctrine of God*, vol. 2 of *Church Dogmatics*, trans. T. H. L. Parker et al., ed. G. W. Bromiley and T. F. Torrance (Edinburgh: T&T Clark, 1957), 1:360.
13. Barth, *Doctrine of God*, 1:364.
14. Cf. Barth, *Doctrine of God*, 1:351–68.
15. Patrick D. Miller, *The Way of the Lord: Essays in Old Testament Theology* (Grand Rapids: Eerdmans, 2004), 51–67.
16. Implicit in the Decalogue is the *imago Dei*.
17. Th. C. Vriezen, *An Outline of Old Testament Theology* (Oxford: Basil Blackwell, 1970), 297, 300.
18. See Philip P. Jenson, *Graded Holiness: A Key to the Priestly Conception of the World*, JSOTSup 106 (Sheffield: Sheffield Academic, 1992), 43–45; Joseph Dan, *On Sanctity: Religion, Ethics and Mysticism in Judaism and Other Religions* (Jerusalem: Magnes, 1998), 14 (in Hebrew); Alan

Mittleman follows Hilary Putnam, who in turn follows John Dewey, in distinguishing between a *dichotomy* and a *distinction*,[19] and he rightly argues that the holy-profane distinction is just that, a distinction and not a dichotomy.[20] As Mittleman astutely observes, if we make it a dichotomy,

> it is but a small step to the belief that the profane is broken, fallen, corrupt, contemptible, or worse. So our ordinary lives in the profane sphere are fundamentally flawed or wanting. Access to the sacred compensates for the truncated possibilities of life in the mundane. The world is *entzaubert*, disenchanted, but if we allow ourselves to achieve a special "mode of being," enchantment awaits. Ours is a misbegotten world from which we must be saved.
>
> But if the antipode of the holy is the *unclean*, then there is no durable profane world that opposes it. . . . Rather than one-half of a dichotomy, holiness is a spectrum or field. It maps onto stronger and weaker expressions over a range. The "holy of holies" in the Tabernacle is more sacred than the utensils on the altar outside it—which then grade off further into various stages of purity and impurity.[21]

To express the point in different language, the fact that parts of the creation are holy does not for a moment distract from God's evaluation of his creation as "very good" (Gen. 1:31). That one day is set aside as special does not make the other six days unimportant. Indeed, the whole idea of the Sabbath is to cast its light on the whole of the week as terrain in which to serve God. This difference between a false dichotomy and a legitimate distinction is vital when it comes to the relationship between wisdom and holiness, for, as has often been noted, wisdom is rooted in a theology of creation and explores God's ways

---

L. Mittleman, *Does Judaism Condone Violence? Holiness and Ethics in the Jewish Tradition* (Princeton, NJ: Princeton University Press, 2018), 28–30.

19. Mittleman, *Does Judaism Condone Violence?*, 197n10.
20. On this and related vocabulary in Leviticus, see Gordon J. Wenham, *The Book of Leviticus*, NICOT (Grand Rapids: Eerdmans, 1979), 18–25. Wenham draws on the rich work of Mary Douglas, *Purity and Danger* (London: Routledge, 1966).
21. Mittleman, *Does Judaism Condone Violence?*, 29 (emphasis original).

in the everyday. A false dichotomy between the holy and the profane takes us down the slippery slope of Gnosticism, in which the material reality of the world is viewed as second rate and evil, from which we need to be saved. Far too much evangelicalism has fallen prey to this dualism, a dualism that is catastrophic for the church's public witness.

WISDOM

In a chapter on OT wisdom and atonement, I set out the key characteristics of OT wisdom as follows.[22] Proverbs is the foundational OT wisdom book, and in it, we see that wisdom:

- is an attribute of God (8:22–31);
- is how God created the world (3:19–20), such that his wisdom is built into the fabric of creation and cries out to be heard by humans in all areas of life (1:20–21);
- is needed by humans in every area of life to flourish in creation (3:13–18);
- has its starting point and foundation in the fear of YHWH (1:7, etc.); and
- is the opposite of folly, an ever-present reality (see ch. 9, on Lady Wisdom's and Lady Folly's houses).

Wisdom is a comprehensive concept. It is not just about wise activities but about how such activities fit within God's order for creation and the *erōs* that directs our lives.

PROVERBS AND HOLINESS

YHWH is called "the Holy One" in two places in Proverbs—namely, in 9:10 and 30:3:

- "The fear of the Lord is the beginning of wisdom, and the knowledge of the Holy One is insight."
- "I have not learned wisdom, nor have I knowledge of the Holy One."

22. Craig G. Bartholomew, "Wisdom Books (Old Testament)," in *T&T Clark Companion to Atonement*, ed. Adam J. Johnson (London: Bloomsbury T&T Clark, 2017), 801–6.

The first of these, 9:10, is particularly interesting since it articulates the motto or theme of Proverbs 1–9 and forms an inclusio with 1:7. The second verse, 1:7, also forms an inclusio with 31:31, flagging the fear of YHWH as the theme of the entire book. In 9:10 the fear of YHWH and the knowledge of the Holy One are in parallel, thereby equating the fear of YHWH with the knowledge of the Holy One. In 30:3 wisdom is in parallel with the knowledge of the Holy One.

Intriguingly, all the major commentaries I have consulted for the present essay either ignore this holiness terminology or simply point out that, as with the fear of YHWH, it implies that wisdom is religious. Such commentary seems to me inadequate. By far, the most frequent use of "Holy One" for God is in Isaiah, and of course, Isaiah 6:1–7 is a rich text for understanding YHWH's holiness. In his excursus on the fear of YHWH, Roland Murphy notes that although this motto is central to OT wisdom, it permeates the Bible. He writes:

> It seems undeniable that fear of God is rooted in a basic attitude of mortal beings before the Numen. That is simply the fear that the Bible expresses so often and in so many ways. . . . One of the prime examples is the Sinai revelation and the reaction of the people indicated in Exod 19:16; 20:15–18. The role of nature in the theophany intensifies the awfulness of these events. . . . The concept of the "holiness" of the Lord is another expression associated with fear of the Lord. It is a characterization of the divinity as totally other, as being in a sphere of its own that differs from the level in which mortals find themselves. Both the Numinous and the Holy beget certain standards if one is to be able to live in their proximity.[23]

Sinai is *the* generative event of the OT, then the Israelites' experience of YHWH at Sinai illuminates what is involved in the fear of YHWH. In the course of Sinai is a development in their experience of YHWH, from terror to covenant and thus communion and wonder, without losing the aspect of profound awe and reverence. Oliver O'Donovan perceptively points out the centrality of wonder in OT

23. Roland E. Murphy, *Proverbs*, WBC 22 (Nashville: Thomas Nelson, 1998), 255.

wisdom,[24] and C. S. Lewis can help us in this respect. In his analysis of the medieval era, "Lewis perceived that . . . the natural world, like so many stained-glass windows, was, as it were, transparent to a light from beyond this world. What are for us merely natural processes seemed to our ancestors phenomena that pointed beyond themselves. The whole world felt like a cosmic cathedral."[25] Profound respect for YHWH and communion with him issue forth in wonder at his ways in creation, and the desire to know those ways is at the heart of OT wisdom.[26]

Now it might be argued that Proverbs knows nothing of covenant and Torah and, thus, that the link with Sinai is tenuous.[27] However, as Michael Fox points out, the epistemology of Proverbs is not empiricism.[28] The book's observations are informed by values, and as I have argued elsewhere, these values demonstrably come from Sinai. Furthermore, a growing body of literature is emerging that shows Proverbs is indeed aware of covenant and, thus, Torah.[29]

It should also be noted that Proverbs is fully aware of cultic activity; indeed, a theme of Proverbs is the danger of engaging in cultic activity while not living accordingly (7:14; 15:8; 20:25; 21:3, 27). The language of cleanness also occurs in the book (20:9, 30; 30:12).

JOB AND HOLINESS

God is referred to as the Holy One in Job in only one place—namely, in 6:10: "This would be my comfort; I would even exult in pain unsparing, for I have not denied the words of the Holy One." This verse comes in the context of Job's response to Eliphaz, in which he defends

24. Oliver O'Donovan, "Response to Craig Bartholomew," in *A Royal Priesthood? The Use of the Bible Ethically and Politically; A Dialogue with Oliver O'Donovan*, ed. Craig Bartholomew et al., SHS 3 (Grand Rapids: Zondervan Academic, 2002), 113–15.

25. Jason M. Baxter, *The Medieval Mind of C. S. Lewis: How Great Books Shaped a Great Mind* (Downers Grove, IL: IVP Academic, 2022), 20.

26. See the noteworthy chapter "The Self-Revelation of Creation," in Gerhard von Rad, *Wisdom in Israel*, trans. James D. Martin (London: SCM, 1972), 144–76. I disagree with von Rad on certain points in this chapter, but his insights are generally remarkable. Commenting on the way in which wisdom plays in Prov. 8:31, for example, von Rad observes that "already in old wisdom one could constantly discern a desire for fun in the vicinity of truth, a delight, a fascination for a truth that entices men" (170n30).

27. Cf. here von Rad, *Wisdom in Israel*, 175. This is one of those points on which I disagree with him.

28. Michael V. Fox, *Qoheleth and His Contradictions*, JSOTSup 71 (Sheffield: Almond, 1989), 90–95.

29. See, e.g., Bernd U. Schipper, *The Hermeneutics of Torah: Proverbs 2, Deuteronomy, and the Composition of Proverbs 1–9*, AIL (Atlanta: SBL, 2021).

the legitimacy of his complaint. Job is described in 1:1 in characteristic wisdom terminology as "one who feared God and turned away from evil" (cf. 28:28). David Clines seeks to diminish the religious nature of Job's character: "Nothing in the present text entitles us to assert that Job's fear of God was the secret of his moral and social equilibrium."[30] On 1:5—Job's practice of sacrificing for his children, in case they have sinned—Clines asserts that "in general, as Job's account of his innocent life silently testifies, relationship with God is primarily a matter of right behavior and not of religious exercises."[31] According to Clines, "it is only in those parts of the book most obviously folkloristic and unbegotten by the wisdom tradition (the prologue and the epilogue) that sacrifice appears"; "in this the dialogues of the book are wholly at one with the stance of the wisdom teaching of Proverbs and Ecclesiastes."[32] Clines adds, "How much this stance represents an alternative posture in Israelite religion and how much it is consciously one-sided or legitimate only within the broader Israelite framework of history, covenant, and cult, is impossible to say."[33]

Our discussion above shows that, on the contrary, it is indeed possible to say. Job is an unusual book, set outside Israel with a non-Israelite main character, but the worldview of the book is precisely that of the OT and of OT wisdom in particular. Neither in Job nor in Proverbs and Ecclesiastes can a right relationship with God be reduced to ethical behavior. Reading Job as a literary whole, we discover that the prologue and epilogue are an essential part of the book. As C. L. Seow notes, "Without the prose tale, the poetry lacks context; without the poetic middle, the story lacks theological depth and vibrancy. The prose narrative by itself is not a complete story, and neither is the poetic middle."[34] What commentators do not seem to notice is that, intriguingly, a sacrifice inclusio frames the book (1:5; 42:7–9). As a

30. David J. A. Clines, *Job 1–20*, WBC 17 (Dallas: Word, 1989), 12.

31. Clines, *Job 1–20*, 17.

32. Clines, *Job 1–20*, 17.

33. Clines, *Job 1–20*, 17.

34. C. L. Seow, *Job 1–21: Interpretation and Commentary*, Illuminations (Grand Rapids: Eerdmans, 2013), 29. On the unity of the book, Seow perceptively observes that "there are all sorts of literary tensions within the book. Hence, instead of performing textual surgeries to suit modern preconceptions of coherence, it is necessary to give the ancient narrator-poet the benefit of the doubt and to grapple with those dissonances and asymmetry that may well be part of how the book means" (*Job 1–21*, 38).

complex narrative, Job invites its readers to reflect on a range of issues, and one of those issues is sacrifice.

In Job 1, Job offers burnt offerings (*ʿōlâ*), and in chapter 42, his friends do the same. Clines is adamant that here the word is a generic term for sacrifice,[35] but if, as I think likely, it is being used in the same sense as in Leviticus 1:1–17, then "burnt offering" fits with Job's concern because this sacrifice "propitiates God's wrath against sin,"[36] the possible sin of Job's children and the actual sin—note the reference to God's "wrath" in 42:7—of Job's friends. Wrath is closely and inseparably related to God's holiness, and Job's cultic activity manifests an awareness of this. We are invited to reflect on appropriate cultic activity through the difference between Job's sacrifices in 1:5 and those of the friends in 42:7–9, accompanied by Job's prayer.

In my view, the description of Job in 1:1 is too perfect, and the irony of this description comes to the fore in Job's cultic practice (v. 5). Clines rightly observes of verse 5 that "Job's piety is scrupulous, even excessively so, if not actually neurotically anxious. It would not be absurd to see here an almost obsessional *manie de perfection*, a hypersensitivity to detail."[37] Cultic activity has become, for Job, the means of sustaining the status quo. Ironically, Job reduces true religion to what Clines wrongly proposes is that of the wisdom tradition—namely, ethical conduct. What Job must come to grips with is the living God. Although God's holiness is not mentioned by name in Job apart from 6:10, it hovers over all the speeches and comes into clear focus in God's speeches (ch. 38–41). Holiness, as we saw above, is about God's otherness, his power, and his wisdom, and in the speeches, this is established through God's activity in creation. It is Job's encounter with God as the "Holy One" that resolves his crisis and leads him to repentance and peace with God (42:1–6).

ECCLESIASTES AND HOLINESS

The word "holy" only occurs once in Ecclesiastes, in 8:10: "Then I saw the wicked buried. They used to go in and out of the holy place and were praised in the city where they had done such things. This also

35. Clines, *Job 1–20*, 16.
36. Gordon J. Wenham, *The Book of Leviticus*, NICOT (Grand Rapids: Eerdmans, 1979), 57.
37. Clines, *Job 1–20*, 15.

is vanity." Intriguingly, the name YHWH does not occur in the book, although the God in view is clearly YHWH of the OT. Ecclesiastes might therefore be thought to have little to do with the holiness of God, but when the book is read as a whole, that is simply not the case.

Ecclesiastes traces the journey of Qoheleth (the Preacher), who has lost sight of, and connection with, the Holy God of Israel. Source critics see Genesis 1:1–2:4a as coming from the priestly writer or tradition,[38] and as several of us have noted,[39] Ecclesiastes connects intertextually with Genesis 1–2 in a variety of ways. In Genesis 1:31, we read that God saw *all* that he had made, and it was very good.

Seeing is also central to Qoheleth's epistemology, but in relation to Genesis 1:31, nothing prepares one for the "son of David's" conclusions that *all* is utterly enigmatic (*hakōl hābel*). The two approaches to "the all" of creation are utterly opposed and indicate the excruciating situation in which Qoheleth has found himself. The characteristic expression in Ecclesiastes, "under the sun," evokes the oppressiveness of Qoheleth's experience. In 9:2 we see what cultic activity looks like through Qoheleth's troubled state: "It is the same for all, since the same event happens to the righteous and the wicked, to the good and the evil, to the clean and the unclean, to him who sacrifices and him who does not sacrifice. As the good one is, so is the sinner, and he who swears is as he who shuns an oath."

If this were all one could say about Qoheleth, then Ecclesiastes would have little to contribute to our theme of wisdom and holiness. But Ecclesiastes tracks Qoheleth's journey as he finds his way out of the contradictory juxtaposition of *hebel* and an awareness that life is good, as seen in the so-called carpe diem passages. A key turning point comes in 5:1–2 [HB 4:17–5:1], precisely related to the cultus: "Guard

38. Jürg Hutzli, "Tradition and Interpretation in Gen 1:1–2:4a," *JHebS* 10 (2011): https://doi.org/10.5508/jhs.2010.v10.a12.

39. Charles C. Forman, "Koheleth's Use of Genesis," *JSS* 5 (1960): 256–63; Hans Wilhelm Hertzberg, *Der Prediger* (Gütersloh: Verlagshaus Gerd Mohn, 1963), 46, 111, 227–31; Russell L. Meek, "The Meaning of הבל in Qohelet: An Intertextual Suggestion," in *The Words of the Wise are Like Goads: Engaging Qohelet in the 21st Century*, ed. Mark J. Boda, Tremper Longman III, and Cristian G. Rata (Winona Lake, IN: Eisenbrauns, 2013), 241–56. See also Robert Gordis, *Koheleth, the Man and His World: A Study of Ecclesiastes*, 3rd (augmented) ed. (New York: Schocken, 1968), 43 (unchanged from the 1951 ed.); Hagia Witzenrath, *Süss ist das Licht* (St. Ottilien: EOS Verlag, 1979), 40–43; Michael A. Eaton, *Ecclesiastes: An Introduction and Commentary*, TOTC 18 (Downers Grove, IL: IVP Academic, 2009), 46; and R. N. Whybray, *Ecclesiastes*, OTG (Sheffield: Sheffield Academic, 1989), 28–30.

your steps when you go to the house of God. To draw near to listen is better than to offer the sacrifice of fools, for they do not know that they are doing evil. Be not rash with your mouth, nor let your heart be hasty to utter a word before God, for God is in heaven and you are on earth. Therefore let your words be few."[40]

Other major turning points come in 7:23–29 and then in 11:7 onward. Qoheleth's epistemology in his quest for meaning in life is based on reason, observation, and experience, quite different from that of Proverbs (cf. Prov. 1:7). Resolution finally comes when that epistemology is replaced with one comparable to Proverbs's fear of the Lord as the beginning of wisdom—namely, "Remember . . . your Creator" (12:1). This leads to the exhortation in 12:13 to fear God and keep his commandments, language profoundly reminiscent of Sinai.

By tracing the journey of Qoheleth in this way, Ecclesiastes exposes the way in which we can become disconnected from the Holy God. It also shows us the way out of a dilemma like that of Qoheleth, finding our way back to trust and obedience *coram Deo*.

CONCLUSION

OT wisdom is grounded in a theology of creation (Prov. 3:19–20; 8:22–31). It is because YHWH is one and transcends the creation, while remaining immanently involved in it—unlike the thousands of ANE gods, who are viewed as part of creation—that his unified ways, originating in a single source, are written into creation and are discoverable by humans—created in his image. It is by his wisdom that God has created the world, and therefore humans can discover that wisdom built into the world, live accordingly, and thus become wise. Wisdom is the discovery and the following of God's ways in his world. God's transcendence, or otherness, and his immanence, or availability for communion, are central to the biblical notion of divine holiness, as we saw above. Thus, far from being alien to wisdom, *God's holiness is the very thing that makes (human) wisdom possible*. Far from OT wisdom being somehow separate from Sinai and the legal, prophetic, and cultic traditions of the OT, it is different from but integrally related to them.

40. Reading Ecclesiastes as a whole is challenging, as is life. On these turning points, see Craig G. Bartholomew, *Ecclesiastes*, BCOTWP (Grand Rapids: Baker Academic, 2009).

The legal, prophetic, cultic, and wisdom traditions are all woven from the same cloth, and that cloth is Sinai.

The link between wisdom and holiness also illumines God's call to us to become holy. Being holy means finding and following God's ways in every area and aspect of life as God has made it. The valiant woman of Proverbs 31 exemplifies this with her manifestation of wisdom in all areas of life, from being a wife and a homemaker to planting a vineyard and trading in textiles. She shows us what a holy woman, a woman who fears the Lord (v. 30), looks like, and it is a wonderfully attractive picture.

CHAPTER 7

HOLINESS AND THE ARRANGEMENT OF THE PSALMS

TERRANCE R. WARDLAW JR.

The book of Psalms calls for singing, shouts, jubilation, and cries of lament, based on both traditional and novel styles at the time of composition. It calls for strings, trumpets, and percussion instruments, and it ranges in style from lamentation in forsakenness (ch. 22) to ecstatic praise in the presence of God (ch. 146–50). Yet the one prophetic demand of holy obedience to the covenant (ch. 106–7) permeates the entire concept of worship projected by the book. On this point, the Psalter allows no room for diverse opinions or preferences. We are to be holy in worship (15:2; 24:4) because God is holy (99:3, 5, 9). To understand how the concept of holiness within the Psalms unfolds, we will first identify the psalmists' received beliefs about holiness; second, we will examine the canonical structure of the book, alongside a linear reading of words for "holy" within this structure; and third, we will briefly discuss the concept of holiness in relation to the main themes of the book.

THE PSALMISTS' RECEIVED BELIEFS REGARDING HOLINESS

Walter Kaiser observes that holiness is the central organizing feature of OT ethics.[1] God is holy and therefore demands that the redeemed also be holy (Lev. 11:44–45).[2] First, "holiness" refers to both the divine

1. Walter C. Kaiser Jr., *Toward Old Testament Ethics* (Grand Rapids: Zondervan, 1983), 139. For studies of words for "holy," see R. B. Girdlestone, *Girdlestone's Synonyms of the Old Testament* (1871; repr., Peabody, MA: Hendrickson, 2000), 195–202; W. Kornfeld, "קדשׁ," *TDOT* 12:521–444; H. P. Müller, "קדשׁ," *THAT* 2:589–609, esp. 594; Thomas E. McComiskey, "1990 קָדַשׁ," *TWOT*; Jackie A. Naudé, "קדשׁ," *NIDOTTE* 3:877–87; Hon-Lee Kwok, "Holiness," in *Lexham Theological Wordbook*, ed. Douglas Mangum (Bellingham, WA: Lexham, 2014). For an exegetical and theological treatment of holiness, see John N. Oswalt, *Called to Be Holy: A Biblical Perspective* (Nappanee, IN: Evangel, 1999).

2. Rolf Rendtorff, *Theologie des Alten Testaments: Ein kanonischer Entwurf* (Neukirchen-Vluyn, Germany: Neukirchener, 2001), 1:61–64; 2:119–21.

quality of not being common and, from the earthly or human perspective, being set apart or consecrated to the Lord. Second, this primary quality of belonging to God then becomes a condition and personal quality of ritual and moral purity, corresponding to the nature of God (e.g., Lev. 17–26). Third, Girdlestone observes that the emphasis on the moral and spiritual qualities of "holiness" often overshadows the relationship existing between God and the person or thing consecrated to him, which serves as a corrective to the legalistic notion that holiness is an end in itself apart from God's grace and presence.[3] Fourth, the quality of divine holiness also includes an element of fear: "The unapproachable majesty of the divine, convincing every creature of its own nothingness by the exercise of supramundane miraculous power, evokes that most profound of all forms of terror, which cannot be further explained or derived, and which yet as an overwhelming primal feeling seizes the whole of life and shakes it to its foundations" (e.g., Exod. 3:5–6).[4]

The book of Psalms both assumes and applies this concept of holiness from the Mosaic covenant to worship and prayer.[5] The emergence of law (*tôrâ*) at key structural points in the book leads the ideal reader to make this connection (ch. 1, 19, 119). Or articulated in terms of cognitive semantics and oral-traditional culture, words and concepts associated with holiness in the Psalter profile against holiness concepts developed within the traditional materials of the Pentateuch. For example, the Lord is to be praised because he is holy (99:9; Lev. 11:44), and in Psalm 24, the psalmist observes the necessity of personal holiness when he asks, "Who shall ascend the hill of the Lord? And who shall stand in his holy place?" The answer then immediately follows: "He who has clean hands and a pure heart, who does not lift up his soul to what is false and does not swear deceitfully" (vv. 3–4 ESV; Lev. 11:44). Thus, both

3. Girdlestone, *Synonyms of the Old Testament*, 195.

4. Walther Eichrodt, *Theology of the Old Testament*, trans. J. A. Baker, OTL (Philadelphia: Westminster, 1961), 2:270.

5. The priority of the Pentateuch, which is assumed by the Psalms, is discussed by Patrick Fairbairn, *The Revelation of Law in Scripture* (1869; repr., Grand Rapids: Zondervan, 1957), 190–95; W. H. Gispen, *Indirecte gegevens voor het bestaan van den Pentateuch in de Psalmen?* (Zutphen, Netherlands: Nauta, 1928); Gordon J. Wenham, *Psalms as Torah: Reading Biblical Song Ethically*, STI (Grand Rapids: Baker Academic, 2012); and Terrance R. Wardlaw Jr., *Elohim within the Psalms: Petitioning the Creator to Order Chaos in Oral-Derived Literature*, LHBOTS 602 (London: Bloomsbury T&T Clark, 2015), 26–31.

individual holiness and corporate holiness prove foundational to prayer and worship in the Psalms. Holiness describes one attribute of God, and those who worship him are called to be like him.

MAJOR PSALM GROUPINGS AND HOLINESS

One of the key insights guiding the study of the Psalms since 1985 flows from Gerald R. Wilson's Yale dissertation exploring the canonical organization and collection of the Psalter. Whereas earlier scholars categorized psalms on the basis of genre, similar forms independent of canonical placement, and historical usage within the temple (form criticism), and whereas some also sought to identify the editorial activity and layers behind individual or smaller groups of psalms (redaction criticism), Wilson instead identified contiguous groups of psalms based on their superscriptions and thus set in motion the exploration of their canonical shape.[6] Subsequent scholars have applied Wilson's insights in more detailed readings of psalm placement and order.[7] Although evangelical commentaries since 2014 introduce these developments as commonplace, larger structural insights do not seem to influence detailed exegesis. Therefore, the following discussion will examine the basic structure of the book of Psalms in order to explore the context and backdrop of holiness as it emerges within the book. Moreover, in keeping with developments in Psalms discussions, a linear or sequential reading of words for "holy" within each of the major units acknowledged by scholars will suggest the emergence of an implied narrative by which holiness in prayer and worship is understood.[8] This linear reading represents the accrued reading knowledge or text comprehension of the ideal reader.

6. Gerald H. Wilson, *The Editing of the Hebrew Psalter*, SBLDS 76 (Chico, CA: Scholars, 1987). The historical validity of the superscriptions has been challenged by David Willgren Davage, "Why Davidic Superscriptions Do Not Demarcate Earlier Collections of Psalms," *JBL* 139 (2020): 67–86.

7. J. Clinton McCann, ed., *The Shape and Shaping of the Psalter*, JSOTSup 159 (Sheffield: JSOT Press, 1993); Jerome F. D. Creach, *YHWH as Refuge and the Editing of the Hebrew Psalter*, JSOTSup 217 (Sheffield: Sheffield Academic, 1996); Jerome Creach, *Discovering the Psalms: Content, Interpretation, Reception* (Grand Rapids: Eerdmans, 2020), 101–46; David C. Mitchell, *The Message of the Psalter: An Eschatological Programme in the Book of Psalms*, JSOTSup 252 (Sheffield: Sheffield Academic, 1997); Jean-Luc Vesco, *Le psautier de David: Traduit et commenté*, 2 vols., LD 210–11 (Paris: Cerf, 2008); Nancy L. deClaissé-Walford, ed., *The Shape and Shaping of the Book of Psalms: The Current State of Scholarship*, AIL (Atlanta: SBL, 2014); O. Palmer Robertson, *The Flow of the Psalms: Discovering Their Structure and Theology* (Phillipsburg, NJ: P&R, 2015); Peter C. W. Ho, *The Design of the Psalter: A Macrostructural Analysis* (Eugene, OR: Pickwick, 2019).

8. David G. Firth cautions against overinterpreting an emergent narrative in the course of a canonical reading of the Psalter and instead speaks in terms of overarching themes while employing the

The Overarching Structure of the Book of Psalms and Holiness

To begin, the doxological refrains appearing at key points in the Psalms suggest the end of major units (*ʾāmēn wəʾāmēn*, "Amen and amen," 41:14; 72:19; 89:53; 106:48). On this basis, five basic psalm divisions have been recognized: book 1 (1–41), book 2 (42–72), book 3 (73–89), book 4 (90–106), and book 5 (107–50). Although scholars in the past related these five divisions to the five books of Moses, Wilson doubted a strong connection between the Pentateuch and these corresponding units.[9] Nevertheless, it is conceivable that this fivefold division itself alludes to the five books of the Pentateuch, and this allusion functions as a cohesive structural device alongside the prominence of *tôrâ* in Psalms 1, 19, and 119.

Across these five books, other units and groupings have also been identified. Psalms 1 and 2 are generally regarded as an introduction to the book as a whole, while Psalms 146–50 function as the concluding climax of praise.[10] Psalm 1 introduces the Psalter by centering praise on the distinction between the righteous and the wicked as defined by *tôrâ* (v. 2). This theme emerges in many psalms, especially Psalms 19 and 119, thereby forming the first prominent theme of the book. The second major theme emerges in Psalm 2, which is a messianic psalm looking to the ideal and victorious Davidic king to come. The first occurrence of "holy" in 2:6 refers to the holy place of Mount Zion, "my holy mountain" (NIV), where the Lord appoints or sets the anointed king. The juxtaposition of *tôrâ* and the Messiah in these introductory psalms indicates both their prominence in everything that follows and the foundation of the Messiah's rule on the Mosaic law. Psalms 2 and 89 bracket books 1–3 and cast a messianic and eschatological shadow across the book as a whole, while Psalm 110 extends this structural link into book 5.[11] The

---

analogy of musical harmony ("Reading Psalm 46 in Its Canonical Context: An Initial Exploration in Harmonies Consonant and Dissonant," *BBR* 30 [2020]: 22–40).

9. Wilson, *The Editing of the Hebrew Psalter*, 199–203. However, the themes of God's presence, atoning sacrifice, and purity in book 2 (esp. ch. 42, 50–51) correspond well with the same themes in Leviticus, and the themes of Israel in the wilderness and theocracy in book 5 (ch. 90–106) correspond well with the book of Numbers. These observations suggest the need for further comparison of the contents of the Pentateuch and Psalms.

10. Robert L. Cole, "Psalms 1 and 2: The Psalter's Introduction," in *The Psalms: Language for All Seasons of the Soul*, ed. Andrew J. Schmutzer and David M. Howard Jr. (Chicago: Moody, 2013), 183–96.

11. Christoph Rösel, *Die messianische Redaktion des Psalters: Studien zu Entstehung und Theologie der Sammlung Psalm 2–89*, CTM 19 (Stuttgart: Calwer, 1999); Christopher A. Maronde, "'You Are

Septuagint's translation of the Hebrew superscription *lamnaṣṣēaḥ*, "for the choir director," as "for the end" (*eis to telos*) attests an eschatological understanding of these psalms as early as 250 BCE.[12] Other messianic psalms within Books 1–3, such as Psalms 22 and 45, indicate that the Messiah will suffer and serve as a sovereign and universal ruler. Book 3 closes in Psalm 89 with the downfall of the Davidic kingship on the one hand, and the promise of the eternal reign of David on the other. Yet the voice of David again in Psalms 101, 103, 108–10, 118, 122, 124, 131, 133, and 138–45, looks beyond the historical David to the messianic king to come.[13] NT quotations of psalms both develop and apply this messianic understanding (e.g., Ps. 2:7; Matt. 3:17; 17:5).

Holiness in Psalms 1–41 (Book 1)

Moving beyond Psalms 1 and 2, scholars identify smaller groupings within book 1, such as Psalms 3–14.[14] The divine title *ʾĔlōhîm*, which is associated with creation in Genesis 1:1–2:3, occurs within this unit in Psalm 8.[15] This psalm functions as the center or pivot point celebrating the Creator amid the chaotic laments of Psalms 3–7 and 9–14.

Most occurrences of key terms for "holy" in book 1 refer to a place of divine habitation, beginning with the reference to "my holy

---

My Beloved Son': The Foundations of a 'Son of God' Christology in the Second Psalm," *CTQ* 85 (2021): 313–40; S. D. Ellison, "Old Testament Hope: Psalm 2, the Psalter, and the Anointed One," *Them* 46 (2021): 534–45. Daniel Fletcher argues on the basis of Luke 24:44–47 that *all* of the OT, including psalms not mentioning the Messiah explicitly, points toward Christ (*Psalms of Christ: The Messiah in Non-Messianic Psalms* [Eugene, OR: Wipf & Stock, 2018]); cf. Daniel J. Estes, "How Reading the Psalms Christologically Resembles *Where's Waldo?* and How It Does Not," *BSac* 177 (2020): 269–85.

12. This rendering of the *piel* participle *lamnaṣṣēaḥ* plays on the meaning "enduring" and seems to be related to the noun *nēṣaḥ*, "enduring, everlastingness, perpetuity," in reference to the final age. See Pss. 4:1; 5:1; 6:1; 8:1; 9:1; 11:1; 12:1; 13:1; 14:1; 18:1; 19:1; 20:1; 21:1; 22:1; 31:1; 36:1; 39:1; 40:1; 41:1; 42:1; 44:1; 45:1; 46:1; 47:1; 49:1; 51:1; 52:1; 53:1; 54:1; 55:1; 56:1; 57:1; 58:1; 59:1; 60:1; 61:1; 62:1; 64:1; 65:1; 66:1; 67:1; 68:1; 69:1; 70:1; 75:1; 76:1; 77:1; 80:1; 81:1; 84:1; 85:1; 88:1; 109:1; 139:1; and 140:1.
13. Although Pss. 2, 45, 89, and 110 explicitly refer to the Messiah as part of the messianic structure of the Psalms, this does not preclude an understanding of the references to David throughout the superscriptions as part of the typological movement from the OT to the New. Accordingly, the praise and lament of the historical David prophetically points to a greater typological fulfillment as the praise and lament of the Messiah (the antitype). Moreover, the exemplary prayers of David for worshipers at the temple become the messianic prayers of worshipers following David's son.
14. Frank-Lothar Hossfeld and E. Zenger, *Die Psalmen I: Psalm 1–50*, NEchtB (Würzburg: Echter, 1993), 12, 56; Vesco, *Le psautier de David*, 1:95–173.
15. Terrance R. Wardlaw Jr., *Conceptualizing Words for "God" within the Pentateuch: A Cognitive-Semantic Investigation in Literary Context*, LHBOTS 495 (London: T&T Clark, 2008).

mountain" in 2:6, mentioned above.[16] Then, in Psalms 3–14, three more references to the Lord's holy dwelling place occur. The Lord answers prayer from "his holy mountain" (3:4), the psalmist speaks of bowing down "toward your holy temple" (5:7), and in response to distress, the psalmist declares, "The Lord is in his holy temple" (11:4 NIV). This latter statement implies that the Lord sovereignly reigns from his holy temple and will imminently act in response to the psalmist's cry (cf. Mic. 1:2). Therefore, the Lord dwells in the context of holiness, and his place of worship is holy.

Next, Psalms 15–24 center on God's law in Psalm 19.[17] This unit opens and closes with the holiness of God and the issue of who may dwell on his holy mountain. As with the movement from law to the Messiah in Psalms 1 and 2, there is a movement from the Messiah to law in Psalms 18 and 19. This juxtaposition underscores the close relationship between the law and the Messiah developed throughout the collection.

The unit of Psalms 15–24 builds on the idea of the holy place in Psalms 3–14 by developing the concept that we must be holy to dwell in God's presence. Psalms 15–24 focus on the praise of the law, especially in Psalm 19, which declares its perfection (v. 7) and its function in revealing our sin and guiding us to acceptability in God's sight (vv. 8–14). References to the holiness of the Lord's dwelling place bracket this group: "your holy hill" (15:1 ESV) and "your holy place" (24:3 AT). Therefore, Psalms 15–24 underscore the necessity of obedience to God's law as the condition for living in his presence, and those who keep the moral law actually seek the face of the God of Jacob (24:6).

Four other occurrences of the קדשׁ *lemma* within Psalms 15–24 emphasize the importance of purity. The psalmist declares that God's sanctuary or holy place is the origin of salvation (20:2), and the Lord answers the Messiah from "his holy heavens" (v. 6 AT). Furthermore, the adjective "holy" may also be used as a substantive to refer to the saints or to God. The psalmist, David, takes delight in the saints of the land (16:3), whereas he will not even speak the name of those who run after other gods. The cry of dereliction in 22:1 is familiar to many from

---

16. Rolf Rendtorff provides a discussion of holy places in *Theologie des Alten Testaments* (Neukirchen-Vluyn, Germany: Neukirchener, 1999–2001), 2:91–104.

17. Hossfeld and Zenger, *Psalmen I*, 12; Vesco, *Psautier de David*, 1:175–256.

its quotation by Jesus on the cross (Matt. 27:46; Mark 15:34), and its relation to the recognition of God's holiness in verse 3 will be treated in the thematic discussion below.

These structural markers at the boundaries of Psalms 15–24, the centrality of the law in Psalm 19, and the recurrence of the קדשׁ *lemma* prove suggestive for interpreting and applying psalms where holiness vocabulary does not emerge. For example, Psalm 23 is often prayed as a universal promise of the Lord's guidance and care. However, viewed within the interpretive framework of Psalms 15–24, it becomes a promise for those who have clean hands and a pure heart. Not everyone walking through the valley of the shadow of death should fear no evil (23:4), for it is not necessarily the case that the Lord is with them. Many should have a very real fear of death and evil as they experience the Lord's chastising judgment for rejecting him. Moreover, goodness and mercy (v. 6) are not guaranteed universally to everyone. Rather, the promise is restricted to those who keep covenant with the Lord. Therefore, the overall unit of Psalms 15–24, together with the centrality of the law in Psalm 19, informs the interpretation and restricts the application of these prayers and promises.

Turning to the next unit, Psalms 25 and 34, which are acrostics, form an inclusio that centers on Psalm 29 and the theme of the God who vanquishes chaos, responds to prayers of supplication, and performs deeds of gracious salvation.[18] Within this unit, the קדשׁ*lemma* occurs five times, excluding the reference to the wilderness of Kadesh in 29:8, and the voice of David continues to characterize the Lord and his place of worship as holy (28:2; 30:4; 33:21). Moreover, David builds on this concept by calling those who worship the Lord to worship him in holiness (29:2).[19]

Holiness in Psalms 42–72 (Book 2)

Whereas the use of the Lord's covenant name YHWH predominates in Psalms 1–41, the title *ʾĔlōhîm* occurs more frequently in Psalms 42–83. Accordingly, these psalms, in books 2–3, are known as the

18. Hossfeld and Zenger, *Psalmen I*, 12; Vesco, *Psautier de David*, 1:257–320. In terms of form, acrostics indicate perfection as they move through the Hebrew alphabet letter by letter. Divergences from this structure prove interpretively significant, such as the emphasis on redemption in Pss. 25:22 and 34:22.

19. No words for "holy" occur in Pss. 35–41.

Elohistic Psalter. Additionally, one can note a chiastic arrangement in this collection on the basis of various names mentioned in the superscriptions. The chiastic organization highlights the central element. The Davidic psalms in 51–72 form the center, and they are surrounded by the Psalms of Asaph in Psalms 50 and 73–83, as well as the outer Psalms of Korah in Psalms 42–49 and 84–89.[20] The centrality of David within books 2 and 3 is emphasized by the placement of another Davidic psalm (86) at the center of the final group of Korah psalms (84–89; see table 1).

<table>
<tr><th colspan="7">Table 1. The Structure of Psalms 42–89
(Books 2 and 3) on the Basis of Ascriptions</th></tr>
<tr><th>Korah</th><th>Asaph</th><th>David</th><th>Asaph</th><th colspan="3">Korah</th></tr>
<tr><td rowspan="3">42–49</td><td rowspan="3">50</td><td rowspan="3">51–72
(Solomon, 72)</td><td rowspan="3">73–83</td><td colspan="3">84–89</td></tr>
<tr><td>Korah</td><td>David</td><td>Korah</td></tr>
<tr><td>84–85</td><td>86</td><td>87–89</td></tr>
<tr><td>A</td><td>B</td><td>C</td><td>B′</td><td colspan="3">A′</td></tr>
</table>

As with book 1, most occurrences of the קדשׁ *lemma* in book 2 describe a holy location associated with the Lord's presence (43:3; 46:4; 47:8; 48:1). However, usage changes in Psalm 51, a penitential psalm composed by David after he took Bathsheba and commanded her husband, Uriah, to be killed. In this psalm, David pleads for the Lord's mercy and cleansing from transgression when he confesses his sin against God (vv. 3–4). In verses 10–11, David petitions God: "Create in me a clean heart, O God, and renew a right spirit within me. Cast me not away from your presence, and take not your Holy Spirit [*rûaḥ qādšəkā*] from me" (ESV).

In the OT, the Spirit of the Lord comes on priests, prophets, and kings at their installation. Applied more broadly to all believers under the Christian dispensation (Acts 2; Rom. 8), Psalm 51 situated within larger canonical context indicates, first, that one becomes unclean with

20. Vesco, *Psautier de David*, 1:389–825; Robert L. Cole, *The Shape and Message of Book III (Psalms 73–89)*, JSOTSup 307 (Sheffield: Sheffield Academic, 2000). Parallel psalms provide structural cohesion between book 2 of the Elohistic Psalter (Pss. 42–72) and the remainder of the Psalter. Parallels include Pss. 14 // 53; 40:14–18 // 70:2–6; and 57:8–12 and 60:7–14 // the composite Ps. 108.

the commission of sin and, second, that God's Spirit may depart from one who becomes unclean. Third, one component of repentance and confession consists of petitioning the Lord to cleanse our heart and not to take his Spirit from us. Fourth, with cleansing and restoration comes the joy of salvation and a willing spirit (Ps. 51:12). This process culminates in the forgiven sinner teaching transgressors the ways of God, praising God, and offering the sacrifice of a broken and contrite heart (vv. 13–17). Moreover, the cleansing of the individual sinner issues forth in communal blessing as Zion worships God (vv. 18–19).

Psalm 60 corrects one possible misunderstanding of earlier references to the sanctuary and Zion as the Lord's holy dwelling place and fortress: Zion is not unconditionally impregnable. Verses 1–3 declare that God has rejected his people and broken their defenses in his anger. In contrast, those who fear the Lord may expect salvation and deliverance (vv. 4–5). Next, God speaks "in his holiness," declaring his sovereignty over the tribes of Israel and their allotments, as well as over the surrounding nations (vv. 6–8 ESV). Then the psalmist closes with a declaration that God has rejected his people, a petition for him to grant help, and a pronouncement that he will tread down the foes of his people (vv. 9–12). The reference to God speaking in holiness (v. 6) implies that his people are not holy, which has led to his anger. Thus, holiness is expected of God's people, will result in earthly salvation, and continues the trajectory of covenant obedience in Psalms 1, 15–24, 50, and 51.

Book 2 continues with references to "the holy place" and "your holy temple" (63:2; 65:4). Whereas Psalm 60 describes a people who are weak when God is angry with them, Psalm 68 focuses on God's strength and might, and it implies that his people are to be holy in worship as he is holy, with the result that God will demonstrate power in battle (vv. 5, 17, 24, 35).

Book 2 contains one final address to "the Holy One of Israel" (*qədôš yiśrāʾēl*) in Psalm 71:22. This psalm is a plea for God's salvation from the enemy, and this reference occurs in the final vow of praise in verses 22–24. The psalm assumes that God will deliver the psalmist, and the latter vows to praise God for his faithfulness, righteous help, and putting to shame of those who have attempted to hurt him. This complex implies (1) that we are to address God as holy when we praise him, (2) that God's holiness and righteousness manifest themselves when he delivers his people, and (3) that God demonstrates himself to be holy in judging the enemies of his people.[21] This petition cuts against the grain of anemic theological systems that do not allow for God's wrath against wickedness and unrighteousness, for salvation is a double-edged sword. The salvation of God's elect entails the judgment of the wicked.

Holiness in Psalms 73–89 (Book 3)

Turning to book 3 (Pss. 73–89), the second half of the Elohistic Psalter, the crises of the prosperity of the wicked and the collapse of the Davidic monarchy emerge. Expanding on the theme of Psalm 60, the laments and petitions within this group of psalms correct the errant notion that Zion, the Lord's dwelling place on earth, remains unconditionally invincible through the ages.

The unit opens with three references to the holy place in Psalms 73 and 74. In Psalm 73, the psalmist almost stumbles while watching the wicked prosper, and in discouragement, he begins to think he has kept his heart clean in vain (vv. 1–15). The pivot occurs in verses 16–17: "But when I thought how to understand this, it seemed to me a wearisome task, until I went into the sanctuary of God [*miqdəšê-ʾēl*]; then I discerned their end" (ESV). Thus, entering into worship at God's holy place reorients the psalmist and reminds him of the end of the wicked, who will be destroyed in a moment (vv. 18–28). This psalm underscores the importance of worship for reorienting believers to God's truth and the end of time in a fallen world.

However, the crisis deepens in the lament of Psalm 74 with the destruction of the sanctuary (vv. 3, 7; also 79:1). This destruction issues forth in the praise of God as the judge of the righteous (ch. 75) and the judge of the kings of the earth (ch. 76), and it develops the idea that God will strip everything away from his people to bring them to trust in him entirely and to recognize his complete sovereignty over the earth. In relation to creation and the encompassing Elohistic Psalter, just as God once acted progressively each day, culminating in a sanctified day of rest (Gen. 1:1–2:3), he now uses chastising judgment to create a holy people for himself. The lament in Psalm 77 bears out this

21. Eric Zenger, *A God of Vengeance? Understanding the Psalms of Divine Wrath*, trans. Linda M. Maloney (Louisville: Westminster John Knox, 1995).

functional use of chastisement when the psalmist remembers the days of old and concludes, "Your way, O God, is holy" (*ʾĕlōhîm baqqōdeš darkekā*, v. 13 ESV). Thus, although God's chastisement is not pleasant, it is holy and just. However, the view that God delights in chastising his people distorts his character, and Psalm 78 corrects this error by recounting God's holy response of steadfast love to Israel's repeated rebellion (vv. 41, 54, 69).

Finally, Psalm 83:18 sums up what some consider to be the main theme of the Elohistic Psalter—namely, that the nations "may know that you alone, whose name is the LORD, are the Most High over all the earth" (ESV). Moreover, the intentional placement of Psalms 84–89 at the end of Book 3 aids the transition from the recurrence of *ʾĔlōhîm* in Psalms 42–83 to the themes of humanity's finitude and the kingship of God in book 4 (ch. 90–106). Within the final psalms of book 3, the declaration of the Lord's love for Zion and its holy mountains (87:1–2) turns to darkness in Psalms 88 and 89, which are linked together by the mention of Ethan the Ezrahite in their superscriptions. Psalm 88 petitions the Lord to remain silent no longer amid affliction; this lament then develops in Psalm 89 with the praise of the Lord's steadfast love and salvation (vv. 1–37), especially with a focus on the Lord's eternal covenant with David (vv. 3–4, 19–37). However, the climax of Psalms 1–89 is found in 89:38–52, with the rejection of the Lord's anointed and the defilement of the Davidic crown. The issue of holiness remains foundational in the downfall of Zion, as the root *qdš* is used recurrently (see *qedōšîm* and *qedôš* in vv. 5, 7, and 18). Moreover, the Lord anoints David with his holy oil (*bəšemen qādšî məšaḥtîw*, v. 20) and swears this covenant by his holiness (*nišbaʿtî bəqādšî*, v. 35). Therefore, integrally bound with the downfall of Zion and the defilement of the Davidic crown is the issue of an unholy people defiling worship and the holy dwelling place of the Lord's covenant with profane sacrifices (ch. 50), while also failing to heed the messianic voice calling Israel to confession, repentance, and a holy life (ch. 51) in the chiastic and structural center of books 2–3. Thus, book 3 ends with the crisis of an eternal Davidic promise seemingly contradicted by the downfall of the dynasty.

Holiness in Psalms 90–106 (Book 4)

On the heels of the downfall of the Davidic dynasty in Psalm 89, it is no accident that book 4 (ch. 90–106) begins with a psalm of Moses, who led Israel in the wilderness as an entire generation passed away for rebelling against the Lord and profaning the covenant (Num. 13–Deut. 34). Moses sings to the present generation the lesson they should learn as they once again wander in another wilderness of chastising judgment (ch. 90). Amid judgment, Israel still sings of the Lord's deliverance (ch. 91) and gives thanks to him on the Sabbath, while recognizing that his enemies will perish and that he is upright (ch. 92).

The question echoes following Psalm 89: Will the Lord fail to keep his eternal covenant with David? The answer emerging in Psalms 90–106 and, in particular, the kingship psalms (ch. 93–100) is that the Lord is the universal king of all the earth, with numerous references to holiness in relation to the Lord's character and rule.[22] Thus, the answer to this crisis is to remember the Mosaic theocracy.[23] Moreover, even after the crisis of the downfall of the Davidic dynasty, the voice of David, the messianic type, sounds forth in Psalms 101 and 103. This juxtaposition of the Lord's kingship and the continued voice of David suggests that Israel's Holy God has not forgotten the eternal covenant made with David, and this unit begins to hint at the expanded role and the universal rule of the Davidic Messiah issuing forth from Israel's judgment.[24]

Interestingly, holiness remains one of the key attributes of both the Lord as king and the Lord's subjects in Psalms 93–100 (93:5; 96:6, 9; 97:12; 98:1; 99:3, 5, 9), and the final psalms in book 4 open with David, the messianic voice, pondering the blameless way and purposes to destroy the wicked in the land, while cutting them off from the city of the Lord in Psalm 101. Then the Lord looks down from his holy

22. Vesco, *Psautier de David*, 2:841–1019; David M. Howard Jr., *The Structure of Psalms 93–100*, BJS 5 (Winona Lake, IN: Eisenbrauns, 1997).

23. Sampson S. Ndoga, "Revisiting the Theocratic Agenda of Book 4 of the Psalter for Interpretive Premise," in de Claissé-Walford, *Shape and Shaping*, 147–59.

24. Davage uses the additions of "David" to the superscriptions of Pss. 91–99 and 104 in the LXX to suggest the fluidity of David in the superscriptions of psalm manuscripts. However, these additions instead suggest a messianic understanding for the kingship psalms within the communities that used the LXX ("Davidic Superscriptions," 83–84). The recurrence of the phrase "for the end" within LXX superscriptions, together with the eschatological understanding of this phrase, provides further warrant for this view. Although Davage argues for an ongoing Davidization on the basis of the Qumran and LXX additions, what he actually demonstrates is a growing messianic interpretation and expectation during the Second Temple period. On a similar note, Adam Hensley argues that books 1 and 2 primarily focus on the historical David, whereas books 3–5 have an eschatological David or Davidic monarchy in view ("David, Once and Future King? A Closer Look at the Postscript of Psalm 72:20," *JSOT* 46 [2021]: 24–43).

heights to hear the prayer of the one lamenting (102:19), David calls worshipers to bless the Lord's holy name (103:1), worshipers are called to glory in the Lord's holy name as they remember his works and acts in keeping his holy promise (105:3, 42), and the Lord punishes the men in the camp who are jealous of holy Aaron (106:16). Book 4 then closes with a petition for the Lord to gather worshipers from among the nations, "that we may give thanks to your holy name" (106:47 ESV). Thus, the Lord dwells in a holy place on high, possesses a holy name, has made a holy promise, and has judged those who have opposed his holy priest. In contrast, the people have rebelled and experienced the Lord's righteous judgment for violating the covenant and living in an unholy manner. Nevertheless, this unit ends on the expectant note of a future ingathering of the elect based on the Lord's steadfast love alone (106:47).

Holiness in Psalms 107–50 (Book 5)

Finally, in book 5 (ch. 107–50), the theme of the Lord's eternal and steadfast love recurs throughout Psalms 107–18.[25] Within this unit, Psalms 108–10 are Davidic and messianic, and Psalms 111–17 either begin or end with the call to worship (*haləlû yāh*, "Praise the LORD!"), with the only exception of Psalm 114. The messianic Psalm 118 leads into the extended meditation on the law in the acrostic Psalm 119, and then the first lines of Psalms 120–34 begin with "A Song of Ascents" (ESV).[26] The last Davidic unit occurs in Psalms 138–45, and Psalms 146–50 close the Psalter with a climax of praise. Recent discussion notes the role of the Davidic psalms in the development of messianic expectations within book 5.[27]

Examining book 5 in more detail, we can see that it opens with a call to thank the Lord, with the voice of David in Psalm 108 praising the Lord's steadfast love, describing the manner in which the Lord rules Israel and the surrounding nations as holy in a holy manner, and then petitioning him to defeat Israel's foe. The progression within

25. Vesco, *Psautier de David*, 2:1023–1377.

26. See, e.g., David Noel Freedman, *Psalm 119: The Exaltation of Torah*, with Jeffrey C. Geoghegan and Andrew Welch, BJS 6 (Winona Lake, IN: Eisenbrauns, 1999); Joachim Ringleben, "Das Wort, der Weg und die Weisung: Systematische Analyse von Psalm 119," *Kerygma and Dogma* 65 (2019): 173–201.

27. See, e.g., Michael K. Snearly, *The Return of the King: Messianic Expectation in Book V of the Psalter*, LHBOTS 624 (London: Bloomsbury T&T Clark, 2016).

Psalm 108 suggests that the Lord has not granted Israel's army victory precisely because the nation has failed to live in collective holiness. In the messianic Psalm 110, David describes the people of the Lord as offering themselves in holy dress to his sovereign rule, and he depicts the Messiah as both a king and a priest. This juxtaposition of regal and priestly offices follows Psalms 1–2, 18–19, and 118–19 in uniting themes of the law and the Davidic kingship.[28] By assuming the offices of both king and priest, the Messiah will both rule and sanctify his people. Then, in Psalm 111, the Lord possesses a "holy and awesome" name (v. 9 ESV) because he has established the eternal covenant, and in 114:2, the people of Judah become the Lord's "sanctuary" (*qādəšô*) following the exodus, which proves foundational for Paul's later references to the body as the Lord's temple (1 Cor. 3:16–17; 6:19). Thus, the Lord sets his people free and leads them to inherit the land in order to be his holy dwelling place.

Of note, the extended meditation on the law in Psalm 119 contains no holiness vocabulary. Nevertheless, a messianic psalm (ch. 118) once again occurs in juxtaposition with the theme of *tôrâ* in Psalm 119. Further, the Songs of Ascent (ch. 120–34) culminate with a call for everyone standing by night in the house of the Lord to "lift up [their] hands to the holy place [*qōdeš*] and bless the Lord!" (134:2 ESV). Thus, the meditation on the law in Psalm 119 functions as Israel's foundation for living a holy life and lifting its hands to the holy place in purity under the priestly rule of the Messiah (ch. 110).

The final Davidic section of the Psalter, Psalms 138–45, is bracketed by references to holiness (an inclusio). The voice of David opens by declaring, "I bow down toward your holy temple and give thanks to your name" (138:2 ESV). He then concludes with a messianic declaration and call: "My mouth will speak the praise of the Lord, and let all flesh bless his holy name forever and ever" (145:21 ESV). Therefore, those who pray these laments of David and experience the Messiah's suffering (140:1) are prophetically called to praise the Lord's holy name for all eternity. Moreover, one may infer that suffering for the

28. Jamie Grant provides an extended analysis of the juxtaposition of kingship psalms and *tôrâ* psalms as an intentional interpretive feature of the Psalter: *The King as Exemplar: The Function of Deuteronomy's Kingship Law in the Shaping of the Book of Psalms*, AcBib 17 (Atlanta: SBL, 2004).

Messiah produces holiness and that a holy people are willing to suffer for the Messiah.

Furthermore, the concept of holiness carries through to the very end of the Psalter. The concluding psalms of praise (ch. 146–50) situate the exhortation to praise God "in his sanctuary" (*bəqādšô*, 150:1 ESV) amid the call to praise him with a variety of musical instruments (vv. 3–6).[29]

An implied conceptual narrative or thematic movement tends to emerge following canonical investigations of psalms and larger collections.[30] This implied narrative will be sketched below as it relates to the concept of holiness in the Psalms.

THE CONCEPT OF HOLINESS IN THE PSALMS: THEMATIC CONCERNS

From this linear reading, one may conclude from the text structure that the two main themes organizing the book of Psalms are *tôrâ* (ch. 1) and the Messiah (ch. 2). Moreover, it is precisely the Messiah who fulfills the law and sanctifies his people through it. All genre considerations, poetic devices, and localized subthemes, such as holiness or the kingship of God, develop these two major themes in the context of prayer and worship. The distinction between *etic* and *emic* concerns (an external system of classification and an internally developed framework of understanding, respectively) suggests that *tôrâ* and the Messiah remain the foremost organizing principles indicated by text structure (an emic consideration), whereas the elevation of subthemes or other external concerns for discussion proves to be an etic approach to the text and risks distorting the biblical construction of meaning, both in terms of conceptualization and proportion. Appeal to a theme remains valid when it emerges explicitly and is contextually primed. Otherwise, one risks foisting systematic concerns onto the text and failing to hear the text in its own right. Therefore, we shall now consider the manner in which holiness relates to and augments these

29. Tremper Longman III, "From Weeping to Rejoicing: Psalm 150 as the Conclusion to the Psalter," in Schmutzer and Howard, *Psalms*, 219–28.
30. See Mitchell, *Message of the Psalter*; Robert E. Wallace, "Gerald Wilson and the Characterization of David in Book 5 of the Psalter," in de Claissé-Walford, *Shape and Shaping*, 193; Snearly, *The Return of the King*; and Fletcher, *Psalms of Christ*.

two themes, as well as the recurring senses in which key terms within the semantic domain for holiness occur within the Psalms.

Tôrâ *and Holiness*

Tôrâ is the first major theme, arising in Psalm 1. As noted above, it is prominent in Psalms 19 and 119, and it is precisely the law that defines the nature of holiness.[31] Foremost, the law defines both the attribute of God's holiness and the moral expectations for holy living in response to the covenant. Psalm 1 contrasts the righteous and the wicked, and verse 2 leads the praying worshiper to declare that one is truly blessed who delights in the law of the Lord and meditates on it day and night. Praying this psalm within the new covenant, Jesus similarly underscores the centrality of covenant ethics in the Sermon on the Mount, where he declares that the law will not pass away until all is accomplished and that the righteousness of his disciples must surpass that of the scribes and Pharisees (Matt. 5:17–20). Therefore, the depiction of the law at the outset of the Psalms indicates that a thoroughgoing knowledge of it (both its theology and its ethics), a disposition to delight in it, and obedience to it.

Moreover, within the larger unit focusing on holiness and purity in Psalms 15–24, Psalm 19 particularizes both the nature and the role of the law in the believer's life (esp. vv. 7–14). Within these verses, the law of the Lord is described as perfect, sure, pure, true, and enduring forever. Moreover, the law revives the soul, makes wise the simple, causes the heart to rejoice, enlightens the eyes, and warns the Lord's servant so that obedience to it will result in great reward. Furthermore, the law enables the worshiper to discern errors and hidden faults in order to avoid presumptuous sins (vv. 12–13). This praise of the law climaxes with the psalmist's petition that the words of his mouth and the meditation of his heart be acceptable in the Lord's sight (v. 14). Thus, under the Christian covenant, a discerning knowledge of sin (Rom. 3:20) and obedience to God's law by the power of the Spirit (Rom. 8) will result in acceptable praise and meditation in the sight of the Lord.

Furthermore, Psalm 119 functions as a prominent structural feature pointing toward both the role and the nature of the law in the life of the

---

31. Wenham, *Psalms as Torah*, 77–137.

saints. This extended praise of the law in acrostic form serves as the solution to Israel violating the covenant, experiencing the curses of the Mosaic law, and losing the Davidic kingship (ch. 89, 105–6).[32] Moreover, Psalm 119 both particularizes the delight expressed in 1:2 and prepares the heart for ascending into the Lord's presence (ch. 120–34). Psalm 119 contains several key ideas that prove foundational for understanding holiness. First, just as the Lord calls Israel to love him with their whole heart (Deut. 6:5), the psalmist repeatedly pairs keeping the Lord's commandments with seeking him with a whole heart (e.g., Ps. 119:2, 10, 34). Second, worshipers vow to meditate on the Lord's commandments (e.g., vv. 15, 27, 97); learning them will result in praising God with an upright heart (v. 7). Third, the psalmist implicitly assumes that we do not have the ability either to understand or to keep the law. Rather, the Lord both gives understanding and enables us to obey (e.g., vv. 33–40, 133, 176). Fourth, the psalmist acknowledges an inability to obtain the Lord's favor through obedience and instead asks him to be gracious and keep him from straying (e.g., vv. 58, 176). Fifth, the psalmist acknowledges that chastising affliction helps teach the Lord's statutes when we go astray (e.g., vv. 65–72). Sixth, the psalmist's obedience functions as the grounds for petitioning the Lord for deliverance from his oppressor (e.g., vv. 121–28). Seventh, the law is wonderful and upright (e.g., vv. 129, 137).

Finally, the link between the creation narrative (Gen. 1:1–2:3) and the Elohistic Psalter (Pss. 42–89), developed with the recurrent use of the title *ʾĔlōhîm*, "God," provides further background against which the theme of *tôrâ* profiles within the Psalms (conceptual blending).[33] Just as God systematically and progressively separates light from darkness and dry land from the waters in order to create life, culminating in the sanctified seventh day, the Creator now uses chastisement, lament, and praise in order to separate the

32. The acrostic form itself points toward wholeness and completion.

33. Conceptual blending is a term used in cognitive semantics and refers to the process by which the mind construes meaning in processing words in a text. The specific sense of a word, concept, or traditional theme profiles against a semantic frame. For example, with the metaphor "lion of Judah," David profiles against the figure of a strong lion. This conceptual blending indicates David is strong and victorious. Similarly, elements of discourse may profile against traditional themes to evoke an inferred interpretation. For example, prophetic call narratives (e.g., Isa. 6; Jer. 1; Ezek. 1–3) echo elements from Moses's call at the burning bush (Exod. 3:1–4:17). This conceptual blending leads to the inference that each of these prophets falls within the Mosaic tradition (Deut. 18:15).

righteous from the wicked in order to systematically and progressively create a holy people for himself. The movement from Psalms 1–89 into 90–150 issues forth from chaos to life-giving moral order as the Lord transforms a rebellious people into sanctified followers of the Messiah (ch. 110, 119) who will ascend Zion (ch. 120–34) and worship the Lord for all eternity (ch. 146–50).

The Messiah, Future Expectations, and Holiness

The second major theme dominating the book of Psalms emerges in the introductory Psalm 2, appears throughout with references to the anointed one (2:2; 18:51; 20:7; 28:8; 45:8; 84:10; 89:21, 39, 52; 105:15; 132:10, 17) and the king (e.g., 2:6; 45:5, 14, 15), recurs with references to the historical David in many of the superscriptions (e.g., ch. 3–41), and is developed with references to the Davidic covenant promising a son to sit on the throne forever (e.g., ch. 89 and 132). As was noted above, the increasing attribution of kingship psalms (ch. 93–100) to David within Septuagint and Qumran manuscripts suggests the growing messianic expectation among psalm interpreters during the intertestamental period. Moreover, alongside the book of Isaiah, NT authors frequently appeal to the book of Psalms to provide a prophetic context for understanding the ministry and person of Jesus Christ as our King and sanctifying Priest. Understanding the Messiah in the Psalms remains central for an orthodox Christology. Therefore, we shall examine a few select psalms and how they feature in the messianic structure of the Psalter.

Psalm 2 initially depicts the nations and their kings in opposition to the Messiah, which was understood by the apostles as the Holy Spirit speaking through David about Herod and Pilate's crucifixion of Jesus (Ps. 2:1–2; Acts 4:25–26). In contrast, the Lord holds the nations' kings in derision (Ps. 2:4) and declares that he has begotten the king (v. 7). The early church applied this ANE kingship language to Jesus in relation to his resurrection, sonship, and priesthood (Acts 13:33; Heb. 1:5; 5:5). Moreover, this psalm indicates the universal rule of the Messiah and calls rulers to submit lest they face his wrath (Ps. 2:8–12). Therefore, the nations stand against Christ, who rules universally, is God's Son, and will express wrath against rulers and those who rebel.

Then, in Psalm 22, David augments the depiction of the sovereign Messiah from Psalm 2 by expressing the lament of a suffering king. The well-known cry of dereliction (22:1; Matt. 27:46; Mark 15:34) leads into the psalmist's complaint against those mocking and wagging their heads, which the apostles applied to the mockery at Jesus's suffering (Ps. 22:6–8; Matt. 27:39–43; Mark 15:29–32; Luke 23:35–36). David continues by lamenting, "They have pierced my hands and feet" (Ps. 22:16 ESV), which was understood as a reference to the nails piercing Jesus's hands and feet (Matt. 27:35; Mark 15:24; Luke 23:33; John 19:23). Likewise, evildoers cast lots for the king's clothing (Ps. 22:18), which was fulfilled by the Roman soldiers taking Jesus's garment (John 19:24). Nevertheless, the recognition of God's holiness proves to be a turning point (Ps. 22:4). The cry of lament is heard (v. 24), and the king's suffering shall issue forth in the ends of the earth turning to the Lord, who rules over the nations, and posterity serving him (vv. 27–31). Therefore, the suffering of the Messiah inaugurates the manifest extension of the Lord's rule to the ends of the earth, as well as the proclamation of the Lord's righteousness to posterity.

In Psalm 45, a love song, the sons of Korah sing of God's eternal rule and its uprightness (v. 6), as well as of the king loving righteousness and hating wickedness (v. 7). The writer of Hebrews understood this as a reference to the holy nature of Christ's rule (Heb. 1:8–9). Furthermore, the chiastic structure of the Elohistic Psalter (books 2 and 3) focuses on the central unit of the Davidic psalms (ch. 51–72), which particularizes this righteous and holy nature of the Messiah's reign from Psalm 45. David's opening prayer of repentance in Psalm 51 functions as an exemplary prayer for those who desire God's mercy and cleansing from sin in order to submit to the eternal rule of a Messiah who loves righteousness and hates wickedness. This psalm casts a long shadow across the remaining Elohistic psalms in holding up the penitent ideal for those following the Anointed One.

Although righteousness characterized David's reign, and the Lord's eternal covenant with him required obedience, David's children violated the covenant statutes. This resulted in the downfall of the kingship (Ps. 89:28–52). However, this downfall was not permanent, and the Lord kept his steadfast love for David by promising a throne that would endure forever (89:33–37). Therefore, after prayers focusing on the Lord's kingship (ch. 93–100), the voice of David once again emerges in Psalms 101, 103, 108–10, 122, 124, 131, 133, and 138–45. This voice expresses future hope for the Davidic reign and a victorious king to sit on the throne of Zion. According to Psalm 108, salvation will come, and God promises this deliverance "in his holiness" (v. 7 ESV) issuing forth in the victory over and the division of the nations.

In response to the opposition against the Messiah, the plea for salvation, and the vow of praise (Ps. 109), salvation issues forth in Psalm 110, one of the most-quoted psalms in the NT. This psalm opens with David declaring, "The Lord says to my Lord: 'Sit at my right hand, until I make your enemies your footstool'" (Ps. 110:1 ESV).

Thus, the earlier lament of Psalm 109 turns to the subjugation of the Lord's enemies in Psalm 110. David quotes the Lord speaking to "my Lord" (*nəʾum yhwh laʾdōnî*), and Jesus quotes the Lord's speech here when contending with the Pharisees that the Messiah is more than David's son (Matt. 22:44; Mark 12:36; Luke 20:42–43). Peter and the writer of Hebrews likewise refer to this passage as proof of Jesus's identity as the Messiah (Acts 2:34–35; Heb. 1:13). Moreover, in Psalm 110, the Lord's people will be clothed in holy garments ("holy splendor") when they offer themselves to him (v. 3 NIV). In addition to the Lord's identity as king (vv. 2, 5–7), the messianic figure will be "a priest forever after the order of Melchizedek" (v. 4 ESV). Thus, the priestly office entails the Messiah making both atonement and intercession (Lev. 1–17), in addition to judging the nations as King. The writer of Hebrews applies this priestly identity to Christ, suggesting that he offers prayers and supplications, secures eternal salvation, saves to the uttermost, makes supplication, and sacrifices once for all, a Son perfect forever (Heb. 5:5–10; 7:11–28). Whereas Psalm 22 depicts a suffering Messiah who is sovereign over the nations, Psalm 110 depicts a conquering Messiah executing judgment among the nations and shattering their leaders (vv. 5–7). Moreover, Psalm 110 unites the messianic offices of both king and priest, as the Lord both rules and sanctifies his people forever.

Following the extended meditation on the law in Psalm 119, David sings in the Psalms of Ascent (ch. 122, 124, 131, and 133) and leads future generations to worship in the Lord's presence. Moreover, Psalm 132 reminds worshipers of David's commitment to build the Lord's place of worship (vv. 1–7), reflects upon the righteousness of the priests and the holiness of God's people (vv. 9, 16), refers to the Messiah ("the anointed one," vv. 10, 17 ESV), and declares again the eternal Davidic covenant (vv. 11–18). Therefore, the Messiah will both reign forever and lead his people to worship in the presence of God in Zion.

The final Davidic unit (Pss. 138–45) functions as a reprise for many of the themes and phrases occurring up to this point in the collection. In Psalm 138, the psalmist gives thanks and declares that the Lord will fulfill his purpose for David. Moving beyond Psalm 51, David notes the Lord's complete knowledge of his inward thoughts and petitions him to search him and know his heart in Psalm 139. In Psalms 140–44, David laments and pleads for deliverance, and then in Psalm 145, he closes with a model of praise for his people. Therefore, David voices these prayers for the king and priest of Psalm 110, both to make intercession for his saints and to lead them in prayer and worship in God's presence.

With these thoughts in mind, we now turn from the two main themes of the Psalms to discuss three thematic uses of holiness vocabulary in the Psalter.

The Holy Place

The קדשׁ *lemma* occurs most frequently in the Psalter in constructions referring to holy places. This usage is based on the pentateuchal conceptualization of God's holy place. In the book of Exodus, the exodus (ch. 6–14) leads to the Mosaic covenant and the revelation of moral, civil, and ceremonial law at Sinai (ch. 19–24).[34] The law reveals the Lord's expectations of holy living in preparation for the revelation of instructions for building the tabernacle (ch. 25–31), the tabernacle's actual construction (ch. 35–40), and the resulting presence of God (40:34–38). In Leviticus, the tabernacle is the place of atonement (ch. 1–17), which calls for holy living (ch. 18–27). Moreover, Numbers tells of God's presence leading his people toward the promised land, and Deuteronomy recounts the covenant as the people prepare to enter the land. Psalms 15–24 reflect this concern for holy living in the presence of the Lord with a life centered on the law (ch. 19).

34. Critiques of this tripartite division of biblical law abound, as well as the assertion that it is alien to the text itself. However, Walter Kaiser answers these criticisms and demonstrates the usefulness of this classification within a Christian hermeneutic for both interpreting and applying legal texts (*Toward Old Testament Ethics* [Grand Rapids: Zondervan Academic, 1983], esp. 44–48). The present author finds Kaiser's approach helpful for understanding the enduring nature of Mosaic law within the Christian covenant (e.g., Matt 5:17–20).

First, in Psalm 2, the Lord declares that he has installed his king on Zion, "my holy mountain" (v. 6). The Lord's holy mountain refers to Zion, the Temple Mount from the time of Solomon (tenth century BC) to the destruction of Jerusalem (sixth century BC), which later became the site of the second temple. This is the place where the psalmist prays in distress (3:5), and it is a place where only the blameless may dwell (15:1). Only God's light and truth (i.e., the revealed covenant) can lead those experiencing oppression into the joy of worship at the altar on the holy hill (43:3). This is the city of the great King (48:2), as well as the place where the Lord's people are called to worship (99:9). The phrase "the holy mountains" likewise refers to the mountains in and around Jerusalem (87:1), the city God loves.

Second, David speaks of entering the "holy temple" to worship (Ps. 5:7 ESV), which is the location of the Lord's presence (11:4; 65:4). Moreover, Asaph laments the nations entering and defiling the Lord's holy temple (79:1). Under the Christian covenant, Paul identifies the body of Corinthian believers as the temple of the Holy Spirit (1 Cor. 3:16–17; 6:19). In 1 Corinthians 3:16–17, Paul begins his discussion with a plural reference to the believers in Corinth (v. 16), shifts to singular forms in the conditional clause in verse 17a, and then ends with plural forms in verse 17b. These plurals may be understood ambiguously either as referring to the Holy Spirit dwelling within their corporate midst, or as a collective plural with the Holy Spirit dwelling in the body of each individual believer. The reference to "the body (of believers [PL])" in 6:19 likewise remains ambiguous. Nevertheless, this identification implies that Christians are called to remain pure at all times because individuals may defile the temple. Since believers are now the locus of God's presence, they may always worship and pray because the body is his temple.

Third, the קדשׁ *lemma* occurs in various constructions referring to the sanctuary or holy place. The Lord sends help from the sanctuary (Pss. 20:3; 68:6) and answers from his holy heavens (20:7; 102:20).[35] Moreover, only those with clean hands and a pure heart may enter the holy place (24:3). Those who cry out in prayer lift their hands to the

35. The parallel nature of the Lord's earthly presence in the earthly temple and his heavenly presence in the heavenly temple or sanctuary is suggested by Pss. 11:4 and 20:3, 7. This distinction between the earthly and heavenly temples comes to fruition in the distinction between Christ's perfect work in the heavenly sanctuary and the imperfect sacrifices in the earthly sanctuary under the Mosaic covenant (Heb. 9).

holy of holies or prostrate themselves toward it (28:2; 134:2; 138:2). Moreover, the holy place or tabernacle, where the Lord dwells, is a place of joy (46:5), and it is the place he manifests strength and glory (63:3; 68:18, 25, 36; 96:6). The Lord is the one who leads his people to the holy place, and he also builds his sanctuary (78:54, 69). At the sanctuary, the Lord reorients those who struggle in a world where the wicked prosper (73:17). Furthermore, the wicked of the nations do not respect the holy place, and they readily defile and destroy it (74:3, 7). However, the people of God become the sanctuary of the Lord following redemption (114:2). The Psalter climaxes with a call to praise God in his sanctuary (150:1), which is made possible by the great high priest (ch. 110). The sons of Korah use kingship imagery and refer to the Lord's heavenly dwelling place as his "holy throne" (47:8 ESV), where he rules over the nations.

Above all, the institution of the earthly sanctuary functions as a type pointing toward the necessity of holiness and purity as Christians worship the Lord from the temple of the body. This purity begins with repentance and the restoration of the Holy Spirit (Ps. 51, esp. v. 11). The Lord reigns in us and through us by the presence of his Spirit, and the process of chastisement leads to lament and praise, to turning from dependence on all earthly institutions and powers (ch. 3–89), and to a recognition of the Lord's kingship (ch. 90–106). This recognition of the Lord's kingship, in turn, results in purification and obedience to the covenant (ch. 107–19), which leads into the Lord's presence (ch. 120–34) and jubilant praise for all eternity (ch. 146–50). Thus, holy living, prayer, and praise should result in the manifestation of the divine glory and salvation associated with the holy place within believers, both corporately and individually.

The Holy One

Names in the OT often reveal the nature of the one to whom they are given, and they often relate to narrative development. In particular, divine names reveal God's nature. Along these lines, the psalmists highlight the Lord's nature when they refer to him as "the Holy One" (Pss. 71:22; 78:41; 89:19), when they describe him as "holy" (e.g., 22:4; 99:3, 5, 9), and when David pleads with him not to take away his Holy Spirit (51:13). The psalmists call worshipers to "give thanks to his holy remembrance" (30:4; 97:12), at which recent translations render as a reference to the divine name (e.g., NKJV, NASB, ESV, NIV, and NET). The psalmists frequently refer explicitly to the Lord's "holy name" (*šēm qādəšô*), in which they trust (33:21) and which we are called to worship and thank (99:3; 103:1; 105:3; 106:47; 145:21). The Lord manifests his holiness when he redeems his people and commands the covenant (111:9); similarly, the manner in which the Lord delivers his people leads the psalmist to refer to "his holy arm" working salvation (98:1 ESV). "Holy" characterizes how God speaks as the sovereign King over the nations (60:8; 108:8), and it also characterizes the greatness with which he acts (77:14). God has sworn an oath to David in holiness and therefore cannot lie by breaking it (89:36). Similarly, the Lord remembers his "holy promise" to Abraham (105:42 ESV).

Therefore, God possesses a nature of holiness, which manifests itself in truth, faithfulness to promises, glory, might, and acts of salvation and deliverance. Moreover, the Holy Spirit manifests his presence when God's people repent and live in purity (Ps. 51:13). This indicates that the holy nature of God requires holiness from those with whom he dwells.

The Saints

The preceding section notes both the holiness of God and his requirement of holiness from his people. Thus, the psalmists refer to the Lord's people as "saints" (*qədôšîm*). David and the Messiah delight in the saints (Ps. 16:3), who are called to fear the Lord (34:10; 89:7) and praise his faithfulness (89:5). However, such delight does not mean that the Lord delights in all praise from the willfully sinful and impenitent. The Lord's call to worship stipulates a life of holiness, such that the saints may worship the Lord "in the splendor of holiness" (29:2; 96:9 ESV). Moreover, the Lord zealously loves the saints and is aware of opposition as they serve him. The psalmist characterizes Aaron, the first high priest, as "the holy one of the LORD," and the Lord defends him from his jealous opponents by causing the earth to swallow them (106:16 ESV).

SUMMARY AND CONCLUSIONS

In sum, this investigation has first noted the background assumptions about holiness in the Psalms. Second, canonical discussions make it possible to observe thematic progressions emerging from the arrangement of the Psalter, and these progressions form the context for a linear reading of words for "holy." Third, this analysis has noted that an implied conceptual narrative emerges from the canonical arrangement of the Psalter and that this narrative centers on the relation between the law in Psalm 1 and the Messiah in Psalm 2. The voice of David throughout the book functions as a type pointing to the eschatological antitype to come. David leads his people in praise and lament (ch. 3–41, 51–71), as well as confession (ch. 51). Moreover, the eclipse of the monarchy in Psalm 89 and the connection between monarchic Israel and the wilderness generation (ch. 90–106) set a trajectory for understanding the kingship of God (ch. 93–100) in relation to the voice of David (ch. 101 and 103). The prominence of David (ch. 108–10, 118, 132–33, 138–45) and the law (ch. 119) in book 5 (ch. 107–50) suggests the restoration of holiness and covenant ethics through messianic rule, the ascent of the elect to worship in holiness (ch. 120–34), the willingness of a holy people to suffer for the Messiah (ch. 138–45), and the eternal praise of the elect in holiness (ch. 146–50). References to the holy place, the Holy One, and the saints augment these two main themes in the book in order to characterize how the Messiah will rule his people as King and sanctify them as Priest.

Chapter 8

HOLINESS IN THE PROPHETS: BY THE BRANCH, FOR THE WORLD

PETER C. W. HO

When the people of Israel first come to Sinai, God gives them a vision of what it means to be delivered and what it means to be in a covenantal relationship with him. Israel is to be (1) God's treasured possession among all the peoples, (2) a kingdom of priests, and (3) a holy nation (Exod. 19:5–6; 22:31). This vision has a threefold character and a logical sequence: First, by God's own pleasure, he has chosen a people to belong to him, not as slaves but as his beloved people.[1] Second, God rules this people through chosen leaders who are to administer justice, lead battles, and preside over the entire cultus of worship and sanctification in Israel. This priesthood is envisioned to grow beyond the selected few so that the entire nation can fulfill the priestly role and the nations become beneficiaries.[2] Third, this vision speaks of holiness—a divine quality of utter majesty, purity, perfection, and separation from all that is profane or sinful. Significantly, the holiness of God's people functions as the critical link between God and the nations (Isa. 61:6). Uche Anizor and Hank Voss put the matter succinctly: "Priesthood connotes a dignity before God and a responsibility to creation."[3] But how does this Exodus vision (i.e., the vision of Israel as a kingdom of priests and a holy nation) find its way through a period of about eight

1. In contrast, consider the depiction of humans created as laborers to provide food for the gods in Atrahasis 1:1–6. See Bernard F. Batto, *In the Beginning: Essays on Creation Motifs in the Ancient Near East and the Bible*, Siphrut 9 (Winona Lake, IN: Eisenbrauns, 2013), 27, 143.
2. Although the priesthood was originally chosen from the family line of Aaron, as a nation of priesthood, this hierarchy in the cultus may no longer be clearly distinguished with the Jews' return from Babylon. In this context, as Isa. 61:5–6 suggests, Israel is to fulfill her destiny "as a nation that serves the other nations as priest." (Martha Himmelfarb, *A Kingdom of Priests: Ancestry and Merit in Ancient Judaism* [Philadelphia: University of Pennsylvania Press, 2006], 2).
3. Uche Anizor and Hank Voss, *Representing Christ: A Vision for the Priesthood of All Believers* (Downers Grove, IL: IVP Academic, 2016), 15. This work is a helpful biblical-theological study of the priesthood of believers.

hundred years from Israel's monarchy, to its divided nationhood, and subsequently through its destruction and captivity? In this essay, we will trace the motif of holiness in the Latter Prophets via the vision of Exodus 19:5–6.

In doing so, my approach is to trace words connected to holiness and the priesthood within their larger structural-rhetorical contexts in view of the Exodus vision.[4] Specifically, we will observe their occurrences across the main structural sections of a major prophetic corpus, with special attention to how Israel fulfills the Exodus vision of becoming a kingdom of priests and a holy nation. Admittedly, ascertaining these main structural sections is a major undertaking, enjoying no clear consensus. In general, these sections are assessed by scholars through "formal patterning."[5] We take a more synchronic approach, even if we do not jettison the diachronic approach altogether. A synchronic approach undertakes analysis of the text as it stands in its final form while a diachronic approach, focuses on the historical compositional development of the text. Our methodology in this essay is synchronic but moves beyond mere lexical analysis and is not necessarily reader-oriented because observed textual features still guide our interpretation.[6]

The holiness motif is first established in the Pentateuch. There the Israelites have a firsthand encounter with the holiness and power of God at Sinai, where they receive covenantal laws and instructions to build a tabernacle. The entire purification cultus is established so that Israel can live before a holy God (Lev. 10:3; 11:44–45; 19:2; 20:7;

4. My assumption is that the Prophetic Books have a coherent message and unity. Such issues are well treated elsewhere. See Daniel C. Timmer, *The Non-Israelite Nations in the Book of the Twelve: Thematic Coherence and the Diachronic-Synchronic Relationship in the Minor Prophets*, BibInt 135 (Leiden: Brill, 2015), 10.

5. Formal patterns include repeated speech forms such as woe oracles, salvation oracles, or hymnic invocations. Robert H. O'Connell, *Concentricity and Continuity: The Literary Structure of Isaiah*, JSOTSup 188 (Sheffield: Sheffield Academic, 1994), 20–21, 22.

6. For a detailed lexical study of "holiness," see David P. Wright, "Holiness: Old Testament," *ABD* 3:237–49. See also John Barton, "*Déjà lu*: Intertextuality, Method or Theory?," in *Reading Job Intertextually*, ed. Katharine Dell and Will Kynes, LHBOTS 574 (New York: Bloomsbury T&T Clark, 2013), 2. It has been shown that reader-oriented strategies can also function as hermeneutical tools. See Archibald L. H. M. van Wieringen, "The Reader-Oriented Position of Babel and Assur within the Framework of Isaiah 1–39," in *'Enlarge the Site of Your Tent': The City as Unifying Theme in Isaiah*, ed. Archibald L. H. M. van Wieringen and Annemarieke van der Woude, OtSt 58 (Leiden: Brill, 2011), 49–62.

22:19).[7] But by the book of Numbers, Israel has profaned her calling to be holy, and the nation perishes in the desert. When we arrive at Deuteronomy, Exodus 19:6 is envisioned for a *new* generation of God's people (Deut. 7:6). Israel's (future) kings will have to copy the book of the law, approved by the Levitical priests (17:18). We see clearly that when God's people keep the covenant, foreigners share in his justice and blessings (14:21). In this way, the entire people of Israel function as intermediaries of God's justice and blessings for the foreigners among them (26:19; 28:9).

The failures of God's people and their profanity of God's holiness in the Pentateuch perpetuate and are accentuated in the Historical Books. Israel's pre-monarchic leaders, or judges, spiral into moral decadence. By Jephthah and Samson, the Israelites behave no differently from the Canaanites. Israel's first king disobeys God (1 Sam. 15:22–23), and Judah's last king continues to break YHWH's covenant laws. One by one, Israel's and Judah's kings are measured against their covenantal commitments, and all of them come up short. The lack of holiness, from leaders to the people, is stark in this context. Figure 8.1 shows that the Historical Books[8] (i.e., the Former Prophets) have fewer instances as compared to the Pentateuch and the Latter Prophets, per thousand words, of terms based on the root *qdš*.[9] Many of these terms are connected to physical objects and places of the cultus (e.g., "sanctuary").[10] As such, they are linked to the motif of holiness directly or indirectly.

7. The term "Israel" refers to different entities in different contexts. We will adopt a general meaning of "the people of God" in this essay. This term may be used interchangeably with "Judah," especially in contexts set after 722 BCE.

8. Scholars often refer to the books of 1–2 Chronicles, Ezra, Nehemiah, and Esther (set in the postexilic period) as the Chronistic History and the books of Deuteronomy, Joshua, Judges, 1–2 Samuel, 1–2 Kings (the Former Prophets) as the Deuteronomistic History.

9. Such words may appear as nouns, proper nouns, verbs, adjectives, and so on. My electronic search for the root *qdš* in the Lexham Hebrew Bible turns up 880 occurrences in the OT, and more than two-thirds of these occurrences are in the nominal form (e.g., "holiness," "something holy," "sanctuary"). About fifty or so occurrences are proper nouns (e.g., "Kadesh") and references to cult prostitutes. See Helmer Ringgren, "קדשׁ [*qdš*]," *TDOT* 12:530–43.

10. "Sanctuary" is signified by the Hebrew *miqdāš* (Exod. 15:17; Lev. 12:14) and *haqōdeš*, both of which use the root *qdš*. The latter is the nominal form of "holy" with a prefixed article (Exod. 30:24; Lev. 4:6).

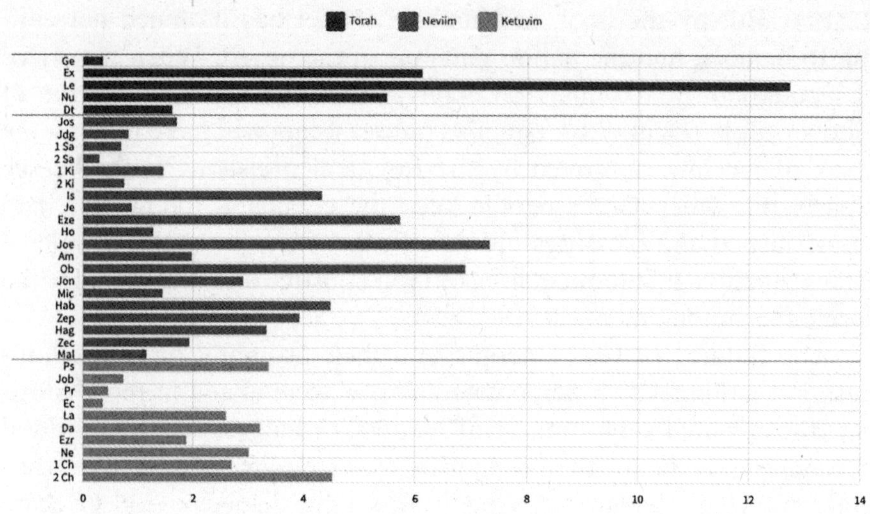

Figure 8.1. Occurrences of Terms with the Root *qdš* per Thousand Words in the OT[11]

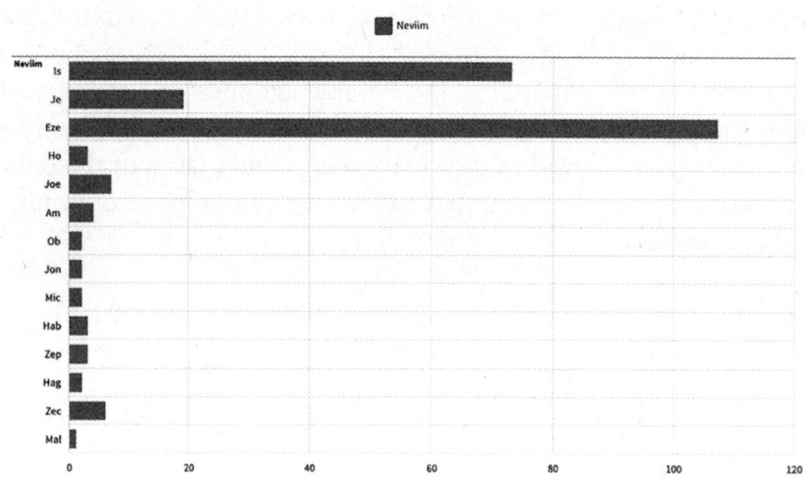

Figure 8.2. Occurrences of Words with the Root *qdš* in the Latter Prophets

Figure 8.2 shows absolute numbers in the Latter Prophets: 73 instances of words with the root occur in Isaiah (31.2%), 19 occur in Jeremiah

11. Figures in this essay have been generated by Logos 10 and then adapted and edited for clarity.

(8.1%), 107 occur in Ezekiel (45.7%), and 35 occur in the Book of the Twelve (15%). Although the four corpora are similar in length, such words occur with different frequencies in them. As a whole, the prophetic literature (including the Former and the Latter Prophets) depicts how Israel and Judah have failed to be a kingdom of priests and a holy nation. Not only have they disobeyed and broken their covenantal commitments; they have also despised the Holy One and profaned the Sabbath and the holy things of God. The people persist in such profanity to the point that Jerusalem and the temple are completely ruined by foreigners (an event that dates to 587 BCE). The Exodus vision, then, turns completely on its head. But a number of texts in the Latter Prophets show YHWH's resolve to vindicate his reputation and name, which have been profaned by his people. In these texts (esp. those in Ezekiel), we see YHWH determined to make the original vision of Exodus 19:6 a reality—namely, that his people would be holy, mediating his justice and blessings to the nations.

ISAIAH

The book of Isaiah has been traditionally divided into three main segments (i.e., ch. 1–39, 40–55, and 56–66), corresponding roughly to three time periods in the eighth through sixth centuries BCE.[12] Beyond these major units, various nuanced proposals proliferate.[13] Most scholars recognize Isaiah 1 as the introduction to the book. The first segment (ch. 1–39) may be further divided (e.g., into ch. 1–6; 7–12; 13–23; and 24–35), with chapters 36–39 functioning as a bridge to the second segment (ch. 40–55). Likewise, chapter 55 serves as a link to the third segment (ch. 56–66).[14] These three major structural divisions are possibly intentional. Many have noticed how chapters 6–39 are bound by narratives concerning two Judean kings, Ahaz and Hezekiah. Whereas the former faces the invasion of the Syro-Ephraimite alliance, the latter experiences the Assyrian expansion (ch. 6–8, 36–39).[15] These

12. For other structural proposals, see Marvin A. Sweeney, *Isaiah 40–66*, FOTL (Grand Rapids: Eerdmans, 2016), 10–11; William H. Brownlee, *The Meaning of the Qumran Scrolls for the Bible with Special Attention to the Book of Isaiah* (New York: Oxford University Press, 1964), 247–49.

13. O'Connell, *Concentricity and Continuity*, 20–21.

14. Chapters 32–33 and 34–35 may function as bridges as well. See Brevard S. Childs, *Isaiah: A Commentary*, OTL (Louisville: Westminster John Knox, 2001), 8.

15. Sehoon Jang, "Is Hezekiah a Success or a Failure? The Literary Function of Isaiah's Prediction at the End of the Royal Narratives in the Book of Isaiah," *JSOT* 42 (2017): 126.

narratives show how Ahaz and Hezekiah respond to national crises in similar yet contrasting ways. They also record the kings' personal interactions with the prophet Isaiah.

Isaiah 40–66 reflects a different historical context, one set more than a century after the Assyrian siege. Elsewhere, I have shown that the asymmetrical use of several lexemes in the latter half of Isaiah (usually divided into ch. 40–48, 49–55, and 56–66) reflects a new stage of hope for the nations.[16] This hope for the nations is directly related to a transformed holy Zion that will minister as a city of priests to the nations.

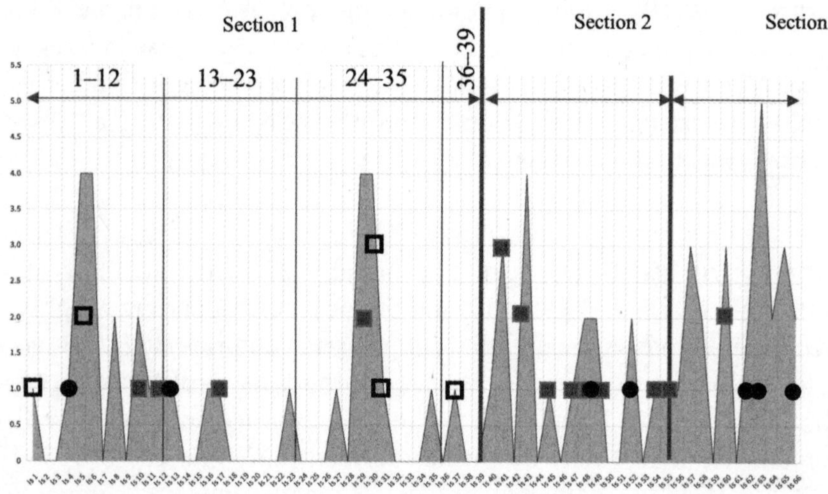

Figure 8.3. Occurrences of Words with the Root *qdš* in the Major Sections of Isaiah

The distribution of seventy-three words based on the root *qdš* across Isaiah is shown by the triangular peaks in figure 8.3.[17] The three major sections of Isaiah are also marked. Notice a higher concentration of the

16. Peter C. W. Ho, "Hope for the Nations in the Psalms, Deuteronomy, and Isaiah: An Intertextual Study," in *Hope for the World from the Old Testament: Essays in Honor of Gordon McConville on His Seventieth Birthday*, ed. Jamie Grant, Alison Lo, and David Firth (Wilmore, KY: GlossaHouse, forthcoming).

17. These seventy-three instances occur in sixty-four verses. The underlined references below refer to "the Holy One of Israel," and those in bold refer to the holy people of God (e.g., "his consecrated ones" or the metaphorical "city"): Isa. 1:4; **4:3**; 5:16, <u>19</u>, <u>24</u>; 6:3, 13; 8:13, 14; 10:17, <u>20</u>; 11:9; <u>12:6</u>; **13:3**; 16:12; <u>17:7</u>; 23:18; 27:13; <u>29:19</u>, <u>23</u>; <u>30:11</u>, <u>12</u>, <u>15</u>, 29; <u>31:1</u>; 35:8; <u>37:23</u>; 40:25; <u>41:14</u>, <u>16</u>, <u>20</u>; <u>43:3</u>, <u>14</u>, 15, 28; <u>45:11</u>; <u>47:4</u>; **48:2**, <u>17</u>; <u>49:7</u>; 52:1, 10; <u>54:5</u>; <u>55:5</u>; 56:7; 57:13, 15; 58:13; 60:9, 13, <u>14</u>; 62:9, **12**; 63:10, 11, 15, **18**; 64:10, 11; 65:5, 11, 25; **66:17**, 20.

relevant words occurring in Isaiah 1–12 and 40–66. At the beginning of the book, Zion is envisioned as a kingdom of priests that will teach the law, judge the nations, and decide disputes to bring peace among the nations (2:1–4). But in the same breath, Isaiah shows Israel rebelling against YHWH by failing to know its master, acting corruptly (1:3; 3:8), and despising the Holy One of Israel (1:4; 5:24). The nation's sin includes its pride, failure to administer justice, and vanity in worship (1:11–17). Accordingly, Israel's priesthood is rejected right off the bat (vv. 13–15). What was originally established as a faithful city, full of righteousness, has become a prostitute and a murderer (v. 21). And in these first twelve chapters, YHWH, who is holy and righteous, has turned against his own possession (v. 25; 3:24–25; 9:11–12). Fewer words based on the root *qdš* occur in Isaiah 13–23, a collection of woe oracles against the nations.

In Isaiah, the phrase "the Holy One of Israel" is distinctive.[18] Repeated twenty-six times and located predominantly in chapters 25–35 and 40–55, this phrase is marked by square boxes in figure 8.3 (whether hollow □ or filled ■). The hollow squares are negative expressions representing the people's rejection of the Holy One and are found mainly within Isaiah 1–39.

Interestingly, juxtapositions of the phrase "the Holy One of Israel" with the word "Redeemer" only occur in the second major segment of Isaiah (40:14; 43:14; 47:4; 48:17; 49:7; 54:5). The occurrences of these two terms in chapters 40–55 show how vocabulary choices and the macrostructural design of Isaiah are linked. In these chapters, we see God redeeming his people through a Suffering Servant who brings light and salvation to the nations and bears their iniquities (49:5–7; 53:11). Through this Servant, the Holy One of Israel will endow God's people with splendor (55:5), and they will begin to fulfill their ministering roles to the nations.

Circles ● in figure 8.3 symbolize references to the "holy people" of God, which give us the clearest intertextual reference to the Exodus vision.[19] Such references occur only in the beginning and in the third major segment of Isaiah (4:3; 62:9, 12; 63:18; 66:17). Transformed and enabled by the Servant, the people of God mourn and humble themselves in Zion:

18. For a good study of this phrase, see esp. John N. Oswalt, *The Holy One of Israel: Studies in the Book of Isaiah* (Eugene, OR: Cascade Books, 2014).

19. Anizor and Voss, *Representing Christ*, 39.

> Strangers shall stand and tend your flocks;
> foreigners shall be your plowmen and vinedressers;
> but *you shall be called the priests of the Lord*;
> *they shall speak of you as the ministers of our God*;
> you shall eat the wealth of the nations,
> and in their glory you shall boast.
> (Isa. 61:5–6, italics added)[20]

At the end of Isaiah 61, it is said that God will "cause righteousness and praise to sprout up before all the nations" (v. 11). God's people will also be sent to the nations to proclaim the glory of God, and the nations will bring their offerings to Zion, the holy mountain. Some of the foreigners will even be priests and Levites (66:18–21)!

In short, what is purposed in Exodus 19:6 for the people of God is shown to have failed because of their sins. The people's sins involve not only their rejection of the Holy One of Israel but also their corruption and their lack of knowledge and understanding. Spectacularly, their sin is likened to making a covenant with death (Isa. 28:15). Accordingly, they are unable to fulfill their role as God's holy priesthood. But their covenant with death will eventually be annulled (v. 18). A reversal of the condition of God's people is gloriously heightened from chapter 40 on (with a preview in 2:1–4). It is made possible by God through redemption and the Suffering Servant, who is also the Holy One of Israel. In fact, the Servant himself is a covenant given to the people and a light to the nations (42:6; 49:6). God's people will become holy and empowered to fulfill their intended role as a kingdom of priests. The ministry of the Suffering Servant is transferred to God's people,[21] and the nations will see the righteousness of God's holy people and the glory of their kings (62:1–12).

JEREMIAH

The structural shape of Jeremiah is somewhat of an enigma. John Bright notes that the book comprises a "hopeless hodgepodge thrown together without any discernible principle of arrangement at all."[22]

20. Bible quotations in this essay are from the ESV, unless otherwise indicated.
21. Anizor and Voss, *Representing Christ*, 41.
22. John Bright, *Jeremiah*, AB 21 (Garden City, NY: Doubleday, 1965), lvi.

Leslie Allen likens the book to "an old English country house, originally built and then added to in the Regency period, augmented with Victorian wings, and generally refurbished throughout the Edwardian years."[23] Indeed, "the structure of the book of Jeremiah, while clear in some respects, is finally something of a puzzle."[24] Barring the difficulties, there is a long-standing consensus that a division occurs at the end of chapter 24, with chapter 25 functioning as the hinge to the second half of the book.[25] To a large extent, the two major segments (ch. 2–24 and 26–51) are distinguishable. The first consists mostly of poems, indictments, and laments on Judah or Jerusalem. The second includes a hopeful unit in chapters 30–33 (often called the Book of Consolation), oracles against the nations, and narratives concerning the final days of Jerusalem. Also, most scholars agree that chapters 1 and 52 function as the prologue and the epilogue, respectively.[26] These chapters frame the book of Jeremiah with a siege motif. What begins as a prophetic vision of the siege of Jerusalem (1:15–16) becomes a narrated reality at the close of the book (52:1–30).

For the most part, Jeremiah is a prophet of doom for Judah. Rather than becoming a holy nation and a kingdom of priests, Judah, because of its sinfulness, has become a curse for the nations (Jer. 24:9; 26:6; 29:18), who also incur the wrath of God (ch. 46–51). But Jeremiah is also a prophet of hope. The Book of Consolation speaks of a future in which a new covenant will be made between YHWH and his people. The people and the city of God will be healed and restored in those days, and such restoration will be renowned among the nations (33:9). These texts look forward to a righteous Branch of David who will execute justice and righteousness. Here we see the development of a perpetual Davidic kingship and an expanded Levitical priesthood:

23. Leslie C. Allen, *Jeremiah: A Commentary*, OTL (Louisville: Westminster John Knox, 2008), 11.

24. Terence E. Fretheim, *Jeremiah*, SHBC 15 (Macon, GA: Smyth & Helwys, 2002), 17.

25. Most scholars are aligned on this delimitation. William L. Holladay breaks his magisterial two-volume commentary between chapters 1–25 and 26–52: *Jeremiah: A Commentary on the Book of the Prophet Jeremiah, Chapters 1–25*, ed. Paul D. Hanson, Hermeneia (Minneapolis: Fortress, 1986); *Jeremiah 2: A Commentary on the Book of the Prophet Jeremiah, Chapters 26–52*, ed. Paul D. Hanson, Hermeneia (Minneapolis: Fortress, 1989).

26. See, e.g., Allen, *Jeremiah*, 12–14; Robert P. Carroll, *Jeremiah: A Commentary* (Philadelphia: Westminster John Knox, 1986), 86–88; and Patrick D. Miller, "The Book of Jeremiah," *NIB* 6:570–72.

> In those days and at that time I will cause a righteous Branch to spring up for David, and he shall execute justice and righteousness in the land. In those days Judah will be saved, and Jerusalem will dwell securely. And this is the name by which it will be called: "The LORD is our righteousness."
>
> For thus says the LORD: David shall never lack a man to sit on the throne of the house of Israel, and the Levitical priests shall never lack a man in my presence to offer burnt offerings, to burn grain offerings, and to make sacrifices forever. . . .
>
> As the host of heaven cannot be numbered and the sands of the sea cannot be measured, so I will multiply the offspring of David my servant, and the Levitical priests who minister to me. (33:15–18, 22)

As in Isaiah, here we see God as the agent of transformation for his people (cf. "I will cause" and "I will multiply" in vv. 15 and 22). In the future, God's people will know the law because God will have put it in their minds and written it on their hearts (31:33). They will fear God with singleness of heart and action (32:39). Likewise, the subsequent oracles against the nations speak of a restoration of the nations (Egypt, Moab, Ammon, and Elam).

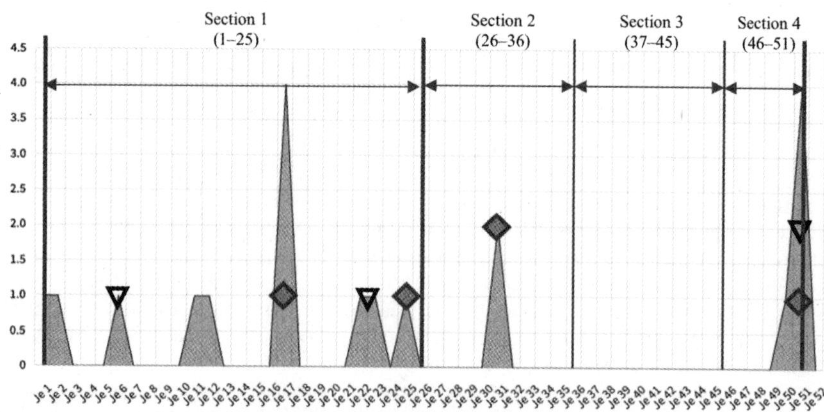

Figure 8.4. Occurrences of Words with the Root *qdš* in the Major Sections of Jeremiah

The triangular peaks (some with a truncated top) in figure 8.4 identify the nineteen *qdš* words in Jeremiah. Most of these words are used negatively and appear in Jeremiah 2–25, where we find indictments of Jerusalem and YHWH's judgments.[27] These chapters show us that the priesthood is clearly defunct and decadent (2:8, 26; 4:9). The recurring phrase "from prophet to priest" also emphasizes the failure of Israel's spiritual leaders; it appears primarily in the first half of Jeremiah (6:13; 8:10; 14:18; 23:11, 33; 26:7–18). The high peaks of chapters 17 and 51 depict Jerusalem's profaning of the Sabbath and its invasion. The use of these words in their immediate contexts aligns well with the macrostructural shape of Jeremiah.

In figure 8.4, the diamond-shaped markers ◆ identify the holy habitation (i.e., the hill or sanctuary) of YHWH that the nations seek to defile. Except for Jeremiah 17:12 and 31:23, where YHWH's holy habitation is highly exalted, all references to the sanctuary or hill express human violation of YHWH's holy place. In other words, Zion, God's holy habitation, is not a place of peace or blessing for the nations; rather, it is a place of warfare and curses. A number of *qdš* words describe the consecration of people for battle or destruction (marked by the inverted hollow triangles ▽ in fig. 8.4: see 6:4; 22:7; 51:27, 28). Noted above, the main place where hope is sustained for Israel's priesthood is in the Book of Consolation (33:17–22).

In sum, Jeremiah shows us that the people of God are an unholy nation and their priesthood and influence on the nations are defunct. God's holy hill is portrayed as a place of warfare. Words linked to the root *qdš* within negative contexts occur primarily in the first half of Jeremiah. Nonetheless, like Isaiah, we find hope in a small number of texts (e.g., in the Book of the Consolation), which highlight Israel as God's chosen and treasured people (32:38–41). We also see the future transformation of God's people through the messianic figure called the Branch, who will enact God's righteousness and justice. For the people of Judah, Jeremiah shows us that God will heal their holy city, restore their fortunes, and cleanse the guilty of their sin (33:6–7). Jeremiah

27. Jer. 1:5; 2:3; 6:4; 11:15; 12:3; 17:12, 22, 23, 24, 27; 22:7; 23:9; 25:30; 31:23, 40; 50:29; 51:5, 27, 28, 51. The negative contexts also appear in the last three chapters, where we see Babylon rejecting the Holy One of Israel and invading Jerusalem.

offers the promise of perpetual kingship and immeasurable priesthood that clearly resonates with the Exodus vision.

EZEKIEL

More consensus exists in the academic community concerning Ezekiel's structural shape. While the book can be divided into two main halves (ch. 1–24 and 25–48),[28] we can view it in four main parts, with two parts in each half: Ezekiel's call (ch. 1–3) and prophecies against Judah and Jerusalem (ch. 4–24) in the first half, together with oracles against the nations (ch. 25–32) and visions of hope and restoration concerning the temple and the people of God (ch. 33–48) in the second half.[29] The book may also be organized around three visions in which God's glory is manifested (1:1–3:15; 8–11; and 40–48).[30] But the repeated recognition formula "know that I am YHWH," which highlights the knowledge of God, is distinctively Ezekielian.[31] This formula is expressed in both contexts of disaster and restoration and is applied to Judah (or Israel) and the foreign nations.[32] Occurring in about eighty verses across the book (except in the call of Ezekiel and the vision of restoration in ch. 40–48),[33] the formula is used in settings of dispersion and destruction, inviting Judah and the nations to know God.[34]

This relationship between Judah and the nations in connection to holiness in Ezekiel is pertinent for our purposes. Historically and theo-

---

28. For instance, see the two separate volumes in the NICOT and Hermeneia series. Walther Zimmerli, *Ezekiel 1: A Commentary on the Book of the Prophet Ezekiel, Chapters 1–24*, Hermeneia (Philadelphia: Fortress, 1988); *Ezekiel 2: A Commentary on the Book of the Prophet Ezekiel, Chapters 25–48*, Hermeneia (Philadelphia: Fortress, 1988); Daniel I. Block, *The Book of Ezekiel: Chapters 1–24*, NICOT (Grand Rapids: Eerdmans, 1997); *The Book of Ezekiel: Chapters 25–48*, NICOT (Grand Rapids: Eerdmans, 1998).
29. Lamar Eugene Cooper Sr., *Ezekiel: An Exegetical and Theological Exposition of Holy Scripture*, NAC 17 (Nashville: Holman, 1994), 17.
30. Margaret S. Odell, *Ezekiel*, SHBC 16 (Macon, GA: Smyth & Helwys, 2005), 1; Zimmerli, *Ezekiel 1*, 28.
31. Apart from Ezekiel, Exodus uses this formulaic phrase as well (see Exod. 6:7; 7:5, 17; 8:22; 10:1–2; 14:4, 18; 16:12; 29:46).
32. Zimmerli finds fifty-four instances of the pure form of the expression, "I am YHWH," and about seventy-eight instances where the phrase is found with a finite verb, noun, participle, or prepositional phrase (Zimmerli, *Ezekiel 1*, 37–38).
33. In contrast, this phrase (or a close parallel) occurs only four times in Isaiah (45:3; 49:23, 26; 60:16) and just twice in Jeremiah (9:23; 24:7).
34. This formulaic expression is elsewhere found with some frequency in the book of Exodus, in similar contexts of divine action (judgment or restoration, directed at Israel or a foreign nation). See Exod. 6:7; 7:5, 17; 8:22; 10:2; 14:4, 18; 16:12; 29:46; 31:13.

logically, Israel was grounded on four pillars: (1) YHWH's covenant with Israel, (2) YHWH's covenant with David, (3) YHWH's residence in Jerusalem, and (4) YHWH's ownership of the land.[35] The people were strongly convinced of an "inseparable bond among national patron deity (Yahweh), territory (land of Canaan), and people (nation of Israel)."[36] In Ezekiel these pillars are all apparently broken. As with Isaiah and Jeremiah, Ezekiel's prophecies explain how Judah has acted more wickedly than the nations (5:5–8; 11:12) and has to be broken (5:14–16). Judah is clearly an unholy nation. Eventually rejected by YHWH, without land, and scattered among the nations, Judah's honor among the nations will be as good as her kingdom—gone! The Exodus vision is clearly in crisis.

What is different in Ezekiel (in comparison to Jeremiah) is the presentation of YHWH's *determination* to vindicate his holiness and to restore the temple and the priesthood. From a macrostructural view of Ezekiel, this determination is heightened in chapters 33–39 and 40–48. In these chapters, Ezekiel notes that YHWH will turn to his people and make an everlasting covenant of peace with them (34:35; 37:26; cf. 20:9, 14, 22) and take away their reproach (34:29–30). These remarkable promises serve to vindicate YHWH's holy name, which has been profaned among the nations (36:16–38; 39:25). Daniel Block points out that the central focus of the message of hope in Ezekiel 36:16–38 (esp. v. 32) is the vindication of God's reputation rather than the deliverance of Israel.[37] As we have seen in Jeremiah 31:31–34, YHWH will accomplish this transformation of a new covenant by cleansing his people and giving them a new heart and spirit so that they can walk according to his statutes and laws (Ezek. 36:26–28).[38]

The vindication of YHWH's holiness by judging, sanctifying, and restoring Judah will result in people knowing YHWH as God (Ezek. 37:27–28). Hence, *holiness and the knowledge of God are inseparable* (38:16, 23).[39] Put differently, theodicy lies at the heart of Ezekiel. The heart of theodicy is the holiness of God, and the effect of theodicy is

35. Block, *Book of Ezekiel: Chapters 1–24*, 8.
36. Block, *Book of Ezekiel: Chapters 1–24*, 7.
37. Block, *Book of Ezekiel: Chapters 25–48*, 343.
38. Zimmerli, *Ezekiel 2*, 249.
39. God's jealousy for his reputation is "fueled not by an exploitative need to dominate but by ardor for the well-being of the object" (Block, *Book of Ezekiel: Chapters 1–24*, 13).

the knowledge of YHWH and how he relates to his people (39:21–23, 28). In Ezekiel this determination and this restoration are sustained from chapter 33 onward and envisioned for a future time.

Lexically, one can find 107 instances of *qdš* in Ezekiel, and their distribution is tilted toward the end of the book.[40] In figure 8.5, we see that most of these occurrences are concentrated in chapter 33 onward, in alignment with the positive shift in the macrostructure of the book.

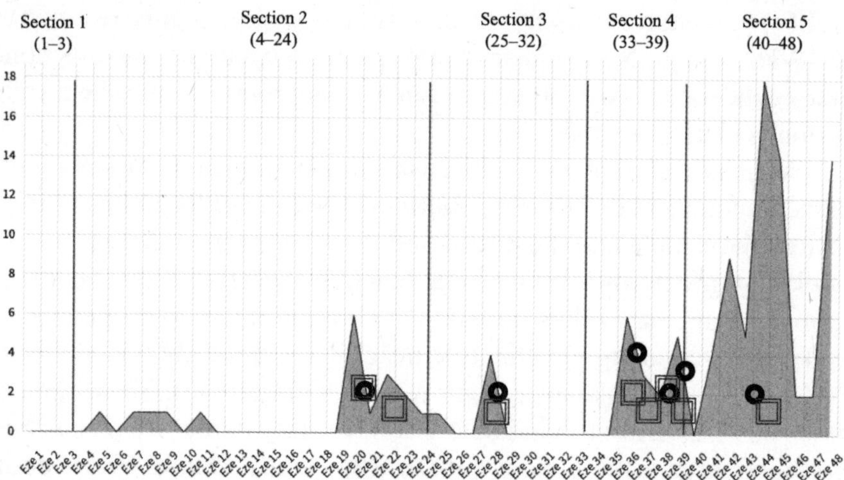

Figure 8.5. Occurrences of Words with the Root *qdš* in the Major Sections of Ezekiel

In addition, more than half of the relevant words refer to places or objects associated with the cultus (e.g., the sanctuary, the holy mountain, the chambers, and the holy of holies).[41] The higher frequency of such words within Ezekiel 40–48 comports with these chapters' focus on the restoration of the Jerusalem temple, worship, and the priesthood. It also suggests that Israel's holiness and priestly functions are critical in Ezekiel's telos.

---

40. Ezek. **5:11**; **7:24**; **8:6**; **9:6**; **11:16**; 20:12, 20, 39, **40**, 41; **21:2[7]**; **22:8**, **26**; **23:38**, **39**; **24:21**; **25:3**; **28:14**, **18**, 22, 25; 36:20, 21, 22, 23, **38**; **37:26**, **28**; 38:16, 23; 39:7, 25, 27; **41:4**, **21**, **23**; **42:13**, **14**, **20**; 43:7, 8, **12**, **21**; **44:1**, **5**, **7**, **8**, **9**, **11**, **13**, **15**, **16**, **19**, 23, 24, **27** [2x]; **45:1**, **2**, **3** [2x], **4** [3x], **6**, **7** [2x], **18**; **46:19**, 20; **47:12**, 19; **48:8**, **10**, 11, **12**, **14**, **18** [2x], **20**, **21** [3x], 28. Bold references are places or objects associated with the cultus.
41. See the references in bold above.

Words related to cultic places and objects aside, we find references to God's holiness and his holy name concentrated within Ezekiel 33–39. Such references are marked by black rings **O** in figure 8.5 (20:39, 41; 28:22, 25; 36:20, 22, 23 [2x]; 38:16, 23; 39:7, 25, 27; 43:7, 8). Furthermore, words associated with holiness and words associated with knowledge, especially with the nations as the subject, appear in the same areas of the book (20:12, 20; 22:26; 28:22; 36:23, 38; 37:28; 38:16, 23; 39:7; 44:23). Such references are marked by hollow squares in figure 8.5.

These observations suggest that the distribution of *qdš* is closely linked to the macrostructural shape of the book. If Ezekiel 33–39 captures the determination of YHWH to fulfill his purposes for his people (linking earlier chapters of judgment to later chapters of restoration), then these chapters, which focus on the knowledge of God and his holiness, are at the heart of the book of Ezekiel. The Babylonian captivity, the destruction of Jerusalem, the scattering of the people of God, and their subsequent restoration all serve to vindicate YHWH's holiness.

While we see a defunct priesthood that disregards the difference between the profane and the holy in the first half of Ezekiel (22:26), the priests eventually teach God's people the difference between the two and show them how to distinguish between the clean and the unclean (44:23). The restored people also live righteously by the agency of God's Spirit and his sanctification (20:12; 37:28). Before chapter 33, Israel's priests are portrayed as wicked (7:26) and as abusers of the law (22:26). The latter chapters depict them positively and as ministering in the new temple (43:18–19, 24, 27). This depiction reaches a high point at the end of the book, in 48:11, where the consecrated priests, the sons of Zadok, are said to remain faithful to YHWH even when the rest fall into apostasy.

Beginning especially in chapter 33, Ezekiel looks forward to the people of God becoming a holy nation and a kingdom of priests through divine determination and action so that the nations can know YHWH. In this way, Ezekiel makes sense of the experience and the horrors of the exile and maintains the vision of Exodus 19:6 for the people of God.

BOOK OF THE TWELVE

Although the Minor Prophets consist of twelve independent books, scholars have long viewed these books as a unified collection. Since the

1990s, several studies have appeared analyzing various catchwords (e.g., "the LORD roars from Zion" in Joel 3:16 and Amos 1:2) and repeated motifs across consecutive books of the Twelve. James Nogalski's works, for instance, have sparked a lot of interest in the redactional shaping of the individual books.[42] Many have already observed how the Twelve is framed with the motif of marriage as a metaphorical expression of YHWH's covenantal relationship with his people (cf. Hos. 1–3; Mal. 2:14–16).[43] A theological metanarrative can also be perceived across the collection. Paul House has argued that "the Twelve are structured in a way that demonstrates the sin of Israel and the nations, the punishment of the sin, and the restoration of both from that sin."[44] The three stages of sin, punishment, and restoration can be generalized in the following way: (1) Hosea, Amos, Obadiah, Jonah, Micah, and especially Joel clarify the sins of Israel, Judah, and the world; (2) Nahum, Habakkuk, and Zephaniah spell out the punishment that the nations and Judah will face, especially on the day of YHWH; and (3) Haggai, Zechariah, and Malachi capture the historical return of God's people and the rebuilding of God's house. These latter three books also prequel the final restoration of God's people through the work of a messianic figure (esp. in Zechariah). At the end of the Twelve, Malachi shows that Israel's full restoration remains in the future.

No hard evidence exists for an intentional macrostructural shaping of the Twelve, nor does a clear consensus exist on House's interpretation currently.[45] What we can say is that the Twelve follows a loose (rather than an absolute) narratival trajectory that traces Israel's

42. James D. Nogalski, *Literary Precursors to the Book of the Twelve*, BZAW 217 (Berlin: De Gruyter, 1993); *Redactional Processes in the Book of the Twelve*, BZAW 218 (Berlin: De Gruyter, 1993); Paul R. House, *The Unity of the Twelve*, BLS 27 (Sheffield: Sheffield Academic, 2009); James D. Nogalski and Marvin A. Sweeney, eds., *Reading and Hearing the Book of the Twelve*, SymS 15 (Atlanta: SBL, 2000); Paul L. Redditt and Aaron Schart, eds., *Thematic Threads in the Book of the Twelve*, BZAW 325 (Berlin: De Gruyter, 2003).

43. See, e.g., Jason T. Lecureux, *The Thematic Unity of the Book of the Twelve*, HBM 41 (Sheffield: Sheffield Phoenix, 2012), 11–12; Marvin A. Sweeney, "Sequence and Interpretation in the Book of the Twelve," in Nogalski and Sweeney, *Reading and Hearing*, 49–64; and John D. W. Watts, "A Frame for the Book of the Twelve: Hosea 1–3 and Malachi," in Nogalski and Sweeney, *Reading and Hearing*, 209–17.

44. House, *The Unity of the Twelve*, 68.

45. Many scholars today reject an overarching macrostructural logic, opting instead for an anthological approach or neither. See the first two essays in Heiko Wenzel, ed., *The Book of the Twelve: An Anthology of Prophetic Books or the Result of Complex Redactional Processes?*, OSJCB 4 (Göttingen: Vandenhoeck & Ruprecht, 2018).

and Judah's sin, destruction, and future restoration, from preexilic to postexilic settings.[46]

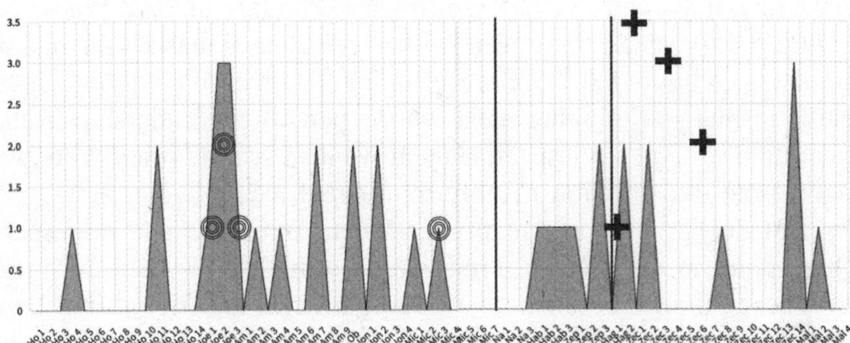

Figure 8.6. Occurrences of Words with the Root *qdš* in the Major Sections of the Twelve

As shown in figure 8.6, about thirty-five instances of *qdš* can be found in the Twelve, with a spread across the corpus.[47] On first sight, no significant distributional peculiarity draws our attention. About half of these occurrences refer to places or objects associated with the cultus. There are only seven verbal forms, and six of them are associated with the consecration of people for battle, a fast, or a sacrifice (Joel 1:14; 2:15, 16; 3:9; Mic. 3:5; Zeph. 1:7). These references (marked with rings ◎ in fig. 8.6) are all found in the context of YHWH's judgment and are located mostly in the first half of the Twelve.

What is more interesting is the characterization of the priesthood in the Twelve, which is overwhelmingly negative. For example, Israel's priests are always depicted as wicked in Hosea (4:4, 6, 9; 5:1; 6:9; 10:5). In Joel all priest-referring verses portray them as mourning (1:9, 13; 2:17). Likewise, references to priests in Amos, Micah, and

46. Like Isaiah, the Twelve skips over the exilic period. Habakkuk sees the Babylonian captivity as an impending event, and Zephaniah highlights the destruction of Jerusalem in view of the day of YHWH. Haggai begins with the exile as a past event.

47. In the following list, references marked in bold are associated with the cultus or the sanctuary: Hos. 4:14; 11:9, 12; Joel 1:14; **2:1**, 15, 16; 3:9, **17**; Amos 2:7; 4:2; **7:9**, **13**; Obad. **16**, **17**; Jonah 2:4, **7**; Mic. **1:2**; 3:5; Hab. 1:12; **2:20**; 3:3; Zeph. 1:7; 3:4, **11**; Hag. **2:12**; Zech. **2:12**, **13**; **8:3**; 14:5, 20, **21**; Mal. **2:11**.

Zephaniah are all negative. The priests are described as murderers, bribe takers, and idolaters, who profane what is holy (Amos 7:10; Mic. 3:11; Zeph. 1:4; 3:4). At the end of the Twelve, the postexilic priesthood remains problematic (Mal. 1:6).

Structurally, however, the postexilic references to priests in the books of Haggai and Zechariah differ starkly. Only in these places do we find positive depictions of Judah's priests. I have marked them with plus signs in figure 8.6.[48] We see specific references to a Zadokite high priest, Joshua son of Jehozadak, who is part of the leadership in the restoration of God's house. In Haggai we also see the priests' knowledge of the transmission of holy things (1:1, 12, 14; 2:2, 4, 11, 12, 13). But Zechariah's presentation of Joshua is unique and represents a high point in the Twelve. First, we see a high priest who is sinful but whose iniquity is taken away. His garments are filthy,[49] but they are replaced with pure vestments (3:3–5).[50] Again, God is the agent of transformation. Conditioned upon obedience, Joshua is promised the rule of God's house and courts, and amazingly, he is given an "enduring role" in the heavenly courts (v. 7).[51]

Second, we find messianic overtones in Zechariah in connection to royal and priestly functions. The messianic title "Branch" (Isa. 4:2; 11:1; Jer. 23:5; 33:15; Ezek. 17:22–24; Zech. 3:8; 6:12) describes the messianic king as one from the line of David, who brings about human flourishing with his powerful, victorious, and righteous rule (esp. Jer. 23:5; 33:15).[52] Consider the following two passages in Zechariah:

> Hear now, O Joshua the high priest, you and your friends who sit before you, for they are men who are a sign: behold, I will

48. Consider the following references to priests in the Twelve, especially the positive references, which are in bold: Hos. 4:4, 6, 9; 5:1; 6:9; Joel 1:9, 13; 2:17; Amos 7:10; Mic. 3:11; Zeph. 1:4; 3:4; Hag. **1:1, 12, 14**; **2:2, 4, 11, 12, 13**; Zech. **3:1, 8**; **6:11, 13**; 7:3, 5; Mal. 1:6; 2:1, 7.

49. Perhaps with excrement. See *BHS*'s marginal note in 2 Kings 18:27. George L. Klein, *Zechariah: An Exegetical and Theological Exposition of Holy Scripture*, NAC 21B (Nashville: B&H, 2008), 119.

50. If the high priest ministers in sin and filth, in contravention to Levitical law (Lev. 22:3), how much more will the rest of the priests and the people live in sin! The filthiness of Joshua son of Jehozadak (of "Jeshua" in Ezra 2:2 and Neh. 7:7; cf. 2 Kings 25:18 and 1 Chron. 40–41) is the basis of Satan's accusation in Zech. 3:1–2 (Klein, *Zechariah*, 114).

51. Mark J. Boda, *The Development and Role of Biblical Traditions in Zechariah*, vol. 2 of *Exploring Zechariah*, ANEM 17 (Atlanta: SBL, 2017), 65–66.

52. Andrew E. Hill, *Haggai, Zechariah, Malachi: An Introduction and Commentary*, TOTC 28 (Downers Grove, IL: IVP Academic, 2012), 151–52.

> bring my servant the Branch [*ṣemaḥ*]. For behold, on the stone that I have set before Joshua, on a single stone with seven eyes, I will engrave its inscription, declares the Lord of hosts, and I will remove the iniquity of this land in a single day. In that day, declares the Lord of hosts, every one of you will invite his neighbor to come under his vine and under his fig tree. (3:8–10)

> And say to him, "Thus says the Lord of hosts, 'Behold, the man whose name is the Branch [*ṣemaḥ*]: for he shall branch out [*ṣāmaḥ*] from his place, and he shall build the temple of the Lord. It is he who shall build the temple of the Lord and shall bear royal honor, and shall sit and rule on his throne. And there shall be a priest on his throne, and the counsel of peace shall be between them both.' . . . And those who are far off shall come and help to build the temple of the Lord. And you shall know that the Lord of hosts has sent me to you. And this shall come to pass, if you will diligently obey the voice of the Lord your God." (6:12–13, 15)

These passages highlight both a distinctive person (not Joshua), called the Branch, who will rule and build the temple, and the inclusion of other people (near and far) to build the temple.[53] A separate individual (a priest) is on the throne.[54] We see a supernatural removal of iniquity that will happen "in one day." The outward effect of this restoration will impact Judah's immediate neighbors and foreigners from all nations (cf. Zech. 8:3, 22–23).[55] Also, Zechariah paints an eschatological image that is remarkably centripetal, with Zion at the center. A cleansing of sin will take place (13:1), and God's people will once again be recognized as God's own possession (v. 9). God will rule victoriously and universally, and the nations will come to his holy mountain to worship him (14:9–19).

53. Boda, *Development and Role*, 76.
54. Boda, *Development and Role*, 59–60, notes that throughout the monarchical period, the king, the priest, and the prophet were key functionaries in the sociological structure of Judah (e.g., Jer. 37). But the relationships between them were not constant and were strained toward the end of the Southern Kingdom.
55. Joyce G. Baldwin, *Haggai, Zechariah, and Malachi: An Introduction and Commentary*, TOTC (Downers Grove, IL: IVP Academic, 1972), 137.

At the end of Zechariah, we see the inscription "Holy to the Lord" on the bells of horses (Zech. 14:20).[56] Surprisingly, every pot in Jerusalem and Judah shall be holy to the Lord of hosts (v. 21). Here we see a "new ritual condition of Jerusalem and Judah in which everything is consecrated for worship."[57] This expansion of the ministerial conditions fits remarkably well with the Exodus vision. From the vantage point of postexilic Israel, the Twelve, like the other books of the Latter Prophets, sustain the hope of the Exodus vision.

CONCLUSION

In this essay, we have studied the motif of holiness in the Latter Prophets in light of the Exodus vision (19:6). Our approach has been to track words connected to holiness and the priesthood within their macrostructural-rhetorical contexts. We find that the occurrences of these words largely follow the macrostructural shaping and trajectory of books within this corpus. Although these books generally indict Israel and Judah for their failure to be holy and their defunct priesthood, we repeatedly find highly positive texts that keep the Exodus vision in perspective (esp. Isa. 61–66; Jer. 30–33; Ezek. 33–39; and Zech. 3, 6, 9–14). Repeatedly, we see the motif of God's sinful people transformed by God himself. God's people simply cannot be holy on their own. A distinct set of texts also identifies a servant-like, messianic Branch, through whom a transformed state of affairs—the Exodus vision—will be fulfilled.

In Isaiah the holiness of God's people is brought about only through the redemption of the Suffering Servant and the Holy One of Israel. God's people are then enabled to fulfill their intended covenantal roles as members of a holy nation and a kingdom of priests. Jeremiah looks forward to future days when the Davidic kingship and the Levitical priesthood are perpetual. The people of God will have a new heart to obey the laws of God written therein. The hope of holiness will be accomplished by the messianic Branch. Ezekiel shows us YHWH's determination for his people to fulfill their Exodus vision—a determination that includes the captivity, the destruction of Jerusalem, the

---

56. Note that horses are considered unclean in the OT.

57. Mark J. Boda, *Haggai, Zechariah*, NIVAC (Grand Rapids: Zondervan Academic, 2004), 529. The only other place in the OT where "Holy to the Lord" is inscribed is Exod. 28:36–38. But in Exodus, only utensils made for the tabernacle can be used in the sacrifices.

scattering of his people, and their subsequent restoration, all of which vindicates his holiness. The latter chapters of Ezekiel depict the people of God positively, ministering in the new temple (43:18–19, 24, 27). The effect is that the nations know YHWH. In the Twelve, especially in Zechariah, we observe eschatological imagery with Zion at the center. Through a messianic figure called the Branch, there will be cleansing of sin and God's people will be reestablished as his own possession (Zech. 13:1, 9). The nations will be drawn to God in worship at his holy mountain (Zech. 14:9–19).

The theological implications of the above study can be crystallized in the following three points: (1) Repetitions in the structural-thematic shaping of the Latter Prophets highlight the continuity of the Exodus vision of what it means to be a kingdom of priests and a holy nation. We now see with greater definition how it is accomplished. In other words, the contours of this vision are clarified by the Latter Prophets by detailing what it means to fail as God's people, nation, and priests. Yet despite that failure, there is a recurring depiction of God rising to vindicate his holiness, especially through the Branch, the messianic Servant-King, who will remove the iniquity of God's people and transform them to live righteously and fulfill the Exodus vision.

(2) The previous point means that the NT's understanding of Jesus as the Messiah is formidable and cogent. Jesus is understood as the Branch, the Redeemer, the Holy One of Israel, and the righteous Priest-King, all of which are left ambiguous in the Latter Prophets (Mark 15:32; Luke 1:35; Heb. 7:26).[58] Paul and the author of Hebrews shows that these titles refer to "Jesus Christ, who gave himself for us to redeem us from all lawlessness and to purify for himself a people for his own possession who are zealous for good works" (Acts 13:35; Titus 2:13–14; Heb. 7:21–28). Christ vindicates the holiness of God and redeems a people to be God's chosen possession, a royal priesthood, and a holy nation (1 Peter 2:9–10). Through Jesus Christ, the Exodus vision is realized. We find that Christ has "ransomed people for God from every tribe and language and people and nation, and [he has] made them a kingdom and priests to our God, and they shall reign

58. Consider other NT references in Rom. 12:1–2; Phil. 2:17; Heb. 10:19–25; 13:1–3; Rev. 1:5–6, 13–18; and 20:4–6.

on the earth" (Rev. 5:9–10). In other words, we find a high degree of continuity between the OT and the NT.

(3) The christological interpretation and the continuity noted above mean that we can now read ourselves into the story of God's people and the Exodus vision. Our sinfulness, pride, selfishness, covenantal unfaithfulness, empty worship, and outright acts of wickedness mirror what we see in the Latter Prophets. Like Joshua the high priest, with filthy garments (Zech. 3:3), our righteousness is as good as filthy rags (Isa. 64:6). Apart from God's transformative work through his Holy One, we are unable to rid ourselves of this predicament. But God is determined to purge us of our sin for his name's sake and for our flourishing. He remains patient with his people and has offered the Servant to secure the Exodus vision. Our redemption in Jesus Christ, our adoption as God's children, and our sanctification in the Spirit (John 16:8) show us how we can truly become God's treasured possession and holy "nation." Through Christ, we also reverse our futile worship and service. Accordingly, we can begin to spread the love and the knowledge of the Holy One (Hos. 6:6; 2 Cor. 2:14), thereby fulfilling the originally intended priestly role of the people of God—the temple of God—through whom the world can come to know him and flourish in him.

Part 3

THEMATIC ANALYSES

CHAPTER 9

HOLINESS AND ATONEMENT IN THE OLD TESTAMENT

VICTOR P. HAMILTON

INTRODUCTION

"Christ has for sin atonement made" is the opening phrase in Elisha Hoffman's "What a Wonderful Savior," penned in the 1890s. Philip Bliss's "'Man of Sorrows,' What a Name" concludes one of its stanzas with the words "Full atonement, can it be? Hallelujah! What a Savior!" Augustus Toplady's famous "Rock of Ages" contains the words "all for sin could not atone, thou must save and thou alone." And who can forget these words from Charles Wesley's majestic "Arise, My Soul Arise": "His blood atoned for all our race, and sprinkles now the throne of grace"? All four of these hymns employ either the noun *atonement* or the verb *atone*.

Each of these great hymns celebrates the atonement made possible by and through Jesus Christ. What precisely do we mean when we use the word *atonement*? Here is a working definition: the reconciliation and repair of the once sin-damaged relationship between God and humans, made possible by the substitutionary death of Jesus on the cross.

This essay explores how the concept of atonement does not appear as a new concept on the pages of the NT but rather as one deeply embedded in the OT. If nothing else, atonement language should tell us that. The word "atonement" appears in the NIV 105 times, all of which are in the OT except for three (Rom. 3:25; Heb. 2:17; 9:5). Furthermore, the majority of those 102 occurrences (i.e., 89%) appear in three OT books: Exodus (17x), Leviticus (56x), and Numbers (18x). The question this essay will address is this: Could an ancient Israelite sing along with Charles Wesley, "O for a heart to praise my God, a heart from sin set free"? If the answer is yes, how so?

ATONEMENT THROUGH SACRIFICE

Sacrifice for sin and divine forgiveness in the OT are available only to the Israelite, he or she who is a part of God's chosen family. Not a word exists about atonement or forgiveness for any Philistine or Moabite. In other words, *sacrifice is not a way of establishing a relationship with God.* Rather, it is a means of expressing or remedying an already-existent relationship between God and a person, be that relationship healthy (expressing) or blemished (remedying). The OT sacrificial system, then, deals with what Wesleyans call "sin in believers." If followers of God fall, what steps must be taken to restore an unbroken fellowship with the Holy One?

A key to answering that question is found in the notion represented by verb *kpr* which we will render as "make atonement for." *Kpr* occurs in the *qal* stem only once in the Bible, with the meaning "cover." That one reference is Genesis 6:14, where God instructs Noah to "coat," "cover," or "smear" the ark with pitch. However, in the *piel* stem, the root (appearing as *kipper*) takes the meaning "make atonement." Does *kipper* mean "rub on" or "rub off"? Is sin *covered*, or is sin *removed*? Based on the Hebrew cognate and the Akkadian *kuppuru*, "rub off" seems more likely. Every occurrence of the Akkadian *kuppuru* (that I am aware of) denotes "rub off." Interestingly, the basic stem of this verb in Akkadian (*kapāru*)—like Hebrew *qal kāpar* in Genesis 6:14—means "rub on." Hence, we can say that the often-heard idea that under the old covenant, sin is only covered (from God's eyes), whereas under the new covenant, sin is removed, is an *inaccurate* idea. The two covenants have major differences (and similarities), but this is not one of them.

In favor of the meaning "remove" against "cover," one could also note other verbs with which *kipper* is used in parallel lines. For example, see Jeremiah 18:23: "Do not make atonement for [*kipper*] their crimes, or blot out [*māḥâ*] their sins from your sight" (AT). See also Isaiah 27:9: "By this, then, will Jacob's guilt be atoned for [*kipper*], and this will be the full fruitage of the removal [*sûr*] of his sin" (AT). Note, however, in the case of Jeremiah 18:23 that very similar language surfaces in Nehemiah 4:5 [3:37]: "Do not cover up [*kāsâ*] their guilt or blot out [*māḥâ*] their sins from your sight" (NIV). Thus, at least in this one instance, the Hebrew verb for "blot out" may stand in parallel to both *kipper* ("wipe off") and *kāsâ* ("wipe on").

There is a possible objection against this argument, though, and that is to be found in the Hebrew word for the cover over the ark in the holy of holies. That Hebrew word is *kappōret*, as found in Leviticus 16:2: "Tell your brother Aaron not to come whenever he chooses into the most holy place, behind the curtain in front of the cover [*kappōret*] on the ark" (AT). This noun refers to the golden, sculptured lid for the ark, fashioned with two cherubs facing each other.[1] Phonetic and epigraphic similarities between *kappōret* and *kipper* may suggest some kind of connection between atonement or purgation and the covering of the ark. The challenge for the translator is how best to render the word in a language other than the original Hebrew. The Greek Septuagint translates *kappōret* with *hilastērion*, "instrument of propitiation." The Vulgate reproduces the same word in Latin as *propitiatorium*. As for some of the renderings in English Bible translations, one of the most common is "cover," as in the translations of Brevard Childs and Robert Alter in their Exodus commentaries.[2] This translation is as old as the Targum fragments on Leviticus from Qumran (4QtgLev), with their use of *ksy*ʾ. The NIV extends this rendering with "atonement cover," and the NLT does so too with its "the ark's cover—the place of atonement." Another popular rendering is "mercy seat" (see KJV, NKJV, RSV, NRSV, and the Amplified Bible). The CEV is close with "place of mercy."[3]

The problem with translating this word as "[atonement] cover" or "mercy seat" is that the verb form from which *kappōret* is formed never conveys by itself the notion of "mercy" or "cover." As I have written elsewhere, "To the best of my knowledge, there is no single text that assigns to the *kappōret* an explicit, expiatory function."[4] On the Day of Atonement, the high priest sprinkled blood on this piece of furniture (Lev. 16:15b), so perhaps this object came to be called the *kappōret* because of what it received on that day. If this lid

1. For particulars see Exod. 25:17–22 and 37:6–9.
2. Brevard S. Childs, *The Book of Exodus: A Critical, Theological Commentary*, OTL (Louisville: Westminster John Knox, 2004), 524. Childs is open to translating the Hebrew word as "cover," but in the end opts for "propitiatory." Robert Alter, *The Hebrew Bible: A Translation with Commentary* (New York: Norton, 2019), 318.
3. Not surprisingly, one esteemed Hebraist once threw up his arms on this Hebrew word and declared it untranslatable!
4. Victor P. Hamilton, *Exodus: An Exegetical Commentary* (Grand Rapids: Baker Academic, 2011), 460.

covered anything, then most obviously it was the contents inside the ark. It would have prevented anyone from viewing the ark's contents, whether that be Aaron when he entered the holy of holies on the Day of Atonement or the Kohath Levites when they carried the "most holy" items on their wilderness journey. And as we learn from the story of the Philistine residents of Beth Shemesh, looking into the ark was a deadly affair (1 Sam. 6:19).

At the heart of OT worship is the material found in the book of Leviticus. Leviticus can be divided into two parts (with ch. 27 as an appendix on vow-making):[5]

1. The way to the Holy One, which is by way of
   a. sacrifice (ch. 1–7) and
   b. priesthood (ch. 8–10).
2. The way to holiness, which is by way of
   a. sanitation (ch. 11–16) and
   b. sanctification (ch. 17–26).

Chapters 1–7 can be divided into two subsections. The first is 1:1–6:7[5:26], which primarily spells out the responsibilities of those who bring or present a sacrifice or offering. Note how this section begins: "The LORD called to Moses out of the Tent of Meeting. He said, 'Speak to *the Israelites* and say to *them*, whenever *any of you* brings an offering'" (1:1–2 at, emphasis added). By contrast, the second subsection (6:8[1]–7:38) begins with these words: "The LORD said to Moses: 'Give *Aaron and his sons* this command'" (6:8–9[1–2] NIV, emphasis added). Thus, the instructions in 1:1–6:7 are for the worshiper, whereas the instructions in 6:8–7:38 are for the priestly officiant.

We can draw at least three basic conclusions from this layout of the material in the first seven chapters of Leviticus. First and foremost, at the heart of worship and atonement is sacrifice or offering. This makes worship something that is much more than an "oozy" inner feeling, an emotional high. There is no such thing in the OT as worship that costs God everything but costs the worshiper nothing. "Nothing in my hands

5. The following outline of Leviticus is borrowed from Norman Geisler's *A Popular Survey of the Old Testament* (Grand Rapids: Baker, 1977), 66.

I bring, simply to thy cross I cling"—while perfectly understandable in a Christian understanding of soteriology—is not a concept a person will find in these opening chapters of Leviticus. Second, worshiping and experiencing God's grace is not something done in the privacy of one's home. To be sure, worship at home can indeed be legitimate. (To this day, among observant Jews, the evening meal in the home at Sabbath's start is a holy moment, what one Jewish writer grippingly describes as "a retreat into restorative magic.")[6] But when it comes to an offering or sacrifice, you head for the house of God. Third, worship by way of sacrifice needs a mediator, a priestly, anointed go-between, someone who can do with your offering what you, the donor, cannot do with it. This moves worship beyond a duet arrangement (God and "me") to a trio arrangement (God, a mediator, and "myself" [or ourselves]).

Leviticus 1–5 spells out the details of the five main offerings that constitute the essence of worship under the old covenant. These five are:

1. the burnt offering (ch. 1),
2. the grain or cereal offering (ch. 2),
3. the fellowship offering (ch. 3),
4. the sin offering (4:1–5:13), and
5. the guilt offering (5:14–6:7 [5:14–26]).

When most Christians use the word "sacrifice," they inevitably connect it with sin and sin's elimination. After all, is that not what Jesus's sacrifice of his life is all about? He willingly gave up his life at Calvary as a substitutionary, perfect sacrifice for the salvation of any and all who embrace him. It may then come as a bit of a surprise to some readers to discover that several of the listed sacrifices in the OT have nothing at all or very little to do with atonement. The first three of the above five are nonatonement offerings, with one of them (the burnt offering) maybe marginally related to atonement. It is the last two (the sin and guilt offerings) that are clearly atonement related. I think it is of some import that Leviticus begins not with atonement offerings (nos. 4 and 5) but with nonatonement offerings (nos. 1–3). It is as if Leviticus

6. H. Wouk, *This Is My God: The Jewish Way of Life* (Boston: Little, Brown, & Co., 1988), 46.

begins by assuming that one has a proper and healthy relationship with God, expressed with offerings 1–3. But Leviticus goes on to say, "If you mess up, here's the way (nos. 4 and 5) to fix your relationship and make amends."

What evidence do we have in the biblical text for separating the three sacrifices of Leviticus 1–3 from the two that follow in 4:1–6:7? Let me list five pieces of evidence.

Qorbān

The generic Hebrew term for the sacrifice one brings to God is *qorbān*. It means literally "that which is brought near, presented, offered." The word is a nominal derived from the Hebrew verb *qārab*, which is the verb of choice when one approaches God's sanctuary. Appropriately, the Septuagint translates the Hebrew word as *dōron*, "gift" or "offering." Think, then, of an offering or a sacrifice as a gift given to God for God. The Hebrew word occurs once in transliteration in Mark 7:9–13, where Jesus is involved in a dispute with some Pharisees about their sneaky way of getting around God's commandments in order to follow their own way. He compares their maneuver to a child who uses *qorbān* as a way of getting out of supporting one's (elderly) parents. Jesus says in Mark 7:11–12, "But you say that if a man says to his father or mother, 'Whatever help you might otherwise have received from me is *corban*,' then you no longer let him do anything for his father or mother" (AT). Christians understandably make the prior emphasis on God's gift to us, as in 2 Corinthians 9:15: "Thanks be to God for his unspeakable gift" (AT). But this OT truth compels us to focus on our gift to God.

What we want to notice is how this Hebrew word is distributed over these opening chapters of Leviticus. Here is the breakdown for the verb *qārab*, which often means "draw near, approach," but in the sacrificial context of Leviticus means "offer, present": chapter 1 (7x), chapter 2 (8x), chapter 3 (9x), chapter 4 (2x), chapter 5 (1x), chapter 6 (3x), and chapter 7 (16x) for a total of forty-six times.

One can see easily that the two cognates combined, the verb and the noun, appear much more with the first three offerings than with the last two: fifty-eight times versus eight times, with the fellowship offering standing out and the cereal offering in second place. Hence, we observe that the heavy use of these cognates with the first three offerings, versus its much lesser use with the last two, suggests some distinction between atonement offerings and nonatonement offerings. Perhaps we might be inclined to call the gifts of Leviticus 1–3 "offerings" and those of Leviticus 4–6 "sacrifices."

How *qārab* and *qorbān* are distributed over the opening chapters of Leviticus
Here is the breakdown for the noun *qārab*:
The burnt offering (6x): 1:3 (2x), 10, 14, 7:8 (2x)
The cereal offering (7x): 2:1, 4, 12, 14 (2x); 6:14[7], 20[13]
The fellowship offering (15x): 3:1 (2x), 6, 7 (2x), 12; 7:11, 12 (2x), 13, 14, 16, 18, 25, 29
The sin offering (3x): 4:3, 14; 5:8
The guilt offering (1x): 7:3
Here is the breakdown for the noun *qorbān*:
The burnt offering (4x): 1:3, 10, 14 (2x)
The cereal offering (8x): 2:1 (2x), 4, 5, 7, 13 (2x); 6:20[13]
The fellowship offering (12x): 3:1, 2, 6, 7, 8, 12, 14; 7:13, 14, 15, 16, 29
The sin offering (4x): 4:23, 28, 32; 5:11
The guilt offering (0x)

An Aroma Pleasing to the Lord

The first three sacrifices or offerings reach their climax with the impact they have on God. The particular phrase in view is "an aroma pleasing to the Lord." The Septuagint's translation of "pleasing aroma" is "sweet savor." It occurs ten times with the first three offerings (burnt: 1:9, 13, 17; cereal: 2:2, 9, 12; 6:15, 21; fellowship: 3:5, 16). It appears only once with the last two (sin: 4:31). The last two offerings reach their climax with the impact they have on the donor. The key refrain here is "The priest shall make atonement for him [or them], and he [or they] shall be forgiven." It occurs nine times with the last two offerings (sin: 4:20, 26, 31, 35; 5:10, 13; guilt: 5:16, 18; 6:7). To be sure, the first half of this refrain appears with the burnt offering (1:4), but the telltale second part ("and he [or they] shall be forgiven") is conspicuously absent. It should then be clear that one distinction between the two sets of sacrifices is that the first three seek God's pleasure, whereas the last two seek God's pardon.

Voluntary Versus Mandatory Offerings

None of the first three sacrifices suggest any occasion, any situation, that calls for their offering. They simply begin with something like "If the offering is a burnt offering from the herd," or "When someone brings a grain offering," or "If someone's offering is a fellowship offering." In contrast, the last two sacrifices begin with a specific identification of the misdeed that calls for their offering. The sin offering begins with the words "When anyone sins unintentionally and does what is forbidden in any of the LORD's commands" (Lev. 4:2 NIV). The guilt offering is introduced with this comment: "When a person commits a violation and sins unintentionally in regard to any of the LORD's holy things" (5:15 AT). I will have more to say later about these two important verses, which introduce the last two of the five offerings. What I wish to point out here is that the first three offerings are clearly voluntary and can be brought into YHWH's presence anytime. In contrast, the last two offerings are mandatory. If one commits any sin inadvertently and seeks or desires forgiveness, then this is the one and only path to that outcome. The sin and guilt offerings are not two of several other options available to the suppliant. They are the only options, at least according to Leviticus.

The Donation Versus the Donor

The two sets of offerings are scaled differently. The first three focus on the donation, whereas the last two focus on the donor. Let us use the burnt and sin offerings as examples. Here is the burnt offering: "If the offering is a burnt offering from *the herd*" (Lev. 1:2 at); "If the offering is a burnt offering from *the flock*" (v.10 NIV); "If the offering is a burnt offering of *birds*" (v. 14 AT, emphasis added in all three quotes). By scaling the offerings from larger to smaller creatures, the sacrificial system makes it possible for any person, regardless of means and financial standing, to be able to bring a precious offering to the Lord. More than likely, the cereal offering, which is the only nonanimal, nonblood offering, is for the really poor who do not have even a bird to present. For them, a pinch of fine flour is adequate. By contrast, here is the sin offering: "If *the anointed priest* sins" (4:3 NIV); "If the *whole Israelite community* sins" (v. 13 NIV); "When *a leader* sins" (v. 22 NIV); "If a *member of the community* sins" (v. 27 NIV, emphasis added in all three quotes). The progression is from the most serious offender (a priest) to the least serious offender (a commoner). This last point will lead us into the fifth and final distinction between the two sets of sacrifices.

Blood

All the sacrifices that involve taking the life of an animal or a bird, regardless of their function, have directions about what is to be done with the blood of the slain creature. What we want to notice is that with the sin offering of either the anointed priest or the entire community, there is a much greater distribution of the blood than there is for the sin offering of a leader or commoner. Also, the instructions Leviticus provides for the shedding of the blood are much more detailed for these last two sacrifices than they are for any of the first three. Note Leviticus 4:5–7 (much the same as 4:16–18): "Then the anointed priest shall take some of the bull's blood and carry it into the tent of meeting. He is to . . . sprinkle some of it seven times before the Lord, in front of the curtain of the sanctuary. The priest shall then put some of the blood on the horns of the altar of fragrant incense that is before the Lord" (NIV). Any remaining blood is poured out at the base of the outer altar—that is, the altar of burnt offering. Only here and on the Day of Atonement (16:18) is sacrificial blood dabbed on a part of the inner altar, which is inside the holy place, just in front of the curtain that divides the holy place from the holy of holies, not in the outer courtyard. It is as if Leviticus is saying that the greater the offender, the greater the offense, which calls for a greater use of sacrificial blood if genuine reconciliation between the individual(s) and God is to take place.

We turn our attention now to the two sacrifices mentioned in the Pentateuch that are designed specifically for the atonement of sins. Those two sacrifices are the sin offering (Lev. 4:1–5:13) and the guilt offering (5:14–6:7 [5:14–26]). The translation into English of the two underlying Hebrew terms is open to question. For example, in some instances, an individual is required to bring a "sin" offering when no apparent sin has been committed. Two examples will suffice. The first example is the sin offering required when individuals have completed their tenure as "short-term" Nazirites (Num. 6:14). A second example is the sin offering of the mother who has just given birth to a newborn after she has completed her period of self-imposed isolation (Lev. 12:6–7). In the case of the second example, we read that the priest, on the occasion of her presentation of the offering, is to "make atonement for her" (v. 7 NIV). But tellingly, the phrase "and she shall be forgiven" is absent, for she has no need of forgiveness on this joyous occasion. Perhaps on such occasions it would be better to render the Hebrew word as "purification offering" rather than "sin offering." This insight should indicate to us one basic difference between moral and physical impurity. Moral impurity (as we shall see) is forgiven (*nislāḥ*), whereas physical impurity is purified (*ṭāher*).

When we turn our attention to the introduction of these two sacrifices, one word keeps popping up. That is the word in the phrase "If X sins *unintentionally*." Other translations include "inadvertently" (Complete Jewish Bible), "by accident" (NCV), "unwittingly" (asv and ESV), or "in ignorance" (KJV).[7] To reinforce this element of ignorance or unintentionality, we read the phrase "even though he is unaware of it" three times in conjunction with the sin offering (Lev. 5:2, 3, 4 AT), and twice we read, "when he learns of it" (vv. 3, 4 AT). For the guilt offering, we have the phrase "even though he does not know it" (v. 17 AT). The verb behind this adverbial expression is either *šāgag* or, less frequently in the Torah, *šāgâ*, whose basic meaning is "to err." The expression rendered in English as "unintentionally" is *bišgāgâ*, which comprises the preposition *bə* ("in") prefixed to the noun *šəgāgâ* ("error").

It should be clear from the above discussion that the atonement sacrifices are designed for the forgiveness of unintentional sins. Such sins are due either to ignorance or to negligence. In the case of ignorance, sinners are quite aware of what they have done but are unaware that they have done anything wrong. In the case of negligence, sinners are aware of the seriousness of the law but accidentally violate it. An illustration of the former is Jonathan and his followers eating honey and meat with blood in it (1 Sam. 14:32–34). An illustration of negligence would be an accidental homicide (Num. 35:22–23; Deut. 19:4–6).

7. See Lev. 4:2, 13, 22, 27; 5:15; and 22:14 (NIV: "by mistake"). For a parallel discussion of the sin offering in Num. 15, see vv. 22, 24, 25, 26, 27, 28, and 29.

Both Leviticus and Numbers affirm that if unintentional sinners bring an appropriate offering to the priest, then the priest shall make atonement for them. Note that there is absolutely no concept of self-atonement. One needs a priest, a mediator, and therefore the subject of the Hebrew root *kpr* in Scripture is always a priest. The result of atonement is that sinners are forgiven—but not symbolically forgiven, nor partially forgiven, nor minimally forgiven, nor kind of forgiven—simply *forgiven*. Their sins are blotted out. The Hebrew word for "forgive" in these passages is *sālaḥ* (in the *niphal* [passive] stem). Nobody other than God is ever the subject of this verb in the OT. I would prefer to translate the "and" in "and he shall be forgiven" as "that" ("*that* he shall be forgiven"). Forgiveness is not something we compel God to do by following proper ritual. Forgiveness is a gift of God's grace that flows from his infinitely loving heart, not something divinely automatic as a response to human ritual. Perhaps this is the reason why the prophets railed against those who misunderstood the role of sacrifice as a means of gaining God's favor, regardless of how they were living.

The verb *sālaḥ* for "forgive" is frequent in Leviticus 4–5 (sin offering: 4:20, 26, 31, 35; 5:10, 13; guilt offering: 5:16, 18, 26 [6:7]; 19:22). This verb appears frequently in one other place in the OT, but with one major difference. I refer to Solomon's prayer at the dedication of the temple, recorded in 1 Kings 8 (cf. 2 Chron. 6). Five times Solomon beseeches the Lord to forgive the sin of his people (1 Kings 8:30, 34, 36, 39, 50).[8] What is different is that no mention is made of the need for sacrifice. What is required for forgiveness of sin, however, is candid confession, a turning back to God, and a deeply penitential prayer for mercy. Numbers 14:19 and 20 illustrate that intercession by a godly mediator can move God to forgiveness, even without a corresponding repentance on the part of the sinner(s): "Forgive the sin of these people. . . . The Lord replied, 'I have forgiven them, as you asked'" (NIV).

A related illustration in Scripture is Exodus 32, the infamous golden calf incident. On the heels of gross idolatry, Moses asks God, "But now, please forgive their sin" (v. 32 NIV), again without any summons to the people to own up to their sin and repent of it. What we

8. See also 2 Chron. 6:21, 25, 27, 30, and 39.

want to notice is that the Hebrew Moses uses for "forgive" is not *sālaḥ*, as discussed in the previous paragraph. Rather, it is *tiśśāʾ ḥaṭṭāʾtām*, meaning "carry [away] sin or iniquity." This is a most interesting phrase. When a person is the subject of this phrase, it means something like "be held responsible," which is how the NIV translates the phrase in Leviticus 5:1, 17; 17:16; 19:8; and Numbers 18:1, 23. The NIV's rendering of this expression in Numbers 9:13 is closer to the mark: "They will bear the consequences of their sin." Hebrew words for "sin" refer not only to the trespass itself but to the fallout from those trespasses. Thus, the concept of sin and the wages of sin are conveyed by the same word.

On the other hand, when this same phrase is used with God as the subject, it means "remove sin or iniquity," as in Exodus 32:32.[9] Carrying over the idea of consequence mentioned above, we can say that when God forgives sin(s), he does two things. First, he removes the sin, and second, he removes iniquity. He not only gets rid of the locusts, but he also restores the years of harvest that the locusts have consumed (Joel 2:25). Does God not only forgive the repentant alcoholic, but in addition also eliminate, or at least curb, that addiction so that the individual need not be plagued by his addiction for the remainder of his life? To be sure, sin, as Scripture shows, can exact a high price on a person or community over the long haul. A parade example of this would be King David. Notwithstanding his repentance over his sin against Bathsheba, God still took the life of the newborn child David fathered with Bathsheba, even though David implored his God to spare the life of the child.

There are three places in the OT where a person asks another person for forgiveness using the idiom under discussion:

1. Genesis 50:17, where Joseph's brothers ask him for forgiveness;
2. Exodus 10:17, where a beleaguered Pharaoh asks Moses for forgiveness; and
3. 1 Samuel 15:25, where Saul, a rejected and disobedient king, asks the prophet Samuel for forgiveness.

9. See also Exod. 34:7; Num. 14:18; Isa. 33:24; Hos. 14:2[3]; and Mic. 7:18.

In each case, the person requesting forgiveness is powerless and is throwing himself on the mercy of the person who has the power to forgive. It works that way with God too.

I have been discussing at length atonement for unintentional sin as I spelled out in the discussion on the Levitical code. What about other manifestations of sin? Is not all sin the same? Can we not just keep things simple? What about sins that do not fall into the unintentional category? In simplified form, let me suggest that the OT places sin in three categories. The first two of those are (1) unintentional, accidental sin and (2) intentional, deliberate sin. Here is an illustration to distinguish between the two. One can run a stop sign in two ways: One way is to miss it (unintentionally), as perhaps leaves from a nearby tree hide the sign from a driver's view. Another way is to ignore it (intentionally), as maybe the driver is too hurried to get elsewhere or is preoccupied on a cell phone. Both are wrong and break a law. Both are potentially catastrophic. For both infractions, the driver, if apprehended, must be held accountable. The difference between the two is that only the second instance, choosing deliberately to ignore the stop sign, is evil.

If atonement is offered only for the unintentional sinner, what about those who are guilty of intentional sin? Must such an individual carry his or her sins into eternity unremitted? A clue to the answer to this question is found in the two passages of Leviticus that list specific infractions for which either the sin or the guilt offering is mandated. For the sin offering, the relevant passage is Leviticus 5:1–4. For the guilt offering, the passage is Leviticus 6:1–7 [5:20–26]. These passages clearly indicate that the infractions listed are anything but unintentional. On the contrary, they are very deliberate. For example, the sin offering covers a case in which a person refuses to come forward and deliberately withholds important evidence in some kind of judicial process (5:1). The infractions listed that call for the guilt offering are even more obvious; for example, "if anyone sins . . . by deceiving a neighbor about something entrusted to them or left in their care or about something stolen, or if they cheat their neighbor . . ." (6:2 [5:21] NIV). That is hardly unintentional!

The explanation for how deliberate sins fall under the category of unintentional sins (for which expiation can be made) is as follows. The key lies in a word that occurs only four times in the Pentateuch.

That word is the *hithpael* form of *yādâ*, meaning "confess." Other portions of the OT use words like "repent" or "(re)turn to," along with "confess," but the Torah employs "confess" exclusively. The four relevant occurrences are:

1. Leviticus 5:5, in conjunction with the sin offering;
2. Numbers 5:7, which parallels the account of the guilt offering in Leviticus;
3. Leviticus 16:21, in conjunction with the Day of Atonement;
4. Leviticus 26:40, a portion of Moses's homily.

These four passages are the closest the Torah comes to having a "sinner's prayer." What all these four "confession" passages have in common is that they all occur in a context of intentional sin. I submit that genuine confession and repentance somehow turns intentional sin into unintentional sin, for which atonement can be made. Deliberate sinners are not in trouble with God; rather, unrepentant sinners are. We will meet "confess" again in the same Hebrew *hithpael* form in Ezra 10:1; Nehemiah 1:6; 9:2–3; and Daniel 9:4, 20. These confession passages in Leviticus and Numbers may not go as far as 1 John 1:9—"If we confess our sins, he is faithful and just and will forgive us our sins and purify us from all unrighteousness" (NIV)—but they are certainly moving in that direction. Interestingly, the Septuagint renders "confess" in these Pentateuch passages with a Greek verb that means "declare (openly)," *exagoreusei*, "he shall confess." The use of the reflexive *hithpael* stem for *yādâ* reinforces this sense of openness, for a literal rendering would be "reveal oneself." There is no such thing as private, secretive confession. Confession is all about being honest with God, honest with others, and honest with oneself.

I said above that, broadly speaking, the OT divides sin into three categories. I have discussed the first two, unintentional and intentional sins. The third can be looked at briefly. It appears in Numbers 15:30–31: "But anyone who sins defiantly . . . blasphemes the Lord and must be cut off from the people of Israel. Because they have despised the Lord's word and broken his commandments, they must surely be cut off" (NIV). Here is the case of a sinner who has brazenly violated the word of God and shows absolutely no remorse or any degree of contrition for his or her trespass. That individual shall be "cut off" (*kārat*—

with "cut off" having a range of possible meanings such as "die," "be excommunicated," "have no descendants." The Hebrew behind "defiantly" is *bəyād rāmâ* ("high-handedly"). The phrase appears in Exodus 14:8 and Numbers 33:3 to describe the defiant departure of the Israelites from Egypt (NIV: "boldly"), what we could call an in-your-face-Mr. Pharaoh exodus from their captivity. I am inclined to link the passage in Numbers 15, about the sin that is not forgivable—mentioned only this one time in the entire OT—with Mark 3:28–29 (cf. Matt. 12:31–32), where Jesus speaks about the sin against the Holy Spirit that is never forgivable. While there is no clear-cut textual connection between these Old and New Testament passages, it is difficult to come up with a sin that is more brazen, more high-handed, more defiant than demonizing Jesus and his saving, delivering ministry. The plaintiffs are guilty of the charges they have brought against the defendant, Jesus.

Leviticus 16 is devoted to a description of the Day of Atonement (Yom Kippur), still the most sacred day of the year for those of Jewish faith. The question that needs to be asked at the beginning is why a special day of atonement is even needed, when at least two sacrifices, already addressed in Leviticus, provide for atonement and sin's forgiveness. Cannot every and any day be a day of atonement for the penitent Israelite? Part of the answer to that question is to examine Leviticus 16 to see how the unique events of this day separate it from any other day in which one might seek expiation from God. A number of items can be pointed out.

First, there is a reference to "confession" of sin on this day (Lev. 16:21), but with one basic difference. In the other confession references (Lev. 5:5; Num. 5:7), the individual sinner confesses. Here the high priest confesses the sins of the Israelites, but not just their sins. Leviticus 16:21 informs us that he confesses (with two hands lying on the live goat, different from the donor's laying one hand on his sacrifice) "all the wickedness and rebellion of the Israelites" (NIV). "Rebellion" (*mārâ*) is the most serious word for any kind of sin in the OT, and "wickedness" (*riš'â*) is just a notch below it. These are hardly unintentional sins! Hence, we can see that atonement is available on this day even for the most blatant and vile type of sins, so long as there is confession. That insight may explain another unique feature of this special day. These venial sins are placed on the head of the live goat, which is then dispatched into the wilderness, never to return. What happens to that live goat once it reaches its destination is a mystery. There is no reference to the scapegoat being slaughtered or put on an altar. In any case, the idea of sin being carried away surely anticipates Jesus's identity as "the Lamb of God, who takes away the sin of the world" (John 1:29 NIV).

I wish to identify one more unique element about Yom Kippur. That is, it is only on this day that the high priest may enter the holy of holies, and it is the only day on which sacrificial blood is brought into this inner sanctum (see Lev. 16:12–15). Why? Because on this day atonement is made not only for sinners and sins as blatant as "transgressions" but also for sacred places and pieces of furniture that have been defiled by those sinners, as odd as that may sound to Christian ears. Sin, Yom Kippur teaches, not only contaminates persons, but sin also contaminates objects, even sometimes the holiness of objects. The Old Testament knows not only of a defiled individual but of a defiled temple, causing even the Holy One to abandon it as we read in Ezekiel 10. In conclusion, we may say that there are two distinct procedures for dealing with sin on the Day of Atonement. One is blood sacrifice; the other is riddance. And this supremely holy day involves the entire nation, not simply individuals, as in Leviticus 1–7.

In some ways, this annual Day of Atonement parallels the Day of Prayer, also observed annually in many churches in America. The latter is a time when Christian believers call on God on behalf of the nation, asking for national forgiveness and the outpouring of God's blessing and leadership on the country. One commentator has appropriately called the Day of Atonement a "cultic drainage system."[10] That's the good news of this sacred day known in Jewish rendition as Yom Kippur. God, in his mercy, has set aside one day per year when his people, all his people, can unload all the junk and garbage in their lives. Note the use of "all" in Leviticus 16:21 ("*all* the wickedness and rebellion of the Israelites—*all* their sins"), as well as in verse 30 ("you will be clean from *all* your sins") and verse 34 ("Atonement is to be made . . . for *all* the sins of the Israelites," NIV, emphasis added).

10. R. S. Kawashima, "The Jubilee Year and the Return of Cosmic Purity," *CBQ* 65 (2003): 372.

HOLINESS

If Exodus ended with chapter 24 (i.e., the sealing and ratification of the covenant between YHWH and Israel), then one might conclude that what God is primarily interested in is his people's obedience to the law of Sinai. But a long section beginning with Exodus 25 talks about worship and meeting with God in the sacred tent. The emphasis on obedience is not muted, but it is joined by an emphasis on worship and the experience of the divine presence in the community. Similarly, if Leviticus ended with chapter 16, one might conclude that this book focuses exclusively on sin and its removal. But as with Exodus, a long section fills the rest of Leviticus (all but perhaps the last chapter). Atonement language, so pervasive in chapters 1–16, is almost completely absent in chapters 17–26. The one exception is the important 17:11 ("For the life of a creature is in the blood, and I have given it to you to make atonement for yourselves on the altar; it is the blood that makes atonement for one's life," NIV). What we find prolifically in chapters 17–26 is holiness or sanctification language. In fact, words related to "holy" or "sanctify" occur so frequently in this unit that many scholars have dubbed it the "Holiness Code." Atonement language occurs only once in Leviticus 17–26 (see the reference above to 17:11), then only one reference in 1–16 enjoins holiness. See 11:44–45: "consecrate yourselves and be holy, because I am holy. . . . I am the Lord, who brought you up out of Egypt to be your God; therefore be holy, because I am holy" (NIV). Interestingly, this call to be holy occurs at the end of a lengthy chapter about clean and unclean food. Holiness in this instance is all about making the right choices when nobody is looking. There are no kosher police peering in your window, making sure you have no pork on your table.

Contrastingly, holiness references occur frequently in chapters 17–26. Before we look at some of those references, we need to observe how this section of Leviticus is introduced in 17:1. In chapters 1–16, we read often that Moses is either to "speak to the Israelites" or to "speak to Aaron [and his sons]." Some of the instructions are meant for the laity, and some are meant for the clergy. And while this distinction continues throughout 17–26, a unique formula appears at the head of 17:2: "Speak to Aaron and his sons and to all the Israelites" (NIV). Here is the one place where both clergy and laity are joined into one audience. It is as if Leviticus is saying that when it comes to holiness, there is no distinction between these two groups. "Be holy, because I am holy" is no more the Lord's word to the high priest than it is to the farmer or the homemaker.

Let us start our canvas of holiness language in Leviticus with 19:2: "Be holy because I, the LORD your God, am holy" (NIV, almost the same as 11:44–45, referenced above).[11] This is such an important teaching that it calls for extra comment.

First, these are words that YHWH instructs Moses to relay to "the entire assembly of Israel" (Lev. 19:2 NIV) So Moses is quoting YHWH to YHWH's people. When YHWH instructs the Israelites to be holy, one must assume that they are, somehow, capable of fulfilling that instruction. God does not ask his people to do the impossible or to become the impossible. He is never the God of the absurd.

Second, it is striking that of all God's attributes—and they are legion—the only one he calls Israel to emulate is holiness. Certainly, nobody can emulate his incommunicable attributes (e.g., eternality, omniscience, and omnipotence). But what about the host of God's communicable attributes? It is not inconceivable to hear the Lord saying, "Be righteous, for I am righteous," or "Be compassionate, for I am compassionate," or "Be loving, for I am loving." The restriction of *imitatio Dei* to holiness is not only an indication that holiness is God's most descriptive and foundational quality. It also suggests that holiness is to be the defining characteristic of those who are followers of the one who calls himself holy. How can the holy and the unholy ever be in a healthy, covenantal relationship?

Third, be careful not to misread the verse. It does not say, "Be as holy as I am." The insertion of the little word *as* distorts a precious biblical truth into something not only impossible but blasphemous. There was a group of Jewish scholars in the Middle Ages, known as the Masoretes, who, between 500 and 900 AD, added vowel points to the Hebrew text, which was totally consonantal beforehand. They did so in order to make the text more readable. Because they were dealing with such a sacred text, they could not simply invent new vowel letters, like our *a*, *e*, *i*, *o*, and *u*, and add them to the text. Instead, their vowels were indicated by dots and dashes above and below the consonants. We call this process vocalization. Here is why

11. See also 20:7, 26; and 26:8 for identical language.

I bring this up under my third comment. It is very interesting to see how these scholars vocalized the word *qādôš* ("holy") when used about God in the second part of Leviticus 19:2 (and the parallel verses I mention above), as well as how they vocalized the word when it refers to an Israelite in the first part of the verse. When "holy" appears in reference to humankind, the Masoretes pointed the "o" in *qādôš* with a *holem* (i.e., an *ō*; *qādōš*). But when "holy" appears in reference to YHWH in the same verse, they pointed the text with a *holem vav* (i.e., an *ô*; *qādôš*). The first is a short "o" (what Hebrew grammarians call a defective spelling). The second is a long "o" (what Hebrew grammarians call a plene ["full"] spelling). This was the Masoretes' way of distinguishing between YHWH's holiness and the holiness of his people. Divine holiness and human holiness are similar, but they are certainly not identical. Holiness confers character. It does not confer incommunicable divine attributes or divinity itself. This point calls to mind a quote I think is from Oswald Chambers, the exact source of which I cannot identify: "It's alright to talk about holiness just as long as you remember whose holiness you are talking about."

Fourth, building on my remarks in the previous paragraph, a distinction in the vowel only occurs when a single verse, such as Leviticus 19:2, references both divine and human holiness. In places where God's covenant people stand alone and are described as "holy," there the Masoretes were content to vocalize the "o" in *qādôš* with the long or full "o."

Fifth, Leviticus and Deuteronomy use "holy" in a perceptibly different way. As we have seen in the passages cited above (Lev. 11:44–45; 19:2; 20:7, 26; 26:8), the language is "You shall be holy" (AT). In Deuteronomy the language is "You are a holy people" (AT; see 7:6; 14:2, 21; 26:19; 28:9). In one we find, "You shall be"; in the other, "You are." In Leviticus holiness is a goal, a challenge to be taken up and pursued. In Deuteronomy holiness is a present reality, a description of who one is. That difference appears throughout the epistolary literature of the NT. On many occasions, the addressees of the letters are called "saints," or more literally "holy ones." By virtue of their position in Christ, they are "set apart." At the same time, these "holy ones" are challenged to be holy. It is as if Paul and Peter are saying, "You need to live up to your name!" Two examples will suffice.

The first is from Peter. In 1 Peter 1, the apostle references his audience as "God's elect, . . . chosen . . . through the sanctifying work of the Spirit" (vv. 1–2 NIV). But just a few verses later, we read, "Just as he who called you is holy, so be holy in all you do" (v. 15 NIV), quoting Leviticus 19:2. Hence, in the first few verses of 1 Peter, the apostle is mirroring the way holiness language is used in Deuteronomy. In later verses of the chapter, though, he mirrors the way such language is used in Leviticus. Yet we know that the Corinthian church was replete with all sorts of misbehaviors that should not be a part of any Christian community. To such misguided believers Paul will point out to them a "more excellent way" (1 Cor. 12:31b ESV).

Sixth, many years ago, Rudolf Otto famously defined the holiness of God as a metaphysical distinction exclusively (see the discussion and evaluation in this volume by John Oswalt and his take on Otto's interpretation of holiness).[12] That is, to call God holy is to designate him as the "Wholly Other." To label God as such is akin to having an awareness of his presence, which is numinous, a *mysterium tremendum* (to use a phrase popular with Otto). I have just a few remarks to make on Otto's position. What Otto says certainly has an element of truth. Approaching God can be—and should be—an awesome experience. To enter the presence of the Holy One on bended knee may cause one to put a hand over an opened mouth. Yet it seems to me that Otto seriously shortchanges the moral stratum in God's holiness. When YHWH says through Moses, "Be holy, for I am holy," surely he is not saying, "Be wholly other, for I am wholly other," or "Invoke a sense of dread, for I invoke a sense of dread." Interestingly, in the Leviticus passages I have mentioned, the people are never said to respond with dread or wonder when God tells them to emulate his holiness. I would argue that a sense of God's wholly otherness is produced by the revelation of his majesty, not the revelation of his holiness. The spectacular, pyrotechnic revelation of YHWH at Sinai, recorded in Exodus 19, is a parade illustration of that truth. The bottom line is, I suggest, that the biblical emphasis on the holiness of YHWH is good, joyful news, not fearful news.

Leviticus 17–26 refers to the Lord making someone holy at least on seven occasions (20:8; 21:8, 15, 23; 22:9, 16, 32)—a warning

12. Rudolph Otto, *The Idea of the Holy: An Inquiry into the Non-rational Factor in the Idea of the Divine and Its Relation to the Rational*, trans. John W. Harvey, 9th ed. (Oxford: Oxford University Press, 1928).

against the false idea that holiness is something one can achieve. Any thinking that redemption is by grace, whereas holiness is by works and effort, cannot be further from the truth. Just as Exodus 25–40 moves the emphasis beyond simple obedience to joyful worship, without dismissing the importance of the former, so also Leviticus 17–26 advances the emphasis from atonement for sin to living a holy, godly life, without dismissing the importance of the former. Yes, God is still in the sin-forgiving business. But lest we be content with nothing more than serial sinning and serial repentance, the divine imperative is that God's followers strive to be like him. Leviticus 17–26 spells out what that means and involves.

The emphasis on atonement and holiness is surely not limited to a couple of books in the Torah. When, for example, we turn to the vast corpus of the Prophets, it becomes transparent that Isaiah, among all the prophets, was the "holiness preacher" par excellence. He has a special name for the Lord: "the Holy One of Israel." It appears almost two dozen times in Isaiah, ten times in the first major section (ch. 1–39) and twelve times in the second (ch. 40–66). To this we can add the expression the "Holy One" in Isaiah 40:25; 43:15; and 49:7. By contrast, the epithet "the Holy One of Israel" appears only once in Jeremiah (51:5) and only once in Ezekiel (39:7). It is appropriate that Isaiah so emphasized the holiness of the God for whom he spoke. After all, he had an encounter with the Holy One that radically transformed his life, resulting in, among other things, his sins being purged (see Isa. 6).

Two other key words are restricted to Isaiah 40–66: "Redeemer" and "redeemed." "Redeemer" appears thirteen times in chapters 40–66, starting with 41:14 and ending with 63:16. Furthermore, it appears in parallel with "the Holy One of Israel" in 41:14; 43:14; 47:4; 48:17; 49:7; and 54:5. The verb "redeemed" appears only three times in chapters 1–39 but nine times in 40–66, starting with 43:1 and ending with 63:9. Similarly, Isaiah 43:3 couples "the Holy One of Israel" with "Savior" or "Rescuer." Another word that occurs in conjunction with "the Holy One of Israel" is "Maker" (45:11; 54:5), using the all-important Hebrew root *br'*, so familiar to us from the opening few chapters of Genesis. In fact, the greatest cluster of occurrences of this root ("create") is in Isaiah 40–66 (19x).

One would think that the prophet is not interested in the doctrine of creation per se. Rather, the emphasis on creation provides a solid foundation for the message of redemption. The connection between the two is not difficult to miss. Perhaps one could say that God's work in redemption fulfills God's work in creation. There is a parallel between God bringing forth dry land from a watery mass in creation, and his bringing forth dry land from a watery mass as God redeemed the Hebrews from their bondage in Egypt.

In Isaiah 40–66, the emphasis on redemption is twofold (recalling that the Hebrew *gā'al*, whether applied to God or to a human redeemer like Boaz in the book of Ruth, means doing something for someone else who is in a hopeless situation, from which they cannot free themselves). On the one hand, God will redeem his people from their bondage in captivity hundreds of miles away. They will return to Zion from Babylon. But that is just half the redemption story. YHWH desires not only the redemption of his chosen people from captivity, but he also yearningly desires their return, their redemption, from the things that brought about the exile in the first place. Hence, the return is not only geographical, but it is also, if not more so, a return to a robust, healthy relationship with the Lord. And who makes possible such a magnificent return not only to *where* the people should be living but also *how* they should be living? None other than the Holy One of Israel.

CONCLUSION

It should be clear by now that both similarities and differences exist in the presentation of atonement and holiness in the OT and the NT. Among the differences are some obvious ones: the sacrificial blood of a perfectly innocent person (as already adumbrated in the great passage from Isa. 52:13–53:12), who never needs to make atonement for himself; the once-for-all and all-sufficient sacrifice of the Messiah; and so forth. Another difference is not mentioned as often. Four main words for "love" exist in the Greek language: (1) *storgē*, (2) *philia*, (3) *erōs*, and (4) *agapē*. Christian tradition and theology place *agapē* at the top of this quartet, for the kind of love signified by this term is all about God's undifferentiated and all-inclusive love, which is at the heart of the NT's teachings. In Jewish theology, however, at least in some writings I have examined,[13] *erōs* is privileged above the other three. The reason for that is that all references to God's love in the OT relate to

13. For example, Michael Wyschogrod, *Body of Faith* (North Vale, NJ: Jason Aaronson, 1983).

his exclusive, passionate love for his chosen Israel. YHWH has indeed chosen Abraham and his descendants to be both a model and a medium for experiencing his blessing(s). But one is challenged to find an OT reference that speaks of God's love for the Philistine or the Hittite. In light of this reality, when it comes to sacrifice and atonement, the best Moses or Aaron can say is "Behold the lamb, which taketh away the sin of the Israelite." They cannot duplicate John the Baptist's "Behold the Lamb of God, which taketh away the sin of the world" (John 1:29 KJV). Similarly, the divine imperative to be holy, first addressed exclusively to one nation, chosen Israel, is now addressed to the worldwide bride of Christ in every nation.

CHAPTER 10

THE SPIRIT OF GOD AND HOLINESS IN THE SAMSON STORY

DAVID G. FIRTH

Readers coming to the OT from the NT might initially be surprised to note that key motifs about the Spirit do not occur with any great frequency in the former. Perhaps the most obvious difference is that only two texts refer to the "Holy Spirit" (Ps. 51:11; Isa. 63:10–11),[1] and both might also be translated as "Spirit of Holiness," depending on how we interpret the construct relationship. However, since either rendering leaves a clear association between the Spirit and holiness, we have no need to linger over the nuances of translation here. But given that there are more than three hundred occurrences of *rûaḥ* in the OT, of which approximately a hundred probably refer to God's Spirit,[2] the above observation does demonstrate that the OT's language of the Spirit is significantly different from that of the New. This difference is at heart driven by the different points of emphasis found in each Testament. In short, although holiness is a motif associated with the Spirit in the OT, this association is only a relatively minor one; by contrast, such an association is much more common in the New. It is therefore more appropriate when focused on the OT to speak of "the Spirit of God [or YHWH]," since such language is more typical of this Testament and can help us avoid the problem of reading developments found in the NT back into the Old. The opposite danger is to assume that the OT has nothing to contribute to our understanding of the Spirit, but this too is something to be avoided, since the OT's presentation of the Spirit is arguably both distinctive (and so worthy of reflection on its own terms)

1. See Daniel J. Estes, "Spirit and the Psalmist in Psalm 51," in *Presence, Power and Promise: The Role of the Spirit of God in the Old Testament*, ed. David G. Firth and Paul D. Wegner (Nottingham: Apollos, 2011), 122–34. For the importance of Isa. 63:10–11 in the understanding of the Spirit, see John R. Levison, *The Holy Spirit before Christianity* (Waco, TX: Baylor University Press, 2019).
2. See Roedolf J. duPlooy, "Die Teologiese Gebruik van רוח יהוה in die Ou Testament" (PhD thesis, Northwest University, 2004), 88–103.

and fundamental to understanding the NT's presentation.[3] That is, rather than reading back from the NT to the Old, we should read from the Old to the New and so understand why the language of holiness became so closely associated with the Spirit. This essay aims to lay a foundation for that project. It explores the Samson story (Judg. 13–16) as an early account of the Spirit in Israel's life to demonstrate some of the OT's distinctive contributions to our understanding of the Spirit, while also showing that this presentation exhibits a move toward holiness. It is important to note that although holiness can be understood solely in terms of something or someone belonging to God, the OT also understands holiness as a positive disposition toward God and his purposes.[4] This latter understanding will guide our discussion. Although explicit holiness language can be an important marker along the way, patterns of disposition and behavior can point to holiness (or its absence) in relation to the presence of the Spirit as well. Thus, even though Samson might seem an unusual choice for an exploration of holiness, we will observe ritual elements in the story that are clearly linked to the motif of holiness.

Of course, speaking of "earlier" and "later" texts in the OT raises an acute question—How can we date the various texts that we consider? In many respects, this is an intractable and finally unanswerable question, amply demonstrated by the various dates scholars assign to different parts of the OT. However, it is at least possible to date the context in which a reference to the Spirit is made. So the book of Judges situates itself early in Israel's life in the land, in the generations immediately after Israel's arrival in the land. We cannot prove that Judges was actually written in that period—most scholars would date the finished text considerably later—but we can reasonably suggest that the traditions incorporated into the book reach back to that period, even if there was later editing.[5] This is perhaps not an entirely satisfactory answer to the question, but it is sufficient for the argument of this essay. In short, Judges 13–16 reports events that occurred in an early period in Israel's life.

3. On the broader issue of the OT's presentation of the Spirit, see Wilf Hildebrandt, *An Old Testament Theology of the Spirit of God* (Peabody, MA: Hendrickson, 1993); Firth and Wegner, *Presence, Power and Promise*; Jack Levison, *A Boundless God: The Spirit according to the Old Testament* (Grand Rapids: Baker Academic, 2020).

4. For an accessible introduction and overview of this topic, see David P. Wright, "Holiness: Old Testament," *ABD* 3:237–49.

5. For a plausible model, see Brian Neil Peterson, *The Authors of the Deuteronomistic History: Locating a Tradition in Ancient Israel* (Minneapolis: Fortress, 2014), 165–98.

SAMSON—TROUBLED BY THE SPIRIT

Although important references to the Spirit can be found in the Pentateuch,[6] none of these references provide key insights into the theme of holiness. The Spirit's presence in creation is fundamental to how we are to understand the world in which we live,[7] and the Spirit's enabling of craftsmen and elders in Israel demonstrates that even if the Spirit did not indwell all Israelites, Israel's life was shaped by the presence and enabling of the Spirit. This shaping can be seen in Israel's earlier life, though it only comes to a full understanding in later periods.

Since the book of Joshua makes no mention of the Spirit, we can focus our reflections on the Spirit and Israel's early life in the book of Judges. Given the absence of "Spirit" language in Joshua, the emphasis on the Spirit in Judges (and Samuel) might seem surprising. But the context provided by the Pentateuch counteracts such surprise. The Pentateuch demonstrates that creation, Israel's worship, and its leadership were all shaped to some extent by the work of the Spirit. Accordingly, it might seem more of a surprise that Joshua makes no mention of the Spirit, especially given the prominence given to the Spirit in Judges and Samuel. Understanding this literary phenomenon requires attention to certain distinctive features of Joshua. There an important bridge is formed between the Pentateuch and the rest of the Former Prophets, and Joshua 1 is saturated in allusions to both Deuteronomy and Numbers. Within this context, earlier references to Joshua form part of the intertextual background, including most obviously Numbers 27:18, which stresses the presence of the Spirit in Joshua.[8] This means that the book of Joshua is able to present Joshua throughout as a man of the Spirit, though the connections with the Spirit are not made explicit in the book itself. However, when we turn to Judges, we find that references to the Spirit are much more prominent, occurring in the accounts of Othniel (3:7–11), Gideon (6:1–8:35), Jephthah (10:6–12:7), and Samson (ch. 13–16). Othniel is presented as the paradigm judge, against which we evaluate the other judges, though his

6. See, e.g., Gen. 1:2; Exod. 31:1–5; and Num. 11:16–30.

7. Whether we should understand *rûaḥ* in Gen. 1:2 as a reference to the Spirit is much debated (see the NRSV). But for an affirmative defense, see Robert L. Hubbard Jr., "The Spirit and Creation," in Firth and Wegner, *Presence, Power and Promise*, 71–91. This foundation is pivotal for the reference to the Spirit in Ps. 104:30.

8. Cf. David G. Firth, *Joshua*, EBTC (Bellingham, WA: Lexham, 2021), 70.

account is (probably intentionally) colorless,[9] leading readers to later accounts to understand the ways in which the Spirit works.[10] Othniel's experience of the Spirit testifies to the community that he is someone though whom YHWH is working,[11] providing a paradigm for what follows, but the account does not allow us to say more than that.

But if Othniel's account is intentionally colorless, the same cannot be said of Samson's. Samson is the wild man of the judges, a cartoonish figure of violence and sexual drive. Yet his story is also one that is remarkable for its emphasis on the Spirit. Indeed, the narrative reports more experiences of the Spirit for Samson than for any other character in the OT. Samson is also an intriguing character for our purposes, since his life shows hardly any evidence of holiness. This is not to claim that no connection exists between the Spirit and holiness; it is only to claim that such a connection is not reflected in the literary traditions that center on Samson. Nevertheless, we can see that Samson's experiences lay the foundation for understanding the Spirit's association with holiness, albeit in a distinctive manner; the Spirit's work is focused largely on preventing Samson from acting in ways contrary to God's purposes. Hence, although holiness language is not directly present, the Samson narratives demonstrate that a key part of the Spirit's work is to ensure that God's greater purposes prevail, even when doing so prevents God's people from acting as they otherwise intend. This is not a positive presentation of holiness, but it does lay the foundation from which a positive move toward holiness can be made. In addition, a key element of the story is that the Spirit's coming in power is most evident at points where Samson has made himself unclean, acting against his Nazirite status.

As already noted, no individual in the OT is said to have more experiences of the Spirit than Samson. We read about his encounter with the Spirit in four different places (Judg. 13:25; 14:6, 19; and 15:14), though this observation needs to be balanced by the note in 16:20 of YHWH leaving him. Of the four references to Samson's experience of

---

9. See Barry G. Webb, *The Book of the Judges: An Integrated Reading*, JSOTSup 46 (Sheffield: JSOT, 1987), 127, and Barnabas Lindars, *Judges 1–5: A New Translation and Commentary* (Edinburgh: T&T Clark, 1995), 128–30.

10. Cf. Dennis T. Olson, "Judges," *NIB* 2:768.

11. See David G. Firth, "The Spirit and Leadership," in Firth and Wegner, *Presence, Power and Promise*, 270–74.

the Spirit, the first needs to be treated apart from the other three, since it uses a different verb and creates the context for reading the rest of the narrative. Overall, we will see that Samson acts contrary to holiness,[12] which is why he joins Jephthah as one of only two judges who fail to bring rest to the land. He is driven much more by his own desires than holiness. Indeed, Samson seems to actively violate his holiness as a Nazirite when he touches a lion's corpse (14:9).[13] Regardless, YHWH still works through him on behalf of his people, most notably through the Spirit.

CHARACTERIZING SAMSON

It is often the case in OT narratives that a character's introduction sets the scene for what follows.[14] Although Judges 13 has traditionally been regarded as part of the Samson narrative, most of the chapter is preparatory for his birth. Nevertheless, although Samson's birth is not recorded until verses 24–25 of the chapter, the earlier material establishes several motifs that are crucial for what follows. The encounters between Samson's mother and YHWH's messenger throughout the chapter evoke important echoes from earlier accounts in the OT, most obviously the account of Isaac's birth (Gen. 21:1–7). Just as Sarah is said to have been barren, so is Samson's mother, suggesting another miraculous birth.[15] What is striking is that woven into the various encounters of Judges 13 are three separate points where Samson's Nazirite status is highlighted. The first occurs when the messenger appears to Samson's mother and announces his coming birth (vv. 3–5). Although the birth will be miraculous, this element is passed over remarkably quickly, with far more attention given to the child's status as a Nazirite. So important

12. Eugene H. Merrill, "The Samson Saga and Spiritual Leadership," in Firth and Wegner, *Presence, Power and Promise*, 282, describes Samson as a "narcissistic adolescent who at every turn seemed unwilling or unable to comport himself in a holy, upright manner."

13. Lee Roy Martin, *The Unheard Voice of God: A Pentecostal Hearing of the Book of Judges*, JPTSup 32 (Blandford Forum, UK: Deo, 2011), 88, also notes that the feast in Judg. 14:10–20 suggests a consumption of wine on Samson's part, also contrary to his Nazirite status.

14. Leland Ryken, *How Bible Stories Work: A Guided Study of Biblical Narrative* (Bellingham, WA: Lexham, 2015), 43–46, notes that whereas OT narratives sometimes characterize directly (the narrator explicitly commenting on an aspect of character), they more commonly characterize indirectly, through what is reported. In Samson's case, an initial example of direct characterization notably occurs in Judg. 13:24–25; such characterization is then explored through the indirect characterization of the narrative, though with important intrusions.

15. Within the corpus of the Former Prophets, Sasmson's birth also establishes a series of anticipatory links for Hannah and the account of Samuel's birth. Cf. Martin, *Unheard Voice of God*, 235–37.

is this status that his mother is told that she is to consume no wine or fermented drink during her pregnancy. Effectively, the child is set apart as a Nazirite in utero, and his status is formalized after his birth, with the focused note that no razor should be used on his hair, which will prove vital in what follows.[16] As a Nazirite, Samson is dedicated to YHWH (Num. 6), a status meant to mark him out as holy (vv. 5–8).[17]

The reason for this focus on Samson's Nazirite status is then highlighted by the declaration in Judges 13:5 that Samson will "begin" (*ḥll*) Israel's deliverance from the Philistines. Such a statement is unique among the judges; it plausibly indicates that Samson will not see Israel.[18] Lawson Stone has rightly cautioned that the verb can have the sense of initiating a process and, thus, highlighting the first point of an action without requiring completion; accordingly, he believes we should not see this declaration.[19] But since the Samson narrative never reports a completed deliverance or a securing of rest, it is better to see the assertion as an instance of indirect characterization (since it is uttered by the messenger rather than the narrator), which foreshadows the narrative's close.[20] This instance of indirect characterization is then linked with direct characterization following Samson's birth, as the narrator introduces two key elements for understanding what follows, beginning with the note that as Samson grew, he was blessed by YHWH (v. 24). The nature of this blessing is left unstated, but it is certainly a sign of YHWH's presence.

The second key element of direct characterization, introduced in Judges 13:25, is more important for our purposes, since it makes the first explicit connection between Samson and the Spirit (though the interpretation of the verse is not altogether clear). The verb used here

16. Cf. Mark Greene, "Enigma Variations: Aspects of the Samson Story (Judges 13–16)," *VE* 21 (1991): 59.

17. On the importance of allusions to the Nazirite laws for the Samson story, see Jillian L. Ross, *A People Heeds Not Scripture: Allusion in Judges* (Eugene, OR: Pickwick, 2023), 176–89.

18. Prior to the Samson narrative, the verb *ḥll* only appears in the book at Judg. 10:18, though there the expectation is that whoever begins a battle against the Ammonites will see it through to its conclusion. Within the Samson narrative, the term recurs twice in chapter 16, first in verse 19, where Delilah "begins" to subdue Samson, and then in verse 22, where Samson's hair "begins" to grow. The term appears, therefore, to be an important boundary marker in Samson's narrative, though it also occurs three times in chapter 20 (vv. 31, 39, 40).

19. Lawson G. Stone, "Judges," in *Cornerstone Biblical Commentary*, vol. 3, *Joshua, Judges, Ruth*, ed. Philip W. Comfort (Carol Stream, IL: Tyndale House, 2012), 374. This reading of the verb is potentially consistent with its use in Judg. 13:25.

20. With Daniel I. Block, *Judges, Ruth*, NAC 6 (Nashville: Broadman & Holman, 1999), 403–4.

(*pʿm*) occurs in only four other passages in the OT (Gen. 41:8; Ps. 77:5; Dan. 2:1, 3), and it is used nowhere else of the Spirit of God.[21] Although commonly translated as "stir" (cf. NIV, LEB), which might suggest a positive experience, the word more likely has a negative sense here. This is the only instance of the verb occurring in the *qal*, though given the lack of wider distribution, we should not place too much weight on this fact. Three of the other occurrences are in the *niphal* (Gen. 41:8; Ps. 77:5; Dan. 2:3), whereas the fourth is in the *hithpael* (Dan. 2:1). What is notable in each of these instances is that the verb always reports someone who is troubled by something. Taking the *niphal* first, we may link Genesis 41:8 and Daniel 2:3, since both passages report on kings who are "troubled" by dreams they have had and for which they seek an interpretation. In both cases, the king experiences a lack of control and so sends for those who can interpret the dream, seeking a resolution for that which troubles them. The situation in Psalm 77:5 is different, reflecting on a period of distress that has left the psalmist unable to speak. The absence of sleep here may suggest an association between the verb and sleep (esp. given the link with dreams), but the evidence overall is insufficient to make that conclusion. Nevertheless, something negative is experienced in each case, leaving the person involved in a troubled state of mind. This background means that the *hithpael* in Daniel 2:1 is probably best understood as a reflexive factitive,[22] reporting the condition into which Nebuchadnezzar is brought, though in translation terms, we would again understand him as being troubled.

In light of the above evidence, it is probably best to understand Samson as being troubled by God's Spirit. It is not that the Spirit is stirring Samson and so preparing him to (at least) begin the task of delivering the nation. Rather, the narrator here sets a contrast between Samson's own desires and YHWH's purposes for him. The Spirit is urging him toward acts that he resists, most obviously in terms of his own holiness as a Nazirite, and for this reason, he is troubled by the Spirit.[23] The narrator thus sets up the struggle that will dominate

21. In both references from Daniel, though, it refers to Nebuchadnezzar's own spirit.
22. Ronald J. Williams, *Williams' Hebrew Syntax*, rev. and exp. John C. Beckman, 3rd ed. (Toronto: University of Toronto Press, 2007), 64 (§154).
23. Cf. Barry G. Webb, *The Book of Judges*, NICOT (Grand Rapids: Eerdmans, 2012), 359. Isabelle Hamley, *God of Justice and Mercy: A Theological Commentary on Judges* (London: SCM, 2021), 164, observes that there "is almost a sense of Samson fighting against the Spirit."

Samson's life as he begins the deliverance of Israel. Moreover, by introducing the Spirit through direct characterization, readers are alerted to watch for the work of the Spirit in what follows.

THE SPIRIT COMES IN POWER

Given the prominence of the Spirit in Samson's introduction, it is perhaps no surprise that his experience of the Spirit is important in Judges 14–15. The three encounters in these chapters are united by a verb that describes the Spirit's coming on Samson (*ṣlḥ*). Although often translated as "rush" (e.g., ESV), it explicitly refers, when associated with the coming of the Spirit (14:6, 19; 15:14; 1 Sam. 10:6, 10; 11:6; 16:13), to a coming in power that enables the persons in view to achieve something beyond their normal ability. The only exception to this description is the Spirit's coming on David when he is anointed (1 Sam. 16:13).[24] But given the other usage, we can assume that a sense of empowerment is present, even if it is not described. The coming in power can enable acts of physical prowess or prophecy, though in these early instances, it is not clear that prophecy refers to speaking YHWH's word, since in none of these instances is a prophetic word mentioned, nor does the person affected seem to display ecstatic behavior.

In all three instances relevant to Samson, the Spirit's coming with power enables him to act with great physical strength, each time overcoming the Philistines and, thus, beginning to deliver Israel. Samson's first experience of the Spirit (Judg. 14:6) occurs in the context of his desire to marry a Philistine woman. Since Israel and the Philistines were at war, it is not impossible to consider his marriage as an approved arrangement under the law for war brides (Deut. 21:10–14).[25] However, since the narrative assumes Philistine rule over Israel at the time (Judg. 14:4), it might be better to think of it more as an act of collaboration. In any case, since the Philistines are routinely described as uncircumcised,[26] such a marriage would seem to be highly irregular, a point made by his parents (v. 3). Samson is straining against what

24. The verb is also used of the coming of the baleful spirit on Saul (1 Sam. 18:10), with a similar meaning.
25. So Roger Ryan, *Judges*, RNBC (Sheffield: Sheffield Phoenix, 2007), 103.
26. Though, of course, circumcision only describes males.

is expected.[27] Yet a sense of irony also exists here, because we have a comparatively rare direct comment from the narrator, who points out that Samson's desire for the marriage has come from YHWH (v. 4). That is, Samson's desire, though contrary to holiness, is the means through which YHWH will act against the Philistines.

It is with this background that we have the record of Samson's first experience of the Spirit coming with power (Judg. 14:6), an account that sets up the two that follow. As Samson heads toward Timnah with his parents, a young lion comes roaring toward him. At this point, the Spirit comes upon him in power, enabling him to tear the lion apart without any weapon or tool. Although Samson apparently routinely assumes that his strength is present (cf. his conversations with Delilah in 16:1–21), the narrator here indicates that special endowments can exceed his normal strength. His parents are apparently unaware of this reality, since he does not tell them about it.[28] Perhaps more remarkably, Samson does not seem to think that the matter is important, as he simply continues to Timnah and meets with his prospective wife. The narrator elides the details of their conversation, noting simply that Samson thinks the woman is right for him. Additionally, the narrative quickly moves to the family's journey home, where Samson takes some honey from the lion's carcass, sharing some with his parents (who remain ignorant about it). Doing so may have broken the Nazirite law, since that law precludes contact with a dead body (Num. 6:6), though it is possible that human bodies are primarily in view there.[29] Nevertheless, at the very least, Samson makes himself unclean (Lev. 11:27) and transmits his uncleanness to his parents. Since only the clean can be holy, Samson has clearly moved to a state of ritual unholiness, something that seems to be matched on the moral level by his attitude toward marrying a Philistine woman.

27. David J. H. Beldman, *Judges*, THOTC (Grand Rapids: Eerdmans, 2020), 162, believes that this is not the behavior we would expect to see from one in whom the Spirit is stirring. But if Samson is troubled rather than led by the Spirit, then his choice of a potential wife becomes early evidence of this.

28. Mary J. Evans, *Judges and Ruth: An Introduction and Commentary* (London: Inter-Varsity, 2017), 154, suggests that Samson may have gone to relieve himself, though no doubt other reasons exist as to why he and his parents might not have been together at this point.

29. See Robert B. Chisholm Jr., *A Commentary on Judges and Ruth*, KEL (Grand Rapids: Kregel Academic, 2013), 406–7.

The background provided by this account is essential to understanding Samson's second experience of the Spirit coming in power (Judg. 14:19). At this point, Samson has gone to the wedding feast, which apparently reflects a custom no longer practiced when the account was written (v. 10). While there, the Philistines bring thirty companions to the feast. Samson immediately tells them a riddle, promising to provide a full change of clothes for each companion if they can resolve the riddle. Readers can immediately see that the riddle alludes to the honey taken from the lion, but of course, because the riddle refers to something so specific, the companions are unable to solve it, certainly not within the seven days Samson has specified. On the fourth day, they pressure Samson's wife, who weeps before him for the rest of the feast, until he reveals the answer to her, and she in turn tells her people. Armed with this information, the companions' answer resolves the riddle, though Samson immediately realizes that they could only solve it by consulting his wife. At this point, the Spirit comes in power on Samson, though once again his actions are contrary to holiness, even if he continues to "begin" to deliver Israel. After traveling to Ashkelon (about twenty-five miles away), Samson strikes down thirty people and takes their clothes. Touching animal carcasses sometimes brings about uncleanness, but touching a human corpse always brings uncleanness (Num. 19:11). Again, Samson's ritual uncleanness is matched by his moral uncleanness—he has killed thirty people. In this case, he has unambiguously breached his Nazirite status. But this breach needs again to be read in light of the irony of Judges 14:4, as YHWH continues to prod Samson to act in ways that lead him to begin Israel's deliverance from the Philistines.[30] In a sense, the Spirit's coming in power permits Samson to act in the ways he wants, but the Spirit also prods him to act for Israel's deliverance. Again, we see that the Spirit troubles Samson.

The first two experiences of the Spirit coming in power provide key background to the third instance (Judg. 15:14). By this point in the story, the woman whom Samson has hoped to marry has been given to another, leading him to more acts of violence against the Philistines, though these remain acts of personal revenge, not acts concerned with Israel's deliv-

30. As Block, *Judges, Ruth*, 438, points out, Samson still shows no sign of interest in acting for Israel's deliverance.

erance. Samson's actions then lead to further raids in Israelite territory (this time, in Judah), leading the men of Judah to arrest Samson and hand him over to the Philistines, so that they would withdraw from their land. Samson agrees to be bound by his compatriots (anticipating the Delilah story), who bring him to the Philistine camp. The Philistines then come shouting at him, like the lion before, but at this point, the Spirit again comes in power on Samson. As a result, he is enabled to break the ropes that hold him and to kill a thousand men with a donkey's jawbone. Touching the donkey's bone again renders Samson unclean (Lev. 11:26), and killing a thousand men likewise renders him morally unclean, as with his first two experiences of the Spirit. This time, his moral uncleanness is clearly seen in his boastful song (Judg. 15:16), which makes no mention of God but claims victory only for himself.[31] Samson again acts in line with his own impulses, thus failing to retain the cleanness required of him as a Nazirite, and yet it is the coming of the Spirit with power that moves him toward delivering Israel, even though at this point, he seeks only personal revenge. The Spirit troubles Samson, pushing him toward a vocation that he resists. Even though Samson's actions move away from holiness, once the Spirit comes in power and Samson begins the process of deliverance, he returns to YHWH's purposes and thus to the way of holiness.

SAMSON'S DEATH

No mention of the Spirit is found in Judges 16, though the chapter is replete with allusions to earlier parts of the Samson narrative. For example, Delilah's behavior toward Samson in discovering the secret of his strength (vv. 4–22) is like an expanded edition of the earlier report of his wife in Timnah entreating him for information about his riddle (14:15–18). Likewise, the cords that bind Samson (16:10–12) echo the account of Samson being bound by the men of Judah (15:13–14). These echoes make clear that whatever the compositional relationship of Judges 16 to the rest of the Samson story, the Samson narrative as we now have it is an integrated unit. Moreover, whereas the earlier parts of the story implicitly suggest that Samson goes against the fundamental tenets of his Nazirite status, the fact that he finally

31. Cf. Butler, *Judges*, 343. Hamley, *God of Justice*, 183, notes that Samson "seeks to go down in history on his own merits, alone and separated from human or divine help."

agrees to have his hair shaved is the point where this breach is now made explicit, pointing back to the introductory statements about his head (13:5). Yet strikingly, although these earlier parts of the story are astir with mentions of the Spirit, chapter 16 is notable for the absence of such references, perhaps reflecting Samson's shift from implicit to explicit breaches in his status. However, this is perhaps a point where the absence of evidence is not evidence of absence. Samson's previous experiences of the Spirit are all instances in which the Spirit comes in power, experiences distinct from the Spirit's more consistent troubling of Samson.

The nadir of Samson's experience is undoubtedly the moment he expects to go out once more against the Philistines but is unable to do so because he is unaware that YHWH has left him (Judg. 16:20). Within the overall structure of the story, we should understand Samson's loss as more than just a loss of strength, a loss that occurs because of his rejection of his Nazirite status. Instead, he is also no longer considered YHWH's servant.[32] Indeed, it is possible that his earlier experiences of the Spirit coming in power have misled him, since he makes himself unclean and implicitly breaches his status in the aftermath. That is, Samson would not have had his strength because he was not maintaining his status, and he only had it because of the Spirit coming in power. The use of the verb *ṣlḥ* would thus point to moments of empowerment when Samson expects to act because of his strength but can only do so because of a temporary enabling of the Spirit. But after being shaved, he has effectively repudiated his status, and his real weakness becomes apparent. This is why the narrative then notes that his hair began to regrow; as Samson once more aligns himself with YHWH's purpose for his life, his strength begins to return. In another irony, even though the Philistines know that Samson's hair is related to his strength, his hair begins to grow back while in their custody.[33]

The balance of the account can be passed over briefly for our purposes. Here Samson finally acts against the Philistines, killing about three thousand who have called for him to be brought out and to entertain them at a sacrifice to their god, Dagon. The Samson who

32. Cf. Stone, "Judges," 418.
33. Block, *Judges, Ruth*, 463, rightly points to the link to 13:5. Samson will "begin" to deliver Israel, and as his hair "begins" to grow, the coming of such deliverance is hinted at.

acts here is seemingly a broken man, with his eyes gouged out following his capture. He needs to ask so he can feel the pillars that hold the building up, unable to see the Philistines who watch on as he provides "entertainment." Leaning on the pillars, Samson prays again, though like his earlier prayer (Judg. 15:18–20), it is a self-centered request, one in which he asks to avenge the Philistines for his eyes (16:28). Nevertheless, there is one point of development: he asks YHWH to strengthen him. Unlike before, when he assumed the presence of the necessary strength, this time he knows YHWH must provide it. In addition, since the narrator has mentioned the regrowth of his hair, Samson is no longer in breach of his Nazirite status. For all his failures, he has at least become clean again, and he has also approached the holiness that was meant to mark his life. By the end of the story, he has not done much to begin delivering Israel, but he has at least fulfilled the command to tear down the shrines of the other gods (Deut. 7:1–5), something that allows Israel to worship YHWH again.[34] It is far from full deliverance, but it is a beginning nonetheless, and the man who was once troubled by the Spirit has finally begun to move (however minimally) toward his status as a Nazirite. He may still be troubled by the Spirit, but he no longer needs special bursts of the Spirit's power as he takes his first steps toward deliverance.

SAMSON, THE SPIRIT, AND HOLINESS

Given Samson's overall characterization, can we realistically speak of the Spirit and holiness in his story? Thomas Mann (quite reasonably) characterizes Samson as a playboy, "a combination of Rambo, Paul Bunyan, and Casanova, all rolled into one."[35] Certainly, if we want Samson to be a model of personal holiness, then we will be disappointed. Even in his death, little suggests that he has fully grasped the fundamentals of his status as a Nazirite. Though his death might initiate a process by which Israel is delivered, his last two speeches indicate that he simply wishes to die with the Philistines, seeing his death as a means of avenging them. Samson has had more privilege than any other judge and perhaps more potential too, but in the end, he

34. Cf. Thomas W. Mann, *The Book of the Former Prophets* (Eugene, OR: Cascade Books, 2011), 85.

35. Mann, *Former Prophets*, 80.

disappoints.[36] But this disappointment is surely something intended. His narrative is structured to provide hope through its extended introduction and its emphasis on his Nazirite status. Its repeated stress on his experience of the Spirit, even as readers struggle to know what it means that the Spirit "troubles" him, points to the resources that YHWH lavishes on him. Yet as is also indicated in the story's introduction, Samson only begins to deliver Israel, leaving readers to wonder how a more complete deliverance might have been achieved. But actually, Samson is representative of the Israelites as a whole, since his is a story in which they seemingly accept the right of the Philistines to rule over them (Judg. 15:11). Samson's failures are those of the nation, even if his are painted in far more vivid colors.

Samson's story offers both positive and negative theological insights. Positively, it points to YHWH's continued commitment to a people who continue to disappoint. After Samson's birth, the nation is never shown worshiping YHWH. Although the narrator often mentions YHWH in Judges 14–16, no Israelite names God until Samson tells Delilah that he has been a Nazirite from his mother's womb (16:17). Samson's prayer for vengeance (v. 28) is the only other occasion in which an Israelite names God in the whole story. The story is full of points where YHWH speaks and acts, and Samson's parents are perfectly aware of YHWH's activity in the birth narrative, but the rest of the narrative paints a very different picture. YHWH is active, especially through his Spirit, but Samson and Israel move in a very different direction. Deliverance has a beginning, but if more is to happen, it must come from YHWH.

Negatively, the story demonstrates the problems associated with a lack of holiness. As we have noted, the points at which the Spirit comes in power on Samson are points where he becomes unclean and thus breaches his status as a Nazirite. As a Nazirite, Samson is meant to be holy, but the unclean cannot, by definition, be holy. That the Spirit comes in power at these points may therefore be unexpected. But if we are correct in seeing them as instances in which Samson acts without intending to breach his status, then we can understand the Spirit's work here as a gracious empowerment by YHWH, something

36. Cf. Mary L. Conway, *Judging the Judges: A Narrative Appraisal Analysis*, LSAWS 15 (University Park, PA: Eisenbrauns, 2020), 201–2.

that enables Samson to seek Israel's deliverance. The Spirit troubles Samson because Samson lives in a manner contrary to his Nazirite status. Such troubling is also evidenced in the Spirit's coming in power, as it means that the opportunity to begin deliverance remains, even though Samson is not living up to Nazirite ideals. Samson becomes unholy, but the Spirit brings him back to the task that YHWH has given him. The Spirit thus counters Samson's own proclivities away from holiness, realigning him with YHWH's purposes, until he consciously breaks his Nazirite status. Yet even here, YHWH remains gracious, and as Samson is realigned with his Nazirite status and thus becomes holy, so YHWH again works through him. Samson may not experience a final burst of the Spirit's power, but he is troubled throughout by the Spirit, as the latter pushes him back toward the holiness of his vocation and against his own desires.

Although the issue of holiness may not be evident on the surface of the Samson story, it is nevertheless an important undercurrent within, and the work of the Spirit is crucial in developing it. The story presents a work of the Spirit that is distinct to the OT—Saul and his messengers being the only other figures who are prevented by the Spirit from doing what they want (1 Sam. 19:19–24), though in their case, the issue of holiness is less evident.[37] Yet both of these stories are joined by the facts that YHWH has a greater purpose and that the Spirit is the means by which actions contrary to that purpose are prevented. It is not that the Spirit prevents any action that is contrary to holiness; rather, the Spirit prevents that which is contrary to YHWH's purposes for his people. Holiness has many aspects, but being aligned with those purposes is certainly one aspect of it.

37. See David G. Firth, "Is Saul Also among the Prophets? Saul's Prophecy in 1 Samuel 19:23," in Firth and Wegner, *Presence, Power and Promise*, 294–305.

Chapter 11

HOLINESS AND THE MESSIAH

PAUL D. WEGNER

God is both the source and the ideal manifestation of holiness. R. A. Finlayson describes the all-encompassing nature of this attribute:

> Since holiness embraces every distinctive attribute of the Godhead, it may be conceived of as the outshining of all that God is. As the sun's rays, combining all the colours of the spectrum, come together in the sun's shining and blend into light, so in his self-manifestation all of the attributes of God come together and blend into holiness. Holiness has, for that reason, been called "an attribute of attributes," that which lends unity to all the attributes of God.[1]

But in the context of the OT, holiness presents a dilemma in that a perfectly holy God desires to have fellowship with his unholy creatures. This fellowship is experienced for some time in the garden of Eden, but following the fall in Genesis 3, sin separates humans from God.

The word "holy" "connotes the essential nature that belongs to the sphere of God's being or activity and that is distinct from the common or profane."[2] According to Jackie Naudé, God's holiness "becomes an expression of his perfection of being that transcends everything creaturely."[3] So by definition, God is separate from his own creation and unable to have fellowship with those whom he has created. This disparity is accentuated by the familiar title "the Holy One of Israel" in the book of Isaiah, for it not only suggests God's supremacy but also

1. R. A. Finlayson, "Holiness," *IDB* 2:656.
2. Jackie A. Naudé, "קדש," *NIDOTTE* 3:879. Finlayson describes holiness as "a term for the moral excellence of God and his freedom from all limitation in his moral perfection (Hab. 1:13)" ("Holiness," 656).
3. Naudé, "קדש," 879.

places "the sins of Israel's society in contrast to God's moral perfection (Isa 30:12) and expresses God's absolute separation from evil (17:7)."[4]

So how does a perfectly holy God relate to miserably marred human beings? Throughout the OT, one class of people in fact lives alternately between the profane and the holy spheres at different times, and that class is the priesthood. But only the high priest could have access into God's very presence in the most holy place, and then only once a year on the Day of Atonement (Lev. 16:3–4, 11–16). Other priests served at the altar outside of the most holy place (Lev. 1–7) as they regularly administered sacrifices and offerings. Priests served as intermediaries between God and humans within certain parameters: they were required to consecrate themselves, and "their holiness was only active in the holy area."[5]

The Hebrew root *qdš*, "holiness," appears as a verb, a noun, and an adjective, and it occurs more than 850 times in the OT. However, the noun and the adjective forms are used differently, as Naudé notes:

> While the nom. [noun] simply denotes a state of belonging to the realm of the divine, those things that are typified by the adj. all possess the ability to move things or people into, or at least toward, the realm of the divine. God, as the source of holiness, is also the primary agent of sanctification, but human beings can participate in the rituals of sanctification (e.g., of Aaron and his sons) and therefore are qualified by the adj.[6]

Thus, priests were able to bring sinful humanity into God's presence under certain conditions. Deuteronomy 26:18–19 explains how Israel could have fellowship with a holy God:

> And today the Lord has declared that you are to be a people of his treasured possession, just as he told you; and that you should keep all his commandments; and that he will set you high above all nations, which he has made, for praise, fame,

4. Naudé, "קדש," 882.
5. Naudé, "קדש," 881.
6. Naudé, "קדש," 881–82.

> and glory; and that you will be a people consecrated to the LORD your God, just as he said. (AT)

But the Israelites did not keep all his commandments and continued to sin; thus, their fellowship with God was only temporary. The sanctification process only lasted until their next sin. Because the old covenant could not remedy this dilemma, a new covenant was necessary:

> "Behold, [the] days are coming," declares the LORD, "when I will make a new covenant with the house of Israel and with the house of Judah, not like the covenant which I made with their fathers in the day I took them by the hand to bring them out of the land of Egypt, My covenant which they broke, although I was a husband to them," declares the LORD. "But this is the covenant which I will make with the house of Israel after those days," declares the LORD, "I will put My law within them and on their heart I will write it; and I will be their God, and they shall be My people. They will not teach again, each man his neighbor and each man his brother, saying, 'Know the LORD,' for they will all know Me, from the least of them to the greatest of them," declares the LORD, "for I will forgive their iniquity, and their sin I will remember no more." (Jer. 31:31–34 NASB1995)

Verses 33–34 note three significant improvements in the new covenant: (1) God will put his law on the hearts of his people, which will engender a new relationship between them and God. The NT clarifies that this is accomplished by the Holy Spirit, who comes to live within believers' hearts to enable them to obey God's law (see John 14:16–17; 16:13). (2) Because they will all know the Lord, his people will not need a priest to have a relationship with God; they can all have direct access to him. The Reformers referred to this reality as the "individual priesthood of all believers";[7] and the Messiah's perfect sacrifice for

7. Martin Luther states, "That the pope or bishop anoints, makes tonsures, ordains, consecrates, or dresses differently from the laity may make a hypocrite or an idolatrous oil-painted icon, but it in no way makes a Christian or spiritual human being. In fact, we are all consecrated priests through baptism; as Saint Peter in 1 Peter 2[:9] says, 'You are a royal priesthood and a priestly kingdom,' and as Revelation [5:10] says, 'Through your blood you have made us into priests and kings'"

us granted us this new access to God, which is symbolized in the NT by the ripping of the temple veil from top to bottom (Matt. 27:51).[8] (3) God will forgive his peoples' sins and remember them no more, for they have been obliterated by means of the Messiah's sacrifice. If the sins continued to exist, God, who is omniscient, would know them. Instead, they are truly gone (2 Cor. 7:1; Heb. 10:10, 14; 1 John 1:9), not simply covered over, as they are in the OT (Lev. 16:10, 14–22).

Whereas the first improvement has been secured by the Holy Spirit, the latter two have been accomplished by the Messiah, such that we can be sanctified ("made holy") and have a new relationship with God, thus solving the dilemma as to how a holy God can have a relationship with sinful humanity. The blood of animals sacrificed under OT law served to cover (*kipper*) sin so that the OT God-fearer could temporarily stand in right relationship with the Lord (Lev. 17:11). But the blood of bulls and goats was not sufficient to fully satisfy the justice of God (Heb. 10:4). Only a sinless, perfect sacrifice could do that, as the NT book of Hebrews explains:

> But when Christ appeared as a high priest of the good things that had come, then through the greater and more perfect tabernacle—not made with hands (that is, not of this creation)—and not through the blood of goats and calves but through his own blood, he entered the holy place once for all, thus securing eternal redemption. For if the blood of goats and calves and the ashes of a heifer sprinkling those who have been defiled sanctify for the purification of the flesh, how much more will the blood of Christ, who through the eternal Spirit offered himself without blemish to God, cleanse our conscience from dead works to serve the living God? (Heb. 9:11–14 AT; cf. 1:2–3; 10:11–14)

The blood of goats and calves could ritually cleanse from sin, but according to Hebrews 10:4, it could never take away sins. However, as Philip Hughes writes,

---

(*D. Martin Luthers Werke: Kritische Gesammtausgabe* [Weimar: Hermann Böhlau, 1888], 6:407, lines 19–25 [translation mine]).

8. R. K. Harrison, *Jeremiah and Lamentations: An Introduction and Commentary*, TOTC 19 (Downers Grove, IL: InterVarsity, 1973), 140.

> Christ, the incarnate Son of God, is a fellow human being, partaking of our own human nature (2:14), and therefore, as man, fully qualified to stand in for us as our substitute, and, as one *without blemish*, that is, as a man morally perfect with an undefiled conscience before God (4:15; 7:27), competent to offer up the completely efficacious sacrifice of his own unblemished person in satisfaction for our sins and for the purifying of our consciences.[9]

Therefore, Christ's sacrifice produces an inward change and a purifying of our human conscience so that even our conscience, which condemns us before God as unworthy sinners, can now be purified. The Messiah is the one who provides this sacrifice.

Even though the OT never directly states that the Messiah is holy (*qādôš*), God used the Messiah in history to make a way so that all of his children could be sanctified, a concept that would become progressively clearer until the NT's full revelation. Other terms are used for the Messiah in the OT, highlighting his character as righteous, just, and fair, which makes him an adequate representative for God, and the NT clearly refers to the Messiah's holiness.

THE MESSIAH AS DELIVERER

God begins his plan to restore his people by providing hope for them. He will establish a ruler not only to deliver them from their enemies but also to bring about a kingdom where righteousness, justice, and peace prevail (Isa. 9:1–7 [8:23–9:6]). Both the Deliverer himself and his rule will embody the characteristics of his kingdom. The terms used to describe the Messiah demonstrate the suitability of his character to serve as an emissary for God: (1) "righteous" or "righteousness" (*ṣedeq*, *ṣədāqâ*, *ṣaddîq*: Isa. 9:6[7]; 11:4–5; 16:5; 32:1; 53:11); (2) "just" or "justice" (*mišpāṭ:* 9:6[7]; 16:5); (3) "peace" (*šālôm:* 9:6[7]); (4) "faithful" or "faithfulness" (*ʾĕmûnâ:* 11:5; 16:5); and (5) "fairness" (*mîšôr:* 11:4). The word *ṣedeq* can be defined as "behavior that . . . accord[s] with some standard"[10] and, I would add, with

9. Philip Edgcumbe Hughes, *A Commentary on the Epistle to the Hebrews* (Grand Rapids: Eerdmans, 1977), 357 (italics original).

10. David J. Reimer, "צדק," *NIDOTTE* 3:746.

God's perfect moral standard. The word *ʾĕmûnâ* means "faithfulness"; it "is often associated with the character of Yahweh (predominantly in Israel's praise in the psalms, e.g., Ps 33:4; 92:2[3]; 143:1) and is often linked with the language of 'steadfast love' (*ḥesed*) and 'righteousness' (*ṣedeq*/*ṣᵉdāqâ*)."[11] See also Deuteronomy 32:4, where *ʾĕmûnâ* is connected with *yāšār*, "upright."

Several of these terms overlap in meaning, but they clearly highlight the righteous character of the Messiah and are foundational to his nature. A few other passages also hint at his righteous character. Isaiah 11:3 states that the Messiah will not "judge by what His eyes see, [nor make a decision by what His ears hear" (NASB1995). Rather, his judgments are righteous and his decisions are just (v. 4). The implication is that the Messiah has an inherent sense of justice and is not fooled by appearances or false claims; he has an unerring sense of truthfulness and will judge accordingly. This Deliverer will also set up a kingdom governed by truth and justice; these characteristics will have a profound impact not only on the people (Isa. 32:2–8; Ezek. 37:24–28) but on animals as well (Isa. 11:6–9).

All these terms used for the Messiah have also been used to describe the character of God, as Psalm 36:5–6[6–7] beautifully illustrates: "Your loving kindness [*ḥesed*], O LORD, reaches to the heavens; your faithfulness [*ʾĕmûnâ*] unto the clouds. Your righteousness [*ṣədāqâ*] is like the highest mountains; your justice [*mišpāṭ*] is like the great deep" (AT).

Jeremiah 9:24 also tells us that YHWH not only practices loving kindness (*ḥesed*), justice (*mišpāṭ*), and righteousness (*ṣədāqâ*); he also delights in them. B. A. Milne describes how God's righteousness accords with his holiness: "For the OT God is Creator and therefore he is the ground and guarantor of the moral order. His righteousness is hence intimately related to other more general moral attributes such as his holiness."[12] For example, God could not be holy if he was not righteous, nor could he be holy if he was not just. Unrighteousness is in direct opposition to God's holiness, as are injustice and unfaithfulness.

The Prophets commonly extol the holiness and righteousness of God and portray the effects that his holiness has on his creation. David

11. R. W. L. Moberly, "אמן," *NIDOTTE* 1:429.

12. B. A. Milne, "Righteousness," *IDB* 3:1341.

J. Reimer notes that these consequences are set forth clearly in the book of Isaiah: “The presence of *ṣdq* [“righteousness”] results in *šālôm* [“peace,” “well-being”] (9:2–7[1–6]; 32:16–17; 48:18; 60:17),” and the Prophets “link *ṣdq* to God and the beneficent outworking of the divine *ṣdq* in the world and among God’s people.”[13] It is interesting that several of the passages Reimer mentions describe the ministry of the Messiah; thus, he is a further outworking of the righteousness and peace of God in this world.

Thus, the first step in preparing God’s children to be holy as he is holy (Lev. 11:44–45) is to provide hope in a future Deliverer who will set up a righteous kingdom where God’s holiness can flourish. This Deliverer demonstrates the qualities that God expects from his people and serves as an example of the changes that will occur in people and nature in a righteous kingdom.

THE MESSIAH AS SERVANT

The next crucial step in God’s revelation as to how he will sanctify his people is described in the ministry of the Servant. Even as early as Isaiah 49, the role of the Messiah, pictured as the Servant, is not only to bring the Israelites back to God (v. 5) but also to be a light portraying God’s salvation to the nations (v. 6). In addition, there are hints that the Messiah will suffer (50:6; 52:14; 53:5, 7–12) and be despised by Israel (49:7; 53:3–4) before he completes his ministry. But how will the Servant accomplish his task?

There has been significant disagreement over the meaning of the word *nāzâ* in Isaiah 52:15,[14] but an examination of other biblical occurrences clearly suggests the idea of ritual cleansing (see Exod. 29:21; Lev. 4:6, 17; etc.). Thus, the “Suffering Servant” will fulfill his role by cleansing people from many nations of their sins and bring them to God. But the blood of bulls and goats cannot remove sins (Heb. 10:4); doing so requires a perfect sacrifice, and only this can satisfy the justice of God. However, the only way that Christ’s perfect sacrifice can benefit us is if it can somehow be credited to us (or, more correctly, “imputed to us”) as a substitution for our sinfulness. This

13. Reimer, “צדק,” 764.

14. See Paul D. Wegner, *Isaiah: An Introduction and Commentary*, TOTC 20 (Downers Grove, IL: IVP Academic, 2021), 394–95.

is exactly what Isaiah 53 describes. Verse 4 draws a sharp contrast between the Servant (he) and the people (we). He bore our sorrows and griefs, though we considered him afflicted by God. It is not unusual for a prophet to identify with his people, but the next verse clearly goes beyond this: "He was pierced through because of our transgressions; he was crushed because of our iniquities; the chastening for our well-being was on him, and on account of his scourging, healing was to us" (v. 5 AT). His suffering was on our account—verse 6 makes it clear that he was punished for our iniquities (lit., "but the Lord caused the iniquity of us all to fall on him," AT). Even though R. N. Whybray maintains that this is not a description of "vicarious atonement,"[15] the grammar clearly argues against his view.[16]

Whybray also contends that the phrase in Isaiah 53:8 (NIV), "he was cut off from the land of the living," suggests either a near-death experience (see Lam. 3:54) or that the Servant was "as good as dead."[17] However, a close examination of the term *nāzar* ("to cut off") does not support this: "The phrase 'to cut off' occurs 177 times in the Old Testament, almost all of which mean 'to die' or 'to kill someone.' . . . Smith comments, 'Only dead people are cut off from the land of the living' (2009: 454), an observation that is further supported by the mention of the servant's grave in verse 9."[18]

Other interesting aspects of the nature of the Messiah are found in Isaiah 53:9: "He had done no violence [*ḥāmas*]," and "no deceit [*mirmâ*] was found in his mouth" (AT). The word *ḥāmas*, occurring sixty times in the OT, denotes "a wide range of concepts such as hurt, injury, oppression, violence, or wrong," and it is "virtually always used of sinful violence. Not surprisingly, therefore, God is never the agent involved in such behavior."[19] The word *mirmâ* occurs forty times with the meaning "trick," "fraud," "deceit," "lying," or "betrayal,"[20] but it is most commonly used of "treacherous or deceitful speech" (Gen. 34:13; Pss. 10:7; 17:1; 24:4;

15. R. N. Whybray, *Isaiah 40–66*, NCBC (Grand Rapids: Eerdmans, 1975), 171.
16. Specifically, I have the causal usage of *min* and *bə* in mind. See Ronald J. Williams, *Williams' Hebrew Syntax*, rev. and exp. John C. Beckman, 3rd ed. (Toronto: University of Toronto Press, 2007), 99, 121 (§§247, 319).
17. Whybray, *Isaiah 40–66*, 177.
18. Wegner, *Isaiah*, 398.
19. I. Swart and C. Van Dam, "חמס," *NIDOTTE* 2:177, 178.
20. See *HALOT*, 2:636.

etc.).[21] Used together, the absence of violence, wrong, or deceit suggests that the Suffering Servant will live a righteous and just life.

Isaiah 53:10 draws a contrast with verse 9b in stating that even though the Servant has done nothing wrong, God is pleased to crush (*dākā'*) him and make him sick (*ḥālâ*). But if the Servant is willing to offer himself as a guilt offering (*'āšām*), then he will see his offspring and his days will prosper. This type of offering is entirely fitting:

> According to Leviticus 4–5, the *'āšām* ('guilt offering') was to be offered for an unintentional sin. When made aware of his or her guilt, a person would offer this sacrifice (see Lev. 5:2–7). This is the exact sacrifice the Messiah needed to make on behalf of sinners, who may not recognize their sin until the Holy Spirit reveals it to them.[22]

Isaiah 53 ends with a structure that highlights what the Servant's work will accomplish and is literally translated in the following way:

A Because of the anguish of his soul,
  B he will see
  B′ and be satisfied;
A′ by his knowledge,

[Result:] the righteous one, my Servant, will justify the many, and their iniquities he himself will bear.

A Therefore, I will apportion to him a part
  B with the many
  B′ and with the strong;
A′ he will divide plunder because he emptied himself to the death and was reckoned with the rebellious ones;

[Result:] and he himself carried the sin of the many and interceded for the transgressors.

(Isa. 53:11–12 AT)

21. William White, "רָמָה (*rāmâ*) *II*," *TWOT* 2:849.

22. Wegner, *Isaiah*, 400.

The results in this passage clearly highlight that the role of the Servant is to carry sin and to justify, or make righteous, the many. In verse 11, the Servant (i.e., the Messiah) is even called "the righteous one" (*ṣaddîq*) who will justify (*yaṣdîq*) the many; he accomplishes justification by bearing people's sins on their behalf. God's plan from the beginning was to use the Servant to sanctify his children. This sanctification was something God's children could not achieve on their own. God therefore mercifully provided his own Son as the perfect Redeemer that they needed. The NT clarifies this even further: "For it was fitting for Him, for whom are all things, and through whom are all things, in bringing many sons to glory, to perfect the author of their salvation through sufferings. For both He who sanctifies and those who are sanctified are all from one Father; for which reason He is not ashamed to call them brethren" (Heb. 2:10–11 NASB1995).

THE MESSIAH AS KING

The final step in God's sanctification of his people is pictured in several passages that portray the Messiah as a ruler over a purified kingdom of saints (Isa. 32:1–8; Ezek. 37:24–28)—confirmation that, ultimately, God's children will indeed be sanctified and living in communion with him. The only way that a righteous God can dwell in their midst, as described in Ezekiel 37:26–28, is if they have been purified. The depiction of the Messiah as King appears more frequently than any other concept associated with him (Gen. 49:10; Isa. 9:6–7[5–6]; 16:5; 32:1–8; 33:17–24; Ezek. 37:24–28; Dan. 7:14; Mic. 5:2–5[1–4]; Zech. 9:9–10; Matt. 2:2; 21:5; 27:11; John 1:49; 12:15; 1 Tim. 6:15; Rev. 17:14; 19:16). He is often referred to as the son of David, and the Davidic covenant itself implies that David will have sons on the throne forever (2 Sam. 7:13–17; Pss. 89:36–37; 132:12). The only way that "a son of David would sit on the Davidic throne forever" would be if the Messiah sits on his throne to carry on his reign without end.

These passages inform us that the Messiah will come from the tribe of Judah (Gen. 49:10), more specifically from David's family (Isa. 9:6[7]; 16:5; Mic. 5:2[1]). He will rule in righteousness (Isa. 9:7[6]; 11:4–5; 16:5; 32:1; Zech. 9:9), justice (Isa. 9:7[6]; 16:5), and fairness (11:4) and will bring peace not only to humanity (9:6[7]; 33:18–24; Mic. 5:5[4]; Zech. 9:10), but also to the animal kingdom (Isa. 11:5–9). David J. Reimer points out that a kingdom of peace and righteousness is a natural hope, given the character of the Messiah: "The assumption is that a properly ordered society, one in which *ṣdq* is found, does not allow the powerful to live at the expense of the weak. This issues naturally into the hope for a king who will act according to *ṣdq* (Jer 22:15; 23:5 || 33:15 . . .); these notices complement those of Isaiah associating *ṣdq* with *šālôm*."[23] Thus, a righteous king ruling over a purified kingdom of saints is crucial to God's plan to sanctify his children. Without this step, God could never resume full fellowship with his children.

Daniel 7 also confirms that the Messiah (pictured as "a son of man") will rule over the eternal kingdom of God (pictured as "the Ancient of Days"). Here, in verses 13–14, the Messiah is given dominion (*šolṭān*) over God's kingdom, which will never be destroyed and includes people from all nations (cf. Rev. 11:15). The phrase "a son of man" is used in Ezekiel ninety-three times to refer to a human being; but in Daniel 7, one like a "human being" will rule over God's kingdom, thus hinting that the Messiah is more than merely human. "Son of Man" is the most common title that Jesus applies to himself in the NT (Matt. 8:20; 9:6; 10:23; 11:19; etc.), but he also claims to be the Son of God, allowing the Messiah to be both divine and human. Revelation 11:15 emphasizes the final outcome of God's kingdom when it announces: "The kingdom of the world has become the kingdom of our Lord and of His Christ [*christou*, "Messiah"]; and He will reign forever and ever" (NASB1995). Thus, the NT confirms that Jesus will rule over God's kingdom.

CONCLUSION

God's unfolding plan for humankind's redemption was revealed over time: while the Messiah is never said to be holy, he is God's agent to sanctify or "to make holy" fallen humankind. The book of Hebrews clarifies that Christ is the perfect high priest, the mediator between God and humanity:

> But he holds his priesthood permanently because he abides forever. Therefore also, he is able to save forever those who draw near to God through him, since he always lives to make intercession for them. For it was indeed fitting that we should

23. Reimer, "צדק," 764.

> have such a high priest, holy, innocent, undefiled, separated from sinners and exalted above the heavens; who does not need daily to offer up sacrifices, like those high priests, first for his own sins and then for the sins of the people, because this he did once for all when he offered up himself. For the Law appoints men as high priests who are weak, but the word of the oath, which came after the Law, appoints a Son, made perfect forever. (7:24–28 AT)

Yet if the Messiah is God's means of sanctifying his children, why is the term "holy" never used of him? Some scholars have argued that the essence of holiness is the idea of separateness,[24] and we have likewise argued that God is completely separated from his sinful children. However, John Oswalt argues that the full-orbed concept of holiness includes a variety of ideas: (1) God's nature as mysterious, transcendent, and other; (2) his nature as being set apart from all evil; and (3) his absolute ethical purity.[25] If this is the case, then some aspects of the concept of holiness do not correspond well to the role of the Messiah. God is wholly other and set apart from sinful humanity, but the Messiah serves to bridge this great gulf. He is God's agent for redeeming lost humanity from their sinful plight, and ultimately, he will rule over God's purified kingdom on earth. Whereas moral and ethical purity are definitely part of the Messiah's character as a representative for God, his ministry also entails coming down to earth as a Suffering Servant to deliver God's people (Isa. 52:15; 53:11) and to interact with sinful humanity during his time on earth; thus, he cannot remain wholly other. Other terms, such as "righteous," "just," and "upright," must therefore be chosen to describe the suitability of the Messiah to fulfill the role God has for him in his plan to sanctify humankind.

While the OT does not use the word "holy" to describe the Messiah, the NT does apply it to each person of the Godhead: the Father (Luke 1:49; John 17:11; Rev. 4:8; 6:10; 15:4; 16:5), the Son (Mark 1:24; Luke 4:34; John 6:69; Acts 4:27, 30; 1 Peter 1:15; Rev. 3:7), and especially the Holy Spirit, who not only manifests the holiness of God but also sanctifies God's children (Rom. 5:5; 14:17; 15:16; 1 Cor. 6:19;

24. See BDB, 871; Finlayson, "Holiness," 656; Naudé, "885 ",קדשׁ.

25. See Oswalt's essay at the beginning of this volume.

Titus 3:5).[26] John 17:19 may refer specifically to Jesus's sanctification for us: "and on account of them I sanctify myself, so that they also may be sanctified in truth" (AT).

The NT thus clarifies that the only way God's children can be sanctified is for the perfect Son of God to come to earth and to offer his life as a ransom. The book of Hebrews proclaims that Jesus was a perfect sacrifice: "In the days of his flesh, he offered up both prayers and supplications with loud cries and tears to the one who was able to save him from death, and he was heard on account of his piety. Although he was a son, he learned obedience from that which he suffered. And having been made perfect, he became to all those who obey him the source of eternal salvation" (5:7–9 AT).

For God to offer his only Son on behalf of those who rebelled against him in the garden of Eden demonstrates a truly amazing love. Leonard Ravenhill, an English evangelist and author, articulates the incredible result of God's sanctification of his children: "The greatest miracle that God can do today is to take an unholy man out of an unholy world, and make that man holy and put him back into that unholy world and keep him holy in it."[27] This miracle is largely because of the Messiah's work.

26. Finlayson, "Holiness," 656.

27. Leonard Ravenhill, "Holiness-Quotes, Devotionals, Illustrations," as quoted by *Precept Austin*, last updated January 15, 2020, https://www.preceptaustin.org/holiness_quotes.

Chapter 12

Holiness and Salvation in the Old Testament: God's Presence Making His People Holy

Scott A. Engebretson

Introduction

What do holiness and salvation have to do with one another? Numerous OT studies have focused on one or the other of these concepts, but rarely have the two been intertwined.[1] Yet a legitimate (even warranted) interpretation of the OT lends itself to a bold proclamation: "without holiness no one will see the Lord" (Heb. 12:14 NIV). Throughout the OT, being in God's presence is the intent at creation, and being restored to God's presence is the goal of salvation. Nevertheless, when thinking about salvation, both ends of the biblical narrative speak of God's people in God's presence. The author of Hebrews appears to suggest that to be in God's presence and to see the Lord, holiness is essential. When a person comes into God's presence and encounters his grace, that person is changed and transformed. Thus, holiness, properly understood and as articulated in this volume, is an essential part of understanding biblical salvation. Holiness is not an ancillary or an optional part of God's plan of salvation; rather, it is at the very heart of God's saving work in this world.

A question that undergirds this essay is this: What do people need to be saved from? On the surface, salvation is an easy concept to grasp in the Bible. Salvation occurs when God intervenes to help, deliver, save, or protect people amid troubles. But the nature of salvation in the Bible is more subtle and universal. This chapter will view salvation through the lens of the OT covenants and show a development of salvation that finds its ultimate aim in YHWH's holy presence. Salvation is not

1. For an important exception, see John N. Oswalt, *Called to Be Holy: A Biblical Perspective* (Anderson, IN: Francis Asbury, 1999).

simply an invitation to be in the presence of "the Holy One of Israel" (cf. Pss. 71:22, 89:18; Isa. 12:6; 41:16–20), rather, it is also an invitation to share in that holiness (e.g., Lev. 11:44–45; 19:2, 24; 20:7, 26). This is salvation: to be in YHWH's presence and encounter his character in such a way that he shares his character with us.

This chapter begins with a general overview of the *language* of salvation that is used throughout the OT. Salvation occurs when God intervenes to help, deliver, save, or protect people amid all sorts of troubles and tribulations—both significant and relatively insignificant. Exploring the terminology of salvation will orient us and provide important data for understanding salvation holistically. The vast majority of the terms used for salvation emerge after the exodus event. The exodus event, alongside the return from exile, are quintessential examples of salvation in the OT. For good reason, these experiences shape Israel's understanding of the concept. Nevertheless, Israel's experience of oppression in Egypt and exile in Babylon are the result of a deeper and more universal human problem of sin in the OT narrative.

Thus, after analyzing the language of salvation, this study will turn to Genesis 1–11 to highlight that which lies behind the oppression in Egypt and Babylon. This section will focus on Genesis 1–3. When sin enters God's good creation, something is fundamentally broken. Man and woman are created in God's image to be image bearers in this world (Gen. 1:26–27). Human beings are created in God's image and likeness to represent him throughout the creation. Furthermore, as Christopher Wright suggests, these qualities imply that men and women are "created for a task" to tend and care for God's creation.[2] The entrance of sin into God's good creation not only removes Adam and Eve from the garden—that is, from God's presence—it also distorts their capacity to faithfully embody his image. Genesis 1–3 provides the origin and locus for the need of salvation. These chapters show us the original intent of humans as image bearers (ch. 1–2), and the departure from that plan (ch. 3). Nevertheless, Genesis 1–2 shows us the potential to be restored in God's image. Humans must be saved from their sinfulness and the ripples of sin that touch every part of creation. Salvation in the Bible is thus a reclamation and restoration project. Salvation implies not only rescue from

2. Christopher J. H. Wright, *The Mission of God: Unlocking the Bible's Grand Narrative* (Downers Grove, IL: IVP Academic, 2018), 425–27.

external circumstances but also a return to God's presence *and* a restoration in God's image. This is the relationship between salvation and holiness. To demonstrate this connection, we will explore the covenants, as they show this understanding of salvation in the OT. Ultimately, this study will point to the new covenant and offer a way to understand both salvation and holiness in the NT.

THE LANGUAGE OF SALVATION

To understand holiness in the OT, it is necessary to explore how the OT defines salvation. In his work *Old Testament Theology for Christians*, John Walton suggests that salvation assumes some type of "transition."[3] When God graciously initiates saving actions on behalf of people who are in difficult situations, deliverance occurs, leading to improved circumstances. In the OT, salvation most often occurs when YHWH is the subject and Israel is the object—whether YHWH's activity is direct or through other agents. Claus Westermann suggests that the exodus event (Exod. 12–15) is salvation par excellence.[4] This event uniquely shapes how the OT describes and envisions salvation. With a few exceptions, the specific terms discussed below emerge after the exodus event and then also refer to this defining moment. Thus, building on the experience of crossing the Red Sea, Israel developed a rich vocabulary for salvation and deliverance.[5] Yet it is also clear that other, less significant acts of divine salvation occur in Israel's everyday, ordinary experience. God saves individuals, families, and nations from various trials and circumstances (e.g., Gen. 32:11; 49:18; 2 Sam. 22:1; 2 Kings 17:39; Ezra 8:11; Pss. 21:1–7; 62:1–8, 88; and Isa. 12:2). Yet even these so-called less significant acts of deliverance are largely understood through the lens of the exodus.[6]

---

3. John H. Walton, *Old Testament Theology for Christians: From Ancient Context to Enduring Belief* (Downers Grove, IL: IVP Academic, 2017), 225–26.
4. Claus Westermann, *Elements of Old Testament Theology*, trans. Douglas W. Stott (Atlanta: John Knox, 1982), 36–45.
5. R. W. L. Moberly, "Salvation in the Old Testament," *JTI* 15 (2021): 189–202. As noted above, many of the terms discussed here emerge only after Israel's exodus from Egypt. A few occurrences of these terms can be found in Genesis, but they are used in more general ways—for example, as prayers for God's protection (32:11, 49:18) and as warnings to flee imminent destruction (19:17–22). The one exception is Jacob's blessing of Joseph in 48:16.
6. The return from Babylonian exile is another significant moment of deliverance. Below, we will see how Isaiah uses the exodus to envision exilic hope. The possibility of Israel's return from exile is rooted in the exodus.

Seven Hebrew terms are used more than eight hundred times to describe an act or experience of salvation. The wealth of terms and the frequency of their use suggest that the idea of deliverance is conceptually important for Israel's understanding of YHWH and its relationship with him. The primary terms utilized are *yšʿ*, *nṣl*, *gʾl*, *pdh*, *mlṭ*, *śrd*, and *plṭ*. The two most prevalent Hebrew roots and their derivatives are *yšʿ* and *nṣl*, used 353[7] times and 220 times, respectively. Two other unique terms are *gʾl* ("to redeem"),[8] which occurs just over one hundred times, and *mlṭ* ("to be delivered"), which occurs just under one hundred times.[9] While these terms have significant semantic overlap, each one offers a shade of nuance that helps provide a rich tapestry for understanding salvation in the OT.

The most common Hebrew root for salvation is *yšʿ*. Moberly suggests that "the basic sense of *ysʿ* is an exercise of help to someone in a difficult and unwelcome situation, that which a stronger party does on behalf of a weaker party."[10] The term is used to describe Israel's miraculous deliverance from Egypt (Exod. 14:13, 30; 15:2), where YHWH is a mighty rescuer who delivers his people from oppression and defends them. This term is also common when describing military conflicts and war. Thus, the term appears with some regularity during the tumultuous transition from the judges to the monarchy, as Israel faces military conflicts and various threats (e.g., Judg. 2:16–17; 1 Sam. 2:1; 9:16; 11:13).[11] Similarly, the Prophets, particularly Isaiah and Jeremiah, use this term to describe God acting benevolently on the Israelites' behalf, rescuing them, and defending their cause (Isa. 37:35; 49:26; Jer. 15:20; 30:11). Finally, Psalms overflows with *yšʿ* in its worship and prayers. There the Israelites consistently remember and celebrate God's past acts of deliverance (e.g., 18:3; 44:3; 106:10), which informs their prayers for future acts of deliverance (e.g., 3:7; 20:9; 54:1; 86:2).

The other most common term, *nṣl*, offers a similar but more forceful depiction of deliverance (Exod. 18:8–10; Josh. 24; Judg. 6:9;

---

7. *TWOT*, 414.
8. *TWOT*, 144.
9. *TWOT*, 507.
10. Moberly, "Salvation in the Old Testament," 192. Moberly notes that surprisingly little secondary literature deals with *yšʿ*, the most frequently used term in the OT for "salvation."
11. Robert L. Hubbard Jr., "ישׁע," *NIDOTTE* 2:556–62.

1 Sam. 4:8; 2 Sam. 22:18; Ps. 7:1–2; Hos. 5:14; Amos 3:12; Zech. 3:2). Salvation is envisioned as a "tearing out" from danger.[12] The causative forms particularly display God snatching people out of trouble, rescue in times of turmoil, and dramatic escape from peril. Similar to *yšʿ*, this term also becomes a regular prayer for Israel in the Psalms and elsewhere (e.g., Gen. 32:11; Josh. 2:13; Pss. 22:20; 40:13; 51:14; 143:9).

Two additional terms worth mentioning are *gʾl* and *pdh*. These two roots are related and provide an expanding picture of salvation as redemption and ransom. The term *gʾl* describes a redeemer taking on the responsibility to protect the family line by vindicating and supporting one's household (Ruth 2:20; 3:9–13; 4:1–8).[13] In the story of Ruth, Boaz goes to great lengths and great expense to redeem Ruth. Similarly, *pdh* describes salvation as sparing someone through an act of ransom or a transfer of ownership.

Although this study does not allow for a full treatment of every term, this brief etymological backdrop provides a general outline for how the OT depicts salvation. The various Hebrew terms provide a robust picture of salvation that extends from help to dramatic rescue, freedom, ransom, and being set free for a price. People are delivered from slavery, protected from enemies, and ultimately brought into better places (e.g., Ps. 18). These acts encompass every facet of life—temporal and physical, spiritual, and even inclusive of future promises of deliverance and safety. Salvation is a perpetual need and persistent possibility in the experience of the Israelites. While the different terms exhibit shades of nuance, the concept is clear: God is Israel's Savior, who delivers the nation *from* (or out of) difficult circumstances and helps it *in* times of trouble and despair.

Isaiah 43 offers an instructive example of how the diverse terminology of salvation is brought together to demonstrate the centrality of the exodus and to distinctly shape Israel's understanding of salvation in the face of exile. There the prophet uses a variety of terms mentioned earlier (*yšʿ*, *nṣl*, *gʾl*) to offer a robust promise and formulation of salvation. YHWH is Israel's only Savior (*môšîaʿ*, from *yšʿ*, vv. 3, 11–12), the one who redeems (*gʾl*, vv. 1, 14) and delivers (*nṣl*, v. 13) the people.

12. Westermann, *Elements of Old Testament Theology*, 45.
13. Sandra L. Richter, *The Epic of Eden: A Christian Entry into the Old Testament* (Downers Grove, IL: IVP Academic, 2008), 40–45.

Furthermore, this hope of salvation is rooted in the exodus experience of previous generations (vv. 2, 16). Israel's past experience defines its future hope. This past act of God's gracious salvation enables the prophet to announce the possibility of the otherwise inconceivable return from exile (vv. 5–7, 14–15)—from one great event of salvation to another. Isaiah then takes these major events and applies them to each person. The Redeemer not only rescues Israel from the nations but also blots out sins (vv. 25–27). The diverse language of Isaiah 43 shows that Israel's concept of salvation is informed by the exodus and provides an ever-expanding possibility of salvation in every facet of life. YHWH saves people from oppression, brings them back from exile, rescues them everywhere in-between, and removes their sins.

To summarize this section dealing with the terminology of salvation in the OT, the way Israel envisions salvation and describes God's acts of deliverance in the Old Testament is anchored in the exodus event. This act was a defining moment that shaped the notion of salvation, and it touched every aspect of daily life. While the language of salvation begins with the exodus event, the need of salvation is evidenced in the initial chapters of Genesis, although the terms discussed above are not present. Israel's deliverance from Egypt shapes them profoundly. However, the oppression the Israelites face in both Egypt and Babylon during the exile is the result of a more universal problem of sin described in Genesis 1–11. The following section will turn to Genesis 1–11 to widen the biblical portrait of salvation, understood as restoration.

SALVATION AS RESTORATION

While the OT's language of salvation focuses on various events and circumstances of deliverance, the OT, more broadly, provides a far deeper sense of salvation. Genesis 1–3 offers an understanding of the nature of God, the goodness of his creation, and the impact of the fall, which necessitates a different sense of salvation and restoration. While salvation in the OT addresses external realities, such as being rescued out of Egypt and returning from Babylon, these chapters point to the need of an internal salvation and restoration from the effects of the fall. Genesis 1–2 poetically paints the picture of God's good creation of the whole world and then focuses on the uniqueness of Adam and Eve in the garden. In Genesis 1, God speaks and everything is put in its place. Creation is ordered, harmonious, beautiful, and full of potential.

Adam and Eve are created in God's image, and they are the pinnacle of creation (vv. 26–28). They are placed in the garden and tasked with cultivating, tending, and caring for this world (ch. 2). They have access to God's presence, and God meets with them in the garden.[14] This is the way things should be.

In Genesis 3, however, things shift dramatically. The introduction of sin into God's good creation impacts all things and all people. Adam and Eve listen to the serpent, turn from God, disobey his instructions, and unleash sin and death into his good creation. At this point, everything changes. The order and harmony of creation is broken, and relationships are fractured. Adam and Eve turn on one another. Creation turns on humanity. And most significantly, Adam and Eve's relationship with their Creator is fractured. Because of their decision, they are removed from the garden. They lose the presence of God. The image is also marred, as it has been created for unbroken fellowship with the Creator. Things have gone terribly wrong.

It will be helpful to understand salvation as restoration of what has been lost in Genesis 3. This is where salvation and the concept of holiness are intermeshed. In the introductory chapter of this volume, John Oswalt suggests that *qādôš* in the OT is nuanced and goes beyond the basic ANE concept. YHWH is the uncreated, transcendent Creator of all creation. Genesis 1–2 reveals a God who is uniquely other. Holiness in the OT, however, is not merely a vague understanding of otherness or a unique experience of awe in the presence of the divine.[15] These ANE connotations of *qādôš* are embedded in the biblical use of holiness, but *qādôš* is further defined in the Bible in light of God's moral character. Holiness is perhaps best evidenced in God's immutable goodness, faithfulness, righteousness, justice, peace, purity, and *ḥesed*.[16] This description is most clearly observed in Exodus 34:6–7. There YHWH reveals himself as compassionate, gracious, slow to

14. See G. K. Beale, *The Temple and the Church's Mission: A Biblical Theology of the Dwelling Place of God*, NSBT 15 (Downers Grove, IL: IVP Academic, 2014), and G. K. Beale and Mitchell Kim, *God Dwells among Us: A Biblical Theology of the Temple*, ESBT (Downers Grove, IL: IVP Academic, 2021).

15. Rudolf Otto, *The Idea of the Holy: An Inquiry into the Non-rational Factor in the Idea of the Divine and Its Relation to the Rational*, trans. John W. Harvey, 9th ed. (Oxford: Oxford University Press, 1928).

16. For a more in-depth discussion, see Oswalt, *Called to Be Holy*, 9–100, and Matt Ayars, Christopher T. Bounds, and Caleb T. Friedeman, *Holiness: A Biblical, Historical, and Systematic Theology* (Downers Grove, IL: IVP Academic, 2023).

anger, and abounding in *ḥesed*, forgiveness, and an unwillingness to allow sin to persist. This portrayal of God's character recurs throughout the OT (e.g., Num. 14:18; Deut. 4:31; Neh. 9:17; Ps. 86:5, 15; Joel 2:13; and Jonah 4:2). God is not merely devoted to this way of acting—he *is* holy. As discussed above, while human beings are not transcendent, we are created in the image and likeness of God and are meant to reflect God's character. This is further highlighted in instructions such as "Be holy because I, the Lord your God, am holy" (Lev. 19:2 NIV; cf. 11:44–45, 20:26; 1 Peter 1:16).[17] In addition to the image of God being marred in humanity, holiness (i.e., moral character—namely—steadfast love) is also part of what is lost in Genesis 3.

Genesis 4–11 continues the sordid, post-sin saga, highlighting the universal ramifications of Adam and Eve's sin, which affects all people and all places.[18] Sin intensifies, spreads, and touches every aspect of God's creation. Murder, violence, and revenge are on the rise. Genesis 6:5 describes the problem in the starkest terms—God sees the wickedness of men and women and observes that "every inclination of the thoughts of the human heart [is] only evil all the time" (NIV). Sin has infected all of creation and all people, and the results have contaminated every aspect of life—personal, relational, social, and spiritual. Throughout the OT, sin in the human heart is the problem that requires salvation. Deliverance will have to take place at the heart level.

The flood account demonstrates the pervasive nature of sin as an internal condition and not something that can be rinsed away externally (Gen. 6:5–6). Though Noah is righteous (*ṣaddîq*) and blameless (*tāmîm*) and is in some sense contrasted with the corruption and violence of the world, he is also marked within by the realities of sin. God tasks Noah with building an ark to save his family from the waters and thus begins a process of re-creation. Although the specific language is not used, Noah and his family will be "saved" from the flood waters (cf. 1 Peter 3:20–22). When the flood waters recede,

17. Peter Gentry has rightfully pointed people back to the text to see various aspects of holiness as "consecration" and "devotion." However, it seems that the vast ways the biblical text uses the terminology of holiness goes beyond the themes he addresses in his article. His study would benefit from additional work exploring Lev. 11:44–45, 19:2, and 20:26. See Peter J. Gentry, "The Meaning of 'Holy' in the Old Testament," *BSac* 170 (2013): 400–417.

18. See Thomas H. McCall, *Against God and Nature: The Doctrine of Sin*, ed. John S. Feinberg (Wheaton, IL: Crossway, 2019), and Cornelius Plantinga, *Not the Way It's Supposed to Be: A Breviary of Sin* (Grand Rapids: Eerdmans, 1999).

Noah and his family emerge from the ark and offer a sacrifice, and God promises via covenant never to curse and destroy the earth again by flood (Gen. 8:21; 9:1–17). It is also clear that the flood does not resolve the lingering issue of sin. Genesis 8:21 restates the devastating analysis first announced in Genesis 6:5: "every inclination of the human heart is evil from childhood" (NIV). Sin remains lodged in the human heart. Neither the flood nor Noah's sacrifice can adequately address this problem.

This is an important point as it relates to the nature of sin. John Walton rightly suggests that sin in Genesis 3 "results in alienation" and "disequilibrium" of God's intended order.[19] As noted, the need for salvation does encompass returning people to God's presence. Walton, however, goes on to suggest that Israel's conception of sin (and salvation) is similar to that of its ANE neighbors. In Egypt and Mesopotamia, sin is linked to ritual transgressions of various kinds.[20] Thus, Walton argues that the "Israelites were not looking for salvation from sins; they were expecting resolution of covenant disorder," which is linked to their divine calling.[21] While sin is a ritual matter, Genesis 1–11 is not dealing with Israel's ritual transgressions of the Mosaic covenant but, rather, with the pervasive power of sin that has intruded and infected every part of creation—especially the human heart. Furthermore, numerous passages in the OT connect salvation with the forgiveness of sins (e.g., 2 Chron. 6:21; Pss. 25:5–11; 32:1–11; 51:1–19 [cf. 2 Sam. 12:13]; 79:9; 85; 103:8–13; Isa. 33:24; 40:2; 43:25; 44:22; 55:7; Jer. 50:20; Mic. 7:18; and Zech. 3:4). Israel's idea of sin includes ritual transgressions and breaches of the Mosaic stipulations, but it is broader.

Genesis 1–11 provides important data points for considering Israel's conceptual framework of sin and salvation. The ramifications of sin described in Genesis 3–11 are universal and pervasive. As illustrated with Noah, external measures of deliverance change circumstances but do not fully address the problem that emerges in Genesis 3. The need for salvation runs deeper. The goal of the exodus is not merely to get the people out of Egypt. Rescue from the oppression in Egypt

19. Walton, *Old Testament Theology for Christians*, 187–88.
20. Walton, *Old Testament Theology for Christians*, 188.
21. Walton, *Old Testament Theology for Christians*, 228.

is necessary, but it is not the goal of salvation. As we will see, this is also the case in the exodus narrative. Getting out of Egypt is necessary, but doing so is not the goal of salvation. This leads to a second point for understanding salvation. Sin has alienated humanity from God's presence; therefore, for restoration to be possible, sin must be dealt with in such a way that people may have access to God's holy presence and recapture again the vision of humanity captured in Genesis 1–2—God's image restored in people, for the sake of his world.

THE GOAL OF SALVATION

As noted above, the most devastating consequence of sin in humanity is twofold. Humanity has lost God's presence, and God's image has been marred. Thus, the goal of salvation must address these two realities. One of the ways God addresses both of these issues is through various covenants in the OT, revealing both the way of salvation and holiness and its goal. As is well known, the concept of covenant (*bərît*) is foundational for understanding the Old and New Testaments.[22] In the 1930s, Walther Eichrodt forcibly argued that covenant is *the* central theme of the OT.[23] The claim that the OT has one unifying center has been debated over the last century, but one does not have to argue for such a center to acknowledge that the covenants are integral to Israel's understanding of salvation.[24] John Stek argues that any discussion of salvation in the OT must be understood within the larger narrative.[25] The covenants carry the narrative of biblical salvation. Although the scope of this chapter disallows a full treatment of the concept of covenant, it does permit us to observe that each covenant offers an unfolding development of God's saving work.

Peter Gentry and Stephen Wellum argue that the concept of covenant is the foundational idea undergirding the narrative structure of the

22. See, e.g., Walther Eichrodt, *Theology of the Old Testament*, trans. J. A. Baker, 2 vols. (London: SCM, 1961, 1967); Richter, *Epic of Eden*, 69–91; Walton, *Old Testament Theology for Christians*, 105–42; Peter J. Gentry and Stephen J. Wellum, *Kingdom through Covenant: A Biblical-Theological Understanding of the Covenants*, 2nd ed. (Wheaton, IL: Crossway, 2018); and Moshe Weinfeld, "בְּרִית *bərîth*," *TDOT* 2:253–79.

23. Eichrodt, *Theology of the Old Testament*.

24. For a brief but helpful history of Eichrodt's role in the discipline of OT theology, as well as the differences in approaches between one central theme versus multiple themes, see Brittany Kim and Charlie Trimm, *Understanding Old Testament Theology: Mapping the Terrain of Recent Approaches* (Grand Rapids: Zondervan Academic, 2020), 3–6, 53–88.

25. John H. Stek, "Salvation, Justice and Liberation in the Old Testament," *CTJ* 13 (1978): 164–65.

entire biblical corpus. They write, "*The progression of the covenants* forms the backbone of Scripture's metanarrative, the relational reality that moves history forward according to God's design and final plan for humanity and all creation."[26] Walton highlights the unfolding development inherent in the covenants, which moves from relationship to God's dwelling, then to reigning, and finally to saving.[27] Each covenant advances the way of salvation. Of course, the Mosaic covenant looms large over the biblical text. But even this covenant has a backstory. God intervenes because he has heard the cry of his people and "remembered his covenant with Abraham, with Isaac and with Jacob" (Exod. 2:24 NIV; cf. 3:6, 15–16; 6:3–8; see also Gen. 50:24 and Deut. 26:5–10). The Mosaic covenant also points forward to the Davidic covenant and the new covenant. Below, we will look at facets of each covenant and consider how each one contributes to Israel's robust understanding of salvation and holiness.

Noah: Divine Patience in Salvation

God first makes a covenant in the Bible within the context of the flood and his interaction with Noah, already discussed above (Gen. 6–9).[28] Noah's story suggests that sin is so anticreational that God must start over.[29] The flood comes as a response to the evil of the human heart and the vast wickedness spreading throughout the earth (6:5). Again, when Noah and his family emerge from the ark, the problem remains (8:21).

26. Gentry and Wellum, *Kingdom through Covenant*, 31 (italics original). See also Peter J. Gentry and Stephen J. Wellum, *God's Kingdom through God's Covenants: A Concise Biblical Theology* (Wheaton, IL: Crossway, 2015).
27. Walton, *Old Testament Theology for Christians*, 114–32.
28. Noteworthily, some scholars argue that Gen. 1–3 betrays a formal covenantal structure, even though *bərît* is not used there. See the discussion of a potential "creation covenant" in Gentry and Wellum, *Kingdom through Covenant*, 211–58; *God's Kingdom through God's Covenants*, 69–92. In both places, Gentry and Wellum argue that a significant linguistic difference exists between *kārat bərît* and *hēqîm bərît*. The former is used frequently in the OT to *initiate* a covenant, whereas the latter affirms a *preexisting* covenant. The latter is also used in Gen. 6:18 and 9:9–17, which can only point back to Gen. 1–3. Whether a covenant can be found in Gen. 1–3 or not, it has already been noted that these chapters are instrumental in understanding the need for salvation.
29. This point is observed in how Gen. 9:1–7 mirrors various aspects of God's instructions in Gen. 1. For example, Noah is called to be fruitful and increase in number (9:1, 7), which is the same command given to Adam and Eve in 1:28. Then the divine image, which is the climax of creation in 1:27, is reaffirmed in 9:6. Additionally, Noah is instructed to rule over the animals and all of creation. Each of these examples suggests that God intends the flood to be a re-creational event that allows his original purposes to govern the world again. God institutes a new creation in Gen. 6–9 through Noah and his family.

The floodwaters seemingly touch every aspect of brokenness except the human heart. Thus, the problem and need for salvation remains.

Despite the grim prognosis of Genesis 8:21, God initiates an eternal covenant with Noah, his family, and *all* future generations. Three broad lessons can be learned from the flood story as it relates to salvation. First, sin is insidiously destructive, and second, sin must be remedied. The flood suggests that God desires to rid the world of sin and its consequences. Third and finally, God promises in the Noahic covenant to never again "destroy all living creatures," even though sin remains in the human heart (Gen. 8:21). The Noahic covenant points to two realities: (1) divine patience in the face of sin (cf. 2 Peter 3:5–10) and (2) YHWH's commitment to restore his creation.[30] Through Noah, God offers an ongoing promise despite the human heart, which is marred by sin. As the narrative turns to Abraham, God turns from a widespread flood that had massive implications for people in general to a husband and wife to address the problem of sin in the human heart.

Abraham: Divine Relationship and Trust

The story of Abraham marks a shift in the storyline. The narrative ambit moves from people in general to a single family, aging and childless. The covenant with Abraham and Sarah suggests that God's remedy for sin and the restoration of God's presence begin with relationship.[31] The promise given to Abraham and his family is fourfold. Abraham's family will receive a land, become a great nation, experience God's blessing, and ultimately bless the whole world. The commands given to Adam and Eve and then to Noah are also given to Abraham and Sarah: "Be fruitful," "increase in number," and "fill the earth" (Gen. 1:28; 9:1, 7; 17:5–6 NIV). While this covenant begins with one couple, it is not about a single-family unit but rather an ever-expanding circle of blessing. Abraham and his family are to carry God's blessing to the entire world. In this regard, the Abrahamic covenant is a covenant of mission.[32]

To carry out this mission, an active faith is required. Abraham and Sarah must "go" (Gen. 12:1) and effectively walk with an unknown God into an unknown future. Abraham is asked to give up his country,

30. Christopher J. H. Wright, *The Mission of God: Unlocking the Bible's Grand Narrative* (Downers Grove, IL: IVP Academic, 2018), 326–27.
31. Walton, *Old Testament Theology for Christians*, 115.
32. Wright, *Mission of God*, 327–29.

his people, and the security of his *bêt ʾāb*—which would have included his inheritance, livelihood, and economic security—and go.[33] For an aging, childless couple, doing so would require trusting God's promise of a child (ch. 21). Part of the biblical story of salvation concerns the need for radical *trust* in the face of uncertainty. Throughout their journey, Abraham and Sarah face many detours, but at every stage, Abraham is asked to exhibit an active, embodied faith by giving up his identity and being obedient. Ultimately, after Isaac is born, Abraham is asked to give him up in Genesis 22:1–19. The way of salvation for Abraham and Sarah does not require giving up their worst things (i.e., sins); rather, it requires giving up that which is most important in their lives. This type of trust impacts their way of life and character. As a result of his trust, Abraham's faith becomes the biblical model (e.g., Gen. 12; 15; 22; Rom. 4; Gal. 3:1–9; Heb. 11:8–19; and James 2:20–24). Despite their frailties, Abraham and Sarah exude a faith marked by growing trust within a maturing relationship. The way of salvation requires radical faith, trust, and obedience that reshapes our lives.

Moses: Flourishing in God's Presence

The exodus and the Mosaic covenant are central to any conception of salvation in the OT. But the covenantal narrative also reveals a rich understanding of God's presence and character, which illuminates Israel's calling to be a holy priesthood. As Exodus begins, the people are languishing under the oppressive hand of Egypt. YHWH uses Moses to deliver the Israelite people from their slavery (Exod. 1–15). As already noted, the exodus is the pivotal moment in Israel's salvation experience. But this is only the beginning of its deliverance story. Once again, the external circumstances are not the root issue—freedom from Egypt is necessary but is not the goal. The rest of the story points to God's presence, his character, and Israel's unique calling.

After crossing the Red Sea, the people begin a three-month journey toward Sinai (Exod. 15:22–18:27), where they will be invited into covenant. During this in-between period, other acts of divinely initiated salvation occur. God sustains the people with water (15:22–27; 17:1–7), provides manna and quail (ch. 16), protects and delivers the

33. See Philip J. King and Lawrence E. Stager, *Life in Biblical Israel*, LAI (Louisville: Westminster John Knox, 2001), 36–40.

people from an imposing enemy (17:8–16), and even provides organizational wisdom to sustain Moses as he leads the people (ch. 18). Before a single law of the Mosaic covenant is etched in stone, the people have been delivered out of Egypt and have experienced God's gracious provision in multiple ways. The covenant in Exodus 19–24, including the Ten Commandments and the other instructions, is built on God's prior saving actions on Israel's behalf (19:4).

Subsequently, in light of these gracious acts of deliverance, faithfulness to the terms of the covenant is required so that Israel might live in God's presence, as his treasured possession, and become a kingdom of priests and a holy nation for the sake of the world (Exod. 19:3–6). God has brought the people out of Egypt to himself, that they might be different (holy) and stand between him and the people of the world (as priests). Once the Israelites agree to the terms of the covenant (19:8; 24:3, 7) and the instructions and stipulations of the covenant are expressed, the rest of Exodus shifts toward the tabernacle. The tabernacle is the structure that symbolizes YHWH's dwelling place with the people. As Victor Hamilton points out, roughly a third of Exodus is dedicated to the building of the tabernacle, which highlights the importance of God's presence among his people.[34] The climax of the book is Exodus 40:34–38, where God's presence and glory fill the tabernacle. This is the goal of the covenant and the aim of salvation: that God's presence might consistently dwell among his people. Numbers 1–10 locates the tabernacle at the center of the people, and throughout the rest of the Pentateuch, this structure is the focal point of the community, symbolizing God's presence at the center of his people.[35]

At this point, one can see the intertwining of salvation and holiness. Being in God's presence again is one part of the equation of salvation. As people are in God's presence, humans will increasingly reflect his character. God's presence is multidimensional. The tabernacle not only houses God's glory and represents his presence among the people, but God's presence also demands that people know and experience his

34. Victor P. Hamilton, *Exodus: An Exegetical Commentary* (Grand Rapids: Baker Academic, 2011), 449. In ch. 25–31, God provides the blueprints for the tabernacle. Chapters 35–40 detail the construction of this portable tent and its various components. The interruption of the golden calf incident in ch. 32–34, as well as the question of God's presence continuing with the people (33:12–23), will be discussed in the next section.

35. J. N. Oswalt, "Theology of the Pentateuch," *DOTP* 857–58.

character. The presence of YHWH among his people is not a talisman relic, a military safeguard, or a nominal symbol. The people are to encounter God's presence in such a way that his character shapes (and reshapes) them in his likeness (i.e., Exod. 34:6–7). It is not enough to journey with the Holy One on the way to the promised land. He wants his people to also be like him. This requires proximity and awareness of his nature. Thus, the Israelites' unique access to God's presence gives them unique insight into his character, which ultimately makes distinctive demands on their lives. Outward and inward sin must be dealt with to remain in God's presence.

Immediately after God's glory fills the tabernacle, Leviticus provides a divinely initiated, five-part framework for retaining his presence. First, the people are given a series of offerings and sacrifices that allow them to express thanks, restore peace, and relieve the burdens of their sin and guilt (ch. 1–7). The sin and guilt offerings assume that the people will not be sinless. Second, chapters 8–10 reveal the importance of the priesthood. This group of people stands between God and his people to mediate his presence, and it also serves as a model for Israel's larger vocation of serving as a kingdom of priests (Exod. 19:6). The next two divisions in Leviticus, chapters 11–17 and 18–27, highlight Israel's calling to be a holy and distinct nation. Chapters 11–15 encourage the Israelites to be different from their surrounding neighbors, and chapters 16–17 note that such holiness requires blood atonement. Through atonement, the Holiness Code of chapters 18–27 offers specific instructions concerning obedience and various facets of holy living. The Mosaic covenant tells a story of salvation that culminates in God's holy presence. Building on the gracious deliverance from Egypt, Israel is called to persistently remain in God's presence. The goal of salvation is that people are restored to God's presence and, as a result, his character and holiness are shaped in them.

David: A Sacrificial King

Whereas the Mosaic covenant was meant to facilitate the presence of God and to make a way for the people to come near with sacrifices and offerings, it is also true that the sacrificial system was unable to address the reality of sin entirely. This inability required a new covenant. But these gaps are particularly evident in the Judges period, when persistent sin devolved into spiritual, social, and moral chaos (cf. Judg.

17–21). The failures of the judges and the priests created the impetus for and the development of the Israelite monarchy. A king and a kingdom were anticipated since the time of the patriarchs (e.g., Gen. 17:6–7, 16; 49:10). Furthermore, the Mosaic covenant provided the parameters for this kingdom (e.g., Exod. 19:6; Num. 24:17–19; Deut. 17:14–20). An Israelite king would be chosen from the Israelite people, and he would intentionally limit himself with respect to military resources, political alliances, and economic pursuits (vv. 14–17). Power would not come in typical ANE fashion. Israel's king would be subservient to YHWH and constrained by the Mosaic covenant (vv. 18–20). The king would be accountable to an established standard. This is why the request for a king like the nations (1 Sam. 8:5, 20) was a rejection of God. The desire for a king was not the issue; rather, the type of monarchy that Israel desired was the problem. Israel needed a different kind of leader, one who would govern in righteousness and justice and through whom God could indeed bless the world.

Saul, the first Israelite king, fits the pattern and looks the part (e.g., 1 Sam. 9:2). Initially, he plays the part (1 Sam. 11:1–11). Yet his leadership quickly spirals into failure. After Saul, David is chosen and anointed the next king. Instead of his building God a house, God promises to build David a "house," which will be "established forever" for the sake of God's name (2 Sam. 7:12–16). Throughout 2 Samuel 7, there are indications that God is harkening back to previous covenants in this promise. For instance, he recalls the Abrahamic covenant when he says that he will make David's "name great" (v. 9 NIV). He also evokes the covenant with Moses when he states that he will establish a kingdom and a throne (vv. 12, 16).

How does this promise relate to salvation? Interestingly, while 2 Samuel 7 offers an enduring promise, the word for "covenant" (*bərît*) is not used in the passage; nevertheless, the term is found in 2 Samuel 23:5. Furthermore, Psalm 89 (see vv. 3, 28, 34, 39), Psalm 132:11, 2 Chronicles 13:5, and Isaiah 55:3 do specifically use covenant language.[36] In the first part of Psalm 89, the psalmist highlights the enduring love and faithfulness of God in his covenant with David, even when everything else is unstable. The line of kings since Saul and the fractured kingdom following Solomon's death have left much uncer-

36. Gentry and Wellum, *God's Kingdom through God's Covenants*, 190.

tainty. Nevertheless, an assuring security can be felt in God's covenant with David. Isaiah 55 is the concluding part of a larger section in Isaiah dealing with the Servant of the Lord and addressing how and through whom God will ultimately deal with Israel's sin (ch. 49–55). Salvation will come through the free work (55:1) of a Suffering Servant (52:13–53:12), who will stand in contrast to the previous kings of Israel and Judah and transform a splintered kingdom into a beacon for the nations. Through the sacrificial act of this Suffering Servant, Isaiah 55 suggests that David's covenant will be reconstituted and renewed.

To review, the need for salvation arises from the fact that sin separates us from God and mars his image in his people. The goal of salvation is that people might experience his presence again because their sins have been addressed. Noah's covenant offers a portrait of God's patience and his desire to protect and restore creation. This covenant, however, does not deal with the core issue of sin in the human heart. Abraham, then, is invited to trust God for the sake of the world—through faithful obedience. The Mosaic covenant highlights the importance of God's holy presence amid a kingdom of priests who live differently in the world. The promise to David and his house underscores the necessity of a king who will come to remedy the brokenness of the human heart through righteousness and justice. When all these covenants are brought together, they evince a comprehensive view of salvation that includes an experience of God's presence again and a restoration of his image in humanity. When people encounter God's presence, he graciously shares his holy character with them and they become holy.

CONCLUSION

As has been argued, the need for salvation emerges from the loss of God's presence and the marring of God's image, both of which are caused by sin in Genesis 3. It has been argued that through the OT covenants, YHWH has established a framework of salvation and provided a way for the people to encounter his presence and live differently. Proximity to God's presence is meant to clarify who God is and who his people should become. The covenants not only shape Israel's view of salvation but also provide access to God so that his people might be (re)shaped in his presence. This is the essence of the repeated command in Leviticus: "Be holy because I, the Lord your God, am holy" (19:2 NIV; cf. 11:44–45; 20:26; and 1 Peter 2:16). Much more can be said about how each covenant points to different facets of salvation. To summarize, the way of salvation requires divine patience in the face of sin (as in the case of Noah), radical trust (as in the case of Abraham), freedom from oppression and access to God's holy presence (as in the case of Moses), and ultimately a sacrificial king who will make a way for people to truly experience God's presence and be transformed by his holiness (as in the case of David). Accordingly, salvation in the OT points forward while also providing the conceptual backdrop for the relationships between salvation and holiness in the NT.

Many interpreters detect different trajectories of salvation in the Old and New Testaments. While differences certainly exist, it is often claimed that the differences are vast and that the presentations of salvation are at times disconnected. Some argue that the OT envisions salvation as communal and temporal, whereas the NT views it as personal (or individual) and eschatological.[37] In response, one can note that the NT does focus on personal salvation from sins and eternal life through forgiveness. However, the conception of salvation in the OT offered above is embedded in Jesus's teaching, death, and resurrection, as well as in concepts of salvation within the new covenant. When NT soteriology is disconnected from the OT, it offers a disembodied and truncated view of salvation. Salvation in the Bible is an embodied way of life in which God continuously gives us access to his presence through atonement, which enables us to be holy, as he is holy.[38] As stated at the outset of this essay, "without holiness no one will see the Lord" (Heb. 12:14 NIV). The OT gives us the trajectory. A person can become holy by coming into the presence of the Holy One. In this encounter with God's presence, humanity's sins are blotted out (Isa. 43:25), and God's image is restored.

37. See Walton, *Old Testament Theology for Christians*, 227–37, and James K. Zink, "Salvation in the Old Testament," *Encounter* 25 (1964): 405.

38. In recent years, various works have reexplored ideas of salvation that are influenced by the OT and have offered models for an embodied obedience and faithfulness. See Matthew W. Bates, *Salvation by Allegiance Alone: Rethinking Faith, Works, and the Gospel of Jesus the King* (Grand Rapids: Baker Academic, 2017); and Thomas H. McCall, Caleb T. Friedeman, and Matt T. Friedeman, *The Doctrine of Good Works: Reclaiming a Neglected Protestant Teaching* (Grand Rapids: Baker Academic, 2023).

CHAPTER 13

"A HOLY PEOPLE BELONGING TO YHWH YOUR GOD": HOLINESS AND COVENANT IN DEUTERONOMY

DANIEL I. BLOCK

INTRODUCTION

When we think of holiness in the First Testament, we do not readily think of Deuteronomy. In a composition consisting of 14,294 words,[1] the root *qdš* appears only seventeen times (twenty-three if we count the place name Kadesh)—that is, once every 680 words. This contrasts sharply with Leviticus, where the root (*qdš*) occurs 152 times—that is, once every 79 words. Deuteronomy is obviously less interested than Leviticus (or Exodus and Numbers, for that matter) in the technicalities of sacred sites, rites, objects, and personnel, but this does not mean that Deuteronomy is less interested in holiness. Indeed, one could argue that whereas Exodus 25–Numbers 29 functions as a sort of handbook on holiness, Deuteronomy offers an ecclesiology of holiness.

YHWH introduces the notion of holiness in Exodus 19:6, declaring Israel within his missional agenda as his "kingdom of priests and holy nation"[2] (*mamleḵeṯ kōhănîm wəḡôy qāḏôš*). However, this notion is not fully developed until we get to Deuteronomy. Instead of referring to the place of worship as a "sanctuary" (*miqdāš*), Deuteronomy frequently depicts YHWH inviting Israelites to his presence (*ləp̄ānāyw*), at the place he will choose "to imprint" (*śîm*) or "establish" (*šāḵan*) his name (12:5, 11; 14:23; 16:2, 6, 11; 26:2). Equally remarkably, Moses never refers to Israel's high priest in his final valedictory addresses—though as we shall see, five times he alludes to the inscription on the medallion of the high priest's turban (*qōdeš*

1. Statistical data is derived from H. P. Müller, "קדשׁ *qdš* holy," *TLOT* 3:1106.
2. Unless otherwise indicated, all Scripture references in this chapter are the author's translation (AT).

layhwh, Exod. 28:36; 39:3) with variations of the phrase *ʿam qāḏôš layhwh*, "a holy people belonging to YHWH" (Deut. 7:6; 14:2, 21; 26:19; 28:9). Through the covenant-renewal ritual on the plains of Moab, Moses supervises the process whereby the offspring of the exodus generation are formally set apart and "branded" the holy people of YHWH. What the high priest is to the nation of Israel, Israel is to be to the world (cf. 26:19; 28:9).

This paper will explore in greater detail Deuteronomy's vision of the covenantal significance of Israel's sanctification on the one hand, and the sanctifying significance of YHWH's establishment of his covenant with them on the other. The covenantal moment on the plains of Moab marks the climax of a series of events through which YHWH "sets Israel apart" (*qdš*) for his mission: choosing them (*bāḥar*), designating them his crown jewel (*ʿam səḡullâ*), identifying them as the objects of his affection (*ḥāšaq*), demonstrating his covenant commitment (*ʾāhēḇ*, "love") by rescuing them from the bondage of Egypt, and now, through this ritual, declaring this generation of Israelites "the people of YHWH your God" (*ʿām layhwh ʾělōhêḵā*, Deut. 27:9). While this process creates "the indicative" of Israel's holy status, this covenant also calls the nation to "the imperative" of holiness—that is, demonstrating its status as YHWH's people to a watching world. In the *tôrâ* that Moses proclaims to the people and transcribes on a scroll (31:9–13, 24–29), he provides the holy covenant people with a resource to guide them in the pursuit not only of "righteousness, only righteousness" (*ṣeḏeq ṣeḏeq tirdōp̄*, 16:20) but also of "holiness, only holiness" (*qōḏeš qōḏeš*). In so doing, he also provides them with a resource to ensure the fulfillment of their mission as agents of sanctification for the world. Given the limitations of space in this essay, following a review of the vocabulary of holiness in Deuteronomy, I shall limit my discussion to the five texts that deal with Israel as YHWH's holy people.

THE VOCABULARY OF HOLINESS IN DEUTERONOMY

Apart from the usage of *qāḏeš* (Kadesh) as a toponym—Meribah Kadesh or Kadesh Barnea[3]—the root *qdš* appears four times as a verb,[4]

3. Meribath Kadesh occurs in 32:51; Kadesh Barnea in 1:2, 19; 2:14; 9:23; and the abbreviated form "Kadesh" in 1:46.

4. The stative *qal* (*qāḏaš*, "to be or become holy, sacrosanct") can be found in 22:9; the factitive *piel* (*qiddaš*, "to treat or honor as holy") in 5:12 and 32:51; and the causative *hiphil* (*hiqdîš*, "to make

six times as a noun,[5] and seven times as an adjective in Deuteronomy.[6] Each occurrence contributes to the broader picture, but rather than focus on the forms of the words, we may survey who or what is holy in this book and what implications the answers might have for understanding Israel's covenant. In so doing, we may not only establish a taxonomy of sanctity but also grasp the center of gravity of holiness in Moses's farewell addresses in Deuteronomy. The persons and objects that are characterized by the root *qdš* reflect the dimensions of the notion of holiness in this book.

The Holiness of YHWH, the God of Israel, in Deuteronomy

References to YHWH's holiness are ubiquitous in the account of his establishment of his covenant with Israel at Sinai and his revelation of the stipulations of that covenant in the books of Exodus and Leviticus.[7] By contrast, in Moses's addresses and poetic utterances in Deuteronomy, he never speaks of YHWH as holy. The only allusion to YHWH's holiness occurs from his own mouth in 32:51, where YHWH bars Moses and Aaron from entrance into the promised land because they have failed to treat him as holy (*lōʾ-qiddaštem ʾōtî*) at Meribah Kadesh.

Holy Space in Deuteronomy

The closest Moses comes to speaking of sacred space involves his reference to YHWH's heavenly "residence" as holy (*māʿôn qoḏšəḵā*, 26:15) and to the need for maintaining the sanctity of Israel's camp as a prerequisite for YHWH "walking about in the midst of your camp [*miṯhallēḵ bəqereḇ maḥănekā*] to rescue you from their enemies before you" (23:14[15]). Although Moses refers to "the place that YHWH would choose" to imprint his name and where the Israelites would come to worship him more than twenty times, he never refers to this either as YHWH's *miqdāš* or *qōḏeš*, "holy place," "sanctuary."

---

holy, consecrate") in 15:19. On the distinction between the factitive *piel* and the causative *hiphil*, see *IBHS*, §§24.2; 27.1.

5. Occurrences are as follows: *qōḏeš*, "holy object" (12:26; 26:13), "holy heavenly courtier" (33:2); *qəḏōšîm*, "holy ones" (33:2); *qāḏēš*, "consecrated man," and its feminine counterpart, *qəḏēšâ*, "consecrated woman" (23:18[17]).

6. *Qāḏôš*, "holy," appears in relation to Israel in 7:6; 14:2, 21; 26:19; 28:9; YHWH's heavenly dwelling in 26:15; and Israel's (military) camp in 23:14[15].

7. See Lev. 11:44, 45; 19:2; 20:26; 21:8. Note also the space devoted to the "sanctuary" (*miqḏāš*) as YHWH's holy residence in Exod. 25–31; 35–40.

Holy Heavenly Beings in Deuteronomy

In the exordium to Moses's benediction of the twelve tribes, he speaks of YHWH coming from Sinai, dawning from Seir, and beaming forth from Mount Paran, accompanied by "myriads of holy ones [*ri<u>b</u>ə<u>b</u>ōt qo<u>d</u>eš*] with fire emanating from his right" (33:2). Here the singular *qō<u>d</u>eš* functions as a collective for "holy ones" (*qədōšîm*), which occurs in verse 3. These "holy ones" are the angelic host who serve YHWH in and from his heavenly court and who accompany the divine warrior as a royal entourage.

Holy People in Deuteronomy

Moses often speaks of the role of Levitical priests,[8] but he never characterizes them or Aaron as holy in this book. The closest he comes to characterizing persons as holy is his reference to a "consecrated man" and a "consecrated woman" in 23:18[17], but in this instance, he repudiates their legitimacy: "Among you there may not be any consecrated woman [*qə<u>d</u>ēšâ*] chosen from the daughters of Israel; and there may not be any consecrated men [*qa<u>d</u>ēš*] chosen from the sons of Israel." While most interpreters and translations understand these persons as male and female cult prostitutes,[9] it is preferable to see here a reference to an indiscriminate selection of cult personnel from the general population of the Israelites. "Consecrated" women and men seem to have been young women and men dedicated for service to the gods at the local shrines, as opposed to divinely chosen and ordained Levites.[10]

Instead of identifying specific cultic persons as holy, Moses democratizes the notion. In the exordium to his tribal blessings, he follows up his reference to YHWH's "myriads of holy ones" (*ri<u>b</u>ə<u>b</u>ōt qō<u>d</u>eš*) with the following general description: "O [you] who love the peoples [*ḥō<u>b</u>ē<u>b</u> ʿammîm*], all his holy ones [*qə<u>d</u>ōšāyw*] were in your hand. So they followed in your steps, receiving orders from you" (Deut. 33:3). Whereas the opening colon highlights YHWH's disposition toward the people, the characterization of the Israelites as "holy ones . . . in

---

8. Deut. 10:8–9; 17:9, 18; 18:1–8; 21:5; 24:8; 27:1, 9–12; 31:9, 25–26; 33:8. Elsewhere Moses names the Levites as an economically marginalized group, along with resident aliens (*gērîm*), widows (*ʾalmānâ*), and the fatherless (*yā<u>t</u>ôm*): 12:12, 18–19; 14:27, 29; 16:11, 14; 26:11–13.
9. As I did in Daniel I. Block, *Deuteronomy*, NIVAC (Grand Rapids: Zondervan Academic, 2012), 544–47.
10. For fuller discussion, see Daniel I. Block, *The Gospel according to Moses: A Commentary on Deuteronomy* (Hong Kong: Inspirata, 2023), 2:362–68.

your hand" underscores their status as "a holy people belonging to YHWH" (*ʿam qāḏôš layhwh*)[11] their security in YHWH's protective care, and their being under his authority; they follow at YHWH's feet and receive orders from him. God's affectionate disposition toward Israel, reflected in "you who love the peoples" (v. 3), is reinforced by his special epithet for Israel, *Jeshurun* (meaning "[my] little one made straight").[12] Since the repeated expression "a holy people belonging to YHWH your God" represents the center of gravity for Moses's reflections on holiness, I shall return to a fuller discussion below of the five critical texts where it occurs. But first, we must complete our survey of the taxonomy of "holy" entities in the book.

Holy Objects in Deuteronomy.

On four occasions in his addresses, Moses refers to holy items devoted to YHWH. He identifies these objects as *haqqōḏeš*, "the consecrated item" (26:13), and *qoḏāšêkā*, "your consecrated items" (12:26). These are objects that have been dedicated (*hiqdîš*) as gifts to YHWH, which means that they cannot be used for common everyday functions, like food eaten at home or livestock as draft animals or sheared for their wool (15:19). As with the offerings listed in 12:6 and 11, the Israelites are to bring healthy firstborn annually to "the place that YHWH would choose" (to establish his name), and there YHWH invites entire households to feast in his presence (v. 20): whole burnt offerings (*ʿōlōṯ*), sacrifices (*zāḇāḥîm*), tithes (*maʿśərot̠*), tribute offerings (*tərûmot̠*), votive offerings (*nədārîm*), freewill offerings (*nədāḇot̠*), and the firstborn of your herd and of your flock (*bəḵōrōṯ*)—in short, all the select gifts (*miḇḥar*) that people vow (*nāḏar*) to give (i.e., consecrate) to YHWH (v. 11). To these texts, we must add Deuteronomy 22:9, which uses the *qal* form of *qāḏaš*, "to be holy," distinctively: "You must not plant two kinds [of seed] in your vineyard, lest the produce [*məlēʾâ*]—the seed you sow and the yield of the vineyard—become sacrosanct [*tiqdaš*]." Whereas

11. An expression that recurs in Deut. 7:6; 14:2, 21; 26:19; 28:9. Cf. YHWH's repeated calls to the Israelites to be a holy people (*qəḏōšîm*) in Lev. 11:44, 45; 19:2; 20:7, 26; Num. 15:40; esp. 16:3: "The whole congregation, all of them are holy ones." The present form, "his holy ones" (*qəḏōšāyw*), occurs also in Ps. 34:9[10].

12. The epithet occurs only four times in the Hebrew Bible: Deut. 32:15; 33:5, 26; Isa. 44:2. For further discussion of the etymology and significance of the name, see Daniel I. Block, *Covenant: The Framework of God's Grand Plan of Redemption* (Grand Rapids: Baker Academic, 2021), 232–33, 377. Cf. also M. J. Mulder, "יְשֻׁרוּן *yᵉšurûn*," *TDOT* 6:472–77.

Leviticus 19:19 prohibits mixing two kinds of seed in a field, here Moses disallows sowing different kinds in a vineyard and therefore declares this off limits to the farmer and his family.[13] It seems that the grain and wine produced in vineyards where another crop had been sown was confiscated by the priests and set apart for sanctuary use.[14]

Holy Times in Deuteronomy.

The annual festivals of Passover and Unleavened Bread (*Pesaḥ*), Weeks (*Šāvū ʿōṯ*), and Booths (*Sukkōṯ*) called for in Deuteronomy 16:1–16 were obviously holy times in the Israelite calendar. These festivals carry heavy implications for holiness, including: (1) the centrality of sacrifices at these festivals; (2) their location "at the place that YHWH chooses [to establish his name]" (vv. 2, 6, 7, 11, 15, 16); (3) the invitation to celebrate Weeks and Booths "before YHWH" (*lip̄nê yhwh*, v. 11; *ʾeṯ-pənê yhwh*, v. 16) and to celebrate Passover and Unleavened Bread as "a holiday [dedicated] to YHWH" (*ʿăṣereṯ layhwh*, v. 8); (4) the prohibition of any normal "workday" work (v. 8). However, in Deuteronomy, Moses never calls these observances holy (*qdš*).[15] He reserves that status for the divinely proclaimed Sabbath ordinance in the Decalogue: "Guard the Sabbath day by sanctifying [*ləqaddəšô*] it, as YHWH your God has commanded you. Six days you shall labor and do all your work, but the seventh day is a Sabbath belonging to YHWH your God" (5:12–14). Ironically, the seventh-day Sabbath was a domestic observance celebrated in people's homes and villages, rather than in the central sanctuary before YHWH. Because YHWH had designated the seventh-day Sabbath as the sign (*ʾôt ṯ*) of his covenant with Israel (Exod. 31:12–17), in Deuteronomy Moses might have clarified the relationship between this Sabbath and the Israelite covenant, especially the role of the tabernacle and its rituals in maintaining

13. Many English versions read "forfeited" (ESV, NRSV, NLT, NJPS), meaning "prohibited from human use because of the violation of a taboo."

14. So also Jacob Milgrom, "Law and Narrative and the Exegesis of Leviticus xix 19," *VT* 45 (1995): 56; idem, *Leviticus 1–16: A New Translation with Introduction and Commentary*, AB 3 (New York: Doubleday, 1991), 548–49.

15. Cf. the repeated characterization of these sorts of observances in Exodus–Numbers as a *miqrāʾ qōdeš*, "a holy proclamation." For discussion of this expression, see Daniel I. Block, "'O Day of Rest and Gladness': Rediscovering the Gift of Sabbath," in *The Triumph of Grace: Literary and Theological Studies in Deuteronomy and Deuteronomic Themes* (Eugene, OR: Cascade, 2017), 206–8.

of covenant relationship. However, instead of doing so, he reserves his fullest comments on holiness for announcements of Israel as "the holy people belonging to YHWH your God," a subject to which I now turn.

THE DIMENSIONS OF THE HOLINESS OF YHWH'S COVENANT PEOPLE

As noted above, five critical texts represent the conceptual center of gravity in Deuteronomy for the notion of holiness, and they offer significant insight into the relationship between Israel's status as a holy people and her status as YHWH's vassal covenant partner: Deuteronomy 7:6; 14:2, 21; 26:18–19; and 28:9. Moses bound these texts conceptually with common vocabulary, especially the phrases "a holy people" (*ʿam qāḏôš*), "belonging to YHWH your God" (*layhwh ʾĕlōhêḵa*), and "a treasured people" (*ʿam səḡullâ*). While these expressions represent a conceptual common core for these five texts, Moses's vision of Israel as YHWH's holy and treasured people was inspired by YHWH's own vision statement in his first words to Moses and his people once they had arrived at Sinai:

> You yourselves have seen what I did to the Egyptians, how I carried you on wings of eagles and brought you to myself. Now then, if you will listen to my voice and keep my covenant, you shall be my treasured possession [*səgullâ*] out of all the peoples. Indeed, the whole earth is mine, but you shall be for me a kingdom of priests and a holy nation [*gôy qādôš*]. (Exod. 19:4–6)

This divine utterance set the stage for YHWH's establishment (*hēqîm*) of the covenant that he had previously made (*kāraṯ*) with Abraham (Gen. 17:7–8) with his descendants at Sinai. It also transferred to the exodus generation and its descendants the commission to which he had called the patriarch and which served as a preamble to all the revelation they would receive in the next eleven months at Sinai (cf. Exod. 19:1 and Num. 10:11). Through his covenant with Israel, YHWH intended to create a society that was paradigmatic for the world and that was based on covenant rather than law. YHWH's foundational declaration in Exodus 19:4–6 focused on his covenant relationship with the Israelites and his mission for them. The stipulations came later as gifts graciously revealed, so that they might respond to YHWH's grace in ways that pleased their divine Redeemer and demonstrate what it meant to be a kingdom of priests and a holy nation before a world under the curse of death. When we look more closely at Moses's five statements, we discover a profound theology of communal and individual holiness that derives from YHWH, Israel's holy God, who had brought the nation to himself and was sending it out on a holy mission.

Moses's First Call to Holiness (7:1–16)

Moses embedded his first call to holiness in the second of four farewell pastoral addresses to his people on the plains of Moab (4:45–11:32). Following Moses's opening recitation of the Decalogue (5:1–22) and his recollection of his official installation as prophetic mediator (5:23–6:3), the center of gravity of this address is represented by two "Shema segments" signaled by separate calls to listen ("Hear, O Israel," *šəmaʿ yiśrāʾēl*, 6:4; 9:1). The first of these segments (6:4–8:20) opens with a formal Shema (6:4–9), which calls Israel to uncompromised covenant commitment to YHWH as the verbal mark of its identity as his people alone. Moses follows up this statement with an essay on the tests and marks of Israel's fidelity to YHWH and his covenant. While forbidding Israel to test (*nissâ*) the fidelity of the divine Suzerain (v. 16), Moses describes two tests instituted by the Suzerain to test Israel's fidelity to him: (1) an internal test, represented by his blessing and their flourishing in the land (vv. 10–15; 8:1–20), and (2) an external test, represented by the Canaanite populations, whom YHWH would hand over to them. However, rather than destroying them supernaturally in a flash, YHWH would challenge the Israelites to demonstrate their fidelity to him by destroying every vestige of pagan Canaanite culture (6:17–19; 7:1–26). Moses's first call for Israel's holiness appears as part of the presentation of the latter test in 7:6–11.

The Background to the Call (7:1–5)

Building on Exodus 23:20–33, Deuteronomy 7 opens with Moses's most explicit description of Israel's policy on *ḥērem*, YHWH's call for the total annihilation of the present inhabitants of the land of Canaan. The following list represents the key elements of the policy: (1) the total elimination of the seven people groups that inhabit the land (vv. 1–2a); (2) an absolute taboo on all favorable relationships with these peoples (v. 2b); (3) a prohibition of intermarriage with the current residents (v. 3); and (4) the obliteration of all sites and appurtenances used by the Canaanites in the worship of their gods. In verse 4, Moses provides a rationale for these drastic policies—namely, that sympathy for and intermarriage with Canaanites will jeopardize Israel's fidelity to YHWH and his covenant, in direct violation of the Shema (6:4–5) and leading ultimately to the ignition of YHWH's fury against his own people (cf. 7:10, 16, 25–26). Note especially Moses's summary of Israel's distinctive treatment of the Canaanites in 20:16–18:

> However, in the towns that are part of these peoples that YHWH your God is giving to you as a grant, you may not let anything that breathes survive. No! You must completely destroy them—the Hittite, the Amorite, the Canaanite, the Perizzite, the Hivite, and the Jebusite—just as YHWH your God has commanded you, *to prevent them from teaching you to practice all the abhorrent rituals that they perform for their gods, and from sinning against YHWH your God.* (emphasis added; see also Exod. 23:33; 34:11–17)

Although the Hebrew root *qdš* is missing in the core texts focused on the *ḥērem* policy, absence of lexical evidence is not evidence of the absence of the concept. This was obvious to Moses, for he followed up his announcement of the policy in Deuteronomy 7 with an explicit declaration of its grounds, grammatically signaled by the particle *kî*: "*Because* you are a holy people belonging to YHWH your God" (*kî ʿam qāḏôš ʾattâ layhwh ʾĕlōhêḵā*, v. 6). But what does that mean, and how has Israel become "a holy people belonging to YHWH" and "[his] treasured possession" (*ʿam səgullâ*)? Whereas other texts describe this event as a divine act of sanctification (*qiddēš*),[16] Moses prefers less technical explanations in Deuteronomy.[17] Moses's answers to these questions will clarify the significance of the *ḥērem* policy described in verses 1–5.

16. Exod. 31:13; Lev. 20:8; 21:15, 23; 22:9, 16, 32; Ezek. 20:12; 37:28.
17. The *piel* form of the verb occurs only once in the book and has Moses as the subject; he did not "treat YHWH as holy" (32:51).

The Nature of the Call (7:6–8)

> For you are a holy people belonging to YHWH your God [*kî ʿam qāḏôš ʾattâ layhwh ʾĕlōhêḵā*]. YHWH your God has chosen you out of all the peoples on the face of the earth to be his people as [his] treasured possession. It was not because your population was larger than all the peoples that he set his affection on you or chose you, for your population is the smallest among all the peoples. But it was because YHWH loves you and because he kept the oath that he swore to your ancestors that, with a strong hand, he brought you out and redeemed you from the slave house, from the power of Pharaoh, king of Egypt. (Deut. 7:6–8)

Here Moses highlights the divine actions and motivations that account for Israel's holy status. We may unpack his compilation of ideas and rhetoric by isolating six main clauses and arranging them in pairs as follows:

Verse 6 A
1 YHWH declared Israel to be his holy people (*ʿam qāḏôš layhwh*).
2 YHWH chose Israel to be his treasured people (*ʿam səḡullâ*).

Verse 7 B
1 YHWH set his affection on Israel (*ḥāšaq bāḵem*).
2 YHWH chose Israel out of all the peoples (*wayyibḥar bāḵem*).

Verse 8 C
1 YHWH brought Israel out from the slave house (*hôṣîʾ ʾeṯkem*) with a strong hand.
2 YHWH redeemed Israel (*wayyip̄dəḵā*) from the hand of the king of Egypt.

The first pair announces the status that YHWH has in mind for his people: to be his holy people and his treasured possession. The second pair declares YHWH's antecedent, unmerited election of Israel from all the peoples as the objects of his affection. And the third summarizes his actions for the Israelites that have elevated them to their privileged status. However, with remarkable insight into the divine mind, to the last pair (v. 8) Moses adds two motive clauses. This entire paragraph is cast in elevated prose, which resists complex parallel constructions. We may recognize Moses's logic in verse 8 by realigning the clauses as follows and yielding two more or less parallel statements:

1a ↓Because YHWH loves you,
1b he brought you out of the slave house with a strong hand,
2a ↓and because he kept the oath that he swore to your ancestors,
2b he redeemed you from the hand of Pharaoh, king of Egypt.

The first statement echoes Deuteronomy 4:37–38, whereas the second seems to allude to the oath ritual in Genesis 15:17 and YHWH's promise to Abraham in 15:13–14. But there may be more. The word for "oath" (*šəbûʿâ*) occurs only here in Deuteronomy,[18] but this is also true of the collocation "the oath that he swore to your ancestors" (*haššəḇuʿâ ʾăšer nišbaʿ laʾăḇōṯeḵem*).[19] But what is this oath of which Moses speaks? The verb *nišbaʿ*, "to swear," occurs thirty-three times in Deuteronomy, more often than in any other book in the First Testament, but always in the *niphal* stem. The overwhelming majority (twenty-eight) of occurrences relate to the covenant promises. Since three-fourths (twenty-one) of these, including the one in 7:13, refer to YHWH's promise of land, our first impulse is to link 7:8 with that promise. The fact that both Genesis 26:3 and Jeremiah 11:5, the only other places where the collocation occurs in the Hebrew Bible, involve the promise of land may reinforce this interpretation. However, the absence of any reference to the land in Deuteronomy 7:1–13 and the focus on the people in this part of the chapter suggest that the issue may be the covenant promises generally[20] or, more particularly, YHWH's promise on oath to be the God of Abraham and his descendants and his promise to receive them as his people.[21] Admittedly, in Genesis 26:3, YHWH cited the

18. It appears ten times in the Pentateuch, but only in Gen. 26:3 does it relate to the ancestral covenant promises.
19. This expression applies to YHWH's oath to the ancestors elsewhere only in Gen. 26:3 and Jer. 11:5. Whereas our text speaks of YHWH "keeping" (*šāmar*) the oath, the other two speak of him "establishing" or "confirming" (*hēqîm*) the oath.
20. As in Deut. 4:31; 7:12; 8:18; 13:17[18]; 28:9; and 29:13[12].
21. Sounding quite Mosaic, Jeremiah precedes his reference to YHWH's oath sworn to Israel's ancestors with the following statement: "Thus has YHWH, the God of Israel, said, 'May any persons who do

land promise in verses 3–5, which suggests he had in mind a more comprehensive view of the covenant.

We may scarcely overestimate the significance of Deuteronomy 7:6–8 as the grounds for Israel's *ḥērem* ordinance, particularly YHWH's passion to maintain the spiritual integrity and the purity of the nation. For the Israelites to go after other gods would mean denying their identity as YHWH's chosen, holy, and treasured people, trampling underfoot the grace, affection, and covenant love that he had lavished on them in rescuing them from Egypt, as well as repudiating the sacred mission of being agents of blessing to the world under the curse of sin.

The Theological and Practical Implications of the Call (7:9–16)

Whether or not this interpretation of the oath is correct, Moses's point in Deuteronomy 7:8 is that YHWH was legally and morally bound to redeem his people from their bondage to Pharaoh in Egypt. His doxological reflection on the character of YHWH in the wake of his announcement of Israel's glorious gospel reinforces this conclusion: "So you should know that YHWH your God is *the* God [*hā ʾĕlōhîm*], the faithful El [*hā ʾēl hanne ʾĕmān*], who keeps the covenant of unfailing love [*šōmēr habbərîṯ wəhaḥeseḏ*] to the thousandth generation of those who demonstrate love for him [*lə ʾōhăḇāyw*] and keep his commands" (v. 9).

The expressions "the faithful El" and "the keeper of the covenant and the *ḥesed*" declare that YHWH is always true to his word—and that includes his promises to the ancestors. In the exordium to Israel's national anthem, YHWH includes this quality in his self-description, cast in the third person for a singer to declare:

> The Rock!
> His activity is perfect [*tāmîm po ʿŏlô*];
> see, all his ways—justice [*kol-dərakāyw mišpāṭ*].
> *A God of faithfulness* and without caprice [*ʾēl ʾĕmûnâ wə ʾēn ʿāwel*],
> righteous and upright is he [*ṣaddîq wəyāšār hû ʾ*].
>
> (Deut. 32:4, emphasis added)

---

not heed the words of this covenant, which I charged your ancestors [to keep] when I brought them out of the land of Egypt, from the iron smelter, saying, "Listen to my voice, and put into practice all that I command you; then you will be my people, and I will be your God"'" (Jer. 11:3–4).

Since Moses does not use the language of "sanctification" (*qiddēš*) in declaring YHWH's Israel to be his holy and treasured people, we may summarize the divine *ordo salutis* (order of salvation) reflected in Deuteronomy 7:6–8 as follows: (1) YHWH's election of Abraham as the object of his love; (2) YHWH's formalization of his covenant with Abraham, including his sworn oath to his descendants; (3) YHWH's election of Abraham's descendants in Egypt; (4) YHWH's rescue of the exodus generation from slavery in Egypt; (5) YHWH's establishment of his covenant with those descendants at Horeb (in fulfillment of Genesis 17:7 and by which Abraham's descendants were incorporated into YHWH's covenant with Abraham and into his royal-priesthood commission); and (6) YHWH's declaration of Israel as his holy and treasured vassal people—the goal of the sequence of divine actions.

Given the detailed citation of imperatives in Leviticus 19:2–37—which attend to Israel's status as YHWH's holy people, beginning with "You shall be holy, because I, YHWH your God, am holy"—we may ask what imperatives attend Moses's present description of the *ordo salutis*. Moses offers a clue in Deuteronomy 7:9 when he characterizes the beneficiaries of YHWH's electing and saving action as "those who demonstrate love for him [*ʾōhăḇāyw*] and keep his commands [*šōmərê miṣwoṯāyw*, qere]." He provides motivation for a grateful response to YHWH's past action with promises of future blessing in verses 12–15. In verses 10–11, Moses summarizes the alternative response and its consequences: YHWH will repay to their faces those who reject (*śānēʾ*) him by refusing to act as a holy people. That is, he will act against them directly with just punishment.

Deuteronomy 7:11–12 constitutes Moses's interim "altar call":

> So you must keep the command—that is, the ordinances and stipulations that I am commanding you today—by putting them into practice. Now if you pay attention to these stipulations, and you keep them and put them into practice, YHWH your God will keep with you the covenant of unfailing love [*habbərît wəhaḥesed*], which he promised on oath [*nišbaʿ*] to your ancestors.

After a description of the personal and economic benefits that will result from fidelity to YHWH and his covenant (Deut. 7:13–15), Moses brings his discussion full circle with the reminder of the immediate test of Israel's fidelity: "You must devour all the peoples that YHWH your God hands over to you. You may not look on them with pity, and you must not serve their gods, for that would be a trap for you" (v. 16). In the light of verses 1–5 and 16, the maintenance of Israel's holy-and-treasured-people status depends on its elimination of the Canaanites. To claim the status of a holy people but to tolerate the existence of an unholy population is fundamentally oxymoronic.

While the call to Abraham to be YHWH's agent, the call to his descendants to be saved from the Egyptian slave house, and the privilege of holy-and-treasured-people status have come without moral and ethical preconditions, the blessings that attend the covenant and the fulfillment of the people's commission as his royal priesthood are obviously contingent on their response. The relationship between the conditionality and unconditionality of YHWH's covenants is illustrated in figure 13.1:

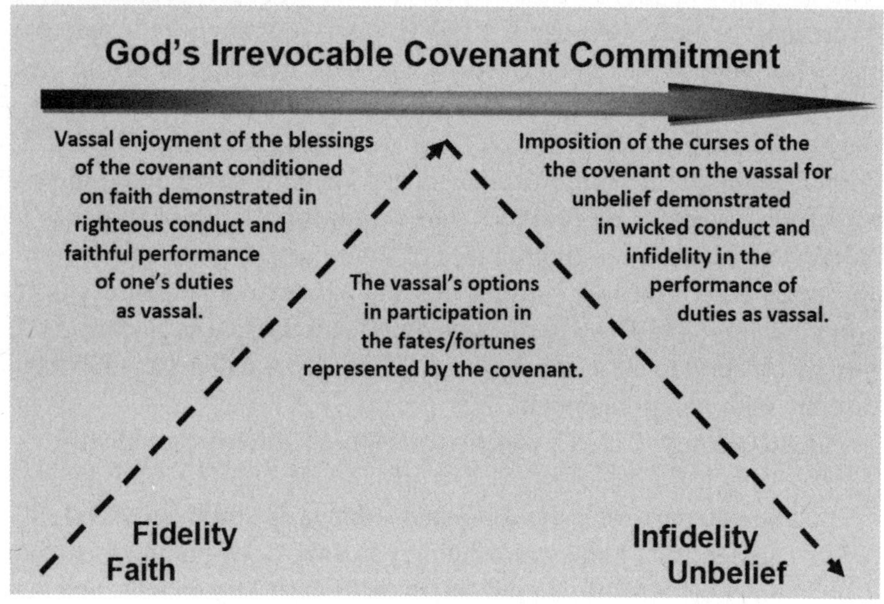

Figure 13.1. God's Irrevocable Covenant Commitment

Moses's Second and Third Calls to Holiness (14:1–21)

> Sons you are to YHWH your God. You must not gash yourselves or shave the front of heads on behalf of the dead, because you are a holy people belonging to YHWH your God [*kî ʿam*

> *qāḏôš ʾattâ layhwh ʾĕlōhêḵā*]. You are the ones YHWH has chosen to be his treasured people [*lihyôt lô ləʿam səgullâ*] out of all the peoples on the face of the earth. (Deut. 14:1–2)
>
> You may not eat any carcass; you may give it to a resident alien in your towns for him to eat, or you may sell it to a foreigner, because you are a holy people belonging to YHWH your God [*kî ʿam qāḏôš ʾattâ layhwh ʾĕlōhêḵā*]. (v. 21)

In Moses's third address (Deut. 12–26, 28), he reemploys the determinative statement found in 7:6 ("because you are a holy people belonging to YHWH your God [*kî ʿam qāḏôš ʾattâ layhwh ʾĕlōhêḵā*]) to frame his version of Leviticus 11's dietary boundaries (Deut. 14:1–21). We hear echoes of 7:6 in Moses's reference to YHWH's election (*bāḥar*) of Israel as his treasured people (*ʿam səgullâ*, 14:2). However, Moses opens with a new element: "Sons you are to YHWH your God" (*bānîm ʾattem layhwh ʾĕlōhêḵem*, 14:1). In 1:31 and 8:5, Moses compares YHWH and Israel to a father and a son, respectively, but here he strengthens the image by using a metaphor rather than a simile: YHWH not only *treats* Israel like a father treats a son; he also *is* Israel's father. While references to God as father are common in the NT,[22] explicit declarations of divine fatherhood are rare in the Hebrew Bible. YHWH provides the most dramatic expression in Deuteronomy 32:6:[23] "Is not he your father, who created [*qānâ*] you, who made [*ʿāśâ*)] you and established [*kōnēn*] you?"[24]

Whereas this characterization of YHWH as Israel's father highlights the nation's origin in him, the metaphor in Deuteronomy 14:1 derives from ANE political relationships that perceived the suzerain as the "father" and the vassal as the suzerain's "son" (cf. 2 Kings 16:7).[25]

---

22. In John, "Father" is the most common designation for God (ca. 120 times; cf. *theos*, which only occurs 108 times). For a variety of studies on God as Father in John, see Adele Reinhartz, ed., "God the Father in the Gospel of John," special issue, *Semeia* 85 (1999).
23. Employing maternal imagery, in Deut. 32:18 YHWH speaks of himself metaphorically as having given birth (*yālaḏ*) to Israel (through labor pains).
24. For additional references to YHWH as Israel's father, see Isa. 63:15–17; 64:1[8]; Jer. 3:19–20; Mal. 2:10; and Ps. 103:13. On Israel as YHWH's firstborn son (*bəḵôr*), see Exod. 4:22, and on Israel as his son in a more general sense, see Isa. 1:2–3; Hos. 11:1–4, 10.
25. In Mesopotamia people viewed the suzerain's status as *abbūtu* ("fathership") and the vassal's status as *mārūtu* ("sonship"). Cf. ARMT 2.119r.8 and *CAD* 10/1:321. See, e.g., the fourteenth-century BCE treaty between Shattiwaza of Mittanni and Suppiluliuma I of Hatti, in Gary Beckman, *Hittite*

In Deuteronomy Moses never speaks explicitly of YHWH's entrance into covenant relationship with Israel with adoptive language, but Jeremiah 3:19–20 does. By opening this unit with "Sons you are to YHWH your God," Moses announces that whatever follows reflects YHWH's acceptance of Israel as his privileged people—which is the antithesis to defection to other gods, Moses's preoccupation in Deuteronomy 13. By juxtaposing these texts, Moses suggests that the Israelites' pursuit of other deities signifies denying their status as YHWH's children.[26] Appearing shortly after YHWH's invitation to the Israelites to bring their offerings to him at the place he would choose to imprint his name (12:5–7, 11–14), here Israel's status as YHWH's adopted sons, his holy people, and his chosen, treasured people provides the basis for participation in table fellowship with him.[27] As his holy people, the Israelites have access to YHWH's presence and his table.

If Moses has provided a profound theology of the Israelites' holiness in Deuteronomy 7:6–18, here he contemplates the celebration of that status whenever they sit at their tables at home and when they eat in YHWH's presence at the sanctuary. This text highlights specific external markers of Israel's internal spiritual identity. The apparently mundane and secular tone of the material between the opening (vv. 1–2) and the closing frame (v. 21) may deceive the uninitiated. However, in this passage, Moses illustrates concretely the Pauline adage "Whether you eat or drink, or whatever you do, do it all for the glory of God" (1 Cor. 10:31 NLT).

As intimated, most of Moses's injunctions in Deuteronomy 14:3–20 are practical rather than explicitly theological. However, the framework imposes theological significance on the notion of Israel's holiness. First, speaking for YHWH, Moses forbids the Israelites from lacerating their bodies or shaving their heads bald for the dead. Both actions seem to involve mourning rites associated with the cult of the dead. Many in the ancient world believed that the deceased continued to exercise both beneficent and malevolent influences over the living and that mortuary rites could secure a favorable influence. However,

Diplomatic Texts, ed. Harry A. Hoffner Jr., WAW 7 (Atlanta: Scholars, 1996), 49. For additional references and discussion, see Moshe Weinfeld, "The Covenant of Grant in the Old Testament and in the Ancient Near East," *JAOS* 90 (1970): 191–94.

26. Mal. 2:11 speaks of non-Israelites as "daughters of a foreign god."

27. See Ps. 23:5 for a poetic portrayal of an Israelite as the privileged vassal eating at YHWH's table.

the present prohibition seems not to allude simply to mourning rites for the dead.[28] Moses hereby insists that his people should scrupulously guard the boundaries between the living and the dead. For this reason, he extends the taboos beyond contact with corpses to contact with the "vital forces" (*nəp̄āsôṯ*) of the deceased.[29] In the closing frame, Moses prohibits not the meat of a specific kind of animal but a specific culinary practice: boiling a kid in its mother's milk (v. 21). This taboo continues to mystify interpreters. Whether the ordinance arose from a humanitarian concern,[30] a perverse violation of natural law—that which is intended for nourishment is used to kill—or a perception of the reddish color of milk rich in colostrum a few days after giving birth and considering meat of a kid cooked in its mother's milk as eating meat with blood,[31] its threefold appearance in the constitutional documents (cf. Exod. 23:19; 34:26) suggests a common pagan practice that fell under the Hebrew rubric of *tô ʿēḇâ*, "abomination," "abhorrent notion," which heads this list of dietary regulations (Deut. 14:3).

Moses's instructions between the frames open with a titular prohibition: "You must not eat anything abhorrent" (*tô ʿēḇâ*, Deut. 14:3). While the category applies to two-thirds of verses 4–21a, Moses punctuates this document with affirmations that give it an essentially positive tone: (1) "These are the animals you may eat" (v. 4); (2) "These you may eat from among all aquatic creatures" (v. 9); (3) "Every clean bird you may eat" (v. 11); "Every clean flying [insect] you may eat" (v. 20). These features suggest Moses's statements signify grants of permission and invitation rather than legal proscriptions. Israel's privileged status as YHWH's covenant people and as guests at his table

28. So also Brian B. Schmidt, *Israel's Beneficent Dead: Ancestor Cult and Necromancy in Ancient Israelite Religion and Tradition* (Winona Lake, IN: Eisenbrauns, 1996), 166–78.

29. First Kings 18:28 and Hos. 7:14 suggest that some pagan rituals involved self-laceration. Jer. 16:5–7; 41:5; 47:5; and Mic. 4:14 associate these rituals with lamentation and the shaving of the head, both common elements in mourning rites.

30. Cf. the prohibitions against slaughtering animals fewer than eight days old (Exod. 22:30[29]; Lev. 22:27); killing a cow or ewe and her calf or lamb, respectively, on the same day (Lev. 22:28); and taking a mother bird and its young or its eggs at the same time (Deut. 22:6–7; cf. Exod. 22:30[29]; Lev. 22:27–28).

31. Such a perception is akin to the prohibition on nonkosher meat from an animal whose blood has not been drained properly (v. 21a). Cf. C. J. Labuschagne, "'You Shall Not Boil a Kid in Its Mother's Milk': A New Proposal for the Origin of the Prohibition," in *The Scriptures and the Scrolls: Studies in Honour of A.S van der Woude on the Occasion of His 65th Birthday*, ed. F. García Martínez, A Hilhorst, and C. J. Labuschagne, VTSup 49 (Leiden: Brill, 1992), 14–15. Earlier attempts to associate this prohibition with a Ugaritic text (*UT* 52.14 = *CTA* 23.14) have proven unfounded.

implicates all aspects of life, including respect for the divine order in creation in as mundane a matter as eating.[32]

In the absence of an explicit declaration of the rationale for the boundaries between clean and unclean food, scholars have speculated endlessly on the underlying premises. However, what characterizes the meat of prohibited animals is its association with filth and carrion and these animals' carnivorous dietary habits. It is also striking that the types of meat authorized for Israelite consumption are precisely the kinds that YHWH invites his people to bring to the sanctuary and to eat in his presence (cf. Deut. 12:6–7, 11–12). This suggests, in a sense, that even meals eaten at home are sacred (cf. the use of *zābaḥ* for domestic slaughter in v. 15) and, for members of YHWH's family (cf. 14:1–3), extensions of their holy communion in YHWH's presence. If that is so, then Moses's present listing of acceptable table fare seeks to remove artificial boundaries between the sacred and the profane. To the Israelites, YHWH's holy people, the sanctity of YHWH in his sanctuary and the people in his presence extend to all their activities when they exit sacred space. Within this theocratic worldview, a holy God has called his people to himself and, in so doing, has sanctified them and granted them territory that

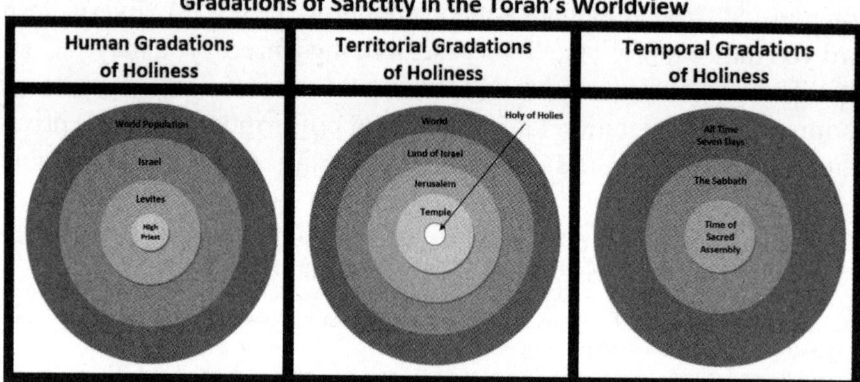

Figure 13.2. Gradations of Sanctity in the Torah's Worldview

32. See Mary Douglas, *Purity and Danger: An Analysis of Concepts of Pollution and Taboo* (London: Routledge & Kegan Paul, 1966).

is an extension of the sacred space he inhabits.[33] Although Moses obviously recognizes gradations of sanctity, for him the concept is comprehensive, governing time, space, and persons (see fig. 13.2).

Moses's Fourth Call to Holiness (26:16–19)

> This day YHWH your God is commanding you to put into practice these ordinances and stipulations; so you must keep the covenant and put them into practice with your whole heart/mind and with your entire being. You have had YHWH declare today to be your God—and you have promised to walk in his ways, to keep his ordinances, his commands, and his stipulations, and to listen to his voice. YHWH has had you declare today to be his treasured people [*ʿam səḡullâ*], as he promised you, and [that you would] keep all his commands—and [he has promised] to install you high above all the nations that he has made, for praise and for a name and for honor—and [you have promised] to be a holy people belonging to YHWH your God [*lihyōṯəḵā ʿam-qāḏōš layhwh ʾĕlōheḵā*], just as he promised. (Deut. 26:16–19)

In Moses's previous calls for holiness, the grammar of "because you are a holy people belonging to YHWH your God" suggests an accomplished fact, a present reality. However, this point raises the question concerning the moment YHWH conferred this status on the people. According to Exodus 19:4–6, the status of a royal priesthood and a holy nation had officially been conferred on the exodus generation at Sinai, in association with YHWH's "establishment" (*hēqîm*) of his covenant with Abraham for his descendants (Gen. 17:7), which he had achieved through the rituals described in Exodus 20–24. However, because that generation had proved itself a faithless and unholy lot of rebels, it had died in the desert and left Israel's future in the hands of its children, born in the following decades. Along with persons under twenty years of age at the time of the covenant ritual at Horeb, this

---

33. Even though the epithet "holy land" appears in English translations of the Hebrew Bible only twice: Ps. 78:54, *gəbûl qodšô*, lit. "territory of his holiness"; and Zech. 2:12[16], *ʾadmat haqqōdeš*, lit. "land of the holiness."

new generation stood before Moses as the addressees of what would later become the Torah orations of Deuteronomy. Since these were the children of faithless parents, and since they had not been circumcised after the custom of Abraham (Gen. 17:9–27; cf. Josh. 5:5),[34] how could Moses identify them as "a holy people belonging to YHWH" and his "treasured people"? Did he recognize in them a "spiritually" circumcised heart (cf. Deut. 10:16), or did he anticipate the short verbal ritual underlying 26:16–19? The latter seems more likely.

Although the covenant blessings and curses preserved in Deuteronomy 28 are still to come, by the time we reach the end of Moses's instructions concerning the private thanksgiving rituals in 26:1–15, the instructions on holy and righteous living in the third address have ended. For the most part, those instructions look forward to Israel's imminent entry and settlement in the promised land beyond the Jordan. However, with Moses's threefold temporal signal "this day" (or "today," *hayyôm* [*hazzeh*]) in 26:16–18, the supervisor of this covenant-renewal ritual brings his audience back to the present.

Within Deuteronomy the significance of these four short verses is disproportionate to their length.[35] In short, they summarize key theological issues in the book and provide a hinge between Moses's lengthy exposition of the covenantal stipulations and his recitation of the consequences of covenantal obedience and disobedience in Deuteronomy 28. Although we may separate 26:16 from verses 17–19 on the basis of style and content, the paragraph is held together by Moses's penchant for triadic constructions, which crosses the divide in at least eight ways.[36]

The opening reference to "ordinances and stipulations" (*haḥuqqîm* and *hammišpāṭîm*) in Deuteronomy 26:16 links this verse with earlier combinations of these terms.[37] Alongside the verbs *šāmar*, "to keep," and *ʿāśâ*, "to do," "to put into practice," this pair of substantives links

34. Contra the Judaizers' characterization of circumcision as a Mosaic custom (*tō ethei tō Mōuseōs*, Acts 15:1) and law (*tērein ton nomon Mōuseōs*, v. 5).

35. For a study of this text and its function, see Steven Guest, "Deuteronomy 26:16–19 as the Central Focus of the Covenantal Framework of Deuteronomy" (PhD diss., Southern Baptist Theological Seminary, 2009).

36. For further details, see Block, *Gospel according to Moses*, 3:93–94n2.

37. In 5:1, 6:1, and 12:1, the pair opens new movements in Moses's addresses; in 5:31, 11:32, and 26:16–17, it signals a conclusion. The pair also occurs four times in the first address (4:1, 5, 8, 14) and three additional times in the second address (5:31; 6:20; 7:11).

the statement stylistically and thematically with 12:1. Together, 12:1 and 26:16 frame Moses's exposition of specific covenantal issues in his third address (12:2–26:15). In the second part of verse 16, Moses exhorts his people to take seriously the previous statement. The call to keep and put into practice the will of YHWH with one's entire heart and mind and with one's whole being derives from the Shema in Deuteronomy 6:4. With this ending, Moses reminds his audience that a satisfactory relationship with YHWH is not expressed merely by creedal confessions or external conformity to the laws; it requires commitment to *doing* the will of YHWH, the covenant Lord.

Deuteronomy 26:17–19 divides into two parts, which, although unequal in size, display a remarkable parallelism (see table 13.1).

Table 13.1. A Synopsis of Deuteronomy 26:17 and 18–19

Deuteronomy 26:17	Deuteronomy 26:18–19
You have had YHWH declare today to be your God,	YHWH has had you declare today to be his treasured people, just as he promised you,
and [you have promised] to walk in his ways, to keep his ordinances, his commands, and his stipulations, and to listen to his voice.	and [you have promised] to keep all his commands– and [he has promised] to install you high above all the nations that he has made —for praise and renown and honor— and [you have promised] to be a holy people belonging to YHWH your God, just as he promised.

Each segment is introduced by a clause involving the only occurrences of the *hiphil* form (*heʾĕmîr*) of the root *ʾmr*, "to speak," by far the most frequently occurring verb in the Hebrew Bible (with more than 5,300 occurrences).[38] English translations and commentaries tend to misconstrue the verbal event by attributing the respective statements to the wrong persons, thereby also contradicting the structure of the

38. Cf. H. H. Schmid, "אמר *ʾmr* to say," *TLOT* 3:159–62.

covenant relationship.[39] The exceptional character of these two *hiphil* forms demands careful attention to the context, but because verbs in this stem usually bear a causative sense, that is our default interpretation here. The text reinforces this approach by fronting the opening sentence in verse 17 with YHWH as the direct object, rather than the subject of the verb, suggesting a meaning like "You have caused YHWH to declare" and recognizing the following infinitive phrase ("to be your God") as a representation of his declaration. YHWH hereby commits himself to being the God of this generation from this moment forward.[40] Meanwhile, YHWH has Israel declare its acceptance of its status as YHWH's own treasured possession.

The term for "covenant" (*bərîṯ*) is missing from this paragraph, but the *hiphil* of *ʾāmar* functions in a quasi-juridical sense, according to which each party to a covenant hears the other party declare its commitment to the stipulations of the agreement. In this instance, YHWH hears the Israelites declare their acceptance of his covenant promises, and the Israelites hear YHWH declare their acceptance of the privileges and obligations that attend this covenant. Given the social distance between YHWH, the divine Suzerain, and Israel, his liberated vassals, the mutuality and reciprocity reflected in these declarations is unparalleled and unprecedented in ancient records.[41] The closest extrabiblical analogue involves a thirteenth-century BCE parity treaty signed by Rameses II of Egypt and the Hittite king Hattusili III after many years of indecisive conflict.[42] Significantly, the Egyptian version

39. The ESV's rendering is typical: "You have declared this day that the LORD is your God" (v. 17); "and the LORD has declared this day that you are his people, his treasured possession" (v. 18). Cf. the CSB, NIV, NASB, and NJPS; among commentators, see Bill T. Arnold and Paavo N. Tucker (*Deuteronomy 12–26: A Handbook on the Hebrew Text*, BHHB [Waco, TX: Baylor University Press, 2022], 195–96), who express awareness of the alternative interpretation but opt for the traditional "You have declared YHWH to be your God today" (v. 17) and "YHWH has declared you to be his treasured people today" (v. 18).

40. Similarly, Richard D. Nelson, *Deuteronomy: A Commentary*, OTL (Louisville: Westminster John Knox, 2002), 304. Although the word order shifts from object, verb (with the embedded subject "you"), and complement in verse 17 to explicit subject, verb (with the embedded object "you"), and complement in verse 18, the latter represents Israel's corresponding declaration. John Goldingay (*The First Testament: A New Translation* [Downers Grove, IL: IVP Academic, 2018], 194) renders these statements appropriately as "You've got YHWH to say today that . . ." (v. 17), and "YHWH has got you to say today that . . ." (v. 18).

41. Cf. M. A. Friedman, "Israel's Response in Hosea 2:17b: 'You Are My Husband,'" *JBL* 99 (1980): 202.

42. For the Egyptian and Hittite texts and a recent translation, see Kenneth A. Kitchen and Paul J. N. Lawrence, *Treaty, Law and Covenant in the Ancient Near East*, vol. 1, *The Texts* (Wiesbaden, Germany: Harrassowitz, 2012), 573–94. For brief commentary, see Kitchen and Lawrence, *Treaty,*

reflects the voice of the Hittite king, whereas in the Hittite version, we hear the voice of the Pharaoh.[43]

Admittedly, Deuteronomy 26:17–19 does not quote YHWH's or the Israelites' declarations but casts the verbal ritual as indirect speech. If Moses functioned as the covenant mediator as he had at Horeb (Exod. 19:3–8), and if he cast this report as direct speech, we may speculate that the verbal exchange looked something like this, with the italicized bold font highlighting the accepted responsibilities and privileges within the covenant relationship and the normal font representing the obligations of the other party:

Table 13.2. A Plausible Reconstruction of the Verbal Ritual in Deuteronomy 26:17–19

Moses's voice:	**Today you have had YHWH declare:**
YHWH's voice:	I will be your God, and you must walk in my ways and keep my ordinances, my commands, and my stipulations. And you must listen to my voice.
Moses's voice:	**Today YHWH has had you [Israel] declare:**
Israel's voice:	We will be your treasured people—just as you promised us— and we will keep all your commands. And you will install us high above all the nations that you have made, for praise and for a name and for honor. And we will be a holy people, belonging to YHWH our God— just as you promised.

Through these declarations, a relationship that did not exist naturally had been created or confirmed.[44] When the Israelites heard YHWH declare

Law and Covenant in the Ancient Near East, vol. 2, *Text, Notes and Chromograms* (Wiesbaden, Germany: Harrassowitz, 2012), 57–60.

43. The treaty has been preserved in both Egyptian and Hittite versions. For discussion of the treaty-making procedure, see Block, *Gospel according to Moses*, 3:98–99; Beckman, *Hittite Diplomatic Texts*, 91.

44. Since the present ceremony seems to have involved the "covenant formula" ("I will be your God, and you shall be my people" [cf. Jer. 7:23]), the *Sitz im Leben* of the present literary form may derive from the context of family law. Thus, Ze'ev W. Falk (*Hebrew Law in Biblical Times: An*

his commitment to be their God, and when YHWH heard the Israelites declare that they will be his treasured people, the generation standing before Moses was (re)constituted as the "people [*ʿam*] of YHWH"[45]—that is, his "treasured people" (*ʿam səḡullâ*, Deut. 26:18)—which links this passage lexically to 7:6 and 14:2, 21. Whatever the original historical and literary relationships between chapter 27, on the one hand, and chapters 26 and 28, on the other, in 27:9 Moses and the Levitical priests formally declare the significance of this event: "Be silent, O Israel, and listen! This day [*hayyôm hazzeh*] you have become the people of YHWH your God" (AT). Remarkably, this is the only place in Moses's valedictory pastoral addresses where he refers to Israel as the "people [*ʿam*][46] Through the present verbal ritual, Moses's earlier statements of potential ("you are YHWH's treasured people, chosen out of all the peoples of the earth," 7:6; 14:2, 21) have been fulfilled.

But what does all this have to do with holiness and Israel's mission as YHWH's royal priesthood? For the former, we may note the emphasis in this ritual on the importance of Israel's response to the privilege of being YHWH's vassal. The Israelites have indeed acknowledged him as their divine Suzerain and accepted their privileged role as "the people of YHWH," but the ritual involves more than the elevation of their status. The preamble to Moses's report of the ritual (Deut. 26:10) and the verbal utterances themselves redundantly specify the obligations to which the Israelites have bound themselves as his vassals: "to walk in his ways, to keep his ordinances, his commands, and his stipu-

---

Introduction, 2nd ed. [Winona Lake, IN: Eisenbrauns, 2001], 136), who views such utterances as representing "a constitutive declaration," by which a relationship could be created, as is the case in marriage rituals. In ancient marriage covenants, the groom would say, "I will be your husband, and you shall be my wife," and the bride would reciprocate. In adoption ceremonies, the father would say, "I will be your father, and you will be my son." For a helpful presentation of the evidence, see Seock-Tae Sohn, "'I Will Be Your God and You Will Be My People': The Origin and Background of the Covenant Formula," in *Ki Baruch Hu: Ancient Near Eastern, Biblical, and Judaic Studies in Honor of Baruch A. Levine*, ed. Robert Chazan, William W. Hallo, and Lawrence H. Schiffman (Winona Lake, IN: Eisenbrauns, 1999), 355–72; and Sohn, *The Divine Election of Israel* (Grand Rapids: Eerdmans, 1991), 62–73.

45. This is suggested by YHWH's declaration that he will be Israel's God (*lihyôt ləḵā lēʾlōhîm*) in verse 17. On the formula, see Rolf Rendtorff, *The Covenant Formula: An Exegetical and Theological Investigation*, trans. M. Kohl (Edinburgh: T&T Clark, 1998).

46. The expression "the people of YHWH" (*ʿam yhwh*) occurs elsewhere only ten times in the First Testament: Num. 11:29; 16:41[17:6]; Judg. 5:11, 13; 1 Sam. 2:24; 2 Sam. 1:12; 6:21; 2 Kings 9:6; Ezek. 36:20; Zeph. 2:10. Judges 20:2 and 2 Sam. 14:13 speak of Israel as "the people of God" (*ʿam ʾĕlōhîm*). Numbers 21:29 and Jer. 48:46 refer to Moabites as "the people of Chemosh" (*ʿam kəmôš*).

lations, and to listen to his voice," (v. 17); "to keep all his commands" (v. 18); and "that you would be a holy people belonging to YHWH your God" (*lihyōṯəḵā ʿam-qāḏōš layhwh ʾĕlōhêḵā*, v. 19). Through this ritual, they have accepted the status of being YHWH's people, but they have also committed themselves to living out that status. They have heard YHWH's covenantal invitation and his voice binding himself to them, and he has heard their acceptance of their role and their voice promising him full allegiance. This verbal ritual reinforces the notion that holiness is not just a state of being, let alone a state of mind; it is life. Moses often reminded the people, and will do so again with incredible rhetorical force in the curses of chapter 28, that if they depart from the course he has laid out and will refuse to listen to YHWH's voice, their claim to special status will count for nothing. Those who demonstrate covenant love to him by putting into practice his charges will be richly blessed (7:9, 12–15), but those who demonstrate their rejection of him by defecting to other gods and rebelling against him will be repaid—not capriciously nor impulsively, but in strict accord with his gracious forewarning (vv. 16, 25–26).

The climactic sentence in Deuteronomy 26:19 highlights one more dimension of Israel's holiness: "and [he has promised] to install you high above all the nations that he has made, for praise and for a name and for honor—and [you have promised] to be a holy people belonging to YHWH your God, just as he spoke." Since Exodus 19:4–6, we have heard little of YHWH's commission for his people—namely, to be YHWH's treasured possession, chosen from all the peoples, to serve him as his holy nation—that is, his kingdom of priests.[47] At Sinai YHWH had transferred Abraham's commission to be a blessing to all the families of the earth (Gen. 12:3; 18:18) to the exodus generation of his descendants (22:18; 26:4; 28:14). The only hint of this agenda in Deuteronomy prior to 26:19 occurs in Moses's first address, where it surfaces almost as a side issue:

> Look, I have taught you ordinances and stipulations, just as YHWH my God commanded me, that you may put them into

47. We recognize the propriety of juxtaposing "holy nation" (*gôy qāḏôš*) and "royal priesthood" (*mamleḵeṯ kōhănîm*) when we realize that in the Hebrew Bible a *gôy* is, by definition, a people headed by a king (*meleḵ*). See further Daniel I. Block, "The Foundations of National Identity: A Study in Ancient Northwest Perceptions" (PhD diss., University of Liverpool, 1982), 115–20, 494–509.

> practice within the land you are entering to possess. So keep them—that is, put them into practice—for this is [the mark of] your wisdom and understanding in the eyes of the nations, who will hear these ordinances and say, "Wow! This great nation is indeed a wise and understanding people." Look, which [other] great nation is there that has a god as near to it as YHWH our God [is to us] whenever we call on him? And which [other] great nation is there that has righteous ordinances and stipulations as this whole Torah that I am presenting to you today? (Deut. 4:5–8)

Here Moses imagines the peoples (*ʿammîm*) observing how the Israelites live and acknowledging their unique privilege in having a god who responds to their prayers and provides them with the Torah—that is, a document that reveals his will and vision for his vassals with unparalleled clarity and unprecedented "righteousness" (*ṣaddîqim*).

Deuteronomy 26:19 implies minimally a paradigmatic role for Israel and maximally a missionary role—declaring to the world what divine grace can achieve and making the nation the envy of the world. Essential to Israel's calling as "a holy people belonging to YHWH" (*ʿam qāḏôš layhwh*) is YHWH's elevation of his people "high above all the nations that he has made, for praise and for a name and for honor" (v. 19). Moses's statement is vague: Whose praise, fame, and honor are in view? Is it Israel's praise, fame, and honor, or YHWH's? Undoubtedly, Israel's status among the nations is at issue, as Moses suggests in 4:6: "What great nation is as wise in the eyes of other nations, and what great nation has a god as near and as responsive as YHWH is to Israel?" However, as Moses emphasizes in 7:6–8 and 9:4–24, Israel's special status is neither earned nor deserved. By sheer grace, YHWH has marked her as the target of his benevolent actions and set her high above the nations, that the latter might be drawn to him when they see what divine grace can achieve. This point will be even more apparent in Moses's last reference to Israel as "a holy people belonging to YHWH," to which I now turn.

Moses's Fifth Call to Holiness (28:1, 16–19)

> If you will listen seriously to the voice of YHWH your God by keeping [the covenant], by putting into practice all his commands that I am commanding you today, YHWH your God

> will install you high above all the nations on earth. All these blessings will come over you and overtake you if you listen to the voice of YHWH your God. . . .
>
> YHWH will command the blessing to be with you where you store your produce and in every task to which you extend your hand. And he will bless you in the land that YHWH your God is giving you.
>
> YHWH will establish you as his own holy people, as he has promised you on oath, if you keep the commands of YHWH your God and walk in his ways. Then all the peoples of the earth will see that YHWH's name is "read" on you, and they will be in awe of you. (Deut. 28:1–2, 8–10, AT)

Deuteronomy 28's opening suggests that in an earlier stage of the book's composition, Moses had presented the blessings and curses of chapter 27 immediately after the account of the verbal covenant-ratification ritual in 26:16–17. The linkage between 26:18–19 and 28:1 is obvious:

Table 13.3 A Synopsis of Select Phrases in Deuteronomy 26:18–19 and Deuteronomy 28:1

Deuteronomy 26:18–19	Deuteronomy 28:1
wəlišmōr kol-miṣwôṯāyw *ûləṯittəḵā ʿelyôn* *ʿal kol-haggôyim ăšer ʿāśâ*	*[lišmōr laʿăśôṯ ʾet-kol-miṣwôṯāyw* *ûnəṯānəḵā yhwh ʾĕlōhêḵā ʿelyôn* *ʿal kol gôyê hāʾāreṣ*
and to keep all his commands, and to install you high above all the nations that he has made.	to keep [the covenant] by doing all his commands, and YHWH your God will install you high above all the nations of the earth.

Deuteronomy 28:9 reinforces this linkage, referring for the last time to Israel as YHWH's holy people, albeit in modified form. As the climactic benefaction that YHWH promises Israel as the consequence of scrupulous fidelity to his will (vv. 1, 9, 13–14), he declares in verse

9: "YHWH will establish you as his own holy people [*yəqîməḵā yhwh lô lə ʿam qāḏôš*], as he has promised you on oath [*ka ʾăšer nišba ʿ laḵ*]" (AT, undoubtedly alluding to the verbal ritual underlying 26:17–19).

Three features of Moses's statement in Deuteronomy 28:9–10 are noteworthy. First, whereas YHWH's invitation to the present covenant relationship is preconditioned only by his gracious acts of election and redemption (7:6–8), here Moses declares unequivocally that the fulfillment of YHWH's promise in 26:19 and Israel's experience of the covenant benefactions will depend on Israel's scrupulous acceptance of its role as his vassal, demonstrated in obedience to the covenant stipulations.[48]

Second, when the Israelites flourish in the land that YHWH has given them, all the peoples of the earth will recognize that they belong to YHWH. Most translations render the critical clause something like "that you are called by the name of YHWH" (*kî šēm yhwh niqrāʾ ʿālêḵā*, v. 10). However, this is contrary to the grammar ("name" is the subject of the verb), and it misses the point. The statement reads literally "the name of YHWH is read on you."[49] The expression derives from the practice of inscribing or branding one's name on property that one owned.[50] Elsewhere in Deuteronomy, Moses usually associates the inscription of YHWH's name with the central sanctuary (e.g., 12:5, 11). Following the command to expunge the names of the Canaanite gods from the land (v. 3), by imprinting his name on the chosen place, YHWH claims ownership of this land, which he has assigned to Israel as its land grant (*naḥălâ*, 4:21, 38, etc.). Through the covenant-ratification ritual, YHWH in effect stamps his people with his name, which means not only that YHWH owns them as their Suzerain[51] but also that their well-being reflects the

48. Whether we interpret the introductory particle *kî* as conditional ("if"), temporal ("when"), or causal ("because"), the conditionality remains. Cf. the more explicit causality in *ʿēqeḇ ʾăšer* in Gen. 22:18 and 26:5. *DCH* (4:387) renders it causally.

49. The Hebrew word *qārāʾ* means "to call out," but since texts were always read aloud in ancient times the word also denoted "to read." For discussion of the idiom, see F. L. Hossfeld and H. Lambert-Zielinski, "קרא *qārāʾ*," *TDOT* 13:131–32.

50. For detailed discussion, see Sandra L. Richter, *The Deuteronomistic History and the Name Theology: ləšakkēn šəmô šām in the Bible and the Ancient Near East*, BZAW 318 (New York: De Gruyter, 2002). On the practice of branding slaves with the name of an owner in ancient Mesopotamia, see M. A. Dandamaev, *Slavery in Babylonia from Nabopolassar to Alexander the Great (626–331 BC)*, rev. ed. (DeKalb: Northern Illinois University Press, 1984), 78, 229–34.

51. See also 2 Chron. 7:14; Isa. 44:5; and especially 63:19: "We have become like those whom you have never ruled, on whom your name has not been read."

character of the one whose name they bear.[52] As the second command of the Decalogue suggests (5:11), Israel's bearing the name of YHWH was both a privilege and a challenge.

Third, when all the peoples recognize the link between Israel and YHWH, they will extend the awe (*yārēʾ*) that is rightly expressed before God himself to the people who bear his awesome name. This comment correlates with Moses's declaration in 26:19 that the nations' recognition of Israel will ultimately result in the praise (*təhillâ*), renown (*šēm*), and glory (*tipʾāreṯ*) of YHWH himself.

CONCLUSION

Having examined all the texts that relate to Israel's status as "a holy people belonging to YHWH," we may summarize our findings on the importance of the notion of holiness in the context of YHWH's covenant with Israel in the form of a series of postulates.

Postulate #1. As an essential element of YHWH's covenant with Israel, the creation of "a holy people belonging to YHWH" was a fundamentally monergistic enterprise, dependent entirely on YHWH's initiative. YHWH chose Israel out of all the peoples on the face of the earth; YHWH set his affection on Israel and identified this nation as the object of his love; and YHWH rescued Israel from the slave house of Egypt, that he might sanctify her and declare her his holy covenant people. As a microcosm of humanity as a whole, Israel was to function as YHWH's image, embodying his own sanctity and righteousness. Through the verbal revelation of his will, YHWH declared to Israel the ethical and cultic boundaries of holiness. As was the case with Aaron, the high priest, whose medallion was engraved with the words "holy, belonging to YHWH," through the covenant ritual, YHWH branded Israel with his name, ordained it as his holy nation, and commissioned it as his kingdom of priests to bring the blessing of Abraham to all the families or nations of the earth.

Postulate #2. YHWH's covenant with the Israelites provides a framework through which the indicative of their holiness ("you are a holy people belonging to YHWH") may be matched by the imperative

52. For further discussion, see Daniel I. Block, "Bearing the Name of the Lord with Honor," *BSac* 168 (2011): 20–31; Carmen J. Imes, *Bearing YHWH's Name at Sinai: A Reexamination of the Name Command of the Decalogue*, BBRSup 19 (Winona Lake, IN: Eisenbrauns, 2018), 178–79.

of holiness. Indeed, in Deuteronomy a truly holy state is marked by exclusive, full-bodied, and wholehearted love for God (the Shema, 6:4–5) and the uncompromised pursuit of "righteousness, only righteousness" (the watchword of Moses's third address, 16:20). If the former is demonstrated by action in the interest and according to the agenda of the divine Suzerain, the latter involves action in accord with an established standard, which in this book is essentially the Torah (Moses's addresses in Deuteronomy), which appeals to the ordinances and stipulations revealed earlier as its starting point (law in the interest of covenantal theology and ethics). In this regard, the perspective of Deuteronomy is fully consonant with Jesus's appeals in John 14 and 15: If you are covenantally committed to me (i.e., if you love me), you will keep my commands (14:15).[53]

Postulate #3. While the calls to covenant relationship and holiness are unconditional, both Israel's personal well-being and its fulfillment of the commission for which it has been ordained are contingent on the people demonstrating their holiness and righteousness within the covenant community and before a watching world. To rephrase, when Israel proves her holy status with holy living, YHWH will lavish his blessings on her, and the nations will acknowledge in her well-being the gracious hand of God and extend their awe of YHWH to his people. This is what it means to be YHWH's trophies of grace, his city on a hill, and his light to the world (Matt. 5:14–15).

53. Here *entolas* ("commands") refers to an established body of ordinances, and as YHWH incarnate, Jesus claims to be the authority behind ancient Israel's constitutional documents. Jesus clarifies the status of those who claim to be his (holy) covenant people but refuse to live accordingly in 15:2, 6.